Social Psychology 1

Social Psychology I

Compiled from:

Social Psychology
Eighth Edition
Elliot Aronson, Timothy D. Wilson and Robin M. Akert

Social Psychology
Eleventh Edition
Shelley E. Taylor, Letitia Anne Peplau and David O. Sears

Harlow, England • London • New York • Boston • San Francisco • Toronto • Sydney • Auckland • Singapore • Hong Kong
Tokyo • Seoul • Taipei • New Delhi • Cape Town • Sao Paulo • Mexico City • Madrid • Amsterdam • Munich • Paris • Milan

Pearson Education Limited
Edinburgh Gate
Harlow
Essex CM20 2JE

And associated companies throughout the world

Visit us on the World Wide Web at:
www.pearson.com/uk

Compiled from:

Social Psychology
Eighth Edition
Elliot Aronson, Timothy D. Wilson and Robin M. Akert
ISBN 10: 0-205-79662-1
ISBN 13: 978-0-205-79662-5

Social Psychology
Eleventh Edition
Shelley E. Taylor, Letitia Anne Peplau and David O. Sears
ISBN 0-13-099006-x

ISBN 978-1-78399-318-5

Printed and bound in Great Britain by Ashford Colour Press, Gosport, Hampshire.

Contents

1 Introducing Social Psychology

THE TASK OF THE PSYCHOLOGIST IS TO TRY TO UNDERSTAND AND PREDICT HUMAN BEHAVIOR. Different kinds of psychologists go about this task in different ways, and in this book we attempt to show you how social psychologists do it. Let's begin with a few examples of human behavior. Some of these might seem important; others might seem trivial; one or two might seem frightening. To a social psychologist, all of them are interesting. Our hope is that by the time you finish reading this book, you will find these examples as fascinating as we do.

- Abraham Biggs Jr., age 19, had been posting to an online discussion board for 2 years. Unhappy about his future and that a relationship had ended, Biggs announced on camera that he was going to commit suicide. He took an overdose of drugs and linked to a live video feed from his bedroom. None of his hundreds of observers called the police for more than 10 hours; some egged him on. Paramedics reached him too late, and Biggs died.
- Oscar is a middle-aged executive with a computer software company. As a student, Oscar had attended a large state university in the Midwest, where he was a member of Alpha Beta. He remembers having gone through a severe and scary hazing ritual to join, but believes it was worthwhile, since Alpha Beta was easily the best of all fraternities. A few years ago when his son, Sam, enrolled in the same university, Oscar urged him to pledge Alpha Beta. Sam did and was accepted. Oscar was relieved to learn that Sam was not required to undergo a severe initiation in order to become a member; times had changed, and hazing was now forbidden. When Sam went home for Christmas, Oscar asked him how he liked the fraternity. "It's all right, I guess," he said, "but most of my friends are outside the fraternity." Oscar was astonished. Why had he been so enamored of his fraternity brothers and his son wasn't? Was Alpha Beta now admitting a less desirable group of young men than in Oscar's day?
- In the mid-1970s, several hundred members of the Peoples Temple, a California-based religious cult, immigrated to Guyana under the guidance of their leader, the Reverend Jim Jones. Their aim was to found a model interracial community, called Jonestown, based on "love, hard work, and spiritual enlightenment." But within a few years some members wanted out, and they wrote to their congressman, claiming they were being held against their will. The congressman flew to Jonestown to investigate, but he and several other members of his party were shot and killed by a member of the Peoples Temple on Jones's orders. Jones grew despondent and began to speak over the public address system about the beauty of dying and the certainty that everyone would meet again in another place. The residents lined up in a pavilion, in front of a vat containing a mixture of Kool-Aid and cyanide. According to a survivor, almost all the residents drank willingly of the deadly solution. A total of 914 people died, including 80 babies and the Reverend Jones.

These stories pose fascinating questions about human social behavior: Why would people watch a troubled young man commit suicide in front of their eyes, when, by simply flagging the video to alert the Web site, they might

FOCUS QUESTIONS

- What is social psychology, and how is it different from other disciplines?
- What's more important: personality or situation?
- How did behaviorism and Gestalt psychology contribute to the development of social psychological thought?
- What are the differences between the self-esteem approach and the social cognition approach?
- How can social psychology help solve social problems?

Social Psychology
The scientific study of the way in which people's thoughts, feelings, and behaviors are influenced by the real or imagined presence of other people

Social Influence
The effect that the words, actions, or mere presence of other people have on our thoughts, feelings, attitudes, or behavior

have averted a tragedy? Why did Sam feel so much less attached to his fraternity than his father did? And how could large numbers of people be induced to kill their own children and then commit suicide? In this chapter, we will consider what these examples have in common and how social psychologists go about explaining them.

What Is Social Psychology?

Social psychology is the scientific study of the way in which people's thoughts, feelings, and behaviors are influenced by the real or imagined presence of other people: parents, friends, employers, teachers, strangers—indeed, by the entire social situation (Allport, 1985). When we think of social influence, the kinds of examples that readily come to mind are direct attempts at persuasion, whereby one person deliberately tries to change another person's behavior. This is what happens when advertisers use sophisticated techniques to persuade us to buy a particular brand of toothpaste, or when our friends try to get us to do something we don't really want to do ("Come on, have another beer—everyone is doing it"), or when the schoolyard bully uses force or threats to get smaller kids to part with their lunch money.

These direct attempts at **social influence** form a major part of social psychology and will be discussed in our chapters on conformity, attitudes, and group processes. To the social psychologist, however, social influence is broader than attempts by one person to change another person's behavior. It includes our thoughts and feelings as well as our overt acts. And it takes many forms other than deliberate attempts at persuasion. We are often influenced merely by the *presence* of other people, including perfect strangers who are not interacting with us. Other people don't even have to be present in order to influence us: We are governed by the imaginary approval or disapproval of our parents, friends, and teachers and by how we expect others to react to us. Sometimes these influences conflict with one another, and social psychologists are especially interested in what happens in the mind of an individual when they do. For example, conflicts frequently occur when young people go off to college and find themselves torn between the beliefs and values they learned at home and the beliefs and values of their professors or peers. (See the Try It!)

We will spend the rest of this introductory chapter expanding on these issues, so that you will get an idea of what social psychology is, what it isn't, and how it differs from other, related disciplines.

Our thoughts, feelings, and behaviors are influenced by our immediate surroundings as well as by our cultural and family background. These students share a college identity but differ in ethnicity and religion.

TRY IT! How Do Values Change?

Think of the major values that govern people's lives: love, money, sex, wealth, religion, freedom, compassion for others, security, children, duty, loyalty, and so on. Make three lists of the 10 values that are most important to (1) you, (2) your parents, and (3) your closest friends in college. Note the similarities and differences in your lists. How do these differences affect you? Do you find yourself rejecting one set of values in favor of the other? Are you trying to make a compromise between the two? Are you attempting to form a new set of values that are your own?

Social Psychology, Science, and Common Sense

Throughout history, philosophy has been a major source of insight about human nature. Indeed, the work of philosophers is part of the foundation of contemporary psychology. This has more than mere historical significance: Psychologists have looked to philosophers for insights into the nature of consciousness (e.g., Dennett, 1991) and how people form beliefs about the social world (e.g., Gilbert, 1991). Sometimes, however, even great thinkers find themselves in disagreement with one another. When this occurs, how are you supposed to know who is right? Are there some situations where Philosopher A might be right, and other conditions where Philosopher B might be right? How would you determine this?

We social psychologists address many of the same questions that philosophers do, but we attempt to look at these questions scientifically—even questions concerning that great human mystery, love. In 1663, the Dutch philosopher Benedict Spinoza offered a highly original insight. He proposed that if we love someone whom we formerly hated, that love will be stronger than if hatred had not preceded it. Spinoza's proposition is beautifully worked out. His logic is impeccable. But how can we be sure that it holds up? Does it always hold up? What are the conditions under which it does or doesn't? These are *empirical* questions, meaning that their answers can be derived from experimentation or measurement rather than by personal opinion (Aronson, 1999; Aronson & Linder, 1965).

Now let's take another look at the examples at the beginning of this chapter. Why did these people behave the way they did? One way to answer this question would simply be to ask them. We could ask the people who observed Abraham Biggs's suicide why they didn't call the police; we could ask Sam why he wasn't especially excited about his fraternity brothers. The problem with this approach is that people are not always aware of the origins of their own responses and feelings (Gilbert, 2008; Nisbett & Wilson, 1977; Wilson, 2002). People might come up with plenty of excuses for not calling the police to rescue Biggs, but those excuses might not be the *reason* they did nothing. It is unlikely that Sam could pinpoint why he liked his fraternity brothers less than his father had liked his.

After the mass suicide at Jonestown, everyone had an explanation. Some people claimed (mistakenly) that the Reverend Jones used hypnotism and drugs to weaken the resistance of his followers. Others claimed (also mistakenly) that the people who were attracted to his cult were emotionally disturbed in the first place. As you will learn throughout this book, such speculations are almost always wrong, or at the very least oversimplified, because they underestimate the power of the situation. It is difficult for most people to grasp just how powerful a cult can be in affecting the hearts and minds of otherwise healthy and well-educated people.

If we rely on commonsense explanations of one particular tragic event, moreover, we don't learn very much that helps us understand other, similar ones. The attacks on the World Trade Center and the Pentagon on September 11, 2001, made Americans wonder what kind of "crazy, deranged" people become suicide bombers. Yet the evidence repeatedly finds that the people in suicide cults, like most suicide bombers today, were mentally healthy and, for the most part, bright and well educated. Name-calling may make some people feel better, but it is no substitute for understanding the

British soldiers stand near burning vehicles in Kabul, Afghanistan, after a suicide car bomber killed soldiers on a NATO-led peacekeeping mission. What causes a person to become a suicide bomber? Popular theories say such people must be mentally ill, alienated loners, or psychopaths. But social psychologists would try to understand the circumstances and situations that drive otherwise healthy, well-educated, bright people to commit murder and suicide for the sake of a religious or political goal.

complexities of the situations that caused these people to kill themselves for their leaders or for a political or religious conviction.

Social psychologists are not opposed to folk wisdom—far from it. You will find plenty of wise observations from journalists, social critics, and novelists in the margins of this book. The primary problem with relying entirely on such sources is that, more often than not, they disagree with one another, and there is no easy way of determining which of them is correct. Consider what folk wisdom has to say about the factors that influence how much we like other people. We know that "birds of a feather flock together." With a little effort, each of us could come up with lots of examples where indeed we liked to hang around with people who shared our backgrounds and interests. But folk wisdom also tells us that "opposites attract." If we tried, we could also come up with examples where we were attracted to people with different backgrounds and interests. Well, which is it? Similarly, are we to believe that "out of sight is out of mind" or that "absence makes the heart grow fonder," that "haste makes waste" or that "he who hesitates is lost"?

And which answer best explains why the Jonestown massacre occurred?

- The Reverend Jones attracted people who were already psychologically depressed.
- Only mentally ill people join cults.
- Jones was such a powerful, charismatic figure that virtually anyone—even strong, nondepressed individuals like you or us—would have succumbed to his influence.
- People cut off from society are particularly vulnerable to social influence.
- All of the above.
- None of the above.

Social psychologists would want to know which of these explanations—or another one entirely—is the most likely. To do this, we have devised an array of scientific methods to test our assumptions, guesses, and ideas about human social behavior, empirically and systematically rather than by relying on folk wisdom, common sense, or the opinions and insights of philosophers, novelists, political pundits, and our grandmothers. Doing experiments in social psychology presents many challenges, primarily because we are attempting to predict the behavior of highly sophisticated organisms in a variety of complex situations. As scientists, our goal is to find objective answers to a wide array of important questions: What are the factors that cause aggression? How might we reduce prejudice? What variables cause two people to like or love each other? Why do certain kinds of political advertisements work better than others?

To answer questions like these, the first task of the social psychologist is to make an educated guess, called a *hypothesis*, about the specific situations under which one outcome or the other would occur. Just as a physicist performs experiments to test hypotheses about the nature of the physical world, the social psychologist performs experiments to test hypotheses about the nature of the social world. The next task is to design well-controlled experiments sophisticated enough to tease out the situations that would result in one or another outcome. This enriches our understanding of human nature and allows us to make accurate predictions once we know the key aspects of the prevailing situation. (In Chapter 2 we will discuss the scientific methods that social psychologists use.)

To elaborate, let's return to our discussion about the kinds of people we like and the relationship between absence and liking. Social psychologists would suggest that there are some conditions under which birds of a feather do flock together, and other conditions under which opposites do attract. Similarly, there are some conditions under which absence does make the heart grow fonder, and others under which out of sight does mean out of mind. So each proverb can be true. That statement helps, but is it good enough? Not really, because if you want to understand human behavior, knowing that each can be true is not sufficient. Part of the job of the social psychologist is to do the research that specifies the conditions under which one or another is most likely to take place.

Watch on **MyPsychLab**
To learn more about how psychology helps us understand ourselves, watch the MyPsychLab video ***The Complexity of Humans: Phil Zimbardo.***

How Social Psychology Differs from Its Closest Cousins

If you are like most people, when you read the examples that opened this chapter and started thinking about how those events might have come about, you assumed that the individuals involved had some weaknesses, flaws, and personality traits that led them to respond as they did. What character traits might these be? Some people are leaders and others are followers; some people are public-spirited and others are selfish. Perhaps the people who failed to get help for Abraham Biggs were lazy, timid, selfish, or heartless. Given what you know about their behavior, would you want any of them as a friend?

Personality psychologists study qualities of the individual that might make a person shy, conventional, rebellious, and willing to wear a turquoise wig in public or a yellow shirt in a sea of blue. Social psychologists study the powerful role of social influence on how all of us behave.

Individual Differences
The aspects of people's personalities that make them different from other people

Would you loan them your car or trust them to take care of your new puppy? As for Sam, perhaps he is not as much of an extrovert or joiner as his dad was. And, most seriously, perhaps the people at Jonestown ended their own lives and their children's because they were all conformists or weak-willed or suffered from mental disorders.

Asking and trying to answer questions about people's behavior in terms of their traits is the work of personality psychologists, who generally focus on **individual differences**, the aspects of people's personalities that make them different from others. Research on personality increases our understanding of human behavior, but social psychologists believe that explaining behavior primarily through personality factors ignores a critical part of the story: the powerful role played by social influence. Remember that it was not just a handful of people who committed suicide at Jonestown, but almost 100% of the people in the village. Although it is conceivable that they were all mentally ill or had the same constellation of personality traits, this is highly improbable. If we want a richer, more thorough explanation of this tragic event, we need to understand what kind of power and influence a charismatic figure like Jim Jones possessed, the nature of the impact of living in a closed society cut off from other points of view, and other factors that could cause mentally healthy people to obey him.

Here is a more mundane example. Suppose you go to a party and see a great-looking fellow student you have been hoping to get to know better. The student is looking pretty uncomfortable, however—standing alone, not making eye contact, not talking to anyone who comes over. You decide you're not so interested; this person seems pretty aloof, standoffish, even arrogant. But a few weeks later you see the student again, now being outgoing, funny, and appealing. So which is it? What is this person "really" like? Shy or arrogant, charming and welcoming? It's the wrong question; the answer is both and neither. All of us are capable of being shy in some situations and outgoing in others. A much more interesting question is this: What factors are different in these two situations that have such a profound effect on behavior? That is a social psychological question. (See the following Try It!)

Social psychology is related to other disciplines in the social sciences, including sociology, economics, and political science. Each of these examines the influence of social factors on human behavior, but important differences set social psychology apart—most notably in their level of analysis. For biologists, the level of analysis might be the gene or neurotransmitter. For personality and clinical psychologists, the level of the analysis is the individual. *For the social psychologist, the level of analysis is the individual in the context of a social situation.* For example, to understand why people intentionally hurt one another, the social psychologist focuses on the psychological processes that trigger aggression in specific situations. To what extent is aggression preceded by frustration? Does frustration always precede aggression? If people are feeling frustrated, under what conditions will they vent their frustration with an overt, aggressive act? What factors might preclude an aggressive response by a frustrated individual? Besides frustration, what other factors might cause aggression? We will address these questions in Chapter 12.

TRY IT! Social Situations and Behavior

1. Think about one of your friends or acquaintances whom you regard as a shy person. (You may use yourself!) For a moment, try not to think about him or her as "a shy person," but rather as someone who has difficulty relating to people in some situations but not in others.
2. Make a list of the social situations you think are most likely to bring out your friend's shy behavior.
3. Make a list of the social situations that might bring forth more-outgoing behaviors on your friend's part. Being with a small group of friends he or she is at ease with? Being with a new person, but one who shares your friend's interests?
4. Set up a social environment that you think would make your friend comfortable and relaxed. Pay close attention to the effect that it has on your friend's behavior.

The people in this photo can be studied from a variety of perspectives: as individuals or as members of a family, a social class, an occupation, a culture, or a region. Sociologists study the group or institution; social psychologists study the influence of those groups and institutions on individual behavior.

Other social sciences are more concerned with broad social, economic, political, and historical factors that influence events in a given society. Sociology is concerned with such topics as social class, social structure, and social institutions. Of course, because society is made up of collections of people, some overlap is bound to exist between the domains of sociology and those of social psychology. The major difference is that sociology, rather than focusing on the individual, looks toward society at large. *The level of analysis is the group or institution.* So while sociologists, like social psychologists, are interested in aggression, sociologists are more likely to be concerned with why a particular society (or group within a society) produces different levels of aggression in its members. Why is the murder rate in the United States so much higher than in Canada or Europe? Within the United States, why is the murder rate higher in some social classes and geographic regions than in others? How do changes in society relate to changes in aggressive behavior?

The difference between social psychology and other social sciences in the level of analysis they examine reflects another difference between the disciplines: what they are trying to explain. *The goal of social psychology is to identify universal properties of human nature that make everyone susceptible to social influence, regardless of social class or culture.* The laws governing the relationship between frustration and aggression, for example, are hypothesized to be true of most people in most places, not just members of one social class, age group, or race.

However, because social psychology is a young science that developed mostly in the United States, many of its findings have not yet been tested in other cultures to see if they are universal. Nonetheless, our goal as social psychologists is to discover such laws. And increasingly, as methods and theories developed by American social psychologists are adopted by European, Asian, African, Middle Eastern, and South American social psychologists, we are learning more about the extent to which these laws are universal, as well as cultural differences in the way these laws are expressed (see Chapter 2). *Cross-cultural research* is therefore extremely valuable, because it sharpens theories, either by demonstrating their universality or by leading us to discover additional variables whose incorporation helps us make more-accurate predictions of human behavior. We will encounter many examples of cross-cultural research in subsequent chapters.

In sum, social psychology is located between its closest cousins, sociology and personality psychology (see Table 1.1). Social psychology and sociology share an interest in the way the situation and the larger society influence behavior. But social psychologists focus more on the psychological makeup of individuals *that renders people susceptible* to social influence. And although social psychology and personality psychology both emphasize the psychology of the individual rather than focusing on what makes people different from one another, social psychology emphasizes the *psychological processes* shared by most people around the world that make them susceptible to social influence.

Watch on **MyPsychLab**
Consider social psychology and related fields as you watch the MyPsychLab video ***Alan Kazdin: Would you suggest psychology students keep their eyes open to other disciplines?***

TABLE 1.1 Social Psychology Compared to Related Disciplines

Sociology	Social Psychology	Personality Psychology
The study of groups, organizations, and societies, rather than individuals.	The study of the psychological processes people have in common that make them susceptible to social influence.	The study of the characteristics that make individuals unique and different from one another.

The Power of the Situation

Suppose you stop at a roadside restaurant for a cup of coffee and a piece of pie. The server comes over to take your order, but you are having a hard time deciding which pie you want. While you are hesitating, she impatiently taps her pen against her notepad, rolls her eyes toward the ceiling, scowls at you, and finally snaps, "Hey, I haven't got all day, you know!" Like most people, you would probably think that she is a nasty or unpleasant person.

But suppose, while you are deciding whether to complain about her to the manager, a regular customer tells you that your "crabby" server is a single parent who was kept awake all night by the moaning of her youngest child, who was terribly sick; that her car broke down on her way to work and she has no idea where she will find the money to have it repaired; that when she finally arrived at the restaurant, she learned that her coworker was too drunk to work, requiring her to cover twice the usual number of tables; and that the short-order cook keeps screaming at her because she is not picking up the orders fast enough to please him. Given all that information, you might conclude that she is not necessarily a nasty person, just an ordinary human being under enormous stress.

The key fact, therefore, is that, without important information about a situation, most people will try to explain someone's behavior in terms of the personality of the individual; they focus on the fish, and not the water the fish swims in. But if the water is murky, contaminated, or full of predators, the fish is not going to be very happy. The fact that many people often fail to take the situation into account is important to social psychologists, because it has a profound impact on how human beings relate to one another—such as, in the case of the server, whether they feel sympathy toward another person or impatience and anger.

Thus, the social psychologist is up against a formidable barrier known as the **fundamental attribution error**: the tendency to explain our own and other people's behavior entirely in terms of personality traits and to underestimate the power of social influence. Explaining behavior this way often gives us a feeling of false security. For example, when trying to explain repugnant or bizarre behavior, such as suicide bombers or the people of Jonestown taking their own lives and killing their own children, it is tempting and, in a strange way, comforting to write off the victims as flawed human beings. Doing so gives the rest of us the feeling that it could never happen to us. Ironically, this in turn increases our personal vulnerability to possibly destructive social influences by making us less aware of our own susceptibility to social psychological processes. Moreover, by failing to fully appreciate the power of the situation, we tend to oversimplify the problem, which then decreases our understanding of the causes of many human actions. Among other things, this oversimplification can lead us to blame the victim in situations where the individual was overpowered by social forces too difficult for most of us to resist, as in the Jonestown tragedy.

To take a more everyday example, imagine a situation in which people are playing a two-person game wherein each player must choose one of two strategies: They can play competitively and try to win as much money as possible and make sure their partner loses as much as possible, or they can play cooperatively and try to make sure both they and their partner win some money. We will discuss the details of this game in Chapter 9. For now, just consider that there are only two basic strategies to use when playing the game: competition or cooperation. How do you think each of your friends would play this game?

Few people find this question hard to answer; we all have a feeling for the relative competitiveness of our friends. Accordingly, you might say, "I am certain that my friend Jennifer, who is a hard-nosed business major, would play this game more competitively than my friend Anna, who is a really caring, loving person." But how accurate are you likely to be? Should you be thinking about the game itself rather than who is playing it?

Fundamental Attribution Error

The tendency to overestimate the extent to which people's behavior is due to internal, dispositional factors and to underestimate the role of situational factors

To find out, Lee Ross and his students conducted the following experiment (Liberman, Samuels, & Ross, 2004). They chose a group of students at Stanford University who were considered by the resident assistants in their dorm to be either especially cooperative or especially competitive. The researchers did this by describing the game to the RAs and asking them to think of students in their dormitories who would be most likely to adopt the competitive or cooperative strategy. As expected, the RAs easily identified students who fit each category.

Next, Ross invited these students to play the game in a psychology experiment. There was one added twist: The researchers varied a seemingly minor aspect of the social situation—what the game was called. They told half the participants that the name was the Wall Street Game and half that it was the Community Game. Everything else about the game was identical. Thus, people who were judged as either competitive or cooperative played a game that was called either the Wall Street Game or the Community Game, resulting in four conditions.

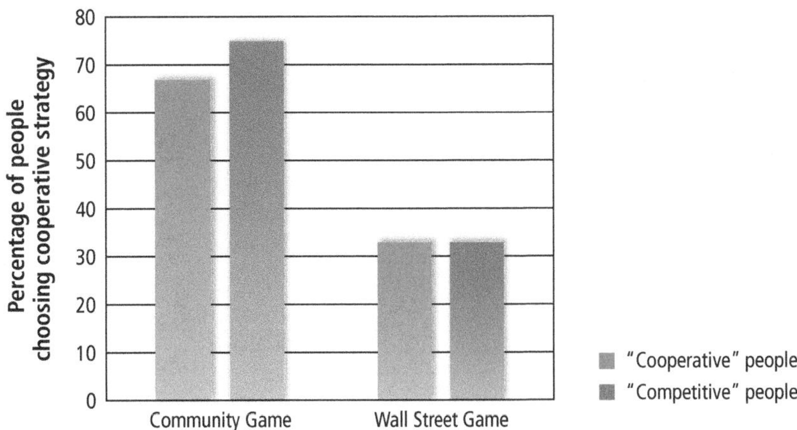

FIGURE 1.1

Why the Name of the Game Matters

In this experiment, when the name of the game was the "Community Game," players were far more likely to behave cooperatively than when it was called the "Wall Street Game"—regardless of their own cooperative or competitive personality traits. The game's title conveyed social norms that trumped personality and shaped the players' behavior.

(Adapted from Liberman, Samuels, & Ross, 2004)

Again, most of us go through life assuming that what really counts is an individual's personality, not something about the individual's immediate situation and certainly not something as trivial as what a game is called, right? Not so fast! As seen in Figure 1.1, the name of the game made a tremendous difference in how people behaved. When it was called the Wall Street Game, approximately two thirds of the students responded competitively, whereas when it was called the Community Game, only a third responded competitively. The name of the game sent a powerful message about how the players should behave. It alone conveyed a social norm about what kind of behavior was appropriate in this situation. In Chapter 7, we will see that social norms can shape people's behaviors in all kinds of remarkable ways.

In this situation, a student's personality made no measurable difference in the student's behavior. The students labeled *competitive* were no more likely to adopt the competitive strategy than those who were labeled *cooperative*. This pattern of results is one we will see throughout this book: Aspects of the social situation that may seem minor can overwhelm the differences in people's personalities (Ross & Ward, 1996). This is not to say that personality differences do not exist or are unimportant; they do exist and frequently are of great importance. But social and environmental situations are so powerful that they have dramatic effects on almost everyone. This is the domain of the social psychologist.

The Power of Social Interpretation

It is one thing to say that the social situation has profound effects on human behavior, but what exactly do we mean by the social situation? One strategy for defining it would be to specify the objective properties of the situation, such as how rewarding it is to people, and then document the behaviors that follow from these objective properties.

This is the approach taken by **behaviorism**, a school of psychology maintaining that to understand human behavior, one need only consider the reinforcing properties of the environment: When behavior is followed by a reward (such as money, attention, praise, or other benefits), it is likely to continue; when behavior is followed by a punishment (such as pain, loss, or angry shouts), it is likely to become extinguished. Dogs come when they are called because they have learned that compliance is followed by positive reinforcement (e.g., food or petting); children memorize their multiplication tables more quickly if you praise them, smile at them, and paste a gold star on their foreheads following correct answers. Psychologists in this tradition, notably the pioneering behaviorist B. F. Skinner (1938), believed that all behavior could be understood by examining the rewards and punishments in the organism's environment. Thus, to understand Sam's lukewarm feelings about his fraternity, Alpha Beta, a behaviorist might

Behaviorism

A school of psychology maintaining that to understand human behavior, one need only consider the reinforcing properties of the environment.

Construal
The way in which people perceive, comprehend, and interpret the social world

Gestalt Psychology
A school of psychology stressing the importance of studying the subjective way in which an object appears in people's minds rather than the objective, physical attributes of the object

analyze the situation to identify the consequences of his actions: Are they rewarded with attention and affection from the other guys or punished by anger and rejection?

Behaviorism has many strengths, and its principles explain some behavior very well, as we will see in our discussion in Chapter 10 of the research on social exchange theory. However, because the early behaviorists chose not to deal with cognition, thinking, and feeling—concepts they considered too vague and mentalistic and not sufficiently anchored to observable behavior—they overlooked phenomena that are vital to the human social experience. They overlooked the importance of *how people interpret their environments.*

For social psychologists, the relationship between the social environment and the individual is a two-way street. Not only does the situation influence people's behavior; people's behavior also depends on their interpretation, or **construal**, of their social environment (Griffin & Ross, 1991; Ross & Nisbett, 1991). In fact, it is often more important to understand how people perceive, comprehend, and interpret the social world than it is to understand its objective properties (Lewin, 1943).

For example, if a person approaches you, slaps you on the back, and asks you how you are feeling, your response will depend not on what that person has done, but how you *interpret* that behavior. You might construe these actions differently depending on whether they come from a close friend who is concerned about your health, a casual acquaintance who is just passing the time of day, or an automobile salesperson attempting to be ingratiating for the purpose of selling you a used car. And your answer will vary also, even if the question about your health were worded the same and asked in the same tone of voice. You would be unlikely to say, "Actually, I'm feeling pretty worried about this kidney pain" to a salesperson, but you might tell your close friend.

This emphasis on construal has its roots in an approach called **Gestalt psychology**. First proposed as a theory of how people perceive the physical world, Gestalt psychology holds that we should study the subjective way in which an object appears in people's minds (the *gestalt*, or whole) rather than the way in which the objective, physical attributes of the object combine. For example, one way to understand how people perceive a painting would be to break it down into its individual elements, such as the exact amounts of primary colors applied to the different parts of the canvas, the types of brushstrokes used to apply the colors, and the different geometric shapes they form. We might then attempt to determine how these elements are combined by the perceiver to form an overall image of the painting. According to Gestalt psychologists, however, it is impossible to understand the way an object is perceived only by studying these building blocks of perception. The whole is different from the sum of its parts. One must focus on the phenomenology of the perceiver—on how an object appears to people—instead of on the individual objective elements of the stimulus.

Simulate on **MyPsychLab**
Learn more about Gestalt principles in the MyPsychLab simulation ***Gestalt Laws of Perception.***

The Gestalt approach was formulated in Germany in the first part of the twentieth century by Kurt Koffka, Wolfgang Köhler, Max Wertheimer, and their students and colleagues. In the late 1930s, several of these psychologists fled to the United States to escape the Nazi regime (Cartwright, 1979). Among the émigrés was Kurt Lewin, generally considered the founding father of modern experimental social psychology. As a young German Jewish professor in the 1930s, Lewin experienced the anti-Semitism rampant in Nazi Germany. The experience profoundly affected his thinking, and, once he moved to the United States, Lewin helped shape American social psychology, directing it toward a deep interest in exploring the causes and cures of prejudice and ethnic stereotyping.

Kurt Lewin: "If an individual sits in a room trusting that the ceiling will not come down, should only his 'subjective probability' be taken into account for predicting behavior or should we also consider the 'objective probability' of the ceiling's coming down as determined by engineers? To my mind, only the first has to be taken into account."

As a theorist, Lewin took the bold step of applying Gestalt principles beyond the perception of objects to social perception: how people perceive other people and their motives, intentions, and behaviors. Lewin was the first scientist to fully realize the importance of taking the perspective of the people in a situation. Social psychologists soon began to focus on the importance of how people construe their environments.

Construal has important implications. In a murder trial, when the prosecution presents compelling evidence it believes will prove the defendant guilty, the verdict always hinges on precisely how each jury member construes that evidence. These construals rest on a variety of events and perceptions that often bear no objective relevance to the case. During cross-examination, did a key witness come across as being too remote or too arrogant? Did the prosecutor appear to be smug, obnoxious, or uncertain?

A special kind of construal is what social psychologist Lee Ross calls "naïve realism," the conviction that all of us share that we perceive things "as they really are." If other people see the same things differently, therefore, it must be because *they* are biased (Ross, 2004, 2010; Ehrlinger, Gilovich, & Ross, 2005). Ross has been working closely with Israeli and Palestinian negotiators. These negotiations frequently run aground because of naïve realism; each side assumes that other reasonable people see things the same way they do. "[E]ven when each side recognizes that the other side perceives the issues differently," says Ross, "each thinks that the other side is biased while they themselves are objective and that their own perceptions of reality should provide the basis for settlement." So both sides resist compromise, fearing that their "biased" opponent will benefit more than they.

Fritz Heider, one of the early founders of social psychology, once observed, "Generally, a person reacts to what he thinks the other person is perceiving, feeling, and thinking, in addition to what the other person may be doing."

In a simple experiment, Ross took peace proposals created by Israeli negotiators, labeled them as Palestinian proposals, and asked Israeli citizens to judge them. The Israelis liked the Palestinian proposal attributed to Israel more than they liked the Israeli proposal attributed to the Palestinians. Ross concludes, "If your own proposal isn't going to be attractive to you when it comes from the other side, what chance is there that the *other* side's proposal is going to be attractive when it comes from the other side?" The hope is that once negotiators on both sides become fully aware of this phenomenon and how it impedes conflict resolution, a reasonable compromise will be more likely.

You can see that construals range from the simple (as in the example of the question "How are you feeling?") to the remarkably complex (international negotiations). And they affect all of us in our everyday lives. Imagine that Jason is a shy high school student who admires Maria from afar. As a budding social psychologist, you have the job of predicting whether or not Jason will ask Maria to the senior prom. To do this, you need to begin by viewing Maria's behavior through Jason's eyes—that is, by seeing how Jason interprets her behavior. If she smiles at him, does Jason construe her behavior as mere politeness, the kind of politeness she would extend to any of the dozens of nerds and losers in the senior class? Or does he view her smile as an encouraging sign, one that inspires him to gather the courage to ask her out? If she ignores him, does Jason figure that she's playing hard to get, or does he take it as a sign that she's not interested in him? To predict Jason's behavior, it is not enough to know the details of Maria's behavior; it is imperative to know how Jason interprets her behavior.

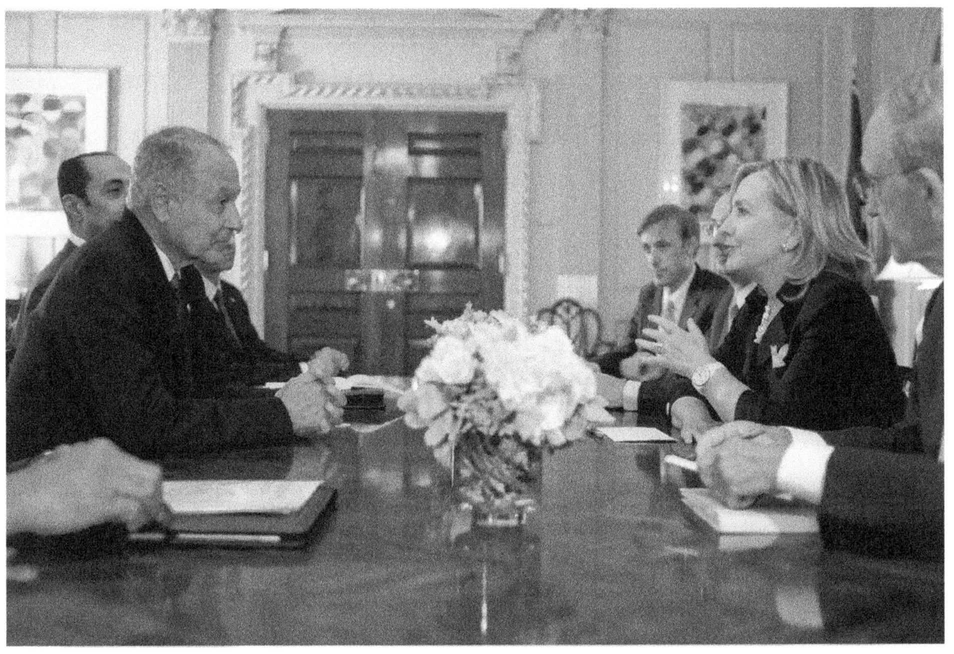

Research by social psychologists on construal shows why negotiation between nations can be so difficult: Each side thinks that it sees the issues clearly but that the other side is "biased."

Now suppose that after class one day, Maria kisses Jason on the cheek. Again, how he responds will depend on how he construes the situation: Does he interpret that kiss as a first step, a sign of romantic interest on Maria's part? Does he see it as an aloof, sisterly signal that Maria wants to be friends but nothing more? Or does he see it as a sign that Maria is interested in him but wants to proceed slowly? Were Jason to misinterpret the situation, he might commit a serious blunder: He might turn his back on what could have been the love of his life, or he might express his own passionate feelings inappropriately. In either case, social psychologists would say that the best strategy for understanding Jason's reaction would be to find a way to determine his construal of Maria's behavior rather than to dissect the objective nature of the kiss itself (its length, degree of pressure, etc.). But how are these construals formed? Stay tuned.

Where Construals Come From: Basic Human Motives

How will Jason determine why Maria kissed him? If it is true that subjective and not objective situations influence people, we need to understand how people arrive at their subjective impressions of the world. What are people trying to accomplish when they interpret the social world? When construing their environments, are most people concerned with making an interpretation that places them in the most positive light (e.g., Jason's believing "Maria is going to the prom with Eric because she is just trying to make me jealous") or with making the most accurate interpretation, even if it is unflattering (e.g., "Painful as it may be, I must admit that she would rather go to the prom with a sea slug than with me")? Social psychologists seek to understand the fundamental laws of human nature, common to all, that explain why we construe the social world the way we do.

We human beings are complex organisms. At any given moment, various intersecting motives underlie our thoughts and behaviors, including hunger, thirst, fear, a desire for control, and the promise of love, favors, and other rewards. (Some of these psychological motives are discussed in Chapters 10 and 11.) Two motives that concern us here are of primary importance: *the need to feel good about ourselves* and *the need to be accurate.* Sometimes, each of these motives pulls us in the same direction. Often, though, these motives tug us in opposite directions, where to perceive the world accurately requires us to face up to the fact that we have behaved foolishly or immorally.

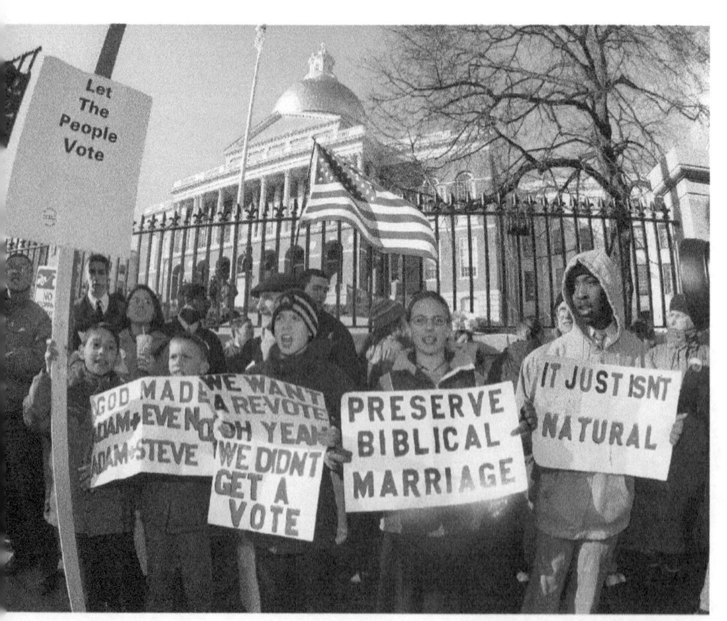

Some people would construe this demonstration as an act of moral protest against same-sex marriage; others would construe it as an act of homophobia and prejudice. Each side is sure that they are right. Where do construals come from, and what are their consequences?

Leon Festinger, one of social psychology's most innovative theorists, was quick to realize that it is precisely when these two motives pull in opposite directions that we can gain our most valuable insights into the workings of the human mind. Imagine that you are the president of the United States and your country is engaged in a difficult and costly war overseas. You have poured hundreds of billions of dollars into that war, and it has consumed tens of thousands of American lives as well as thousands more lives of innocent civilians. The war seems to be at a stalemate; no end is in sight. You frequently wake up in the middle of the night, bathed in the cold sweat of conflict: On the one hand, you deplore all the carnage that is going on; on the other hand, you don't want to go down in history as the first American president to lose a war.

Some of your advisers tell you that they can see the light at the end of the tunnel, and that if you intensify the bombing or add thousands more troops, the enemy will soon capitulate and the war will be over. This would be a great outcome for you: Not only will you have succeeded in achieving your military and political aims, but history will consider you to have been a great leader as well. Other advisers, however, believe that intensifying the bombing will only strengthen the enemy's resolve; they advise you to sue for peace.

Which advisers are you likely to believe? As we shall see in Chapter 6, President Lyndon Johnson faced this exact dilemma in the mid-1970s, with the war in Vietnam; so did George W. Bush in the mid-2000s, when the war in Iraq did not end in 6 weeks as he had predicted when it began in 2003; so did Barack Obama, in deciding in 2009 whether to invest more troops in the war in Afghanistan. Most presidents have chosen to believe their advisers who suggest escalating the war, because if they succeed in winning, the victory justifies the human and financial cost; but withdrawing not only means going down in history as a president who lost a war, but also having to justify the fact that all those lives and all that money have been spent in vain. As you can see, the need to feel good about our decisions can fly in the face of the need to be accurate, and can have catastrophic consequences (Draper, 2008; McClellan, 2008; McNamara, 1995; Woodward, 2008). In Johnson's case, the decision to increase the bombing *did* strengthen the enemy's resolve, thereby prolonging the war in Vietnam.

The Self-Esteem Approach: The Need to Feel Good About Ourselves

Most people have a strong need to maintain reasonably high **self-esteem**—that is, to see themselves as good, competent, and decent (Aronson, 1998, 2007; Baumeister, 1993; Tavris & Aronson, 2007). Given the choice between distorting the world to feel good about themselves and representing the world accurately, people often take the first option.

Justifying Past Behavior Suppose a couple gets divorced after 10 years of a marriage made difficult by the husband's irrational jealousy. Rather than admitting the truth—that his jealousy and possessiveness drove her away—the husband blames the breakup of his marriage on the fact that his ex-wife was not responsive enough to his needs. His interpretation serves a purpose: It makes him feel better about himself (Simpson, 2010). Acknowledging major deficiencies in ourselves is very difficult, even when the cost is seeing the world inaccurately. The consequence of this distortion, of course, is that learning from experience becomes very unlikely. In his next marriage, the husband is likely to recreate the same problems.

We do not mean that people totally distort reality, denying the existence of all information that reflects badly on them; such extreme behavior is rare. Yet it is often possible for people to put a slightly different spin on the existing facts—one that puts them in the best possible light. Consider Roger. He's the guy whose shoes are almost always untied and who frequently has coffee stains on the front of his shirt. Most observers consider Roger a slob, but Roger probably describes himself as casual and noncompulsive. The fact that people distort their interpretation of reality so that they feel better about themselves is not surprising, but the ways in which this motive operates are often startling.

Watch on **MyPsychLab**
To learn more about how we justify our actions, watch the MyPsychLab video ***Carol Tavris: How does cognitive dissonance typically play out in society?***

Suffering and Self-Justification Let's go back to one of our early scenarios: the case of Oscar and his son, Sam. Why was Sam less enamored of his fraternity brothers than Oscar had been when he was in college? Recall that Oscar quickly formed the hypothesis that perhaps his fraternity was not attracting the kinds of wonderful people who were there when he was in college, and that personality psychologists might suggest that father and son differ in their degree of extroversion or other traits. This might be true. But social psychologists would suspect that a far more compelling explanation involves the hazing itself. Specifically, we would contend that a major factor that increased Oscar's liking for his fraternity brothers was the degrading hazing ritual he underwent, a ritual Sam was able to avoid. Why would something so negative cause Oscar to like his fraternity? Don't principles of behaviorism show that rewards, not punishments, make us like things associated with them? Quite so. But as we indicated earlier, social psychologists have discovered that this formulation is too simple to account for human thinking and motivation. Human beings have a need to justify their past behavior, and this need leads them to do many things a behaviorist could not explain.

Self-Esteem
People's evaluations of their own self-worth—that is, the extent to which they view themselves as good, competent, and decent

These first-year students are being "welcomed" to their university by seniors who subject them to hazing. Doing silly or dangerous things as part of a hazing ritual may be, well, silly or dangerous. At the same time, it does build cohesiveness.

Here's how it works. If Oscar goes through a severe hazing to become a member of the fraternity but later discovers unpleasant things about his fraternity brothers, he will feel like a fool: "Why did I go through all that pain and embarrassment to live in a house with a bunch of jerks? Only a moron would do a thing like that." To avoid feeling like a fool, he will try to justify his decision to undergo the hazing by distorting his interpretation of his fraternity experience. In other words, he will try to put a positive spin on his experiences.

Suppose that, having gone through all that hazing, Oscar moves into the fraternity house and begins to experience things that to an outside observer would not be very positive: The fraternity dues make a significant dent in Oscar's budget, the frequent parties take a toll on the amount of studying he can do, and consequently his grades suffer. Whereas an unmotivated observer—someone who didn't go through the hazing—might consider these aspects of fraternity life as definite negatives, Oscar is motivated to see them differently; indeed, he considers them a small price to pay for the sense of brotherhood he feels. He focuses on the good parts of living in the fraternity, and he distorts or dismisses the bad parts as inconsequential. The result of all this self-justification is to make Oscar more kindly disposed toward the fraternity and its members than Sam was, because Sam, not having gone through the hazing, had no need to justify his behavior and thus no need to see his fraternity experiences in a positive light. The end result? Oscar loved his fraternity and Sam did not.

Does this explanation sound far-fetched? How do we know that the people in the fraternity were not objectively nicer when Oscar was a member than when Sam was a member? In a series of well-controlled classic laboratory experiments, social psychologists investigated the phenomenon of hazing: The experimenters held constant everything in the situation, including the precise behavior of the fraternity members; the only thing they varied was the severity of the hazing that the students underwent in order to become members. The results demonstrated conclusively that the more unpleasant the procedure the participants underwent to get into a group, the better they liked the group—even though, objectively, the group members were the same people behaving the same way for everyone (Aronson & Mills, 1959; Gerard & Mathewson, 1966). We discuss this phenomenon more thoroughly in Chapter 6. The important points to remember here are that human beings are motivated to maintain a positive picture of themselves, in part by justifying their past behavior, and that under certain specifiable conditions, this leads them to do things that at first glance might seem surprising or paradoxical. They might prefer people and things for whom they have suffered to people and things they associate with ease and pleasure.

The Social Cognition Approach: The Need to Be Accurate

Even when people are bending the facts to see themselves in as favorable a way as they can, they do not completely distort reality. They know the difference between fantasizing about some hot rock star and believing in the fantasy that the rock star is in love with them. Human beings are quite skilled at thinking, contemplating, and deducing, and these astonishing talents begin early in life. It is impossible to observe the cognitive development of a child without being awestruck. Just think of the vast gains in knowledge and reasoning that occur in the first few years of life, as a child grows from a squirming, helpless newborn who can do little but eat, cry, poop, and sleep into a talkative 4-year-old who can utter complex sentences, hatch diabolical plots to frustrate a younger sibling, and create elaborate imaginary universes.

Social Cognition Given the amazing cognitive abilities of our species, it makes sense that social psychologists, when formulating theories of social behavior, would take into consideration the way in which human beings think about the world. We call this the cognitive approach to social psychology, or **social cognition** (Fiske & Taylor, 1991; Markus & Zajonc, 1985; Nisbett & Ross, 1980). Researchers who attempt to under stand social behavior from the perspective of social cognition begin with the assumption that all people try to view the world as accurately as possible. They regard human beings as amateur sleuths who are doing their best to understand and predict their social world.

Unfortunately, we often make mistakes in that effort to understand and predict, because we almost never know all the facts we need to judge a given situation accurately. Whether it is a relatively simple decision, such as which breakfast cereal offers the best combination of healthfulness and tastiness, or a slightly more complex decision, such as our desire to buy the best car we can for under $18,000, or a much more complex decision, such as choosing a partner who will make us deliriously happy for the rest of our lives, it is usually impossible to gather all the relevant facts in advance. Moreover, we make countless decisions every day. Even if there were a way to gather all the facts for each decision, we lack the time or the stamina to do so.

Does this sound overblown? Aren't most decisions fairly easy? Let's take a closer look. We will begin by asking you an easy question: Which breakfast cereal is better for you, Lucky Charms or Quaker 100% Natural granola with oats, honey, and raisins? If you are like most of our students, you answered, "100% Natural." After all, everybody knows that Lucky Charms is a kids' cereal, full of sugar and cute little marshmallows, with a picture of a leprechaun on the box. Quaker's 100% Natural has a picture of all that healthy granola, the box is the color of natural wheat (light tan), and doesn't *natural* mean "good for you"? If that's the way you reasoned, you have fallen into a common cognitive trap: You have generalized from the cover to the product. A careful reading of the ingredients in small print will reveal that, per one cup serving, 100% Natural has 420 calories, 30 grams of sugar, and 12 grams of fat; no wonder *Men's Health* magazine rated it the worst packaged cereal in America. In contrast, a cup of Lucky Charms has 142 calories, 14 grams of sugar, and 1 gram of fat. Even in the simple world of cereals, things are not always what they seem.

Expectations About the Social World To add to the difficulty, sometimes our expectations about the social world interfere with perceiving it accurately. Our expectations can even change the *nature* of the social world. Imagine that you are an elementary school teacher dedicated to improving the lives of your students. At the beginning of the academic year, you review each student's standardized intelligence test scores. Early in your career, you were pretty sure that these tests could gauge each child's true potential. But after several years of teaching, you have become certain that these tests are accurate. You have come to see that, almost invariably, the kids who got high scores on these tests are the ones who did the best in your classroom, and the kids who got low scores performed poorly in class.

This scenario doesn't sound all that surprising, except for one fact: You might be wrong about the validity of the intelligence tests. It might be that the tests were not very accurate but that you unintentionally treated the kids with high scores and the kids with low scores differently. This is exactly what Robert Rosenthal and Lenore Jacobson (1968) found in their investigation of a phenomenon called the *self-fulfilling prophecy*: You expect that you or another person will behave in some way, so you act in ways to make your prediction come true (see Chapter 3). The researchers entered elementary school classrooms and administered a test. They then informed each teacher that, according to the test, a few specific students were "bloomers" who were about to take off and perform extremely well. In actuality, the test showed no such thing. The children labeled as bloomers were chosen at random by drawing names out of a hat and thus were no different, on average, from any of the other kids. Lo and behold, on returning to the classroom at the end of the school year, Rosenthal and Jacobson found that the bloomers were performing extremely well. The mere fact that the teachers were led to expect these students to do well caused an improvement in their performance. This striking phenomenon is no fluke; it has been replicated a number of times in many different schools (Rosenthal, 1995).

Social Cognition

How people think about themselves and the social world; more specifically, how people select, interpret, remember, and use social information to make judgments and decisions

How did it come about? Although this outcome seems almost magical, it is embedded in an important aspect of human nature. If you were one of those teachers and were led to expect two or three specific students to perform well, you would be more likely to treat those students in special ways: paying more attention to them, listening to them with more respect, calling on them more frequently, encouraging them, and trying to teach them more-challenging material. This, in turn, would almost certainly make these students feel happier, more respected, more motivated, and smarter—and, *voilà*, the prophecy is fulfilled. Thus, even when we are trying to perceive the social world as accurately as we can, there are many ways in which we can go wrong, ending up with the wrong impressions. We will see why in Chapters 3 and 4.

Social Psychology and Social Problems

To reiterate, social psychology can be defined as the scientific study of social influence. But perhaps you are wondering why we want to understand social influence in the first place. Who ca-res? And what difference does it make whether our behavior has its roots in the desire to be accurate or to bolster our self-esteem?

The most basic answer is simple: We are curious. Social psychologists are fascinated by human social behavior and want to understand it on the deepest possible level. In a sense, all of us are social psychologists. We all live in a social environment, and we are all more than mildly curious about such issues as how we become influenced, how we influence others, and why we fall in love with some people, dislike others, and are indifferent to still others. You don't have to be with people literally in order to be in a social environment. Facebook is a social psychologist's dream laboratory because it's all there: love, anger, bullying, bragging, affection, flirting, wounds, quarrels, friending and unfriending, pride and prejudice.

Watch on MyPsychLab
To learn more about cognitive dissonance, watch the MyPsychLab video ***Cognitive Dissonance: Need to Justify Our Actions.***

Leon Festinger: "The way I have always thought about it is that if the empirical world looks complicated, if people seem to react in bewilderingly different ways to similar forces, and if I cannot see the operation of universal underlying dynamics, then that is my fault. I have asked the wrong questions; I have, at a theoretical level, sliced up the world incorrectly. The underlying dynamics are there, and I have to find the theoretical apparatus that will enable me to reveal these uniformities."

Many social psychologists have another reason for studying the causes of social behavior: to contribute to the solution of social problems. From the very beginning of our young science, social psychologists have been keenly interested in such social challenges as reducing violence and prejudice and increasing altruism and tolerance. Contemporary social psychologists have continued this tradition and have broadened the issues of concern to include such endeavors as inducing people to conserve natural resources like water and energy (Dickerson et al., 1992), educating people to practice safer sex to reduce the spread of HIV and other sexually transmitted diseases (Aronson, 1997, 1998; Stone, 1994), understanding the relationship between viewing violence on television and the violent behavior of television watchers (Eron, 1996), developing effective negotiation strategies to resolve international conflict (Kelman, 1997; Ross, 2004, 2010), finding ways to reduce ethnic prejudice and violence in classrooms (Aronson & Patnoe, 1997), raising children's intelligence through environmental interventions and better school programs (Nisbett, 2009), and reducing the high school dropout rate of minority students (J. Aronson, 2010).

The ability to understand and explain complex and harmful social behavior brings with it the challenge to change it. For example, when the American government began to take the AIDS epidemic seriously, it mounted an advertising campaign that seemed intent on frightening people into practicing safer sex. This seems consistent with common sense: If you want people to do something they wouldn't ordinarily do, why not scare the daylights out of them?

This is not a stupid idea. There are many dysfunctional acts (e.g., cigarette smoking, drunk driving) for which the induction of fear can and does motivate people to take rational, appropriate action to preserve their health (Aronson, 2010a; Levy-Leboyer, 1988; Wilson, Purdon, & Wallston, 1988). But, based on years of systematic research on persuasion, social psychologists were quick to realize that in the specific situation of AIDS, arousing fear would almost certainly not produce the desired effect for most people, because most people do not want to think about dying or contracting a horrible illness while they are getting ready to have sex. Moreover, most people do not enjoy using condoms, because they feel that interrupting the sexual act to put on a condom tends to diminish the mood. Given these considerations, when people have been exposed to frightening messages about STDs and AIDS, instead of engaging in rational problem-solving behavior ("How can I protect myself and my partner?"), most tend to reduce that fear by engaging in denial ("It can't happen to me," "Surely no one I'd sleep with is HIV positive").

In this case, as you may have figured out, denial stems not from the desire to be accurate, but from the need to maintain self-esteem. If people can convince themselves that their sexual partners do not carry the HIV virus, they can continue to enjoy unprotected sex while maintaining a reasonably favorable picture of themselves as rational beings. By understanding how this process works, social psychologists have been able to create more effective programs for AIDS education and prevention, as we shall see (Aronson, 1997; Aronson, Fried, & Stone, 1991; Stone et al., 1994).

Social psychology can help us study social problems and find ways to solve them. Social psychologists might study whether children who watch violence on television become more aggressive themselves—and, if so, what kind of intervention might be beneficial.

Throughout this book, we will examine many other examples of the application of social psychology to real-world problems, including the effects of the mass media on attitudes and behavior (Chapter 7), violence and aggression (Chapter 12), and prejudice (Chapter 13). Beginning in the next chapter, you will find an occasional feature called Connections, in which we show how social psychology can be used to understand and solve problems in everyday life. For interested readers, we have also included four final chapters on the application of social psychology to contemporary issues involving health, the environment, law, and education. Finally, we hope that by understanding the fundamental causes of behavior as social psychologists study them, you will also be in a better position to change your own self-defeating or misguided behavior, improve your relationships, and make better decisions.

USE IT! Thinking Like a Social Psychologist

Lately, your once-easygoing, considerate roommate seems to have had a personality transplant, becoming grouchy, thoughtless, and rude. This has been going on for a couple of weeks, long enough to make you think about requesting a shift to a private room or asking for a different roommate. Before you do, what mistake might you be making? Hint: Think of the fundamental attribution error. How likely is it that your roommate's personality has undergone such a drastic change? What might be happening in your roommate's environment or stress levels to cause this change of behavior?

Summary

What is social psychology, and how is it different from other disciplines?

- **What Is Social Psychology?** Social psychology is defined as the scientific study of the way in which people's thoughts, feelings, and behaviors are influenced by the real or imagined presence of other people. Social psychologists are interested in understanding how and why the social environment shapes the thoughts, feelings, and behaviors of the individual.
  - **Social Psychology, Science, and Common Sense** Social psychologists approach the understanding of **social influence** differently from philosophers, journalists, or the layperson. Social psychologists develop explanations of social influence through *empirical methods*, such as experiments in which the variables being studied are carefully controlled. The goal of the science of social psychology is to discover universal laws of human behavior, which is why *cross-cultural research* is often essential.
  - **How Social Psychology Differs from Its Closest Cousins** When trying to explain social behavior, personality psychologists explain the behavior in terms of the person's individual character traits. Although social psychologists would agree that personalities vary, they explain social behavior in terms of the *power of the social situation* to shape how one acts. While social psychology is rooted in the study of the individual's internal

psychological processes, *the level of analysis for social psychology is the individual in the context of a social situation.* In contrast, sociologists focus their analysis on groupings of people organized in social categories such as family, race, religion, and economic class. Social psychologists seek to identify universal *properties of human nature* that make everyone susceptible to social influence regardless of social class or culture. Sociologists seek to explain *properties of societies.*

What's more important: personality or situation?

- **The Power of the Situation** Individual behavior is powerfully influenced by the social environment, but many people don't want to believe this. Social psychologists must contend with the **fundamental attribution error**, the tendency to explain our own and other people's behavior entirely in terms of personality traits and to underestimate the power of social influence. But social psychologists have shown time and again that social and environmental situations are usually more powerful than personality differences in determining an individual's behavior.

How did behaviorism and Gestalt psychology contribute to the development of social psychological thought?

- **The Power of Social Interpretation** Social psychologists have shown that the relationship between individuals and situations is a two-way street, so it is important to understand not only how situations influence individuals, but how people *perceive and interpret* the social world and the behavior of others. These perceptions are more influential than objective aspects of the situation itself. The term **construal** refers to the world as it is interpreted by the individual.

What are the differences between the self-esteem approach and the social cognition approach?

- **Where Construals Come From: Basic Human Motives** The way in which an individual construes (perceives, comprehends, and interprets) a situation is largely shaped by two basic human motives: *the need to be accurate* and *the need to feel good about ourselves.* At times these two motives tug in opposite directions; for example, when an accurate view of how we acted in a situation would reveal that we behaved selfishly.
  - **The Self-Esteem Approach: The Need to Feel Good About Ourselves** Most people have a strong need to see themselves as good, competent, and decent. People often distort their perception of the world to preserve their self-esteem.
  - **The Social Cognition Approach: The Need to Be Accurate** The social cognition perspective is an approach to social psychology that takes into account the way in which human beings think about the world. Individuals are viewed as trying to gain accurate understandings so that they can make effective judgments and decisions that range from which cereal to eat to whom they will marry. In actuality, individuals typically act on the basis of incomplete and inaccurately interpreted information.

How can social psychology help solve social problems?

- **Social Psychology and Social Problems** Social psychological theories about human behavior have been applied effectively to deal with a range of contemporary problems that include prejudice, energy shortages, the spread of AIDS, unhealthy habits, and violence in the schools. The best interventions for serious social problems are those based on scientifically grounded theories about human construal and behavior.

Chapter 1 Test

Study and Review on MyPsychLab

1. The topic that would most interest a social psychologist is
   - **a.** whether people who commit crimes tend to have more aggressive personalities than people who do not.
   - **b.** whether people who commit crimes have different genes from people who do not.
   - **c.** how the level of extroversion of different presidents affected their political decisions.
   - **d.** whether people's decision about whether to cheat on a test is influenced by how they imagine their friends would react if they found out.
   - **e.** the extent to which people's social class predicts their income.

2. How does social psychology differ from personality psychology?
   - **a.** Social psychology focuses on individual differences, whereas personality psychology focuses on how people behave in different situations.
   - **b.** Social psychology focuses on the processes that people have in common with one another that make them susceptible to social influence, whereas personality psychology focuses on individual differences.
   - **c.** Social psychology provides general laws and theories about societies, not individuals, whereas personality psychology studies the characteristics that make people unique and different from each other.
   - **d.** Social psychology focuses on individual differences, whereas personality psychology provides general laws and theories about societies, not individuals.

3. A stranger approaches Emily on campus and says he is a professional photographer. He asks if she will spend 15 minutes posing for pictures next to the student union. According to a social psychologist, Emily's decision will depend on which of the following?
   - **a.** How well dressed the man is.
   - **b.** Whether the man offers to pay her.
   - **c.** How Emily construes the situation.
   - **d.** Whether the man has a criminal record.

4. Researchers who try to understand human behavior from the perspective of *social cognition* assume that
   a. people try to view the world as accurately as possible.
   b. people almost always view the world accurately.
   c. people almost always make mistakes in how they view the world.
   d. people distort reality in order to view themselves favorably.
   e. the need for control is the most important motive behind a person's behavior.

5. The *fundamental attribution error* is best defined as the tendency to
   a. explain our own and other people's behavior entirely in terms of personality traits, thereby underestimating the power of social influence.
   b. explain our own and other people's behavior in terms of the social situation, thereby underestimating the power of personality factors.
   c. believe that people's group memberships influence their behavior more than their personalities.
   d. believe that people's personalities influence their behavior more than their group memberships.

6. Which of the following is least consistent with the *self-esteem approach* to how people view themselves and the social world?
   a. After Sarah leaves Bob for someone else, Bob decides that he never really liked her very much and that she had several annoying habits.
   b. Students who want to take Professor Lopez's seminar have to apply by writing a 10-page essay. Everyone who is selected ends up loving the class.
   c. Janetta did poorly on the first test in her psychology class. She admits to herself that she didn't study very much and vows to study harder for the next test.
   d. Sam has been involved in several minor traffic accidents since getting his driver's license. "There sure are a lot of terrible drivers out there," he says to himself. "People should learn to be good drivers like me."

Answer Key

1-d, 2-b, 3-c, 4-a, 5-a, 6-c

2 Methodology

How Social Psychologists Do Research

IN THIS INFORMATION AGE, WHEN PRETTY MUCH ANYTHING CAN BE FOUND ON THE INTERNET, PORNOGRAPHY IS MORE AVAILABLE THAN EVER BEFORE. One poll found that a quarter of all employees who have access to the Internet visit porn sites during their workdays ("The Tangled Web of Porn," 2008). It is thus important to ask whether exposure to pornography has harmful effects. Is it possible, for example, that looking at graphic sex increases the likelihood that men will become sexually violent?

There has been plenty of debate on both sides of this question. Legal scholar Catharine MacKinnon (1993) argued that "Pornography is the perfect preparation—motivator and instruction manual in one—for . . . sexual atrocities" (p. 28). In 1985, a group of experts, appointed by the attorney general of the United States, voiced a similar opinion, concluding that pornography is a cause of rape and other violent crimes. But in 1970, another commission reviewed much of the same evidence and concluded that pornography does *not* contribute significantly to sexual violence. Whom are we to believe? Is there a scientific way to determine the answer? We believe there is, and in this chapter we will discuss the kinds of research methods social psychologists employ, using research on pornography as an example.

We will also discuss another example, this one having to do not with the causes of violence, but how people react to it when they see it. If you happen to witness someone being attacked by another person, you might not intervene directly out of fear for your own safety. Most of us assume that we would help in some way, though, such as by calling the police. But there are so many examples of witnesses failing to help that it has acquired a name: the *bystander effect*. On March 11, 2011, in Bethesda, Maryland, Jayna Murray was brutally murdered by a coworker inside the clothing store where they worked. Two employees in an Apple store next door heard the murder through the walls, including cries for help from Murray, but did nothing to help (Johnson, 2011). In October of 2011 in Southern China, a 2-year-old girl was run over by two vans, minutes apart, and lay in the street dying. Neither car stopped, and a dozen people walked or rode past the girl without stopping to help (Branigan, 2011).

Perhaps the most famous case was the murder of Kitty Genovese, who was assaulted in the alley of an apartment complex in Queens, New York, in 1964. The attack lasted 45 minutes, and at the time the media reported that as many as 38 of the apartment residents either saw the attack from their windows or heard Genovese's screams, and yet no one attempted to help her, not even by calling the police. Although the details of this account have been called into question (Manning, Levine, & Collins, 2007), there is no doubt that bystanders often fail to help in emergencies, and the Genovese murder triggered a great deal of soul searching as to why. Some concluded that living in a metropolis dehumanizes us and leads inevitably to apathy, indifference to human suffering, and lack of caring. Is this true? Did big-city life cause the bystanders to ignore Kitty Genovese's screams for help, or was there some other explanation? How can we find out?

FOCUS QUESTIONS

- How do researchers develop hypotheses and theories?
- What are the strengths and weaknesses of the various research designs used by social psychologists?
- What impact do cross-cultural studies, the evolutionary approach, and research in social neuroscience have on the way in which scientists investigate social behavior?
- What is the basic dilemma of the social psychologist, and how do social psychologists solve this dilemma?

In October of 2011, a 2-year-old girl was struck by two vans in a row. A dozen people walked or rode past her. Why didn't they stop to help?

Social Psychology: An Empirical Science

A fundamental principle of social psychology is that many social problems, such as the causes of and reactions to violence, can be studied scientifically (Reis & Gosling, 2010; Wilson, Aronson, & Carlsmith, 2010; Reis & Judd, 2000). Before we discuss how social psychological research is done, we begin with a warning: The results of some of the experiments you encounter will seem obvious because social psychology concerns topics with which we are all intimately familiar—social behavior and social influence (Richard, Bond, & Stokes-Zoota, 2001). This familiarity sets social psychology apart from other sciences. When you read about an experiment in particle physics, it is unlikely that the results will connect with your personal experiences. We don't know about you, but we have never thought, "Wow! That experiment on quarks was just like what happened to me while I was waiting for the bus yesterday," or "My grandmother always told me to watch out for positrons and antimatter." When reading about the results of a study on helping behavior or aggression, however, it is quite common to think, "Come on. I could have predicted that. That's the same thing that happened to me last Friday."

The thing to remember is that, when we study human behavior, the results may appear to have been predictable—in retrospect. Indeed, there is a well-known human tendency called the **hindsight bias**, whereby people exaggerate how much they could have predicted an outcome *after* knowing that it occurred (Fischhoff, 2007; Nestler, Blank, & Egloff, 2010; Sanna & Schwarz, 2007). After we know the winner of a political election, for example, we begin to look for reasons why that candidate won. After the fact, the outcome seems inevitable and easily predictable, even if we were quite unsure who would win before the election. The same is true of findings in psychology experiments; it seems like we could have easily predicted the outcomes—after we know them. The trick is to predict what will happen in an experiment before you know how it turned out. To illustrate that not all obvious findings are easy to predict, take the Try It! quiz on the next page.

I love games. I think I could be very happy being a chess player or dealing with some other kinds of games. But I grew up in the Depression. It didn't seem one could survive on chess, and science is also a game. You have very strict ground rules in science, and your ideas have to check out with the empirical world. That's very tough and also very fascinating.

—Leon Festinger, 1977

Formulating Hypotheses and Theories

Research begins with a hunch, or hypothesis, that the researcher wants to test. There is lore in science that holds that brilliant insights come all of a sudden, as when Archimedes shouted, "Eureka! I have found it!" when the solution to a problem flashed into his mind. Although such insights do sometimes occur suddenly, science is a cumulative process, and people often generate hypotheses from previous theories and research.

Inspiration from Earlier Theories and Research Many studies stem from a researcher's dissatisfaction with existing theories and explanations. After reading other people's work, a researcher might believe that he or she has a better way of explaining people's behavior (e.g., why they fail to help in an emergency). In the 1950s, for example, Leon Festinger was dissatisfied with the ability of a major theory of the day, behaviorism, to explain why people change their attitudes. He formulated a new approach—dissonance theory—that made specific predictions about when and how people would change their attitudes. As we will see in Chapter 6, other researchers were dissatisfied with Festinger's explanation of the results he obtained, so they conducted further research to test other possible explanations. Social psychologists, like scientists

Hindsight Bias

The tendency for people to exaggerate how much they could have predicted an outcome after knowing that it occurred

TRY IT! Social Psychology Quiz: What's Your Prediction?

Answer the following questions, each of which is based on social psychological research.

1. Suppose an authority figure asks college students to administer near-lethal electric shocks to another student who has not harmed them in any way. What percentage of these students will agree to do it?
2. If you give children a reward for doing something they already enjoy doing, they will subsequently like that activity (a) more, (b) the same, or (c) less.
3. Who do you think would be happiest with their choice of a consumer product such as an art poster: (a) people who spend several minutes thinking about why they like or dislike each poster or (b) people who choose a poster without analyzing the reasons for their feelings?
4. Repeated exposure to a stimulus—such as a person, a song, or a painting—will make you like it (a) more, (b) the same, or (c) less.
5. You ask an acquaintance to do you a favor—for example, to lend you $10—and he or she agrees. As a result of doing you this favor, the person will probably like you (a) more, (b) the same, or (c) less.
6. When making a complex decision, is it best to (a) decide right away without any further thought, (b) think carefully about the different options, or (c) find something unrelated to distract you for a while and then make up your mind?
7. In the United States, female college students tend not to do as well on math tests as males do. Under which of the following circumstances will women do as well as men: (a) when they are told that there are no gender differences on the test, (b) when they are told that women tend to do better on a difficult math test (because under these circumstances they rise to the challenge), or (c) when they are told that men outperform women under almost all circumstances?
8. Which statement about the effects of advertising is most true? (a) Subliminal messages implanted in advertisements are more effective than normal, everyday advertising; (b) normal TV ads for painkillers or laundry detergents are more effective than subliminal messages implanted in ads; (c) both types of advertising are equally effective; or (d) neither type of advertising is effective.
9. In public settings in the United States, (a) women touch men more, (b) men touch women more, or (c) there is no difference—men and women touch each other equally.
10. Students walking across campus are asked to fill out a questionnaire on which they rate the degree to which student opinion should be considered on a local campus issue. Which group do you think believed that students should be listened to the most? (a) Those given a light clipboard with the questionnaire attached; (b) those given a heavy clipboard with the questionnaire attached; (c) the weight of the clipboard made no difference in people's ratings.

See page 45 for the answers.

in other disciplines, engage in a continual process of theory refinement: A theory is developed; specific hypotheses derived from that theory are tested; based on the results obtained, the theory is revised and new hypotheses are formulated.

Hypotheses Based on Personal Observations Social psychology deals with phenomena we encounter in everyday life. Researchers often observe something in their lives or the lives of others that they find curious and interesting, stimulating them to construct a theory about why this phenomenon occurred—and to design a study to see if they are right.

Consider the murder of Kitty Genovese that we described earlier. At the time, most people blamed her neighbors' failure to intervene on the apathy, indifference, and callousness that big-city life breeds. Two social psychologists who taught at universities in New York, however, had a different idea. Bibb Latané and John Darley were talking one day about the Genovese murder. Here is how Latané remembers their conversation: "One evening after [a] downtown cocktail party, John Darley ... came back with me to my 12th Street apartment for a drink. Our common complaint was the distressing tendency of acquaintances, on finding that we called ourselves social psychologists, to ask why New Yorkers were so apathetic" (Latané, 1987, p. 78). Instead of focusing on "what was wrong with New Yorkers," Latané and Darley thought it would be more interesting and important to examine the social situation in which Genovese's neighbors found themselves. Maybe, they thought, the more people who witness an emergency, the less likely it is that any given individual will intervene. Genovese's neighbors might have assumed that someone else had called the police, a phenomenon Latané and Darley (1968) referred to as the *diffusion of responsibility.* Perhaps the bystanders would have been more likely to help had each thought he or she alone was witnessing the murder.

After a researcher has a hypothesis, whether it comes from a theory, previous research, or an observation of everyday life, how can he or she tell if it is true? In science, idle speculation will not do; the researcher must collect data to test a hypothesis. Let's look at how the observational method, the correlational method, and the experimental method are used to explore research hypotheses such as Latané and Darley's (see Table 2.1).

Simulate on **MyPsychLab**
To learn more about observational research, try the MyPsychLab simulation ***Observational Research: Laboratory vs. Naturalistic.***

TABLE 2.1 A Summary of Research Methods

Method	Focus	Question Answered
Observational	Description	What is the nature of the phenomenon?
Correlational	Prediction	From knowing X, can we predict Y?
Experimental	Causality	Is variable X a cause of variable Y?

Research Designs

Social psychology is a scientific discipline with a well-developed set of methods for answering questions about social behavior, such as the ones about violence with which we began this chapter. These methods are of three types: the *observational method*, the *correlational method*, and the *experimental method.* Any of these methods could be used to explore a specific research question; each is a powerful tool in some ways and a weak tool in others. Part of the creativity in conducting social psychological research involves choosing the right method, maximizing its strengths, and minimizing its weaknesses.

In this chapter, we will discuss these methods in detail. We, the authors of this book, are social psychologists who have done a great deal of research. We will therefore try to provide you with a firsthand look at both the joy and the difficulty of conducting social psychological studies. The joy comes in unraveling the clues about the causes of interesting and important social behaviors, just as a sleuth gradually unmasks the culprit in a murder mystery. Each of us finds it exhilarating that we have the tools to provide definitive answers to questions philosophers have debated for centuries. At the same time, as seasoned researchers, we have learned to temper this exhilaration with a heavy dose of humility, because there are formidable practical and ethical constraints involved in conducting social psychological research.

The Observational Method: Describing Social Behavior

Observational Method
The technique whereby a researcher observes people and systematically records measurements or impressions of their behavior

Ethnography
The method by which researchers attempt to understand a group or culture by observing it from the inside, without imposing any preconceived notions they might have

There is a lot to be learned by being an astute observer of human behavior. If the goal is to describe what a particular group of people or type of behavior is like, the **observational method** is very helpful. This is the technique whereby a researcher observes people and records measurements or impressions of their behavior. The observational method may take many forms, depending on what the researchers are looking for, how involved or detached they are from the people they are observing, and how much they want to quantify what they observe.

Ethnography One example is **ethnography**, the method by which researchers attempt to understand a group or culture by observing it from the inside, without imposing any preconceived notions they might have. The goal is to understand the richness and complexity of the group by observing it in action. Ethnography is the chief method of cultural anthropology, the study of human cultures and societies. As social psychology broadens its focus by studying social behavior in different cultures, ethnography is increasingly being used to describe different cultures and generate hypotheses about psychological principles (Fine & Elsbach, 2000; Hodson, 2004; Uzzel, 2000).

Consider this example from the early years of social psychological research. In the early 1950s, a group of people in the Midwest predicted that the world would come to an end in a violent cataclysm on a specific date. They also announced that they would be rescued in time by a spaceship that would land in their leader's backyard. Assuming that the end of the world was not imminent, Leon Festinger and his colleagues thought it would be interesting to observe this group closely and chronicle how they reacted when their beliefs and prophecy were disconfirmed (Festinger, Riecken, & Schachter, 1956). To monitor the hour-to-hour conversations of this group, the social psychologists found it necessary to become members and pretend that they too believed the world was about to end.

The key to ethnography is to avoid imposing one's preconceived notions on the group and to try to understand the point of view of the people being studied. Sometimes, however, researchers have a specific hypothesis that they want to test using the observational method. An investigator might be interested, for example, in how much aggression children exhibit during school recesses. In this case, the observer would be systematically looking for particular behaviors that are concretely defined before the observation begins. For example, aggression might be defined as hitting or shoving another child, taking a toy from another child without asking, and so on. The observer might stand at the edge of the playground and systematically record how often these behaviors occur. If the researcher were interested in exploring possible sex and age differences in social behavior, he or she would also note the child's gender and age. How do we know how accurate the observer is? In such studies, it is important to establish **interjudge reliability**, which is the level of agreement between two or more people who independently observe and code a set of data. By showing that two or more judges independently come up with the same observations, researchers ensure that the observations are not the subjective, distorted impressions of one individual.

Watch on **MyPsychLab**
Watch an interview with a researcher who uses quantitative, qualitative, and ethnographic methods in the MyPsychLab activity ***Academic Achievement and Academic Engagement among Early Adolescents: Diane Hughes.***

Archival Analysis The observational method is not limited to observations of real-life behavior. The researcher can also examine the accumulated documents, or archives, of a culture, a technique known as an **archival analysis** (Mullen, Rozell, & Johnson, 2001). For example, diaries, novels, suicide notes, popular music lyrics, television shows, movies, magazine and newspaper articles, and advertising all tell us a great deal about how a society views itself. Much like our example of aggression, specific, well-defined categories are created and then applied to the archival source. (See the following Try It! exercise.) Think back to the question of the relationship between pornography and violence. One problem with addressing this question is in defining what pornography is. As Supreme Court Justice Potter Stewart put it, "I know it when I see it," but describing its exact content is not easy.

Archival analysis is a good tool for answering this question, because it enables researchers to describe the content of documents present in the culture—in this case, the photographs and fictional stories that represent currently available pornography in the marketplace. One researcher, for example, studied the content of pornography in adults-only fiction paperback books sold at newsstands and regular bookstores (Smith, 1976). Another analyzed photographs posted on Internet Web sites (Mehta, 2001). One disturbing finding was that a lot of pornography involves the use of force (physical, mental, or blackmail) by a male to make a female engage in unwanted sex. Aggression against women is a major theme in some (though not all) pornography.

Observational research, in the form of archival analysis, can tell us a great deal about society's values and beliefs. The fact that sexual violence against women is common in pornography suggests that these images and stories appeal to many readers (Dietz & Evans, 1982; Gossett & Byrne, 2002) and leads to some troubling questions: Is pornography associated with sexually violent crimes against women that occur in our society? Do reading and looking at pornography cause some men to commit violent sexual acts?

Interjudge Reliability
The level of agreement between two or more people who independently observe and code a set of data; by showing that two or more judges independently come up with the same observations, researchers ensure that the observations are not the subjective, distorted impressions of one individual

Archival Analysis
A form of the observational method in which the researcher examines the accumulated documents, or archives, of a culture (e.g., diaries, novels, magazines, and newspapers)

TRY IT! Archival Analysis: Women, Men, and the Media

Try doing your own archival analysis to see how women and men are portrayed in the media. Choose three or four magazines that focus on different topics and audiences, for example, a newsmagazine, a "women's" magazine such as *Cosmopolitan*, a "men's" magazine such as *GQ*, and a literary magazine such as the *New Yorker*. In each magazine, open the pages randomly until you find an advertisement that has at least one picture of a person in it. Repeat so that you look at two or three such ads in each magazine.

Make a note of how much of the image is devoted to the person's face and whether the person in the ad is a woman or a man. Specifically, place the picture of each person into one of these categories, depending on what part of the person you can see: (a) the entire body, (b) from the waist up, or (c) primarily the head and face. Are there differences in the way women and men are portrayed? If so, why do you think this is? Now turn to page 45 to see how actual research of this sort turned out.

To answer these questions, research methods other than archival analysis must be used. Later in this chapter, we will see how researchers have used the correlational method and the experimental method to address important questions about sexual violence against women.

Limits of the Observational Method There are limits to the observational method. Certain kinds of behavior are difficult to observe because they occur only rarely or only in private. For example, had Latané and Darley chosen the observational method to study the effects of the number of bystanders on people's willingness to help a victim, we might still be waiting for an answer, given the infrequency of emergencies and the difficulty of predicting when they will occur.

Instead, Latané and Darley might have used an archival analysis—for example, by examining newspaper accounts of violent crimes and noting the number of bystanders and how many offered assistance to the victim. Yet here too the researchers would have quickly run into problems: Did each journalist mention how many bystanders were present? Was the number accurate? Were all forms of assistance noted in the newspaper article? Clearly, these are messy data. As is always the case with archival analysis, the researcher is at the mercy of the original compiler of the material; the journalists had different aims when they wrote their articles and may not have included all the information researchers would later need.

Perhaps most importantly, social psychologists want to do more than just describe behavior; they want to predict and explain it. To do so, other methods are more appropriate.

The Correlational Method: Predicting Social Behavior

A goal of social science is to understand relationships between variables and to be able to predict when different kinds of social behavior will occur. What is the relationship between the amount of pornography people see and their likelihood of engaging in sexually violent acts? Is there a relationship between the amount of violence children see on television and their aggressiveness? To answer such questions, researchers frequently use still another approach: the correlational method.

With the **correlational method**, two variables are systematically measured, and the relationship between them—how much you can predict one from the other—is assessed. People's behavior and attitudes can be measured in a variety of ways. Just as with the observational method, researchers sometimes make direct observations of people's behavior. For example, researchers might be interested in testing the relationship between children's aggressive behavior and how much violent television they watch. They too might observe children on the playground, but here the goal is to assess the relationship, or correlation, between the children's aggressiveness and other factors, such as TV viewing habits, which the researchers also measure.

Researchers look at such relationships by calculating the **correlation coefficient**, a statistic that assesses how well you can predict one variable from another—for example, how well you can predict people's weight from their height. A positive correlation means that increases in the value of one variable are associated with increases in the value of the other variable. Height and weight are positively correlated; the taller people are, the more they tend to weigh. A negative correlation means that increases in the value of one variable are associated with decreases in the value of the other. If height and weight were negatively correlated in human beings, we would look very peculiar; short people, such as children, would look like penguins, whereas tall people, such as NBA basketball players, would be all skin and bones! It is also possible, of course, for two variables to be completely unrelated, so that a researcher cannot predict one variable from the other (see Figure 2.1).

Surveys The correlational method is often used in **surveys**, research in which a representative sample of people are asked questions about their attitudes or behavior. Surveys are a convenient way to measure people's attitudes; for example, people can be telephoned and asked which candidate they will support in an upcoming election or how they feel about a variety of social issues. Researchers often apply the correlational method to survey results to predict how people's responses to one question predict their other responses. Psychologists often use surveys to help understand social behavior and

Correlational Method
The technique whereby two or more variables are systematically measured and the relationship between them (i.e., how much one can be predicted from the other) is assessed

Correlation Coefficient
A statistical technique that assesses how well you can predict one variable from another—for example, how well you can predict people's weight from their height

Surveys
Research in which a representative sample of people are asked (often anonymously) questions about their attitudes or behavior

FIGURE 2.1

The Correlation Coefficient

The diagrams below show three possible correlations in a hypothetical study of watching violence on television and aggressive behavior in children. The diagram at the left shows a strong positive correlation: The more television children watched, the more aggressive they were. The diagram in the middle shows no correlation: The amount of television children watched is not related to how aggressive they were. The diagram at the right shows a strong negative correlation: The more television children watched, the less aggressive they were.

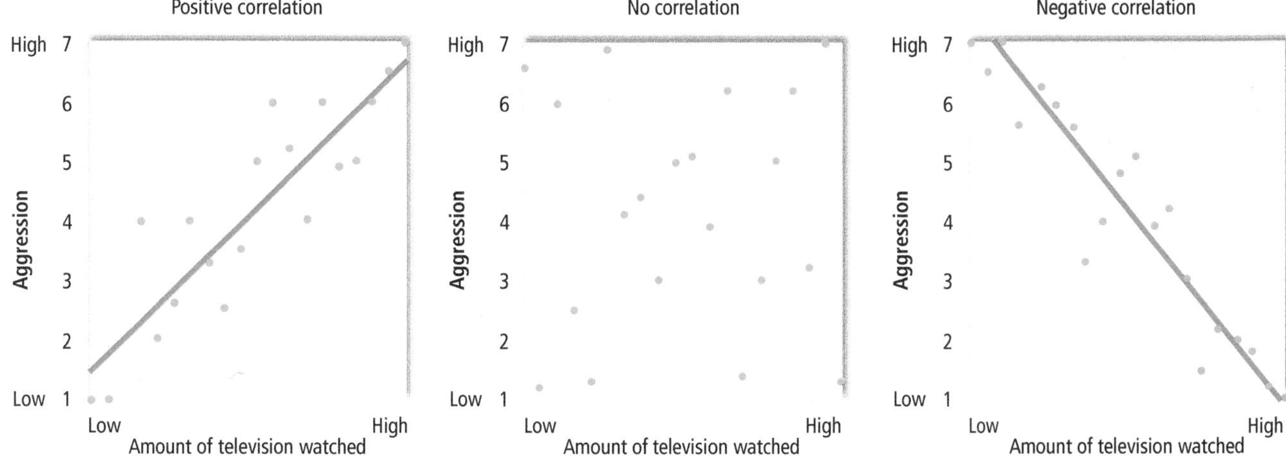

Random Selection

A way of ensuring that a sample of people is representative of a population by giving everyone in the population an equal chance of being selected for the sample

attitudes—for example, by seeing whether the amount of pornography men say they read is correlated with their attitudes toward women.

Surveys have a number of advantages, one of which is allowing researchers to judge the relationship between variables that are difficult to observe, such as how often people engage in safer sex. The researcher looks at the relationship between the questions asked on the survey, such as whether people who know a lot about how HIV is transmitted are more likely than other people to engage in safer sex.

Another advantage of surveys is the capability of sampling representative segments of the population. Answers to a survey are useful only if they reflect the responses of people in general—not just the people actually tested (called the *sample*). Survey researchers go to great lengths to ensure that the people they test are typical. They select samples that are representative of the population on a number of characteristics important to a given research question (e.g., age, educational background, religion, gender, income level). They also make sure to use a **random selection** of people from the population at large, which is a way of ensuring that a sample of people is representative of a population by giving everyone in the population an equal chance of being selected for the sample. As long as the sample is selected randomly, we can assume that the responses are a reasonable match to those of the population as a whole.

CONNECTIONS

Random Selection in Political Polls

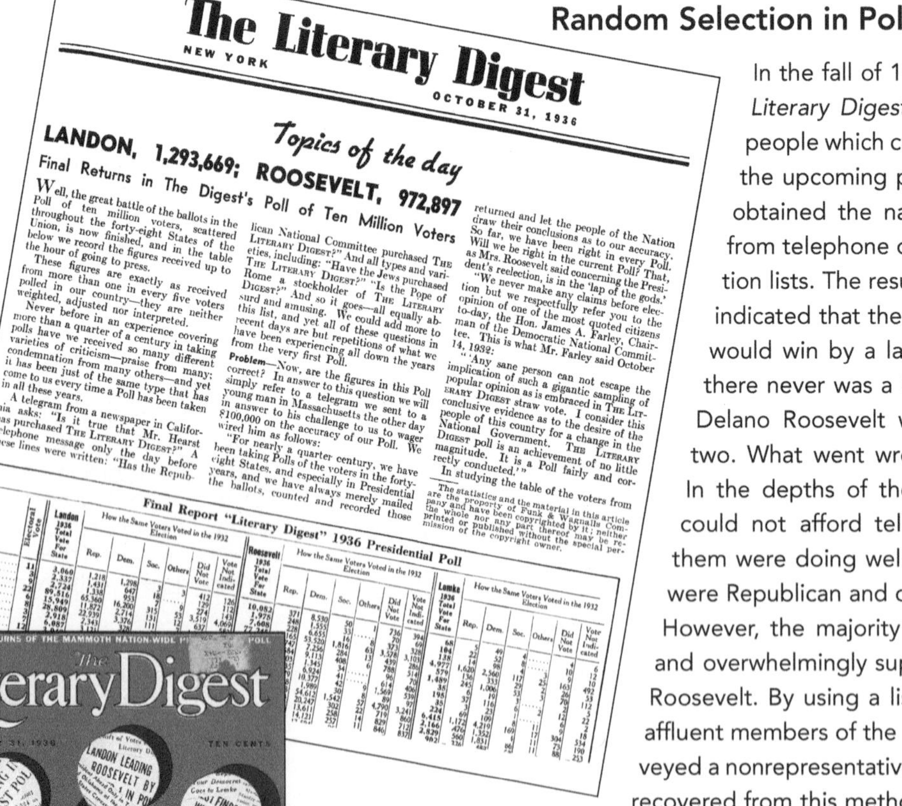

The Literary Digest

NEW YORK

OCTOBER 31, 1936

Topics of the day

LANDON, 1,293,669; ROOSEVELT, 972,897

Final Returns in The Digest's Poll of Ten Million Voters

Well, the great battle of the ballots in the Poll of ten million voters, scattered throughout the forty-eight States of the Union, is now finished, and in the table below we record the figures received up to the hour of going to press.

These figures are exactly as received from more than one in every five voters polled in our country—they are neither weighted, adjusted nor interpreted.

Never before in an experience covering more than a quarter of a century in taking polls have we received so many different varieties of criticism—praise from many; condemnation from many others—and yet it has been just of the same type that has come to us every time a Poll has been taken in all these years.

A telegram from a newspaper in California asks: "Is it true that Mr. Hearst has purchased The Literary Digest?" A telephone message only the day before these lines were written: "Has the Republican National Committee purchased The Literary Digest?" And all types and varieties, including: "Have the Jews purchased The Literary Digest?" "Is the Pope of Rome a stockholder of The Literary Digest?" And so it goes—all equally absurd and amusing. We could add more to this list, and yet all of these questions in recent days are but repetitions of what we have been experiencing all down the years from the very first Poll.

Problem—Now, are the figures in this Poll correct? In answer to this question we will simply refer to a telegram we sent to a young man in Massachusetts the other day in answer to his challenge to us to wager $100,000 on the accuracy of our Poll. We wired him as follows:

"For nearly a quarter century, we have been taking Polls of the voters in the forty-eight States, and especially in Presidential years, and we have always merely mailed the ballots, counted and recorded those returned and let the people of the Nation draw their conclusions as to our accuracy. So far, we have been right in every Poll. Will we be right in the current Poll? That, as Mrs. Roosevelt said concerning the President's reelection, is in the 'lap of the gods.'

"We never make any claims before election but we respectfully refer you to the opinion of one of the most quoted citizens to-day, the Hon. James A. Farley, Chairman of the Democratic National Committee. This is what Mr. Farley said October 14, 1932:

"'Any sane person can not escape the implication of such a gigantic sampling of popular opinion as is embraced in The Literary Digest straw vote. I consider this conclusive evidence as to the desire of the people of this country for a change in the National Government. The Literary Digest poll is an achievement of no little magnitude. It is a Poll fairly and correctly conducted.'"

In studying the table of the voters from

The statistics and the material in this article are the property of Funk & Wagnalls Company and have been copyrighted by it; neither the whole nor any part thereof may be reprinted or published without the special permission of the copyright owner.

Final Report "Literary Digest" 1936 Presidential Poll

Electoral Vote	Landon 1936 Total Vote For State	How the Same Voters Voted in the 1932 Election: Rep.	Dem.	Soc.	Others	Did Not Vote	Vote Not Indicated	Roosevelt 1936 Total Vote For State	How the Same Voters Voted in the 1932 Election: Rep.	Dem.	Soc.	Others	Did Not Vote	Vote Not Indicated	Lemke 1936 Total Vote For State	How the Same Voters Voted in the 1932 Election: Rep.	Dem.	Soc.	Others	Did Not Vote	Vote Not Indicated

In the fall of 1936, a weekly magazine called *The Literary Digest* conducted a large survey asking people which candidate they planned to vote for in the upcoming presidential election. The magazine obtained the names and addresses of its sample from telephone directories and automobile registration lists. The results of its survey of 2 million people indicated that the Republican candidate, Alf Landon, would win by a landslide. Of course, you know that there never was a President Landon; instead, Franklin Delano Roosevelt won every state in the Union but two. What went wrong with *The Literary Digest* poll? In the depths of the Great Depression, many people could not afford telephones or cars. Those who had them were doing well financially; most well-to-do voters were Republican and overwhelmingly favored Alf Landon. However, the majority of the voters were not well off—and overwhelmingly supported the Democratic candidate, Roosevelt. By using a list of names that excluded the less affluent members of the population, *The Literary Digest* surveyed a nonrepresentative sample. (*The Literary Digest* never recovered from this methodological disaster and went out of business shortly after publishing its poll.)

Modern political polls are not immune from such sampling errors. Many polling companies only contact people on their home phones (landlines), because of the difficulty of obtaining directories of cell phone numbers. They do so at their hazard: In a poll conducted in November of 2011, voters were asked who they would vote for for president if Barack Obama were running against Mitt Romney. Among those contacted on landlines, Romney won by 6 percentage points. But among those who did not have a landline and were contacted on their cell phones, Obama won by 22 points ("Obama 46%," 2011).

A potential problem with survey data is the accuracy of the responses. Straightforward questions, regarding what people think about an issue or what they typically do, are relatively easy to answer. But asking survey participants to predict how they might behave in some hypothetical situation or to explain why they behaved as they did in the past is an invitation to inaccuracy (Schuman & Kalton, 1985; Schwarz, Groves, & Schuman, 1998). Often people simply don't know the answer—but they think they do. Richard Nisbett and Tim Wilson (1977) demonstrated this "telling more than you can know" phenomenon in a number of studies in which people often made inaccurate reports about why they responded the way they did. Their reports about the causes of their responses pertained more to their theories and beliefs about what should have influenced them than to what actually influenced them. (We discuss these studies at greater length in Chapter 5.)

Limits of the Correlational Method: Correlation Does Not Equal Causation The major shortcoming of the correlational method is that it tells us only that two variables are related, whereas the goal of the social psychologist is to identify the *causes* of social behavior. We want to be able to say that A causes B, not just that A is correlated with B.

If a researcher finds that there is a correlation between two variables, it means that there are three possible causal relationships between these variables. For example, researchers have found a correlation between the amount of violent television children watch and how aggressive they are (similar to the pattern shown in the graph on the left side in Figure 2.1, though not quite as strong; see Eron, 1982). One explanation of this correlation is that watching TV violence causes kids to become more violent themselves. It is equally probable, however, that the reverse is true: that kids who are violent to begin with are more likely to watch violent TV. Or there might be no causal relationship between these two variables; instead, both TV watching and violent behavior could be caused by a third variable, such as having neglectful parents who do not pay much attention to their kids. (Experimental evidence supports one of these causal relationships; we will discuss which one in Chapter 12.) When using the correlational method, it is wrong to jump to the conclusion that one variable is causing the other to occur. *Correlation does not prove causation.*

Unfortunately, forgetting this adage is one of the most common methodological errors in the social sciences. Consider a study of birth control methods and sexually transmitted diseases (STDs) in women (Rosenberg, Davidson, Chen, Judson, & Douglas, 1992). The researchers examined the records of women who had visited a clinic, noting which method of birth control they used and whether they had an STD. Surprisingly, the researchers found that women who relied on condoms had significantly more STDs than women who used diaphragms or contraceptive sponges. This result was widely reported in the popular press, with the conclusion that the use of diaphragms and sponges caused a lower incidence of disease. Some reporters urged women whose partners used condoms to switch to other methods.

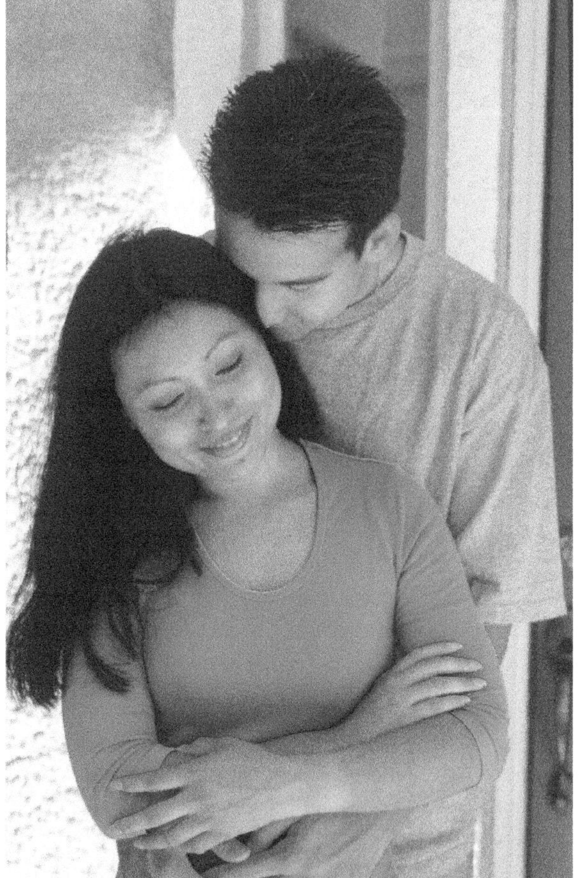

A study conducted in the early 1990s found a correlation between the type of birth control women used and their likelihood of getting a sexually transmitted disease (STD). Those whose partners used condoms were more likely to have an STD than were women who used other forms of birth control. Does this mean that the use of condoms caused the increase in STDs? Not necessarily—see the text for alternative explanations of this research finding.

Can you see the problem with this conclusion? The fact that the incidence of disease was correlated with the type of contraception women used is open to a number of causal interpretations. Perhaps the women who used sponges and diaphragms had sex with fewer partners. (In fact, condom users were more likely to have had sex with multiple partners in the previous month.) Perhaps the partners of women who relied on condoms were more likely to have STDs than were the partners of women who used sponges and diaphragms. There is simply no way of knowing. Thus, the conclusion that the birth control methods protected against STDs cannot be drawn from this correlational study.

Experimental Method
The method in which the researcher randomly assigns participants to different conditions and ensures that these conditions are identical except for the independent variable (the one thought to have a causal effect on people's responses)

As another example of the difficulty of inferring causality from correlational designs, let's return to the question of whether pornography causes aggressive sexual acts against women, such as rape. In one study, male college students at a large midwestern university completed an anonymous survey on which they indicated whether they had ever engaged in sexually coercive behavior as well as the frequency with which they viewed various forms of pornography (Carr & VanDeusen, 2004). The researchers found a small but statistically significant correlation, such that the more pornography the students reported using, the greater the likelihood that they had committed sexual violence.

As suggestive as this finding is, it does not establish that using pornography made the student more likely to commit sexual violence. Can you think of alternative explanations for the correlation? It is possible that men who are aggressive toward women are more interested in pornography; that is, it is their aggression causing their attraction to pornography, and not the pornography causing their aggression (Malamuth et al., 2000). Alternatively, there could be some third variable, such as something in a man's upbringing or subculture, that makes him more likely to commit sexual violence and look at pornography. Other examples of the difficulty of inferring causality from correlational studies are shown in the following Try It!

The Experimental Method: Answering Causal Questions

The only way to determine causal relationships is with the **experimental method**. Here, the researcher systematically orchestrates the event so that people experience it in one way (e.g., they witness an emergency along with other bystanders) or another way

TRY IT! Correlation and Causation: Knowing the Difference

It can be difficult to remember that, when two variables are correlated, it doesn't necessarily mean that one caused the other; correlation does *not* allow us to make causal inferences. For each of the following examples, think about why the correlation was found. Even if it seems obvious which variable was causing the other, are there alternative explanations?

1. A politician extols the virtues of the Boy Scouts and Girl Scouts. In his salute to the Scouts, the politician mentions that few teenagers convicted of street crimes have been members of the Scouts. In other words, he is positing a negative correlation between activity in Scouting and frequency of criminal behavior. Why might this be?
2. A recent study found that college students who have "helicopter parents"—moms and dads who keep close track of their kids' academic life and intervene often—actually get lower grades than college students whose parents do not hover over them so closely. Does it follow that college students would do better in school if their parents backed off a little bit?
3. A study of soldiers stationed on army bases found that the number of tattoos a soldier had was correlated positively with becoming involved in a motorcycle accident. Why?
4. A study found that adolescents who are religious are less likely to commit crimes and more likely to wear seat belts than are adolescents who are not religious. Does religion make people more likely to obey the law?
5. A correlation exists between people's tendency to eat breakfast and how long they live, such that people who skip breakfast die younger. Does eating Wheaties lead to a long life?
6. A study reported that the more milk children drank, the more weight they gained. One researcher concluded that children who need to control their weight should cut down on their milk consumption. Is this a valid conclusion?
7. A recent survey found that people who watch public television have more sex than people who do not. "Who would have thought," the researchers reported, "that National Geographic Specials or Ken Burns' history of baseball could get people in the mood?" How would you explain this correlation?
8. A recent study in Britain found that kids who ate sweets daily at age 10 were much more likely to be arrested for a violent crime later in life than were kids who did not eat sweets daily at 10. Should we limit the number of candy bars that kids eat, so that they don't turn into violent criminals?

See page 45 for the answers.

Theory is a good thing, but a good experiment lasts forever.

—Peter Leonidovich Kapista

(e.g., they witness the same emergency but are the sole bystander). The experimental method is the method of choice in most social psychological research, because it allows the experimenter to make causal inferences.

The experimental method always involves a direct intervention on the part of the researcher. By carefully changing only one aspect of the situation (e.g., group size), the researcher can see whether this aspect is the cause of the behavior in question (e.g., whether people help in an emergency). Sound simple? Actually, it isn't. Staging an experiment to test Latané and Darley's hypothesis about the effects of group size involves severe practical and ethical difficulties. What kind of emergency should be used? Ideally (from a scientific perspective), it should be as true to the Genovese case as possible. Accordingly, you would want to stage a murder that passersby could witness. In one condition, you could stage the murder so that only a few onlookers were present; in another condition, you could stage it so that a great many onlookers were present.

Obviously, no scientist in his or her right mind would stage a murder for unsuspecting bystanders. But how can we arrange a realistic situation that is upsetting enough to be similar to the Genovese case without it being too upsetting? In addition, how can we ensure that each bystander experiences the same emergency except for the variable whose effect we want to test—in this case, the number of bystanders?

Let's see how Latané and Darley (1968) dealt with these problems. Imagine that you are a participant in their experiment. You arrive at the scheduled time and find yourself in a long corridor with doors to several small cubicles. An experimenter greets you and takes you into one of the cubicles, mentioning that five other students, seated in the other cubicles, will be participating with you. The experimenter leaves after giving you a pair of headphones with an attached microphone. You put on the headphones, and soon you hear the experimenter explaining to everyone that he is interested in learning about the kinds of personal problems college students experience.

To ensure that people will discuss their problems openly, he explains, each participant will remain anonymous; each will stay in his or her separate room and communicate with the others only via the intercom system. Further, the experimenter says, he will not be listening to the discussion, so that people will feel freer to be open and honest. Finally, the experimenter asks that participants take turns presenting their problems, each speaking for 2 minutes, after which each person will comment on what the others have said. To make sure this procedure is followed, he says, only one person's microphone will be turned on at a time.

The group discussion begins. You listen as the first participant admits that he has found it difficult to adjust to college. With some embarrassment, he mentions that he sometimes has seizures, especially when under stress. When his 2 minutes are up, you hear the other four participants discuss their problems; then it is your turn. When you have finished, the first person speaks again. To your astonishment, he soon begins to experience one of the seizures he mentioned earlier:

> I—er—um—I think I—I need—er—if—if could—er—er—somebody er—er—er—er—er—er—er—give me a little—er—give me a little help here because—er—I—er—I'm—er—er—h—h—having a—a—a real problem—er—right now and I—er—if somebody could help me out it would—it would—er—er s—s—sure be—sure be good . . . because—er—there—er—er—a cause I—er—I—uh—I've got a—a one of the—er—sei—er—er—things coming on and—and—and I could really—er—use some help so if somebody would—er—give me a little h—help—uh—er—er—er—er c—could somebody—er—er—help—er—uh—uh—uh (choking sounds) . . . I'm gonna die—er—er—I'm . . . gonna die—er—help—er—er—seizure—er (chokes, then quiet). (Darley & Latané, 1968, p. 379)

What would you have done in this situation? If you were like most of the participants in the actual study, you would have remained in your cubicle, listening to your fellow student having a seizure, and done nothing about it. Does this surprise you? Latané and Darley kept track of the number of people who left their cubicle to find the victim or the experimenter before the end of the victim's seizure. Only 31% of the participants sought help in this way. Fully 69% of the students remained in their cubicles and did nothing—just as Kitty Genovese's neighbors failed to offer assistance in any way.

Does this finding prove that the failure to help was due to the number of people who witnessed the seizure? How do we know that it wasn't due to some other factor? We know because Latané and Darley included two other conditions in their experiment. In these conditions, the procedure was identical to the one we described, with one crucial difference: The size of the discussion group was smaller, meaning that fewer people witnessed the seizure. In one condition, the participants were told that there were three other people in the discussion group besides themselves (the victim plus two others). In another condition, participants were told that there was only one other person in their discussion group (the victim). In this latter condition, each participant believed he or she was the only one who could hear the seizure.

Simulate on **MyPsychLab**

Learn more about the "seizure" experiment in the MyPsychLab simulation ***Bystander Intervention.***

Independent and Dependent Variables The number of people witnessing the emergency was the **independent variable** in the Latané and Darley (1968) study, which is the variable a researcher changes or varies to see if it has an effect on some other variable. The **dependent variable** is the variable a researcher measures to see if it is influenced by the independent variable; the researcher hypothesizes that the dependent variable will be influenced by the level of the independent variable. That is, the dependent variable is hypothesized to depend on the independent variable (see Figure 2.2). Latané and Darley found that their independent variable (the number of bystanders) did have an effect on the dependent variable (whether they tried to help). When the participants believed that four other people were witnesses to the seizure, only 31% offered assistance. When the participants believed that only two other people were aware of the seizure, helping behavior increased to 62%. When the participants believed that they were the only person listening to the seizure, nearly everyone helped (85%).

Independent Variable

The variable a researcher changes or varies to see if it has an effect on some other variable

Dependent Variable

The variable a researcher measures to see if it is influenced by the independent variable; the researcher hypothesizes that the dependent variable will depend on the level of the independent variable

These results indicate that the number of bystanders strongly influences the rate of helping, but it does not mean that the size of the group is the only cause of people's decision to help. After all, when there were four bystanders, a third of the participants still helped; conversely, when participants thought they were the only witness, some of them failed to help. Obviously, other factors influence helping behavior—the bystanders' personalities, their prior experience with emergencies, and so on. Nonetheless, Latané and Darley succeeded in identifying one important determinant of whether people help: the number of bystanders that people think are present.

Internal Validity in Experiments How can we be sure that the differences in help across conditions in the Latané and Darley seizure study were due to the different

Independent Variable	Dependent Variable
The variable that is hypothesized to influence the dependent variable. Participants are treated identically except for this variable.	The response that is hypothesized to depend on the independent variable. All participants are measured on this variable.
Example: Latané and Darley (1968)	
The number of bystanders	**How many participants helped?**
Participant + Victim	85%
Participant + Victim + Two others	62%
Participant + Victim + Four others	31%

FIGURE 2.2

Independent and Dependent Variables in Experimental Research

Researchers vary the independent variable (e.g., the number of bystanders people think are present) and observe what effect that has on the dependent variable (e.g., whether people help).

numbers of bystanders who witnessed the emergency? Could this effect have been caused by some other aspect of the situation? This is the beauty of the experimental method: We can be sure of the causal connection between the number of bystanders and helping, because Latané and Darley made sure that everything about the situation was the same in the different conditions except for the independent variable—the number of bystanders. Keeping everything but the independent variable the same in an experiment is referred to as *internal validity.* Latané and Darley were careful to maintain high internal validity by making sure that everyone witnessed the same emergency. They prerecorded the supposed other participants and the victim and played their voices over the intercom system.

You may have noticed, however, that there was a key difference between the conditions of the Latané and Darley experiment other than the number of bystanders: Different people participated in the different conditions. Maybe the observed differences in helping were due to characteristics of the participants instead of the independent variable. The people in the sole-witness condition might have differed in any number of ways from their counterparts in the other conditions, making them more likely to help. Maybe they were more likely to know something about epilepsy or to have experience helping in emergencies. If either of these possibilities is true, it would be difficult to conclude that it was the number of bystanders, rather than something about the participants' backgrounds, that led to differences in helping.

Fortunately, there is a technique that allows experimenters to minimize differences among participants as the cause of the results: **random assignment to condition**. This is the process whereby all participants have an equal chance of taking part in any condition of an experiment; through random assignment, researchers can be relatively certain that differences in the participants' personalities or backgrounds are distributed evenly across conditions. Because Latané and Darley's participants were randomly assigned to the conditions of their experiment, it is very unlikely that the ones who knew the most about epilepsy all ended up in one condition. Knowledge about epilepsy should be randomly (i.e., roughly evenly) dispersed across the three experimental conditions. This powerful technique is the most important part of the experimental method.

Even with random assignment, however, there is the (very small) possibility that different characteristics of people did not distribute themselves evenly across conditions. For example, if we randomly divide a group of 40 people into two groups, it is possible that those who know the most about epilepsy will by chance end up more in one group than in the other—just as it is possible to get more heads than tails when you flip a coin 40 times. This is a possibility we take seriously in experimental science. The analyses of our data come with a **probability level (*p*-value)**, which is a number, calculated with statistical techniques, that tells researchers how likely it is that the results of their experiment occurred by chance and not because of the independent variable. The convention in science, including social psychology, is to consider results *significant* (trustworthy) if the probability level is less than 5 in 100 that the results might be due to chance factors rather than the independent variables studied. For example, if we flipped a coin 40 times and got 40 heads, we would probably assume that this was very unlikely to have occurred by chance and that there was something wrong with the coin (we might check the other side to make sure it wasn't one of those trick coins with heads on both sides!). Similarly, if the results in two conditions of an experiment differ significantly from what we would expect by chance, we assume that the difference was caused by the independent variable (e.g., the number of bystanders present during the emergency). The *p*-value tells us how confident we can be that the difference was due to chance rather than the independent variable.

To summarize, the key to a good experiment is to maintain high **internal validity**, which we can now define as making sure that the independent variable, and *only* the independent variable, influences the dependent variable. This is accomplished by controlling all extraneous variables and by randomly assigning people to different experimental conditions (Campbell & Stanley, 1967). When internal validity is high, the experimenter is in a position to judge whether the independent variable causes

Random Assignment to Condition

A process ensuring that all participants have an equal chance of taking part in any condition of an experiment; through random assignment, researchers can be relatively certain that differences in the participants' personalities or backgrounds are distributed evenly across conditions

Probability Level (*p*-value)

A number calculated with statistical techniques that tells researchers how likely it is that the results of their experiment occurred by chance and not because of the independent variable or variables; the convention in science, including social psychology, is to consider results *significant* (trustworthy) if the probability level is less than 5 in 100 that the results might be due to chance factors and not the independent variables studied

Internal Validity

Making sure that nothing besides the independent variable can affect the dependent variable; this is accomplished by controlling all extraneous variables and by randomly assigning people to different experimental conditions

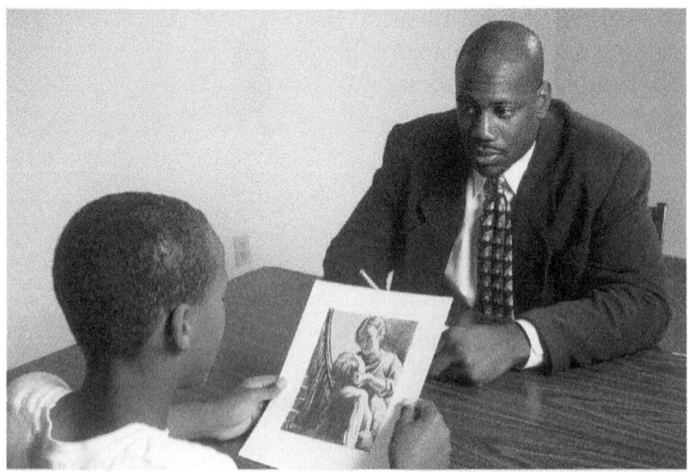

A good deal of social psychological research takes place in laboratory settings. How do social psychologists generalize from the findings of these studies to life outside the laboratory?

the dependent variable. This is the hallmark of the experimental method that sets it apart from the observational and correlational methods: Only the experimental method can answer causal questions, such as whether exposure to pornography causes men to commit violent acts.

For example, researchers have tested whether pornography causes aggression, by randomly assigning consenting participants to watch pornographic or nonpornographic films (the independent variable) and measuring the extent to which people acted aggressively toward women (the dependent variable). In a study by Donnerstein and Berkowitz (1981), males were angered by a female accomplice and then were randomly assigned to see one of three films: violent pornography (a rape scene), nonviolent pornography (sex without any violence), or a neutral film with no violence or sex (a talk show interview). The men were then given an opportunity to act aggressively toward the woman who had angered them, by choosing the level of electric shock she would receive in an ostensibly unrelated learning experiment (the accomplice did not really receive shocks, but participants believed that she would). The men who had seen the violent pornography administered significantly more-intense shocks to the woman than did the men who had seen the nonviolent pornography or the neutral film, suggesting that it is not pornography per se that leads to aggressive behavior, but the violence depicted in some pornography (Mussweiler & Förster, 2000). We review this area of research in more detail in Chapter 12.

External Validity in Experiments For all the advantages of the experimental method, there are some drawbacks. By virtue of gaining enough control over the situation so as to randomly assign people to conditions and rule out the effects of extraneous variables, the situation can become somewhat artificial and distant from real life. For example, one could argue that Latané and Darley strayed far from the original inspiration for their study, the Kitty Genovese murder. What does witnessing a seizure while participating in a laboratory experiment in a college building have to do with a brutal murder in a densely populated urban neighborhood? How often in everyday life do we have discussions with other people through an intercom system? Did the fact that the participants knew they were in a psychology experiment influence their behavior?

These are important questions that concern **external validity**, which is the extent to which the results of a study can be generalized to other situations and other people. Note that two kinds of generalizability are at issue: the extent to which we can generalize from the situation constructed by an experimenter to real-life situations (generalizability across *situations*) and the extent to which we can generalize from the people who participated in the experiment to people in general (generalizability across *people*).

External Validity

The extent to which the results of a study can be generalized to other situations and to other people

Psychological Realism

The extent to which the psychological processes triggered in an experiment are similar to psychological processes that occur in everyday life

When it comes to generalizability across situations, research in social psychology is sometimes criticized for being conducted in artificial settings that cannot be generalized to real life—for example, psychological experiments at a university. To address this problem, social psychologists attempt to increase the generalizability of their results by making their studies as realistic as possible. But this is hard to do in a laboratory setting in which people are placed in situations they would rarely, if ever, encounter in everyday life, such as occurred in Latané and Darley's group discussion of personal problems over an intercom system. Instead, psychologists attempt to maximize the study's **psychological realism**, which is the extent to which the psychological processes triggered in an experiment are similar to psychological processes that occur in everyday life (Aronson, Wilson, & Brewer, 1998). Even though Latané and Darley staged an emergency that in significant ways was unlike those encountered in everyday life, was it psychologically similar to real-life emergencies? Were the same psychological processes triggered? Did the participants have the same types of perceptions and thoughts, make the same types of decisions, and choose the same types of behaviors that they would in a real-life situation? If so, the study is high in psychological realism and we can generalize the results to everyday life.

Psychological realism is heightened if people feel involved in a real event. To accomplish this, experimenters often tell participants a **cover story**—a disguised version of the study's true purpose. Recall, for example, that Latané and Darley told people that they were studying the personal problems of college students and then staged an emergency. It would have been a lot easier to say to people, "Look, we are interested in how people react to emergencies, so at some point during this study we are going to stage an accident, and then we'll see how you respond." We think you'll agree that such a procedure would be very low in psychological realism. In real life, we never know when emergencies are going to occur, and we do not have time to plan our responses to them. If participants knew that an emergency was about to happen, the kinds of psychological processes triggered would have been quite different from those of a real emergency, reducing the psychological realism of the study.

Social psychologists are also concerned with generalizability across people. Latané and Darley's experiment, for example, documented an interesting, unexpected example of social influence whereby the mere knowledge that others were present reduced the likelihood that people helped. But what have we learned about people in general? The participants in their study were 52 male and female students at New York University who received course credit for participating in the experiment. Would the study have turned out the same way if a different population had been used? Would the number of bystanders have influenced helping behavior had the participants been middle-aged blue-collar workers instead of college students? Midwesterners instead of New Yorkers? Japanese instead of American?

The only way to be certain that the results of an experiment represent the behavior of a particular population is to ensure that the participants are randomly selected from that population. Ideally, samples in experiments should be randomly selected, just as they are in surveys. Increasingly, social psychologists are conducting research with diverse populations and cultures, some of it over the Internet (e.g., Lane, Banaji, & Nosek, 2007). But, unfortunately, it is impractical and expensive to select random samples for most social psychology experiments. It is difficult enough to convince a random sample of Americans to agree to answer a few questions over the telephone as part of a political poll, and such polls can cost thousands of dollars to conduct. Imagine the difficulty Latané and Darley would have had convincing a random sample of Americans to board a plane to New York to take part in their study, not to mention the cost of such an endeavor. Even trying to gather a random sample of students at New York University would not have been easy; each person contacted would have had to agree to spend an hour in Latané and Darley's laboratory.

Of course, concerns about practicality and expense are not good excuses for doing poor science. Many researchers address this problem by studying basic psychological processes that make people susceptible to social influence, assuming that these processes are so fundamental that they are universally shared. In that case, participants for social psychology experiments don't really have to come from many different cultures. Of course, some social psychological processes are likely to be quite dependent on cultural factors, and in those cases, we'd need diverse samples of people. The question then is, how can researchers tell whether the processes they are studying are universal?

Field Research One of the best ways to increase external validity is by conducting **field experiments**. In a field experiment, researchers study behavior outside the laboratory, in its natural setting. As in a laboratory experiment, the researcher controls the occurrence of an independent variable (e.g., group size) to see what effect it has on a dependent variable (e.g., helping behavior) and randomly assigns people to the different conditions. Thus, a field experiment has the same design as a laboratory experiment, except that it is conducted in a real-life setting rather than in the relatively artificial setting of the laboratory. The participants in a field experiment are unaware

Cover Story

A description of the purpose of a study, given to participants, that is different from its true purpose and is used to maintain psychological realism

Field Experiments

Experiments conducted in natural settings rather than in the laboratory

Social psychologists are interested in how generalizable their findings are to different kinds of people. What are the challenges in doing so? What approaches do social psychologists take?

that the events they experience are in fact an experiment. The external validity of such an experiment is high, because, after all, it is taking place in the real world, with real people who are more diverse than a typical college student sample.

Many such field studies have been conducted in social psychology. For example, Latané and Darley (1970) tested their hypothesis about group size and bystander intervention in a convenience store outside New York City. Two "robbers" (with full knowledge and permission of the cashier and manager of the store) waited until there were either one or two other customers at the checkout counter. They then asked the cashier to name the most expensive beer the store carried. The cashier answered the question and then said he would have to check in the back to see how much of that brand was in stock. While the cashier was gone, the robbers picked up a case of beer in the front of the store, declared, "They'll never miss this," put the beer in their car, and drove off.

Because the robbers were rather burly fellows, no one attempted to intervene directly to stop the theft. The question was, when the cashier returned, how many people would help by telling him that a theft had just occurred? As it turned out, the number of bystanders had the same inhibiting effect on helping behavior as in the laboratory seizure study: Significantly fewer people reported the theft when there was another customer-witness in the store than when they were alone.

It might have occurred to you to ask why researchers conduct laboratory studies at all, given that external validity is so much better with field experiments. Indeed, it seems to us that the perfect experiment in social psychology would be one that was conducted in a field setting with a sample randomly selected from a population of interest and with extremely high internal validity (all extraneous variables controlled, people randomly assigned to the conditions). Sounds good, doesn't it? The only problem is that it is very difficult to satisfy all these conditions in one study, making such studies virtually impossible to conduct.

There is almost always a trade-off between internal and external validity—that is, between being able to randomly assign people to conditions and having enough control over the situation to ensure that no extraneous variables are influencing the results, and making sure that the results can be generalized to everyday life. We have the most control in a laboratory setting, but the laboratory may be unlike real life. Real life can best be captured by doing a field experiment, but it is very difficult to control all extraneous variables in such studies. For example, the astute reader will have noticed that Latané and Darley's (1970) beer theft study differed from laboratory experiments in an important way: People could not be randomly assigned to the alone or in-pairs conditions. Were this the only study Latané and Darley had performed, we could not be sure whether the kinds of people who prefer to shop alone, as compared to the kinds of people who prefer to shop with a friend, differ in ways that might influence helping behavior. By randomly assigning people to conditions in their laboratory studies, Latané and Darley were able to rule out such alternative explanations.

The trade-off between internal and external validity has been referred to as the *basic dilemma of the social psychologist* (Aronson & Carlsmith, 1968). The way to resolve this dilemma is not to try to do it all in a single experiment. Most social psychologists opt first for internal validity, conducting laboratory experiments in which people are randomly assigned to different conditions and all extraneous variables are controlled; here there is little ambiguity about what is causing what. Other social psychologists prefer to maximize external validity by conducting field studies. And many social psychologists do both. Taken together, both types of studies meet the requirements of our perfect experiment.

Replications

Repeating a study, often with different subject populations or in different settings

Replications and Meta-Analysis **Replications** are the ultimate test of an experiment's external validity. Only by conducting studies in different settings, with different populations, can we determine how generalizable the results are. Often, though, when many studies on one problem are conducted, the results are somewhat variable. Several studies might find an effect of the number of bystanders on helping behavior, for example, while a few do not. How can we make sense of this? Does the number of bystanders make a difference or not? Fortunately, there is a statistical technique called **meta-analysis** that averages the results of two or more studies to see if the effect of an independent variable is reliable. Earlier we discussed *p*-values, which tell us the probability that the findings of one study are due to chance or to the independent variable. A meta-analysis essentially does the same thing, except that it averages the results of many different studies. If, say, an independent variable is found to have an effect in only 1 of 20 studies, the meta-analysis will tell us that that one study was probably an exception and that, on average, the independent variable is not influencing the dependent variable. If an independent variable is having an effect in most of the studies, the meta-analysis is likely to tell us that, on average, it does influence the dependent variable.

Meta-Analysis
A statistical technique that averages the results of two or more studies to see if the effect of an independent variable is reliable

Basic Research
Studies that are designed to find the best answer to the question of why people behave as they do and that are conducted purely for reasons of intellectual curiosity

Applied Research
Studies designed to solve a particular social problem

Most of the findings you will read about in this book have been replicated in several different settings, with different populations; we know, then, that they are reliable phenomena, not limited to the laboratory or to college sophomores. For example, Anderson and Bushman (1997) compared laboratory studies on the causes of aggression with studies conducted in the real world. In both types of studies, violence in the media caused aggressive behavior. Similarly, Latané and Darley's original findings have been replicated in numerous studies. Increasing the number of bystanders inhibited helping behavior with many kinds of people, including children, college students, and future ministers (Darley & Batson, 1973; Latané & Nida, 1981); in both small towns and large cities (Latané & Dabbs, 1975); in a variety of settings, such as psychology laboratories, city streets, and subway trains (Harrison & Wells, 1991; Latané & Darley, 1970; Piliavin, 1981; Piliavin & Piliavin, 1972); and with different kinds of emergencies, such as seizures, potential fires, fights, and accidents (Latané & Darley, 1968; Shotland & Straw, 1976; Staub, 1974), as well as with less-serious events, such as having a flat tire (Hurley & Allen, 1974). Many of these replications took place in real-life settings (e.g., on a subway train) where people could not possibly have known that an experiment was being conducted. We will frequently point out similar replications of the major findings we discuss in this book (Wilson, 2011).

Watch on **MyPsychLab**
To learn more about how psychological research progresses, watch the MyPsychLab video ***Alan Kazdin: What is the coolest thing you have ever discovered?***

Basic Versus Applied Research You may have wondered how people decide which specific topic to study. Why would a social psychologist decide to study helping behavior, cognitive dissonance theory, or the effects of pornography on aggression? Is he or she simply curious? Or does the social psychologist have a specific purpose in mind, such as trying to reduce sexual violence?

The goal in **basic research** is to find the best answer to the question of why people behave as they do, purely for reasons of intellectual curiosity. The researchers aren't trying to solve a specific social or psychological problem. In contrast, **applied research** is geared toward solving a particular social problem. Here, building a theory of behavior is usually secondary to solving the specific problem, such as alleviating racism, reducing sexual violence, or stemming the spread of AIDS.

In social psychology, the distinction between basic and applied research is fuzzy. Even though many researchers label themselves as either basic or applied scientists, the endeavors of one group are not independent of those of the other group. There are countless examples of advances in basic science that at the time had no known applied value but later proved to be the key to solving a significant applied problem. As we will see later in this book, for example, basic research with dogs, rats, and fish on the effects of feeling in control of one's environment has led to the development of techniques to improve the health of elderly nursing home residents (Langer & Rodin, 1976; Richter, 1957; Schulz, 1976; Seligman, 1975).

Most social psychologists would agree that, in order to solve a specific social problem, we must understand the psychological processes responsible for it. Indeed, Kurt Lewin (1951), one of the founders of social psychology, coined a phrase that has become a motto for the field: "There is nothing so practical as a good theory." He meant that to solve such difficult social problems as urban violence or racial prejudice, one must first understand the underlying

There is nothing so practical as a good theory.
—Kurt Lewin, 1951

Watch on MyPsychLab
To learn more about the relevance of social psychology research, watch the MyPsychLab video ***Carol Tavris: Why did you hate your intro to psychology course?***

psychological dynamics of human nature and social interaction. Even when the goal is to discover the psychological processes underlying social behavior, the findings often have clear applied implications, as you'll see throughout this book.

New Frontiers in Social Psychological Research

Cross-Cultural Research
Research conducted with members of different cultures, to see whether the psychological processes of interest are present in both cultures or whether they are specific to the culture in which people were raised

Social psychologists are always looking for new ways of investigating social behavior, and in recent years some exciting new methods have been developed. These methodological advances have been spurred on by new questions about the origins of social behavior, because new questions and new methods often develop hand in hand.

Culture and Social Psychology

Social psychology largely began as a Western science, conducted by Western social psychologists with Western participants. This raises the question of how universal the findings are. To study the effects of culture on social psychological process, social psychologists conduct **cross-cultural research** (Heine, 2010; Kitayama & Cohen, 2007; Nisbett, 2003; Smith & Bond, 1999). Some findings in social psychology are culture-dependent, as we will see throughout this book. In Chapter 3, for example, we will see that Westerners and East Asians rely on fundamentally different kinds of thought to perceive and understand the social world. In Chapter 5, we'll discuss cultural differences in the very way people define themselves. Whether we emphasize personal independence or social interdependence reflects our cultural values (Henrich, Heine, & Norenzayan, 2010).

Some basic psychological processes are universal, whereas others are shaped by the culture in which we live. For example, are people's self-concepts shaped by cultural rules of how people must present themselves, such as the requirement by the Taliban regime in Afghanistan that women cover themselves from head to toe? Cross-cultural research is challenging but necessary for exploring how culture influences the basic ways in which people think about and interact with others.

Conducting cross-cultural research is not simply a matter of traveling to another culture, translating materials into the local language, and replicating a study there (Heine et al., 2002; van de Vijver & Leung, 1997). Researchers have to guard against imposing their own viewpoints and definitions, learned from their culture, onto another culture with which they are unfamiliar. They must also be sure that their independent and dependent variables are understood in the same way in different cultures (Bond, 1988; Lonner & Berry, 1986).

Suppose, for example, that you wanted to replicate the Latané and Darley (1968) seizure experiment in another culture. Clearly, you could not conduct the identical experiment somewhere else. The tape-recorded discussion of college life used by Latané and Darley was specific to the lives of New York University students in the 1960s and could not be used meaningfully elsewhere. What about more subtle aspects of the study, such as the way people viewed the person who had the seizure? Cultures vary considerably in how they define whether or not another person belongs to their social group; this factor figures significantly in how they behave toward that person (Gudykunst, 1988; Triandis, 1989). If people in one culture view the victim as a member of their social group but people in another culture perceive the victim as a member of a rival social group, you might find very different results in the two cultures—not because the psychological processes of helping behavior are different, but because people interpreted the situation differently. It can be quite daunting to conduct a study that is interpreted and perceived similarly in dissimilar cultures. Cross-cultural researchers are sensitive to these issues, and as more and more cross-cultural research is conducted carefully, we will be able to determine which social psychological processes are universal and which are culture-bound (Heine, 2010). For example, there is substantial evidence that playing violent video games makes people act in more aggressive ways and makes them less likely to help others. But is this true just in Western countries? A recent review of the literature compared studies of video games in the United States and Japan. As it happened, the deleterious effects of violent video games were the same in both countries (Anderson et al., 2010).

The Evolutionary Approach

Evolutionary theory was developed by Charles Darwin (1859) to explain the ways in which animals adapt to their environments. Central to the theory is **natural selection**, the process by which heritable traits that promote survival in a particular environment are passed along to future generations, because organisms with those traits are more likely to produce offspring. A common example is how giraffes came to have long necks. In an environment where food is scarce, giraffes that happened to have long necks could feed on foliage that other animals couldn't reach. These giraffes were more likely to survive and produce offspring than were other giraffes, the story goes, and the "long neck" gene thus became common in subsequent generations.

In biology, evolutionary theory is used to explain how different species acquired physical traits such as long necks. But what about social behaviors, such as the tendency to be aggressive toward a member of one's own species or the tendency to be helpful to others? Is it possible that social behaviors have genetic determinants that evolve through the process of natural selection, and, if so, is this true in human beings as well as animals? These are the questions posed by **evolutionary psychology**, which attempts to explain social behavior in terms of genetic factors that have evolved over time according to the principles of natural selection. The core idea is that evolution occurs very slowly, such that social behaviors that are prevalent today are due at least in part to adaptations to environments in our distant past (Buss, 2005; Neuberg, Kenrick, & Schaller, 2010). We will discuss in upcoming chapters how evolutionary theory explains social behavior (e.g., Chapter 10 on interpersonal attraction, Chapter 11 on prosocial behavior, and Chapter 12 on aggression). Here, in our chapter on research methods, it is important to note that a lively debate has arisen over the testability of evolutionary hypotheses. Because current behaviors are thought to be adaptations to environmental conditions that existed thousands of years ago, psychologists make their best guesses about what those conditions were and how specific kinds of behaviors gave people a reproductive advantage. But these hypotheses are obviously impossible to test with the experimental method. And just because hypotheses sound plausible does not mean they are true. For example, some scientists now believe that giraffes did not acquire a long neck in order to eat leaves in tall trees. Instead, they suggest, long necks first evolved in male giraffes to gain an advantage in fights with other males over access to females (Simmons & Scheepers, 1996). Which of these explanations is true? It's hard to tell. On the other hand, evolutionary approaches can generate novel hypotheses about social behavior that can be tested with the other methods described in this chapter.

Evolutionary Theory
A concept developed by Charles Darwin to explain the ways in which animals adapt to their environments

Natural Selection
The process by which heritable traits that promote survival in a particular environment are passed along to future generations; organisms with those traits are more likely to produce offspring

Evolutionary Psychology
The attempt to explain social behavior in terms of genetic factors that have evolved over time according to the principles of natural selection

Social Neuroscience

As we have seen, social psychology is concerned with how people's thoughts, feelings, and behaviors are influenced by the real or imagined presence of other people. Most research studies in social psychology, then, study just that—thoughts, feelings, and behaviors. Human beings are biological organisms, however, and social psychologists have become increasingly interested in the connection between biological processes and social behavior. These interests include the study of hormones and behavior, the human immune system, and neurological processes in the human brain. To study the brain and its relation to behavior, psychologists use sophisticated technologies, including electroencephalography (EEG), in which electrodes are placed on the scalp to measure electrical activity in the brain, and functional magnetic resonance imaging (fMRI), in which people are placed in scanners that measure changes in blood flow in their brains. Social psychologists take these measurements while participants think about and process social information, allowing them to correlate different kinds of brain activity with social information processing. This kind of research

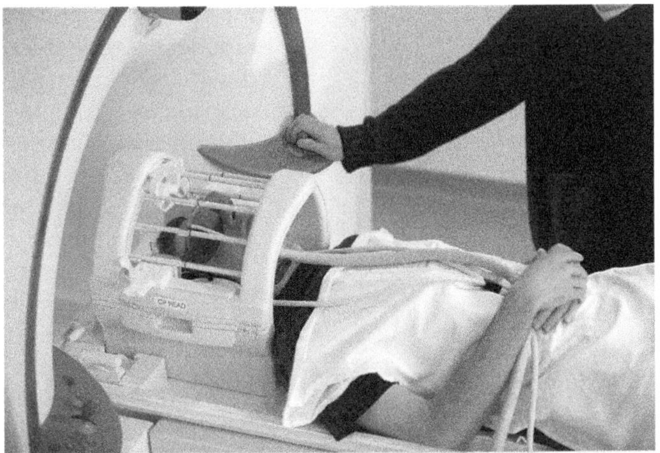

Social psychologists are studying the brain and its relation to behavior. They use technologies such as electroencephalography (EEG) and functional magnetic resonance imaging (fMRI).

Watch on MyPsychLab
To learn more about social neuroscience, watch the MyPsychLab video ***John Cacioppo: Can you tell us about your field?***

promises to open up a whole new area of inquiry into the relationship of the brain to behavior (Chiao et al., 2010; Harmon-Jones & Winkielman, 2007; Lieberman, 2010; Ochsner, 2007).

"DON'T TELL ME THIS NONSENSE DOESN'T VIOLATE THE CODE OF BIOETHICS."

Ethical Issues in Social Psychology

As you read this chapter, did it bother you to learn that researchers sometimes mislead people about the true purpose of their study or that, in Latané and Darley's seizure study, people were put in a situation that might have been upsetting? In their quest to create realistic, engaging situations, social psychologists frequently face ethical dilemmas. For scientific reasons, we want our experiments to resemble the real world as much as possible and to be as sound and well controlled as we can make them. But we also want to avoid causing our participants stress, discomfort, or unpleasantness. These two goals often conflict as the researcher goes about the business of creating and conducting experiments.

Researchers are concerned about the health and welfare of the individuals participating in their experiments. Researchers are also in the process of discovering important information about human social behavior, such as bystander intervention, prejudice, conformity, aggression, and obedience to authority. Many of these discoveries are bound to benefit society. Indeed, given the fact that social psychologists have developed powerful tools to investigate such issues scientifically, many scholars feel it would be immoral not to conduct experiments to explore them. To gain insight into such critical issues, however, researchers must create vivid events that are involving for the participants. Some of these events might make the participants uncomfortable, such as witnessing someone having a seizure. We can't resolve the dilemma by making pious claims that participants never experience discomfort in an experiment or by insisting that all is fair in science and then forging blindly ahead. Clearly, some middle ground is called for.

Informed Consent
Agreement to participate in an experiment, granted in full awareness of the nature of the experiment, which has been explained in advance

Deception
Misleading participants about the true purpose of a study or the events that will actually transpire

Institutional Review Board (IRB)
A group made up of at least one scientist, one nonscientist, and one member not affiliated with the institution that reviews all psychological research at that institution and decides whether it meets ethical guidelines; all research must be approved by the IRB before it is conducted

The dilemma is less problematic if researchers can obtain **informed consent** from their participants prior to their participation. To obtain informed consent, the researcher explains the nature of the experiment to participants before it begins and asks for their permission to participate. If participants are made fully aware of the kinds of experiences they are about to undergo and state that they are willing to participate, the ethical dilemma is resolved. In many social psychology experiments, this sort of description is feasible—and where it is feasible, it is done. But sometimes it is impossible. Suppose Latané and Darley had told their participants that a seizure was about to be staged, that it wouldn't be a real emergency, and that the point was to see if they offered help. Such a procedure would be bad science. In this kind of experiment, it's essential that the participant experience contrived events as if they were real; this is called a *deception experiment*. **Deception** in social psychological research involves misleading participants about the true purpose of a study or the events that transpire. (Note that not all research in social psychology involves deception.)

To ensure that the dignity and safety of research participants are protected, the American Psychological Association (2010) has published a list of ethical principles that govern all research in psychology (see Figure 2.3). In addition, any institution (such as a university) that seeks federal funding for psychological research is required to have an **institutional review board (IRB)** that reviews research before it is conducted. The board, which must include at least one scientist, one nonscientist, and one person who is not affiliated with the institution, reviews all research proposals and decides whether the procedures meet ethical guidelines. Any aspect of the experimental procedure that this committee judges to be overly stressful or upsetting must be changed or deleted

Selected Ethical Principles of Psychologists in the Conduct of Research

1. Psychologists seek to promote accuracy, honesty, and truthfulness in the science, teaching, and practice of psychology.
2. Psychologists respect the dignity and worth of all people, and the rights of individuals to privacy, confidentiality, and self-determination.
3. When psychologists conduct research in person or via electronic transmission or other forms of communication, they obtain the informed consent of the individual.
4. When obtaining informed consent psychologists inform participants about (1) the purpose of the research, expected duration, and procedures; (2) their right to decline to participate and to withdraw from the research once participation has begun; (3) the foreseeable consequences of declining or withdrawing; (4) reasonably foreseeable factors that may be expected to influence their willingness to participate such as potential risks, discomfort, or adverse effects; (5) any prospective research benefits; (6) limits of confidentiality; (7) incentives for participation; and (8) whom to contact for questions about the research and research participants rights.
5. Psychologists have a primary obligation and take reasonable precautions to protect confidential information obtained through or stored in any medium.
6. Psychologists do not conduct a study involving deception unless they have determined that the use of deceptive techniques is justified by the studys significant prospective scientific, educational, or applied value and that effective nondeceptive alternative procedures are not feasible.
7. Psychologists explain any deception that is an integral feature of the design and conduct of an experiment to participants as early as is feasible.
8. Psychologists provide a prompt opportunity for participants to obtain appropriate information about the nature, results, and conclusions of the research, and they take reasonable steps to correct any misconceptions that participants may have of which the psychologists are aware.

FIGURE 2.3

Procedures for the Protection of Participants in Psychological Research

The American Psychological Association, a professional organization that represents psychology in the United States, has established ethical guidelines that psychological researchers are expected to follow. Some of them are listed here.

(Adapted from APA Ethical Principles of Psychologists and Code of Conduct, 2010)

before the study can be conducted. (Note that some of the research described in later chapters was conducted before IRBs were required in the early 1970s. You will need to decide whether you would have approved these studies if you were on an IRB that judged them.)

When deception is used in a study, the postexperimental interview, called the debriefing session, is crucial. **Debriefing** is the process of explaining to the participants, at the end of an experiment, the true purpose of the study and exactly what transpired. If any participants have experienced discomfort, the researchers attempt to undo and alleviate it. During debriefing too the participants learn about the goals and purpose of the research. The best researchers question their participants carefully and listen to what they say, regardless of whether or not deception was used in the experiment. (For a detailed description of how debriefing interviews should be conducted, see Aronson et al., 1990.)

In our experience, virtually all participants understand and appreciate the need for deception, as long as the time is taken in the postexperimental debriefing session to review the purpose of the research and to explain why alternative procedures could not be used. Several investigators have gone a step further and assessed the impact on people of participating in deception studies (e.g., Christensen, 1988; Epley & Huff, 1998; Finney, 1987; Gerdes, 1979; Sharpe, Adair, & Roese, 1992). These studies have consistently found that people do not object to the kinds of mild discomfort and deceptions typically used in social psychological research. In fact, some studies have found that most people who participated in deception experiments reported learning more and enjoying the experiments more than did those who participated in nondeception experiments (Smith & Richardson, 1983). For example, Latané and Darley (1970) reported that, during their debriefing, the participants said that the deception was necessary and that they were willing to participate in similar studies in the future—even though they had experienced some stress and conflict during the study.

Debriefing

Explaining to participants, at the end of an experiment, the true purpose of the study and exactly what transpired

USE IT!

As we have seen in this chapter, social psychologists use empirical methods to test hypotheses about social behavior. Now that you know something about these methods, you are in a good position to judge the quality of research findings you read about in newspapers and magazines. As we saw, for example, one of the most common mistakes is for people to assume that because two variables are correlated with each other, one caused the other. We hope that when you hear about correlational findings in the media, a little light will go off in your head that causes you to challenge any causal conclusions that are drawn. Suppose, for example, that you are browsing through a promotional brochure for the *Consumers Reports on Health* newsletter, as one of us recently was, and you came across this tidbit: "Need more motivation to exercise? Exercise leads to better sex. In one study, men who exercised were five times as likely to achieve normal sexual function as a less-active group." Did the little light go off? This is a correlational finding—men who exercised more functioned better sexually—and we cannot draw the conclusion that it is the exercise that "leads to" (e.g., causes) better sex. Can you think of alternative explanations of this finding? Better yet, can you design an experiment that would test the hypothesis that exercise helps people's sex lives?

Summary

How do researchers develop hypotheses and theories?

- **Social Psychology: An Empirical Science** A fundamental principle of social psychology is that social influence can be studied scientifically.
  - **Formulating Hypotheses and Theories** Social psychological research begins with a hypothesis about the effects of social influence. Hypotheses often come from previous research findings; researchers conduct studies to test an alternative explanation of previous experiments. Many other hypotheses come from observations of everyday life, such as Latané and Darley's hunches about why people failed to help Kitty Genovese.

What are the strengths and weaknesses of the various research designs used by social psychologists?

- **Research Designs** Social psychologists use three research designs: the observational method, the correlational method, and the experimental method.
  - **The Observational Method: Describing Social Behavior** The **observational method**, whereby researchers observe people and systematically record their behavior, is useful for describing the nature of a phenomenon and generating hypotheses. It includes **ethnography**, the method by which researchers attempt to understand a group or culture by observing it from the inside, without imposing any preconceived notions they might have. Another method is **archival analysis**, whereby researchers examine documents or archives, such as looking at photographs in magazines to see how men and women are portrayed.
  - **The Correlational Method: Predicting Social Behavior** The **correlational method**, whereby two or more variables are systematically measured and the relationship between them assessed, is very useful when the goal is to predict one variable from another. For example, researchers might be interested in whether there is a correlation between the amount of violent television children watch and how aggressive they are. The correlational method is often applied to the results of surveys in which a representative group of people are asked questions about their attitudes and behaviors. To make sure that the results are generalizable, researchers randomly select survey respondents from the population at large. A limit of the correlational method is that *correlation does not equal causation.*
  - **The Experimental Method: Answering Causal Questions** The only way to determine causality is to use the **experimental method**, in which the researcher randomly assigns participants to different conditions and ensures that these conditions are identical except for the independent variable. The **independent variable** is the one researchers vary to see if it has a causal effect (e.g., how much TV children watch); the **dependent variable** is what researchers measure to see if it is affected (e.g., how aggressive children are). Experiments should be high in **internal validity**, which means that people in all conditions are treated identically, except for the independent variable (e.g., how much TV children watch). **External validity**—the extent to which researchers can generalize their results to other situations and people—is accomplished by increasing the realism of the experiment, particularly its psychological realism (the extent to which the psychological processes triggered in the

experiment are similar to those triggered in everyday life). It is also accomplished by **replicating** the study with different populations of participants. As in any other science, some social psychology studies are basic research experiments (designed to answer basic questions about why people do what they do), whereas others are applied studies (designed to find ways to solve specific social problems).

What impact do cross-cultural studies, the evolutionary approach, and research in social neuroscience have on the way in which scientists investigate social behavior?

- **New Frontiers in Social Psychological Research** In recent years, social psychologists have developed new ways of investigating social behavior.
    - **Culture and Social Psychology** To study the ways in which culture shapes people's thoughts, feelings, and behavior, social psychologists conduct cross-cultural research. This is not simply a matter of replicating the same study in different cultures; researchers have to guard against imposing their own viewpoints and definitions, learned from their culture, onto another culture with which they are unfamiliar.
    - **The Evolutionary Approach** Some social psychologists attempt to explain social behavior in terms of genetic factors that have evolved over time according to the principles of natural selection. Such ideas are hard to test experimentally but can generate novel hypotheses about social behavior that can be tested with the experimental method.
    - **Social Neuroscience** Social psychologists have become increasingly interested in the connection between biological processes and social behavior. These interests include the study of hormones and behavior, the human immune system, and neurological processes in the human brain.

What is the basic dilemma of the social psychologist, and how do social psychologists solve this dilemma?

- **Ethical Issues in Social Psychology** Social psychologists follow federal, state, and professional guidelines to ensure the welfare of their research participants. These include having an **institutional review board** approve their studies in advance, asking participants to sign **informed consent** forms, and **debriefing** participants afterwards about the purpose of the study and what transpired, especially if there was any deception involved.

Chapter 2 Test

Study and Review on MyPsychLab

1. The basic dilemma of the social psychologist is that
   a. it is hard to teach social psychology to students because most people believe strongly in personality.
   b. there is a trade-off between internal and external validity in most experiments.
   c. it is nearly impossible to use a random selection of the population in laboratory experiments.
   d. almost all social behavior is influenced by the culture in which people grew up.
   e. it is difficult to teach social psychology at 3:30 in the afternoon when people are sleepy.

2. Suppose a researcher found a strong negative correlation between college students' grade point average (GPA) and the amount of alcohol they drink. Which of the following is the best conclusion from this study?
   a. Students with a high GPA study more and thus have less time to drink.
   b. Drinking a lot interferes with studying.
   c. If you know how much alcohol a student drinks, you can predict his or her GPA fairly well.
   d. The higher a student's GPA, the more he or she drinks.
   e. People who are intelligent get higher grades and drink less.

3. A team of researchers wants to test the hypothesis that drinking wine makes people like jazz more. They randomly assign college students who are 21 or over to one room in which they will drink wine and listen to jazz or to another room in which they will drink water and listen to jazz. It happens that the "wine room" has a big window with nice scenery outside, while the "water room" is windowless, dark, and dingy. The most serious flaw in this experiment is that it
   a. is low in external validity.
   b. is low in internal validity.
   c. did not randomly select the participants from all college students in the country.
   d. is low in psychological realism.
   e. is low in mundane realism.

4. Mary wants to find out whether eating sugary snacks before an exam leads to better performance on the exam. Which of the following strategies would answer her question most conclusively?
   a. Identify a large number of students who perform exceptionally low and exceptionally high in exams, ask them whether they eat sugary snacks before exams, and see whether high performers eat more sugary snacks before exams than do low performers.
   b. Wait for exam time in a big class, ask everyone whether they ate sugary snacks before the exam, and see whether those who ate sugary snacks before the exam do better compared to those who didn't.
   c. Wait for exam time in a big class, give a random half of the students M&Ms before the exam, and see whether the students who ate M&Ms perform better.
   d. Pick a big class, give all students sugary snacks before one exam and salty snacks before the next exam; then see whether students score lower on average in the second exam.

5. A researcher conducts a study with participants who are college students. The researcher then repeats the study using the same procedures but with members of the general population (i.e., adults) as participants. The results are similar for both samples. The research has established __________ through __________.
   a. external validity, replication
   b. internal validity, replication
   c. external validity, psychological realism
   d. internal validity, psychological realism
   e. psychological realism, internal validity

6. In the Latané and Darley study, people sat in cubicles and heard over an intercom system someone having a seizure, to test psychological processes thought to be present in the Kitty Genovese murder. All of the following reasons *except one* explain why social psychologists do laboratory studies that differ so much from the real-life events that inspired them. Which one?
   a. It is usually easier to randomly assign people to conditions in controlled laboratory studies.
   b. The participants in lab studies are often more representative of the general population than are the people in the real-life examples.
   c. A great advantage to laboratory studies is the ability to maintain high internal validity and know for sure what is causing what.
   d. To see how much you can generalize from a lab study, you can replicate the study with different populations and in different situations.
   e. It is often possible to capture the same psychological processes in the laboratory as those that occur in real-life settings, if psychological realism is high.

7. Professor X wants to make sure his study of gifted youngsters will get published, but he's worried that his findings could have been caused by something other than the independent variable of who their first-grade teacher was. He is concerned with the __________ of his experiment.
   a. probability level
   b. external validity
   c. replication
   d. internal validity

8. Suppose a psychologist decides to join a local commune to understand and observe its members' social relationships. This is
   a. cross-cultural research.
   b. meta-analysis.
   c. applied research.
   d. an experiment.
   e. ethnography.

9. Mary and Juan want to establish interjudge reliability in their study on child bullying and the amount of time spent playing video games. To ensure interjudge reliability, they should
   a. observe and code the violent behavior together so they can obtain a reliable coding system.
   b. independently observe and code the data to see if they come up with the same observations.
   c. have one of them observe and code the data and then explain his or her system to the other.
   d. have one observe and code child bullying, while the other should observe and code the amount of time the kids play video games.

10. All of the following except one are part of the guidelines for ethical research. Which is not?
   a. All research is reviewed by an IRB (institutional review board) that consists of at least one scientist, one nonscientist, and one person unaffiliated with the institution.
   b. A researcher receives informed consent from a participant unless deception is deemed necessary and the experiment meets ethical guidelines.
   c. When deception is used in a study, participants must be fully debriefed.
   d. There must be a cover story for every study, because all studies involve some type of deception.

Answer Key

1-b, 2-c, 3-b, 4-c, 5-a,
6-b, 7-d, 8-e, 9-b, 10-d

Scoring the TRY IT! exercises

Page 23

1. In studies conducted by Stanley Milgram (1974), up to 65% of participants administered what they thought were near-lethal shocks to another subject. (In fact, no real shocks were administered.)
2. (c) Rewarding people for doing something they enjoy will typically make them like that activity less in the future (e.g., Lepper, 1995, 1996; Lepper, Greene, & Nisbett, 1973).
3. (b) Wilson and colleagues (1993) found that people who did not analyze their feelings were the most satisfied with their choice of posters when contacted a few weeks later.
4. (a) Under most circumstances, repeated exposure increases liking for a stimulus (Zajonc, 1968).
5. (a) More (Jecker & Landy, 1969).
6. (c) Research by Dijksterhuis and Nordgren (2006) found that people who were distracted made the best choices, possibly because distraction allowed them to consider the problem unconsciously but not consciously.
7. (a) Research by Spencer, Steele, and Quinn (1999) and Steele (1997) found that when women think there are sex differences on a test, they do worse. When women were told that there were no gender differences in performance on the test, they did as well as men.
8. (b) There is no evidence that subliminal messages in advertising have any effect; considerable evidence shows that normal advertising is quite effective (Abraham & Lodish, 1990; Chaiken, Wood, & Eagly, 1996; Liebert & Sprafkin, 1988; Moore, 1982; Weir, 1984; Wilson, Houston, & Meyers, 1998).
9. (b) Men touch women more than vice versa (Henley, 1977).
10. (b) People given the heavy clipboard thought that student opinion should be weighed the most (Jostmann, Lakens, & Schubert, 2009).

Page 26

Two teams of researchers (Archer, 1983, and Akert, Chen, & Panter, 1991) performed an archival analysis of portrait art and news and advertising photographs in print and television media. They coded the photographs according to the number of images that were devoted to the person's face. Their results? Over 5 centuries, across cultures, and in different forms of media, men are visually presented in a more close-up style (focusing on the head and face), while women are shown in a more long-shot style (focusing on the body). These researchers interpret their findings as indicating a subtle form of sex-role stereotyping: Men are being portrayed in a stronger style that emphasizes their intellectual achievements, whereas women are being portrayed in a weaker style that emphasizes their total physical appearance.

Page 30

1. The politician ignored possible third variables that could cause both Scout membership and crime, such as socioeconomic class. Traditionally, Scouting has been most popular in small towns and suburbs among middle-class youngsters; it has never been very attractive or even available to youths growing up in densely populated, urban, high-crime areas.
2. Not necessarily. It might be the other way around—namely, that moms and dads are more likely to become helicopter parents if their kids are having academic problems. Or there could be a third variable that causes parents to hover and their kids to have academic problems.
3. Did tattoos cause motorcycle accidents? Or, for that matter, did motorcycle accidents cause tattoos? The researchers suggested that a third (unmeasured) variable was in fact the cause of both: A tendency to take risks and to be involved in flamboyant personal displays led to tattooing one's body and to driving a motorcycle recklessly.
4. It is possible that religion makes people more likely to obey the law. It is equally possible, however, that some other variable increases the likelihood that people will be religious and follow the rules—such as having parents who are religious.
5. Not necessarily. People who do not eat breakfast might differ from people who do in any number of ways that influence longevity—for example, in how obese they are, how hard-driving and high-strung they are, or even how late they sleep in the morning.
6. Not necessarily, because milk drinking may have little to do with weight gain. Children who drink a lot of milk might be more likely to eat cookies or other high-calorie foods.
7. It is possible that watching public television makes people want to have more sex. It is equally possible, however, that some third variable, such as health or education, influences both television preferences and sexual behavior. It is even possible that having sex makes people want to watch more public television. Based on the correlation the researchers reported, there is no way of telling which of these explanations is true.
8. Not necessarily. There could be a third variable that is causing kids to eat a lot of candy and to become violent later in life.

Note: For more examples on correlation and causation, see http://jfmueller.faculty.noctrl.edu/100/correlation_or_causation.htm

8 Conformity

Influencing Behavior

On April 9, 2004, a man called a McDonald's restaurant in Mount Washington, Kentucky, and identified himself as a police detective to the assistant manager, Donna Jean Summers, 51. He told her she had a problem: One of her employees had stolen from the restaurant. He said he had talked to McDonald's corporate headquarters and to the store manager, whom he named correctly. The policeman gave Ms. Summers a rough description of the perpetrator, a teenage female, and she identified one of her employees (whom we will call Susan, to protect her identity). The police detective told the assistant manager that she needed to search Susan immediately for the stolen money, or else Susan would be arrested, taken to jail, and searched there (Wolfson, 2005).

You might be thinking that this all sounds a bit odd. Ms. Summers said later that she was initially confused, but the caller was very authoritative and presented his information in a convincing manner. And, after all, he was a policeman. We're supposed to obey the police. During the phone call, Ms. Summers thought she heard police radios in the background.

So she called Susan into a small room and locked the door. Susan was 18 and had been a perfect employee for several months. The policeman on the phone told Ms. Summers what to do and what to say. Following his instructions, she ordered Susan to take off her clothing, one item at a time, until she was standing naked. Ms. Summers put all the clothes in a bag and put the bag outside the room, as instructed by the caller. Susan was now crying, fearful of the allegations and humiliated by the strip search. It was 5:00 P.M. Unfortunately for Susan, the next 4 hours would involve even further degradation and sexual abuse, all because of orders given by the "policeman" on the phone (Barrouquere, 2006).

Susan was not the first fast-food employee to be victimized in this manner. Phone calls to restaurant managers, ordering them to abuse their employees, had been occurring around the country since 1999. It just took law enforcement some time to put the whole picture together, given that the perpetrator was using a calling card, which is difficult to trace. In all, managers of 70 restaurants, representing a dozen different chains in 32 states, received these phone calls and obeyed the caller's instructions (Barrouquere, 2006; Gray, 2004; Wolfson, 2005). The caller, as you have probably guessed, was not a policeman, but was perpetrating a horrible hoax.

Susan had been standing naked in the small, locked room for an hour. Ms. Summers needed to get back to supervising the cooking area, so the "policeman" told her to find someone else to guard Susan. She called her fiancé, Walter Nix, Jr., 42, who agreed to come to the restaurant. Mr. Nix locked himself into the room with the naked and increasingly terrified teenager. At this point, the events become even more bizarre and disturbing. Mr. Nix also believed the caller was who he said he was, and Mr. Nix proved even more obedient. In a series of escalating demands over 3 hours, the "detective" told Mr. Nix to force Susan to acquiesce to various sexual demands. The caller also talked directly to Susan, threatening her with what would happen if she didn't obey. "I was scared because they were a higher authority to me. I was scared for my safety because I thought I was in trouble with the law," she said (Wolfson, 2005, p. 3).

FOCUS QUESTIONS

- What is conformity and why does it occur?
- How does informational social influence motivate people to conform?
- How does normative social influence motivate people to conform?
- How can we use our knowledge of social influence for positive purposes?
- What have studies demonstrated about people's willingness to obey someone in a position of authority?

Hours later, the caller told Mr. Nix to replace himself with another man. Thomas Simms, a 58-year-old employee, was called into the room. As he put it later, he knew immediately "something is not right about this" (Wolfson, 2005, p. 7). He refused to obey the man on the phone. He called in Ms. Summers and convinced her something was wrong. "I knew then I had been had," she said. "I lost it. I begged [Susan] for forgiveness. I was almost hysterical" (Wolfson, 2005, p. 7). At this point, the "detective" hung up the phone. Susan's abuse was finally over.

After an investigation that involved police detectives in several states, a Florida man, David R. Stewart, 38, was arrested and charged as the telephone hoaxer. Married and the father of five, Stewart worked as a prison guard and was formerly a security guard and volunteer sheriff's deputy. At his trial in 2006, with only circumstantial evidence against him, the jury returned a verdict of not guilty. There have been no further fast-food hoax phone calls (ABC News, 2007). The assistant manager, Donna Summers, and her (no longer) fiancé, Walter Nix Jr., pleaded guilty to various charges. Ms. Summers was sentenced to probation, and Mr. Nix was sentenced to 5 years in prison. Susan, who now suffers from panic attacks, anxiety, and depression, sued the McDonald's corporation for failing to warn employees nationally after the first hoaxes occurred at their restaurants. She was awarded $6.1 million in damages by a Kentucky jury (Barrouquere, 2006; Neil, 2007; Wolfson, 2005).

In one of the saddest comments on this event, Susan's therapist said that Susan followed orders that night because her experience with adults "has been to do what she is told, because good girls do what they are told" (Wolfson, 2005). Indeed, every day people try to influence us to do what they want, sometimes through direct requests and sometimes through more-subtle processes. The most powerful form of social influence produces obedience and occurs when an authority figure gives an order. The fast-food restaurant hoax shows us how overly obedient people can be. A more subtle form of social influence involves conformity. Here, others indicate to us less directly what is appropriate, and we come to sense that it is in our best interest to go along with them. In this chapter, we will focus on the potentially positive and negative effects of these social influence processes.

Conformity: When and Why

Which one of the two quotations on the left do you find more appealing? Which one describes your immediate reaction to the word *conformity*? We wouldn't be surprised if you preferred the second quotation. American culture stresses the importance of not conforming (Hofstede, 1986; Kim & Markus, 1999; Kitayama et al., 2009; Markus, Kitayama, & Heiman, 1996). We picture ourselves as a nation of rugged individualists, people who think for themselves, stand up for the underdog, and go against the tide to fight for what we think is right. This cultural self-image has been shaped by the manner in which our nation was founded, by our system of government, and by our society's historical experience with western expansion—the "taming" of the Wild West (Kitayama et al., 2006; Turner, 1932).

> *Do as most do, and [people] will speak well of thee.*
>
> —Thomas Fuller

> *It were not best that we should all think alike; it is difference of opinion that makes horse races.*
>
> —Mark Twain

American mythology has celebrated the rugged individualist in many ways. For example, one of the longest-running and most successful advertising campaigns in American history featured the "Marlboro Man." As far back as 1955, the photograph of a cowboy alone on the range was an archetypal image. It also sold a lot of cigarettes. Clearly, it told us something about ourselves that we want and like to hear: that we make up our own minds; that we're not spineless, weak conformists (Cialdini, 2005; Pronin, Berger, & Molouki, 2007). More recently, consider the example of Apple Computer, currently the most valuable publicly traded company in the world (Rooney, 2012). For several years, Apple's advertising slogan captured a similar sentiment of simply stated nonconformity: "Think different."

But are we, in fact, nonconforming creatures? Are the decisions we make always based on what we think, or do we sometimes use other people's behavior to help us decide what to do? In spite of Apple's advertising telling customers to "think different," take a careful look around the lecture hall next time you're in class and count how many laptops in the room share the identical glowing Apple logo. The computer of the nonconformist is now everywhere.

On a far more sobering note, as we saw in Chapter 6, the mass suicide of the Heaven's Gate cult members suggests that people sometimes conform in extreme and astonishing ways—even when making such a crucial decision as whether or not to take their own lives. But, you might argue, surely this is an extremely unusual case. Perhaps the followers of Marshall Applewhite were disturbed people who were somehow predisposed to do what a charismatic leader told them to do. There is, however, another, more chilling possibility: Maybe most of us would have acted the same way had we been exposed to the same long-standing, powerful conformity pressures as were the members of Heaven's Gate. According to this view, almost anyone would have conformed in these same extreme circumstances.

If this statement is true, we should be able to find other situations in which people, put under strong social pressures, conformed to a surprising degree. And, in fact, we can. For example, in 1961, activists in the American civil rights movement incorporated Mohandas Gandhi's principles of nonviolent protest into their demonstrations to end segregation. They trained their "Freedom Riders" (so named because they boarded buses and disobeyed "back of the bus" seating rules) in the passive acceptance of violent treatment. Thousands of southern African Americans, joined by a smaller number of northern whites, many from college campuses, demonstrated against the segregationist laws of the South. In confrontation after confrontation, the civil rights activists reacted nonviolently as they were beaten, clubbed, hosed, whipped, raped, and even killed by southern sheriffs and police (Powledge, 1991; Nelson, 2010). Their powerful show of conformity to the ideal of nonviolent protest helped usher in a new era in America's fight for racial equality.

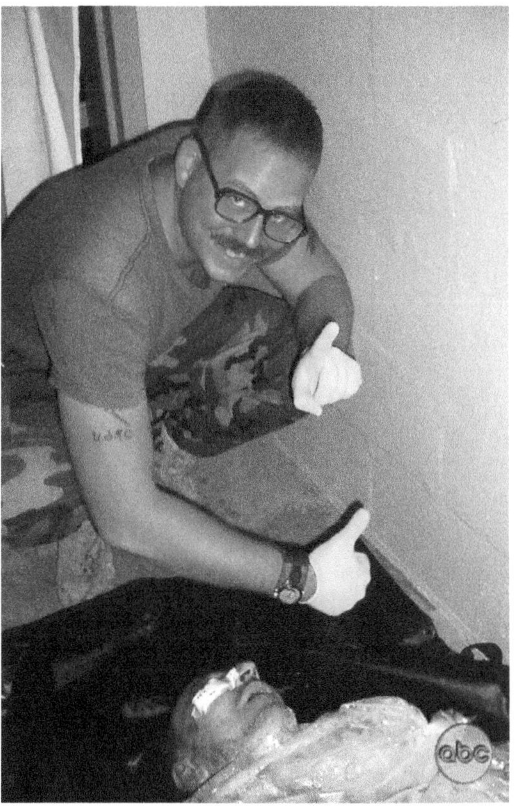

Under strong social pressure, individuals will conform to the group, even when this means doing something immoral. In 2004, American soldiers' degrading abuse of Iraqis held at the Abu Ghraib prison sparked an international scandal and a great deal of soul-searching back home. In this now-infamous photograph, Specialist Charles Graner flashes a thumbs-up sign over the dead body of an Iraqi prisoner. Why did the soldiers humiliate their captives (and seem to enjoy themselves as they did it)? As you read this chapter, you will see how the social-influence pressures of conformity and obedience can cause decent people to commit indecent acts.

But just a few years later, social pressure resulted in a tragic rather than heroic course of events. On the morning of March 16, 1968, American soldiers in Vietnam boarded helicopters that would take them to the village of My Lai. One pilot radioed that he saw Vietcong soldiers below, and so the soldiers jumped off the helicopters, rifles blazing. They soon realized that the pilot was wrong—there were no enemy soldiers, only women, children, and elderly men cooking breakfast over small fires. Inexplicably, the leader of the platoon ordered one of the soldiers to kill the villagers. Other soldiers began firing too, and the carnage spread, ultimately ending with the deaths of 450 to 500 Vietnamese civilians (Hersh, 1970). Similar processes of social influence have been implicated in more-recent military atrocities, including the humiliation of Iraqi captives at the Abu Ghraib prison starting in 2003 (Hersh, 2004), the killing of thousands of Iraqi civilians and destruction of tens of thousands of houses in Fallujah in 2004 (Marqusee, 2005), and American soldiers urinating on the corpses of Taliban fighters in Afghanistan in 2011 (Martinez, 2012).

In all these examples, people found themselves caught in a web of social influence. In response, they changed their behavior and conformed to the expectations of others (O'Gorman, Wilson, & Miller, 2008). For social psychologists, this is the essence of **conformity**: changing one's behavior due to the real or imagined influence of others (Kiesler & Kiesler, 1969; Aarts & Dijksterhuis, 2003). As these examples show, the consequences of conformity can span a wide range, from usefulness and bravery to hysteria and tragedy. But why did these people conform? Some probably conformed because they did not know what to do in a confusing or unusual situation. The behavior of the people around them served as a cue as to how to respond, and they decided to act in a similar manner. Other people probably conformed because they did not wish to be ridiculed or punished for being different from everybody else. They chose to act the way the group expected so that they wouldn't be rejected or thought less of by group members. Let's see how each of these reasons for conforming operates.

Conformity

A change in one's behavior due to the real or imagined influence of other people

Informational Social Influence: The Need to Know What's "Right"

How should you address your psychology professor—as Dr. Berman, Professor Berman, Ms. Berman, or Patricia? How should you vote in the upcoming ballot referendum that would raise your tuition to cover expanded student services? Do you cut a piece of sushi or eat it whole? Did the scream you just heard in the hallway come from a person joking with friends or from the victim of a mugging?

In these and many other situations, we feel uncertain about what to think or how to act. We simply don't know enough to make a good or accurate choice. Luckily, we have a powerful and useful source of knowledge available to us—the behavior of other people. Asking others what they think or watching what they do helps us reach a definition of the situation (Kelley, 1955; Thomas, 1928). When we subsequently act like everyone else, we are conforming, but this doesn't mean we are weak, spineless individuals with no self-reliance. Instead, the influence of other people leads us to conform because we see those people as a source of information to guide our behavior. We conform in such a way because we believe that others' interpretation of an ambiguous set of circumstances is more accurate than ours and will help us choose an appropriate course of action. This is called **informational social influence** (Cialdini, 2000; Cialdini & Goldstein, 2004; Deutsch & Gerard, 1955).

As an illustration of how other people can be a source of information, imagine that you are a participant in the following experiment by Muzafer Sherif (1936). In the first phase of the study, you are seated alone in a dark room and asked to focus your attention on a dot of light 15 feet away. The experimenter asks you to estimate in inches how far the light moves. You stare earnestly at the light and, yes, it moves a little. You say, "about 2 inches," though it is not easy to tell exactly. The light disappears and then comes back; you are asked to judge again. The light seems to move a little more this time, and you say, "4 inches." After several of these trials, the light seems to move about the same amount each time—about 2 to 4 inches.

> *"It's always best on these occasions to do what the mob do." "But suppose there are two mobs?" suggested Mr. Snodgrass. "Shout with the largest," replied Mr. Pickwick.*
>
> —Charles Dickens, *Pickwick Papers*

The interesting thing about this task is that the light was not actually moving at all. It looked as if it was moving because of a visual illusion called the autokinetic effect: If you stare at a bright light in a uniformly dark environment (e.g., a star on a dark night), the light will appear to waver back and forth. This occurs because you have no stable reference point with which to anchor the position of the light. The distance that the light appears to move varies from person to person but becomes consistent for each person over time. In Sherif's experiment, the subjects all arrived at their own stable estimate during the first phase of the study, but these estimates differed from person to person. Some people thought the light was moving only an inch or so; others thought it was moving as much as 10 inches.

Sherif chose the autokinetic effect because he wanted a situation that would be ambiguous—where the correct definition of the situation would be unclear to his participants. In the second phase of the experiment, a few days later, the participants were paired with two other people, each of whom had had the same prior experience alone with the light. Now the situation became a truly social one, as all three made their judgments out loud. Remember, the autokinetic effect is experienced differently by different people; some see a lot of movement and some see not much at all. After hearing their partners give judgments that were different from their own, what did people do?

Over the course of several trials, people reached a common estimate, and each member of the group conformed to that estimate. These results indicate that people were using each other as a source of information, coming to believe that the group estimate was the correct one (see Figure 8.1). An important feature of informational social influence is that it can lead to **private acceptance**, when people conform to the behavior of others because they genuinely believe that these other people are right.

It might seem equally plausible that people publicly conformed to the group but privately maintained the belief that the light was moving only a small amount. For example, maybe someone privately believed that the light was moving 10 inches but

Informational Social Influence

The influence of other people that leads us to conform because we see them as a source of information to guide our behavior; we conform because we believe that others' interpretation of an ambiguous situation is more correct than ours and will help us choose an appropriate course of action

Private Acceptance

Conforming to other people's behavior out of a genuine belief that what they are doing or saying is right

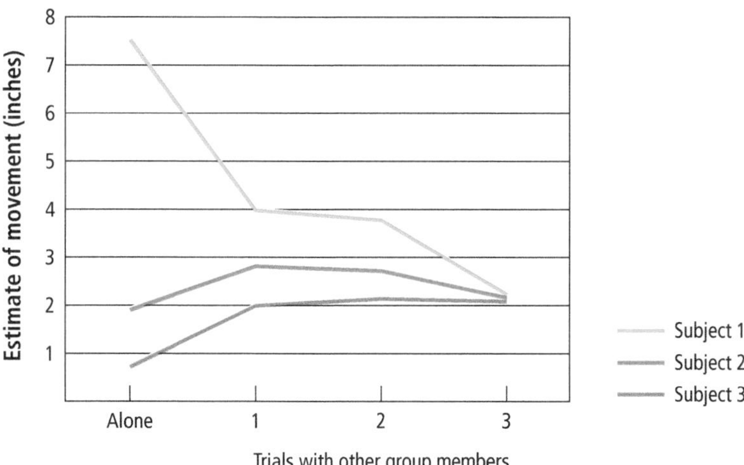

FIGURE 8.1

One Group's Judgments in Sherif's (1936) Autokinetic Studies

People estimated how far a point of light appeared to move in a dark room. When they saw the light by themselves, their estimates varied widely. When they were brought together in groups and heard other people announce their estimates, people conformed to the group's estimate of how much the light moved, adjusting their private beliefs based on the information other group members provided.

(Adapted from Sherif, 1936)

announced that it had moved 3 inches, the group estimate, to avoid standing out from the crowd or looking foolish. This would be a case of **public compliance**, conforming publicly without necessarily believing in what the group is saying or doing. Sherif cast doubt on this interpretation of his study, however, by asking people to judge the lights once more by themselves, after participating in groups. Even though they no longer had to worry about looking silly in front of other participants, they continued to give the answer the group had given earlier. One study even found that people still conformed to the group estimate when they participated individually a year later (Rohrer et al., 1954). These results suggest that people were relying on each other to define reality and came to privately accept the wisdom of the group estimate.

Public Compliance

Conforming to other people's behavior publicly without necessarily believing in what the other people are doing or saying.

The power of conformity to produce private acceptance has been demonstrated in several areas of life, including energy conservation. For example, Jessica Nolan and her colleagues (2008) gave a sample of California residents information urging them to conserve electricity in their homes. The household members received one of four messages. Three of these presented basic reasons to conserve: to protect the environment, to benefit society, or to save money. The fourth message contained information designed to promote conformity: The participants were told that the majority of their neighbors conserved electrical energy. The researchers then measured actual energy usage from the homes' electrical meters. They found that the fourth message, containing information about the behavior of one's neighbors, caused people to conserve significantly more energy than did the other three messages (Nolan et al., 2008). Similarly, Goldstein, Cialdini, and Griskevicius (2008) managed to increase hotel guests' compliance with the "reuse your bath towels and save energy" request, a widely used hotel management technique that hasn't always proved popular with guests. The researchers found that an informational sign in the bathroom, stating that the majority of guests in this room reuse their towels, was significantly more effective than the general appeal for help usually used by hotels ("Help save the environment"; Goldstein et al., p. 473).

Eight thousand pumpkins meet the Eiffel Tower. While the holiday is based on ancient British and Irish traditions surrounding All Hallows' Eve, Halloween as we know it is a completely American phenomenon—until October 1997, that is, when "Ah-lo-ween" was introduced to the French public by retailers in an effort to boost consumer spending to spark a sagging French economy (Cohen, 1997). Informational social influence is how the French literally learned what this holiday is about. As of Halloween 1997, they had no idea of what "treek au treeting" was. However, by Halloween 2000, French shops were decorated in black and orange, carved pumpkins were displayed, and nightclubs held costume competitions.

(Associated Press, 2002)

The Importance of Being Accurate

Later research extended Sherif's classic study on informational conformity in interesting ways (Baron, Vandello, & Brunsman, 1996; Levine, Higgins, & Choi, 2000). This research employed judgment tasks that are more like real life than the autokinetic effect. It also revealed another variable that affects informational social influence: how important it is to the individual to be accurate at the task.

For example, in one study, research participants were given an involving but ambiguous task: eyewitness identification (Baron, Vandello, & Brunsman, 1996). Just like eyewitnesses of a real crime, the participants were asked to pick a "perpetrator" out of a lineup. For each of the 13 tasks, the participants were first shown a slide of a man—the perpetrator. Next they saw a slide of a lineup composed of four men, one of whom was the perpetrator. In the lineup, the perpetrator was sometimes dressed differently than he had been in the prior slide. The participant's job was to pick him out. The task was made very difficult (to the point of ambiguity) by presenting the slides extremely quickly. Participants saw each slide for only half a second. The eyewitness task took place in a group consisting of the participant and three confederates. Each of the four said their answers out loud after viewing each pair of slides. On the critical seven trials, where informational social influence would be measured, the three confederates answered before the participant—and all the confederates gave the same wrong answer.

The researchers also manipulated how important it was to the research participants to be accurate at the task. In the high-importance condition, they were told that the upcoming task was a real test of eyewitness identification ability and that police departments and courts would soon be using it to differentiate good eyewitnesses from poor ones. Participants' scores would therefore establish standards against which future eyewitness performance would be judged. In addition, those who were most accurate at the task would receive a $20 bonus from the experimenters. In contrast, in the low-importance condition, the research participants were told that the study was a first attempt to study eyewitness identification and that the slide task was still being developed. Thus, as the participants began the task, they were in two very different states of mind. Half thought their performance was very important and would have ramifications for the legal community. They were motivated to do well (and earn their $20). The other half saw this as just a regular research study like any other. Their performance didn't seem that important to the experimenters.

Even for judgments of the utmost importance—such as when an eyewitness to a crime later tries to identify the culprit—informational social influence influences our perceptions.

The high-importance condition mirrors the concerns of many situations in everyday life—your judgments and decisions have consequences, and you're motivated to "get things right." Will that make you more or less susceptible to informational social influence? The researchers found that it makes you *more* susceptible. In the low-importance condition, participants conformed to the confederates' judgments and gave the same wrong answers on 35% of the critical trials. In the high-importance condition, participants conformed to the confederates' judgments on 51% of the critical trials.

But relying on other people as a source of information is a strategy that also comes with risks. In a different eyewitness study, pairs of eyewitnesses each watched separate videos of what they believed to be the exact same event (Gabbert, Memon, & Allan, 2003). Unbeknownst to participants, each member of the pair viewed a slightly different video. Among pairs that were allowed to discuss the video before each eyewitness took an individual memory test, 71% of witnesses went on to mistakenly recall having personally seen items that only their partner had actually seen. This experiment illustrates the major risk of using other people around you for information: What if those other people are wrong? Indeed, this is why most police procedures require that eyewitnesses be interviewed individually by investigators (and view lineups individually as well).

When Informational Conformity Backfires

A dramatic form of informational social influence occurs during crises, when an individual is confronted with a frightening, potentially dangerous situation to which he or she is ill-equipped to respond (Killian, 1964). The person may have no idea of what is really happening or what he or she should do. When one's personal safety is involved, the need for information is acute—and the behavior of others is very informative.

Consider what happened on Halloween Night in 1938. Orson Welles, the gifted actor and film director, and the Mercury Theater broadcast a radio play based loosely on H. G. Wells's science fiction fantasy *War of the Worlds*. Remember, this was the era before television; radio was a primary source of entertainment (with music, comedy, and drama programs) and it was the only source for fast-breaking news. That night, the drama that Welles and his fellow actors broadcast—portraying the invasion of Earth by hostile Martians—was so realistic that at least a million listeners became frightened and alerted the police; several thousand were so panic-stricken that they tried to flee the "invasion" in their cars (Cantril, 1940).

Why were so many Americans convinced that what they heard was a real news report of an actual invasion by aliens? Hadley Cantril (1940), who studied this real-life "crisis," suggested two reasons. One was that the play parodied existing radio news shows very well, and many listeners missed the beginning of the broadcast (when it was clearly identified as a play) because they had been listening to a popular show on another station. The other culprit, however, was informational social influence. Many people were listening with friends and family. As the *War of the Worlds* scenario became increasingly frightening, they naturally turned to each other, out of uncertainty, to see whether they should believe what they heard. Seeing looks of concern and worry on their loved ones' faces added to the panic people were beginning to feel. "We all kissed one another and felt we would all die," reported one listener (Cantril, 1940, p. 95).

> *Ninety-nine percent of the people in the world are fools, and the rest of us are in great danger of contagion.*
>
> —Thornton Wilder, *The Matchmaker*

A late-nineteenth-century social scientist Gustav Le Bon (1895) was the first researcher to document how emotions and behavior can spread rapidly through a crowd—an effect he called **contagion** (Fowler & Christakis, 2008; Hatfield, Cacioppo, & Rapson, 1993; Levy & Nail, 1993). As we have learned, in a truly ambiguous situation, people become more likely to rely on the interpretation of others. Unfortunately, in a truly ambiguous and confusing situation, other people may be no more knowledgeable or accurate than we are. If other people are misinformed, we will adopt their mistakes and misinterpretations. Depending on others to help us define the situation can therefore lead us into serious inaccuracies.

> *Yes, we must, indeed, all hang together or, most assuredly, we shall all hang separately.*
>
> —Benjamin Franklin at the signing of the Declaration of Independence, 1776

An extreme example of misdirected informational social influence is **mass psychogenic illness** (Bartholomew & Wessely, 2002; Colligan, Pennebaker, & Murphy, 1982), the occurrence in a group of people of similar physical symptoms with no known physical cause. For example, in 1998, a high school teacher in Tennessee reported the smell of gasoline in her classroom; soon she experienced headache, nausea, shortness of breath, and dizziness. As her class was being evacuated, others in the school reported similar symptoms. The decision was made to evacuate the entire school. Everyone watched as emergency medical workers ushered the teacher and students into ambulances. Local experts investigated and could find nothing wrong with the school. Classes resumed—and more people reported feeling sick. Again the school was evacuated and closed. Experts from numerous government agencies were called in to conduct an environmental investigation. And again nothing was found to be wrong with the school. When it reopened this time, the epidemic of mysterious illness was over (Altman, 2000).

Contagion
The rapid spread of emotions or behaviors through a crowd

Mass Psychogenic Illness
The occurrence in a group of people of similar physical symptoms with no known physical cause

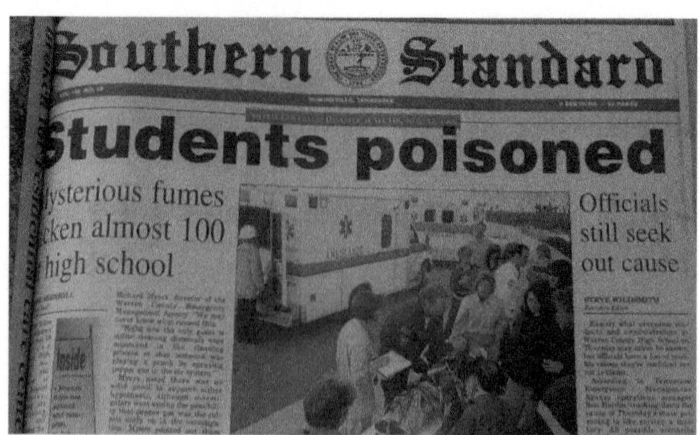

The *Southern Standard* headlined a frightening and mysterious event at a local Tennessee high school. An investigation found that the "poisonings" were a case of mass psychogenic illness.

Discussion regarding the possibility of mass psychogenic illness once again made headlines in early 2012, as more than a dozen students in an upstate New York high school developed a condition resembling Tourette's syndrome (a neurological condition characterized by involuntary tics, body movements, and vocalizations) that seemed to have no identifiable cause (Szalavitz, 2012). What is particularly interesting about incidents like these (as well as other peculiar forms of conformity) is the powerful role that the mass media play in their dissemination. These days, information is spread quickly and efficiently to all segments of the population through not only radio and television, but also texting and social media. Whereas in the Middle Ages it took 2 hundred years for the "dancing manias" (a kind of psychogenic illness) to crisscross Europe (Sirois, 1982), today it takes only minutes for millions of people around the world to learn about an unusual event via computers and smartphones. Luckily, the mass media also have the power to quickly squelch contagion by introducing more-logical explanations for ambiguous events.

When Will People Conform to Informational Social Influence?

Let's review the situations that are the most likely to produce conformity because of informational social influence.

When the Situation is Ambiguous Ambiguity is the most crucial variable for determining how much people use each other as a source of information. When you are unsure of the correct response, the appropriate behavior, or the right idea, you will be most open to influence from others. The more uncertain you are, the more you will rely on others (Allen, 1965; Renfrow & Gosling, 2006; Tesser, Campbell, & Mickler, 1983; Walther et al., 2002). Situations such as the military atrocities discussed above were ambiguous ones for the people involved—ideal circumstances for informational social influence to take hold. Most of the soldiers were young and inexperienced. When they saw a few other soldiers shooting at the villagers or humiliating prisoners, many of them thought this was what they were supposed to do too, and they joined in.

When the Situation is a Crisis Crisis often occurs simultaneously with ambiguity. In a crisis situation, we usually do not have time to stop and think about exactly which course of action we should take. We need to act—immediately. If we feel scared and panicky and are uncertain what to do, it is only natural for us to see how other people are responding and to do likewise. Unfortunately, the people we imitate may also feel scared and panicky and not be behaving rationally.

Soliders, for example, are undoubtedly scared and on edge during their tours of duty. Further, in many wars it is not easy to tell who the enemy is. In the Vietnam War, civilians who were sympathizers of the Vietcong were known to have laid mines in the path of U.S. soldiers, fired guns from hidden locations, and thrown or planted grenades. Similarly, in Iraq and Afghanistan it was difficult to tell if people were civilians or combatants, allies or enemies. It is perhaps not surprising, then, that these soldiers often turned to others around them to gauge the proper course of action. Had these individuals not been in the midst of a chronic crisis situation, and instead had more time to think about their actions, perhaps tragedy and scandal would have been avoided.

When Other People are Experts Typically, the more expertise or knowledge a person has, the more valuable he or she will be as a guide in an ambiguous situation (Allison, 1992; Cialdini & Trost, 1998). For example, a passenger who sees smoke coming out of an airplane engine will probably check the flight attendants' reaction rather than their seatmates'; however, experts are not always reliable sources of information.

Imagine the fear felt by the young man listening to the *War of the Worlds* broadcast who called his local police department for an explanation, only to learn that the police too thought the events described on the radio were actually happening (Cantril, 1940)!

Normative Social Influence: The Need to Be Accepted

The desire to be accepted and liked by others can lead to dangerous behavior. Here, Brazilian teenagers "surf" on top of trains because it has become the popular thing to do in their peer group.

In the 1990s in Rio de Janeiro, Brazil, teenage boys and girls engaged in a dangerous and reckless game: "surfing" on the tops of trains, standing with arms outstretched as the trains sped along. Despite the fact that an average of 150 teenagers died each year from this activity and 400 more were injured by falling off the trains or hitting the 3,000-volt electric cable, the surfing continued (Arnett, 1995). More recently, in the United States and Australia, teenagers surfing on speeding cars has become a growing problem. Severe injuries and deaths from car surfing have been reported in Massachusetts, Ohio, Arizona, Wisconsin, and New South Wales, Australia (Daniel & Nelson, 2004; Ma, 2009).

Why do some adolescents engage in such risky behavior? Why does anyone follow the group's lead when the resulting behavior is far from sensible and may even be dangerous? We doubt that the Brazilian, American, or Australian teenagers risked their lives due to informational conformity. It is difficult to argue that a boy or girl staring at a train would say, "Gee, I don't know what to do. I guess standing on top of a speeding train makes sense." This example suggests that there must be something else besides the need for information that can explain conformity. And there is: We also conform so that we will be liked and accepted by other people (Maxwell, 2002). We conform to the group's **social norms**—implicit (and sometimes explicit) rules for acceptable behaviors, values, and beliefs (Deutsch & Gerard, 1955; Kelley, 1955; Miller & Prentice, 1996). Groups have certain expectations about how the group members should behave, and members in good standing conform to these rules. Members who do not are perceived as different, difficult, and eventually deviant.

Deviant group members are often ridiculed, punished, or even rejected by other group members (James & Olson, 2000; Kruglanski & Webster, 1991; Levine, 1989; Miller & Anderson, 1979). For example, in Japan a whole class (or even the entire school) will sometimes turn against one student perceived as different, alternately harassing and shunning the individual. In a highly cohesive, group-oriented culture such as Japan, this kind of treatment has had tragic results: Twelve teenage victims of bullying killed themselves in one year (Jordan, 1996). Another social phenomenon in Japan is the *hikikomori*, teenagers (mostly male) who have withdrawn from all social interaction. They spend all their time alone, in their bedrooms in their parents' homes. Some hikikomori have remained sequestered for over a decade. Japanese psychologists state that many hikikomori were the victims of severe bullying before their withdrawal (Jones, 2006). Recently, researchers in the United States and Great Britain have begun to study cyberbullying in middle and secondary schools. This form of bullying, using cell phones and the Internet, is increasingly frequent, affecting as many as 11% of middle school children (Kowalski & Limber, 2007; Smith et al., 2008; Wilton & Campbell, 2011).

We human beings are by nature a social species. Few of us could live happily as hermits, never seeing or talking to another person. Through interactions with others, we receive emotional support, affection, and love, and we partake of enjoyable experiences. Other people are extraordinarily important to our sense of well-being. Research on individuals who have been isolated for long periods of time indicates that being deprived of human contact is stressful, traumatic, and psychologically painful (Baumeister & Leary, 1995; Schachter, 1959; Williams & Nida, 2011).

Social Norms

The implicit or explicit rules a group has for the acceptable behaviors, values, and beliefs of its members

Normative Social Influence

The influence of other people that leads us to conform in order to be liked and accepted by them; this type of conformity results in public compliance with the group's beliefs and behaviors but not necessarily in private acceptance of those beliefs and behaviors

Given this fundamental human need for social companionship, it is not surprising that we often conform to gain acceptance from others. Conformity for normative reasons occurs in situations where we do what other people are doing, not because we are using them as a source of information, but so that we won't attract attention, be made fun of, get into trouble, or be rejected. Thus, **normative social influence** occurs when the influence of other people leads us to conform to be liked and accepted by them. This type of conformity results in public compliance with the group's beliefs and behaviors, but not necessarily in private acceptance (Cialdini, Kallgren, & Reno, 1991; Deutsch & Gerard, 1955; Levine, 1999; Nail, McDonald, & Levy, 2000).

You probably don't find it too surprising that people sometimes conform to be liked and accepted by others. You might be thinking, where's the harm? If the group is important to us and wearing the right clothes or using the right slang will gain us acceptance, why not go along? But when it comes to more-important kinds of behaviors, such as hurting another person, surely we will resist such conformity pressures. And of course we won't conform when we are certain of the correct way of behaving and the pressures are coming from a group that we don't care all that much about. Or will we?

Explore on MyPsychLab

To explore social influence further, try the MyPsychLab activity ***Urban Legends***.

Conformity and Social Approval: The Asch Line-Judgment Studies

To find out, Solomon Asch (1951, 1956) conducted a series of now-classic studies exploring the power of normative social influence. Asch devised the studies assuming that there are limits to how much people will conform. Naturally, people conformed in the Sherif studies (see page 200), he reasoned, because the situation was highly ambiguous—trying to guess how much a light was moving. But when a situation was wholly unambiguous, Asch expected that people would act like rational, objective problem solvers. When the group said or did something that contradicted an obvious truth, surely people would resist social pressures and decide for themselves what was going on.

To test his hypothesis, Asch conducted the following study. Had you been a participant, you would have been told that this was an experiment on perceptual judgment and that you would be taking part with seven other students. Here's the scenario: The experimenter shows everyone two cards, one with a single line on it, the other with three lines labeled 1, 2, and 3. He asks each of you to judge and then announce out loud which of the three lines on the second card is closest in length to the line on the first card (see Figure 8.2).

It is crystal clear that the correct answer is the second line. Not surprisingly, each participant says, "Line 2." Your turn comes next to last, and of course you say, "Line 2" as well. The last participant concurs. The experimenter then presents a new set of cards and asks the participants again to make their judgments and announce them out loud.

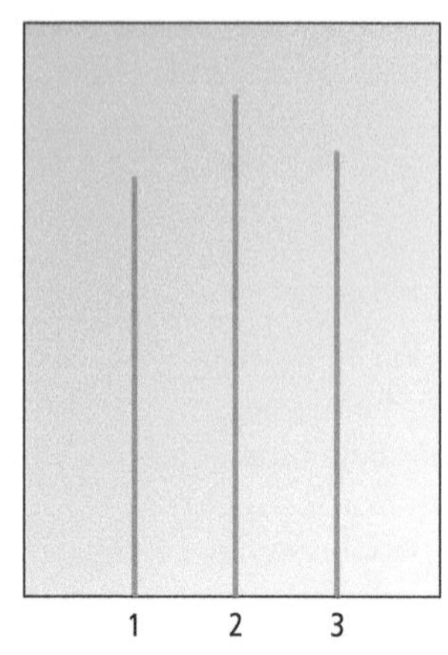

FIGURE 8.2

The Judgment Task in Asch's Line Studies

In a series of studies of normative social influence, participants judged which of the three comparison lines on the right was closest in length to the standard line on the left. The correct answer was always obvious (as it is here). However, members of the group (actually confederates) gave the wrong answer out loud. Now the participant faced a dilemma: Give the right answer and go against the whole group, or conform to their behavior and give an obviously wrong answer?

(Adapted from Asch, 1956)

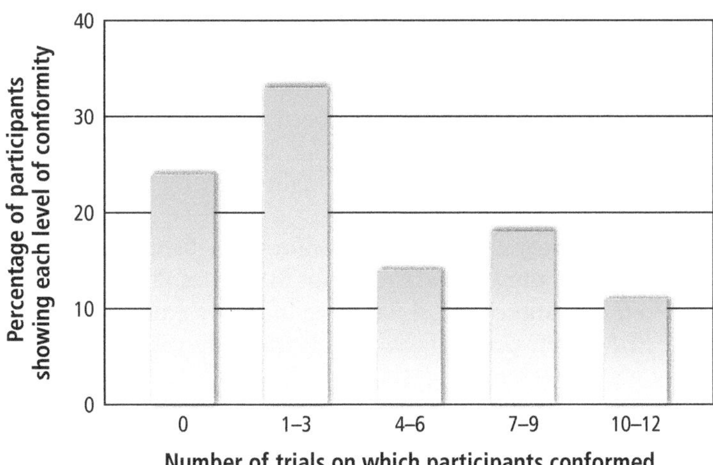

FIGURE 8.3

Results of the Asch Line-Judgment Study

Participants in the Asch line study showed a surprisingly high level of conformity, given how obvious it was that the group was wrong in its judgments. Seventy-six percent of the participants conformed on at least one trial; only 24% of participants never conformed at all (see bar labeled zero). Most participants conformed on one to three of the 12 trials in which the group gave the wrong answer. However, a sizable number of participants conformed to the group's incorrect response nearly every single time (see the two bars on the right).

(Adapted from Asch, 1957)

Again, the answer is obvious, and everyone gives the correct answer. At this point, you are probably thinking, "What a waste of time. I've got a paper due tomorrow. I need to get out of here."

As your mind starts to wander, though, something surprising happens. The experimenter presents a third set of lines, and again the answer is obvious—line 3 is clearly the closest in length to the target line. But the first participant announces that the correct answer is line 1! "This guy must be so bored that he fell asleep," you think. Then the second person announces that line 1 is the correct answer. The third, fourth, fifth, and sixth participants all agree; it's now your turn to judge. Startled at this point, you are probably looking at the lines very closely to see if you missed something. But no, line 3 is clearly the right answer. What will you do? Will you stand up for what you believe to be the truth, blurting out, "Line 3," or will you go along with the group and give the obviously wrong answer, "Line 1"?

As you can see, Asch set up a situation to discover if people would conform even when the right answer was absolutely obvious. In each group, all the individuals except for the actual participant were confederates of the research term who had been instructed to give the wrong answer on 12 of the 18 trials. What happened? Contrary to what Asch expected, a considerable amount of conformity occurred: Seventy-six percent of the participants conformed and gave an obviously incorrect response on at least one trial. On average, people conformed on about a third of the trials on which the accomplices gave the incorrect answer (see Figure 8.3).

Why did people conform so much of the time? Participants couldn't have needed information from others to help them decide, as they did in the Sherif study, because the situation was not ambiguous. The right answers were so obvious that when people in a control group made the judgments by themselves, they were accurate more

It isn't difficult to keep alive, friends—just don't make trouble—or if you must make trouble, make the sort of trouble that's expected.

—Robert Bolt, *A Man for All Seasons*

Participants in an Asch line study. The real participant is seated in the middle. He is surrounded by the experimenter's accomplices, who have just given the wrong answer on the line task.

than 98% of the time. Instead, normative pressures came into play. Even though the other participants were strangers, the fear of being the lone dissenter was so strong that most people conformed, at least occasionally. One participant explained: "Here was a group; they had a definite idea; my idea disagreed; this might arouse anger . . . I was standing out [like] a sore thumb . . . I didn't want particularly to make a fool of myself . . . I felt I was definitely right . . . [but] they might think I was peculiar" (Asch, 1956, Whole No. 416).

These are classic normative reasons for conforming: People know that what they are doing is wrong but go along anyway so as not to feel peculiar or look foolish. Notably, in contrast to informational social influence, normative pressures usually result in *public compliance without private acceptance*; people go along with the group even if they do not believe in what they are doing or think it is wrong.

What is especially surprising about Asch's results is that people were concerned about looking foolish even in front of complete strangers. It is not as if the participants were in danger of being ostracized by a group that was important to them. Yet decades of research since the original Asch study have indicated that conformity for normative reasons can occur simply because we do not want to risk social disapproval, even from complete strangers we will never see again (Bond & Smith, 1996; Cialdini & Goldstein, 2004; Tanford & Penrod, 1984).

In a variation of his study, Asch (1957) demonstrated just how powerful social disapproval can be in shaping a person's behavior. As before, the confederates gave the wrong answer 12 out of 18 times, but in this version participants wrote their answers on a piece of paper instead of saying them out loud. Now people did not have to worry about what the group thought of them, because the group would never find out what their answers were. Conformity dropped dramatically, occurring on an average of only 1.5 of the 12 trials (Insko et al., 1985; Nail, 1986). As Serge Moscovici (1985) observed, the Asch studies are "one of the most dramatic illustrations of conformity, of blindly going along with the group, even when the individual realizes that by doing so he turns his back on reality and truth" (p. 349).

Simulate on **MyPsychLab**
Put yourself in the Asch experiment by trying the MyPsychLab simulation ***Social Influence (1)***.

Research by Gregory Berns and his colleagues has provided biological evidence for just how unpleasant and uncomfortable it is to resist normative social influence (Berns et al., 2005). Berns and his research team used functional magnetic resonance imaging (fMRI) to examine the changes in brain activity of research participants as they either normatively conformed to a group's judgment or maintained their independence and disagreed with the group.

Instead of judgments of line length, the task in this study involved mental rotation. While in the fMRI scanner, participants were shown a three-dimensional figure and then asked if a second figure (rotated in a different direction) was the same as the first figure or different. They indicated their answers by pushing a button. The task was slightly more difficult than Asch's line-judgment task; the baseline error rate, when participants made judgments alone, was 13.8%, compared to Asch's (1951, 1956) baseline error rate of 2%.

Before being placed in the fMRI scanner, participants met and interacted with four other participants who were, as you've probably guessed, actually confederates. These four would be doing the same mental rotation task, but only the participant would have his or her brain activity monitored. During the task, the participant completed one-third of the trials with no knowledge of the answers of the other four people. On the remaining two-thirds of the trials, the participant saw the four group members' answers on a visual display. Half the time the group had all chosen the wrong answer, and the other half of the time they had all chosen the right answer.

Now, what did the participants do, and, most importantly, what areas of their brains were activated when they did it? First, as with the original Asch study, participants conformed to the group's wrong answers some of the time (41% of the trials, to be exact). On the baseline trials, where the participants answered alone, the fMRI results indicated increased activity in the posterior brain areas dedicated to vision and perception. When the participants conformed to the group's wrong

Customs do not concern themselves with right or wrong or reason. But they have to be obeyed; one reasons all around them until [one] is tired, but [one] must not transgress them, it is sternly forbidden.

—Mark Twain

answers, activation occurred in the same areas; however, when participants chose to give the right answer and thus disagree with the group's unanimous wrong answer, the visual/perceptual areas of the brain were not activated. Instead, different areas of the brain became active: the amygdala, an area devoted to negative emotions, and the right caudate nucleus, an area devoted to modulating social behavior (Berns et al., 2005). Thus, this brain-imaging research supports the idea that normative social influence occurs because people feel negative emotions, such as discomfort and tension, when they go against the group (Spitzer et al., 2007).

The Importance of Being Accurate, Revisited

Now, you may be thinking, "OK, so we conform to normative social influence, but hey, only when it's something little. Who cares whether you give the right answer on a line-judgment task? It doesn't matter, nothing is at stake—I'd never conform to the group's wrong answer if something important was involved!" And this would be a very good criticism. Recall our discussion of importance in connection with informational social influence; we found that in ambiguous situations, the more important the decision or choice a person has to make, the more the person conforms for informational reasons. What about in nonambiguous situations? Maybe the more important the decision or choice is, the less the person would conform? When it's important to you to be right, are you strong enough to withstand group pressure and disagree with the group?

Recall the first study of eyewitness identification that we discussed earlier, in which Baron and his colleagues (Baron, Vandello, & Brunsman, 1996) included experimental conditions that triggered social influence. In the study research, participants viewed pairs of slides, one of the perpetrator alone and one of the perpetrator in a lineup. Participants watched the slides in groups with two confederates. When studying informational conformity, the researchers made the task fiendishly difficult and therefore ambiguous—the slides were projected for only half a second. In order to study normative social influence, however, the researchers made the same task ridiculously easy: The participants viewed each slide for a full 5 seconds, and they were shown each pair of slides twice. Now the task becomes analogous to Asch's line-judging task; basically, if you're awake, you'll get the right answer. Baron and colleagues proved that the task was easy, by having individuals in a control group each view the slides alone. The controls answered correctly on 97% of the trials.

Baron and colleagues again manipulated the importance of the participants being accurate, in the same ways we discussed earlier. Half were led to believe that it was very important that they give the right answers, and half were told it really didn't matter how they did. Now how will participants respond when the confederates give the obviously wrong answer? Will they conform to the group on at least some of the trials, as the participants in the Asch study did? Or will the participants who believe accuracy is very important give the correct answers every time, standing up to the group and ignoring the normative pressure to agree with them?

The researchers found that participants in the low-importance condition conformed to the group on 33% of the critical trials—very close to the rate in Asch's line-judgment task. What happened to the participants in the high-importance condition? Instead of standing up to the group across the board, they caved in on at least some trials. They did conform less to the obviously wrong answers of the group; on only 16% of the critical trials did they echo the group's blatantly wrong answer. But they still conformed sometimes! These findings underscore the power of normative social influence: Even when the group is wrong, the right answer is obvious, and there are strong incentives to be accurate, some people still find it difficult to risk social disapproval, even from strangers (Baron et al., 1996; Hornsey et al., 2003). And as the examples of train- and car-surfing demonstrate, this desire to be accepted can have tragic consequences.

Normative social influence most closely reflects the negative stereotype of conformity we referred to earlier: the belief that those who conform are spineless and weak. Ironically, while this type of social pressure can be difficult to resist, people are often quick to deny that they've been influenced by normative considerations. Recall the energy conservation study by Nolan and colleagues (2008) described earlier. In this study, researchers assessed the effectiveness of different arguments for reducing electricity use among Californians. The most persuasive message was telling consumers that their neighbors were conserving energy. But participants *believed* that this message had little effect on them, especially compared to participants who received information regarding protecting the environment or saving money. As Nolan and her coauthors conclude, we often underestimate the power of normative social influence.

But your denial that normative pressures affect you doesn't stop others from trying to exert influence through such processes. How else to explain why some television producers hire professional laughers to sit in the studio audience to make their comedies seem funnier (Warner, 2011)? Or why some sports teams pay abnormally enthusiastic fans to rile up fellow spectators at their home games (Sommers, 2011)? Clearly, the desire to fit in and be accepted is part of human nature, whether or not we're willing to admit it.

The Consequences of Resisting Normative Social Influence

One way to observe the power of normative social pressure is to examine the consequences when people manage to resist it. If a person refuses to do as the group asks and thereby violates its norms, what happens? Think about the norms that operate in your group of friends. Some friends have an egalitarian norm for making group decisions. For example, when choosing a movie, everyone gets to state a preference; the choice is then discussed until agreement is reached. What would happen if, in a group with this kind of norm, you stated at the outset that you only wanted to see *Rebel Without a Cause* and would not agree to watch anything else? Your friends would be surprised by your behavior; they would also be annoyed with you or even angry. If you continued to disregard the friendship norms of the group by failing to conform, two things would most likely happen. First, the group would try to bring you "back into the fold," chiefly through increased communication. Teasing comments and long discussions would ensue as your friends tried to figure out why you were acting so strangely and tried to get you to conform to their expectations (Garfinkle, 1967). If these tactics didn't work, your friends would most likely say negative things to you and about you and start to withdraw from you (Festinger & Thibaut, 1951). Now, in effect, you've been rejected (Abrams et al., 2000; Hornsey et al., 2006; Levine, 1989; Marques et al., 2001; Milgram & Sabini, 1978).

Stanley Schachter (1951) demonstrated how the group responds to an individual who ignores the group's normative influence. He asked groups of college students to read and discuss a case history of "Johnny Rocco," a juvenile delinquent. Most of the students took a middle-of-the-road position about the case, believing that Rocco should receive a judicious mixture of love and discipline. Unbeknownst to the participants, however, Schachter had planted an accomplice in the group who was instructed to disagree with the group's recommendations. The accomplice consistently argued that Rocco should receive the harshest amount of punishment, regardless of what the other group members argued.

Success or failure lies in conformity to the times.
—Niccolò Machiavelli, *The Prince*

How was the deviant treated? He became the target of the most comments and questions from the real participants throughout most of the discussion, and then, near the end, communication with him dropped sharply. The other group members had tried to convince the deviant to agree with them; when it appeared that it wouldn't work, they started to ignore him. In addition, they punished him. After the discussion, they were asked to fill out questionnaires that supposedly pertained to future discussion meetings of their group. The participants were asked to nominate one group member who should be eliminated from further discussions if the group size had to be reduced. They nominated the deviant. They were also asked to assign group members to various tasks in future discussions. They assigned the unimportant or boring jobs, such as taking notes, to the deviant. Social groups are well versed in how to bring a nonconformist into line. No wonder we respond as often as we do to normative pressures! You can find out what it's like to resist normative social influence in the following Try It!

TRY IT! Unveiling Normative Social Influence by Breaking the Rules

Every day, you talk to a lot of people—friends, professors, coworkers, and strangers. When you have a conversation, whether long or short, you follow certain interaction "rules" that operate in American culture. These rules for conversation include nonverbal forms of behavior that Americans consider "normal" as well as "polite." You can find out how powerful these norms are by breaking them and noting how people respond to you; their responses demonstrate the power of normative social influence.

For example, in conversation, we stand a certain distance from each other—not too far and not too close. About 2 to 3 feet is typical in mainstream U.S. culture. In addition, we maintain a good amount of eye contact when we are listening to the other person; in comparison, when we're talking, we look away from the person more often.

What happens if you break these normative rules? Try having a conversation with a friend and stand either too close or too far away (e.g., 1 foot or 7 feet). Have a typical, normal conversation with your friend—only the spacing you use with this person should be different. Note how your friend responds. If you're too close, your friend will probably back away; if you continue to keep the distance small, he or she may act uncomfortable and even end your conversation sooner than usual. If you're too far away, your friend will probably come closer; if you back up, he or she may think you are in a strange mood. In either case, your friend's response will probably include looking at you a lot, having a puzzled look on his or her face, acting uncomfortable or confused, and talking less than normal or ending the conversation.

You have acted in a nonnormative way, and your conversational partner is, first, trying to figure out what is going on and, second, responding in a way to get you to stop acting oddly. From this one brief exercise, you will get the idea of what would happen if you behaved oddly all the time—people would try to get you to change, and then they would probably start avoiding or ignoring you.

When you're finished, "debrief" your friend, explaining the exercise, so that your behavior is understood. The relief you feel upon revealing why you were acting so peculiarly is yet one more demonstration of the strength of normative pressure and the challenge inherent to resisting it.

Normative Social Influence in Everyday Life

Normative social influence operates on many levels in our daily lives. For example, although few of us are slaves to fashion, we tend to wear what is considered appropriate and stylish at a given time. Men's wide neckties, popular in the 1970s, gave way to narrow ties in the 1980s before widening again in the 1990s and seeing a resurgence of skinny ties today; women's hemlines dropped from mini to maxi and then rose again. Normative social influence is at work whenever you notice a particular look shared by people in a certain group, and, no matter what it is, it will look outdated just a few years later until the fashion industry revives it in a new trend.

By 2007, the Crocs fad was in full force as kids (and parents) everywhere could be found out and about in these plastic clogs with Swiss-cheese holes. Five years later, reviews are decidedly more mixed: an anti-Croc page on Facebook currently has more than 1.6 million fans.

Fads are another fairly frivolous example of normative social influence. Certain activities or objects can suddenly become popular and sweep the country. For example, in the late 1950s, every child had to have a Hula Hoop or risk social ostracism, in the 1970s people actually paid for the right to own a Pet Rock, and in the 1990s Beanie Baby mania swept up children and adults alike. College students swallowed live goldfish in the 1930s, crammed as many people as possible into telephone booths in the 1950s, and "streaked" (ran naked) at official gatherings in the 1970s. These fads seem silly now, but ask yourself, could there be "fads" that you are following now?

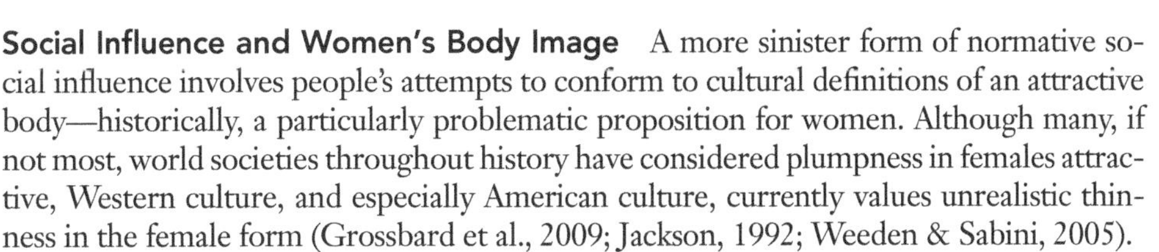

Social Influence and Women's Body Image A more sinister form of normative social influence involves people's attempts to conform to cultural definitions of an attractive body—historically, a particularly problematic proposition for women. Although many, if not most, world societies throughout history have considered plumpness in females attractive, Western culture, and especially American culture, currently values unrealistic thinness in the female form (Grossbard et al., 2009; Jackson, 1992; Weeden & Sabini, 2005).

FIGURE 8.4

What Is the "Ideal" Female Body Across Cultures?

Researchers divided 54 cultures into groups, depending on the reliability of their food supply. They then determined what was considered the "ideal" female body in each culture. Heavy female bodies were considered the most beautiful in cultures with unreliable food supplies. As the reliability of the food supply increased, the preference for a moderate-to-heavy body type decreased. Only in cultures where food was very readily available was the slender body valued more.

(Adapted from Anderson, Crawford, Nadeau, & Lindberg, 1992)

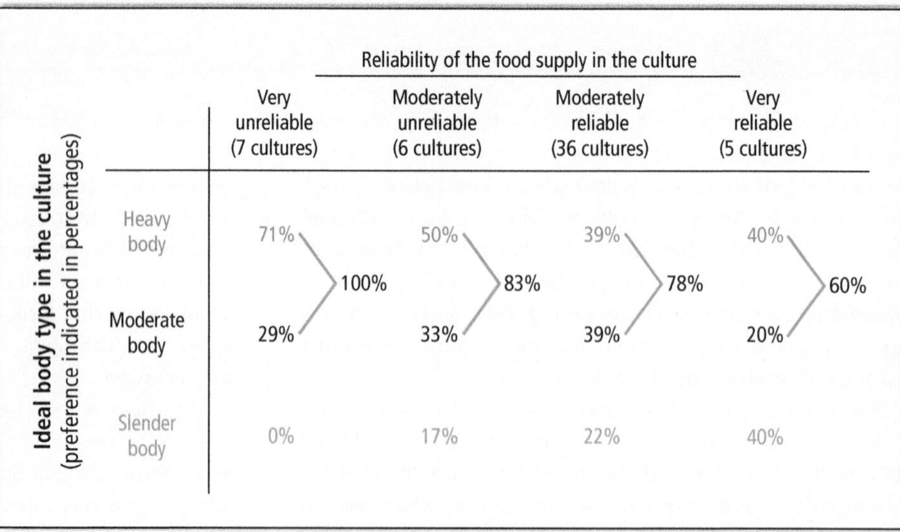

Reliability of the food supply in the culture
Very unreliable (7 cultures)
Moderately unreliable (6 cultures)
Moderately reliable (36 cultures)
Very reliable (5 cultures)
Ideal body type in the culture (preference indicated in percentages)
Heavy body
71%
50%
39%
40%
100%
83%
78%
60%
Moderate body
29%
33%
39%
20%
Slender body
0%
17%
22%
40%

Why should preference for female body type vary by culture? To explore this question, Judith Anderson and her colleagues (Anderson et al., 1992) analyzed what people in 54 cultures considered the ideal female body: a heavy body, a body of moderate weight, or a slender body. The researchers also analyzed how reliable the food supply was in each culture. They hypothesized that in societies where food was frequently scarce, a heavy body would be considered the most beautiful. These would be women who had enough to eat and therefore were healthy and fertile. As you can see in Figure 8.4, their hypothesis was supported. Heavy body types in women were preferred over slender or moderate ones in cultures with unreliable food supplies. As the reliability of the food supply increases, the preference for heavy-to-moderate bodies decreases. Most dramatic is the increase in preference for the slender body across cultures. Only in cultures with very reliable food supplies (such as the United States) was the slender body type highly valued.

No woman can be too slim or too rich.
—Wallis Simpson, Duchess of Windsor

What is the American standard for the female body? Has it changed over time? In the 1980s, Brett Silverstein and her colleagues (Silverstein et al., 1986) analyzed photographs of women appearing in *Ladies' Home Journal* and *Vogue* magazines from 1901 to 1981. The researchers measured the women's busts and waists, creating a bust-to-waist ratio. A high score indicates a heavier, more voluptuous body, while a lower score indicates a thinner, lean body type. Their results show a startling series of changes in the cultural definition of female bodily attractiveness over the course of 80 years (see Figure 8.5).

At the turn of the twentieth century, an attractive woman was voluptuous and heavy; by the "flapper" period of the 1920s, the desired look for women was rail-thin and flat-chested. The normative body changed again in the 1940s, when World War II "pinup girls" such as Betty Grable exemplified a heavier standard. The curvaceous female body remained popular during the 1950s; witness, for example, Marilyn Monroe. However, the "swinging 1960s" fashion look, exemplified by the reed-thin British model Twiggy, introduced once again a very thin silhouette. The average bust-to-waist ratio has been low since 1963, marking the longest period of time in recent history that American women have been exposed to an extremely thin standard of physical attractiveness (Barber, 1998; Wiseman et al., 1992). In fact, a recent meta-analysis of research studies indicates that Americans have adopted the "thin is beautiful" standard for women even more strongly in the 2000s than in the 1990s (Grabe et al., 2008). Though, interestingly, this pattern seems to hold more so for whites; recent analysis of beauty ideals for African American women reveals greater acceptance of larger, more curvaceous body types (Dawson-Andoh et al., 2010).

Interestingly, the standards for physical attractiveness for women in other cultures have also undergone changes in recent decades. Since World War II, the preferred look in Japan has taken on a "Westernized" element—long-legged, thin bodies, or what is

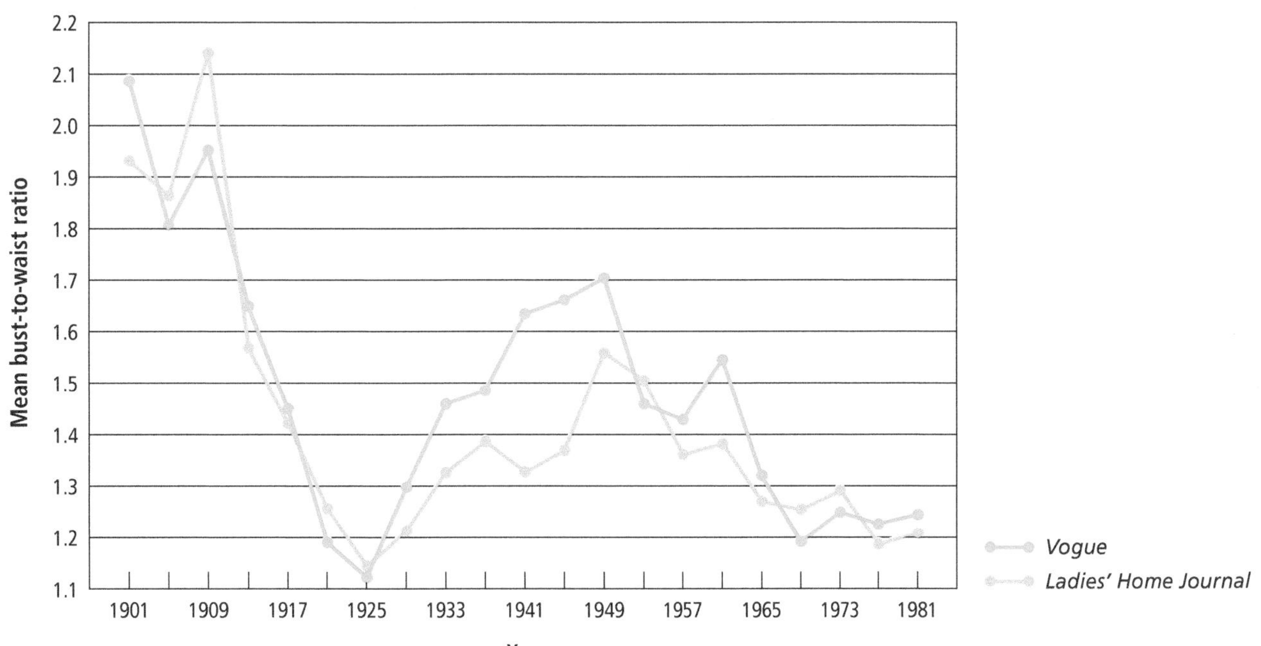

FIGURE 8.5

The Mean Bust-to-Waist Ratios of Models in *Vogue* and *Ladies' Home Journal*, 1901–1981

What is considered an attractive female body changed dramatically during the twentieth century, from heavy women at the beginning of the 1900s, to rail-thin women during the 1920s, to somewhat heavier and more-curvaceous women during the 1940s and 1950s, to a return to very thin women in the 1960s and thereafter.

(Adapted from Silverstein, Perdue, Peterson, & Kelly, 1986)

called the "*hattou shin* beauty" (Mukai, Kambara, & Sasaki, 1998). And this cultural shift has had an effect—Japanese women experience strong normative pressures to be thin (Mukai, 1996). Indeed, researchers have found that Japanese women are even more likely than American women to perceive themselves as being overweight. They also report greater dissatisfaction with their bodies than do American women. All this occurs despite the fact that the Japanese women in the sample were significantly thinner than the American women. In addition, these researchers found that participants' "need for social approval," as measured on a questionnaire, was a significant predictor of eating disorders for the Japanese women but not for the American women. Japanese culture places a greater emphasis on conformity than American culture does, and hence the normative pressure to be thin operates with even more serious consequences for Japanese women (Mukai et al., 1998).

Cultural standards for women's bodies are changeable. Whereas today's female models and movie stars tend to be lean and muscle-toned, the female icons of the 1940s and 1950s, such as Marilyn Monroe, were curvaceous, heavier, and less muscular.

How do women learn what kind of body is considered attractive at a given time in their culture (and how they compare to these standards)? From family and friends and the media. Various contemporary media, from magazine ads to TV sitcoms, have been implicated in sending a message that the ideal female body is thin (Barriga, Shapiro, & Jhaveri, 2009; Cusumano & Thompson, 1997; Fouts & Burggraf, 2000). Women tend to perceive themselves as overweight and as heavier than they actually are (Cohn & Adler, 1992), and this effect is heightened if they've just been exposed to media portrayals of thin women (Bessenoff, 2006; Diedrichs & Lee, 2011; Fredrickson et al., 1998; Grube, Ward, & Hyde, 2008; Strahan et al., 2008). Given that the average U.S. woman is 5'4" and 140 pounds, and the average advertising model in the United States is 5'11" and 117 pounds, this result is not surprising (Locken & Peck, 2005).

The sociocultural pressure for thinness that is currently operating on women has potentially serious consequences. It can even be fatal, as it leads some women to attempt

Has the American cultural ideal of the male body changed over time? Harrison Pope and his colleagues (1999) measured the waist, chest, and biceps of the most popular action-figure toys of the last three decades. The researchers found that the toy figures had grown much more muscular over time, far exceeding the muscularity of even the largest human bodybuilders. The researchers suggest that such unrealistic images of the male body may contribute to body-image disorders in boys.

to attain unrealistic body ideals through unhealthy diet and exercise habits (Bearman, Stice, & Chase, 2003; Crandall, 1988; Stice & Shaw, 2002). The last time that a very thin standard of bodily attractiveness for women existed, in the mid-1920s, an epidemic of eating disorders appeared (Killen et al., 1994; Silverstein, Peterson, & Perdue, 1986). And it is happening again, but with even younger girls: In 2000, the American Anorexia Bulimia Association released statistics indicating that one-third of 12- to 13-year-old girls were actively trying to lose weight by dieting, vomiting, using laxatives, or taking diet pills (Ellin, 2000). Similarly, recent research has indicated that American girls as young as 7 years old are reporting that they are dissatisfied with their bodies (Dohnt & Tiggeman, 2006; Grabe & Hyde, 2006).

Social Influence and Men's Body Image What about cultural definitions of an attractive *male* body? Have these changed over time as well? Do men engage in similar processes of conformity, trying to achieve the perfect-looking body? Until recently, there was very little research on these questions, but studies conducted in the past decade suggest that, yes, cultural norms have changed in that men are beginning to come under the same pressure to achieve an ideal body that women have experienced for decades (Cafri et al., 2005; Cafri & Thompson, 2004; Grossbard et al., 2009; Morry & Staska, 2001; Olivardia et al., 2004; Wojtowicz & von Ranson, 2006; Wiseman & Moradi, 2010).

Specifically, evidence suggests that sociocultural expectations of attractiveness for males have changed over recent decades and that the ideal male body is now much more muscular. For example, Harrison Pope and his colleagues (Pope, Olivardia, Gruber, & Borowiecki, 1999) analyzed boys' toys such as G.I. Joe dolls by measuring their waists, chests, and biceps. The changes in G.I. Joe from 1964 to 1998 are startling, as you can see in the photographs from their research.

They also coded advertisements since 1950 in two women's magazines, *Glamour* and *Cosmopolitan*, for how often male and female models were pictured in a state of undress. For women, the percentage remained at about 20% over the decades, but for men a change was clear. In 1950, fewer than 5% of ads showed men in some state of undress; by 1995, that figure had risen to as much as 35% (Pope, Phillips, & Olivardia, 2000).

Do these presentations of (nearly) naked—and perfect—male bodies affect men's perceptions of themselves? Ida Jodette Hatoum and Deborah Belle (2004) investigated this question by focusing on the relationship between media consumption and bodily concerns in a sample of college men. They found that reading male-oriented magazines such as *Maxim*, *Details*, *Esquire*, *Men's Fitness*, and *Men's Health*—all of which present the "hypermuscular" male body—was significantly correlated with negative feelings about one's own body. In addition, these researchers found that the more men were exposed to these male-directed magazines (as well as to movies), the more they valued thinness in women.

Pope and colleagues (Pope, Gruber et al., 2000) asked men in the United States, France, and Austria to alter a computer image of a male body in terms of fat and muscle until it reflected, first, their own bodies; second, the body they'd like to have; and, finally, the body they thought women would find most attractive. The men were quite accurate in their depiction of their own bodies; however, men in all three countries chose an ideal body that had on average 28 more pounds of muscle than their own. This muscular ideal was also the body they chose for what they thought women would find attractive. (However, when women completed the task, they chose a very normal, average-looking male body as their ideal.)

Researchers have also found that adolescent and young men report feeling pressure from parents, peers, and the media to be more muscular; they respond to this pressure by developing strategies to achieve the ideal, "six-pack" body (Bergstrom & Neighbors, 2006; McCabe & Ricciardelli, 2003a, 2003b; Ricciardelli & McCabe, 2003). For example, results from a number of studies indicate that 21% to 42% of young men have altered their eating habits in order to gain muscle mass and/or weight, while 12% to 26% have dieted in order to reduce body fat/weight. An increasing number are also using risky substances such as steroids or ephedrine to achieve a more muscular physique (Cafri et al., 2005). All these data suggest that informational and normative social influence is now operating on men as well as women, affecting their perceptions of their own bodies' attractiveness.

When Will People Conform to Normative Social Influence?

Social Impact Theory
The idea that conforming to social influence depends on the group's importance, its immediacy, and the number of people in the group

Although conformity is commonplace, people don't always cave in to peer pressure. We certainly do not all agree on many major issues, such as abortion, affirmative action, or same-sex marriage. Exactly when are people most likely to conform to normative pressures? Some answers to this question are provided by Bibb Latané's (1981) **social impact theory**. According to this theory, the likelihood that you will respond to social influence depends on three variables regarding the group in question:

1. *Strength:* How important to you is the group?
2. *Immediacy:* How close is the group to you in space and time during the attempt to influence you?
3. *Number:* How many people are in the group?

Social impact theory predicts that conformity will increase as strength and immediacy increase. Clearly, the more important a group is to us and the closer group members are to us physically, the more likely we will be to conform to its normative pressures.

Social influence operates differently when it comes to group size. As the size of the group increases, each additional person has less of an influencing effect—going from three people to four makes more of a difference than going from 53 people to 54. If we feel pressure from a group to conform, adding another person to the majority makes much more of a difference if the group is small rather than large. Latané constructed a mathematical model that captures these hypothesized effects of strength, immediacy, and number and has applied this formula to the results of many conformity studies (Bourgeois & Bowen, 2001; Latané, 1981; Latané & Bourgeois, 2001; Latané & L'Herrou, 1996).

For example, gay men who lived in communities that were highly involved in AIDS awareness activities (where strength, immediacy, and number would all be high) reported feeling more social pressure to avoid risky sexual behavior and stronger intentions to do so than gay men who lived in less-involved communities (Fishbein et al., 1993). Similarly, a recent study of heterosexual dating couples (a relationship typically high in strength and immediacy) reveals that an individual's own tendency to engage in heavy drinking is significantly predicted by the norm set by his or her partner's drinking tendencies (Mushquash et al., 2011).

Watch on MyPsychLab
To learn more, watch the MyPsychLab video ***Conformity and Influence in Groups***.

Let's see in more detail what social impact theory says about the conditions under which people will conform to normative social pressures.

When the Group Grows Larger At what point does group size stop influencing conformity? Asch (1955) and later researchers found that conformity increased as the number of people in the group increased, but once the group reached four or five other people, conformity does not increase much (Bond, 2005; Campbell & Fairey, 1989; Gerard, Wilhelmy, & Conolley, 1968)—just as social impact theory suggests (see Figure 8.6). In short, it does not take an extremely large group to create normative social influence, but the larger the group, the stronger the social pressure.

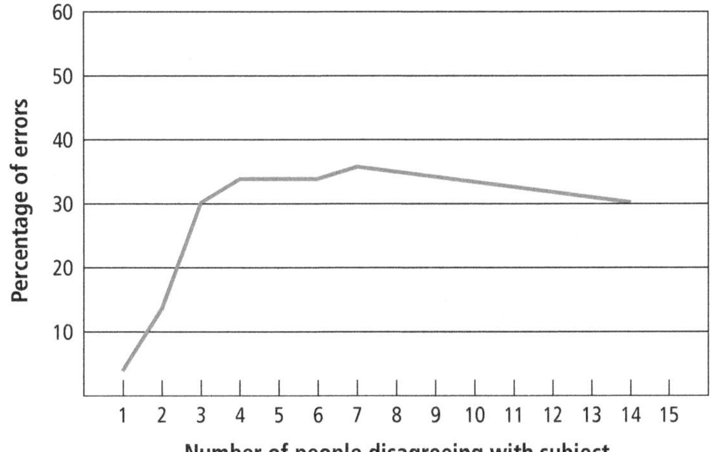

FIGURE 8.6
Effects of Group Size on Conformity
Asch varied the size of the unanimous majority in his study and found that once the majority numbered four, adding more people had little influence on conformity.
(Adapted from Asch, 1955)

When the Group is Important Another tenet of social impact theory is that the strength of the group—defined as how important the group is to us—makes a difference. Normative pressures are much stronger when they come from people whose friendship, love, and respect we cherish, because there is a large cost to losing this love and respect (Abrams et al., 1990; Guimond, 1999; Hogg, 1992; Nowak, Szamrej, & Latané, 1990; Wolf, 1985). One consequence of this conclusion is that it can be dangerous to have policy decisions made by highly cohesive groups, because they care more about pleasing each other and avoiding conflict than arriving at the best, most logical decision. We will see several examples of this phenomenon in Chapter 9.

We should note, however, that the very act of conforming normatively to important groups *most* of the time can earn you the right to deviate occasionally without serious consequences. This interesting observation was made by Edwin Hollander (1960, 1985), who stated that conforming to a group over time earns you **idiosyncrasy credits**, much like putting money in the bank to save for future use. It's as if your past conformity allows you, at some point in the future, to deviate from the group (to "make withdrawals") without getting into too much trouble. Let's say, for example, that your friends are all in agreement that they want to go out for Chinese food. You, however, feel like Mexican food tonight, and rather than simply going along with group consensus, you decide to stick to your guns and lobby for burritos. If you have typically followed their friendship norms in other areas in the past, your friends will be less likely to become upset with you for your current nonconformity, for you've earned the right to deviate from their normative rules in this area on this occasion.

When one has no Allies in the Group Normative social influence is most powerfully felt when everyone in the group says or believes the same thing—for example, when your group of friends all believe that *The Lord of the Rings* was the greatest movie trilogy ever made. Resisting such unanimous social influence is difficult or even impossible, unless you have an ally. If another person disagrees with the group—say, by nominating the original *Star Wars* movies as the best trilogy ever—this behavior will help you buck the tide as well.

To test the importance of having an ally, Asch (1955) conducted another version of his conformity experiment. He had six of the seven confederates give the wrong answer, while one confederate gave the right answer on every trial. Now the subject was not alone. Though still disagreeing with the majority of the group, having one ally helped the subject resist normative pressures. People conformed on an average of only 6% of the trials in this study, compared to 32% when all of the confederates gave the wrong answer. Several other studies have found that observing another person resist normative social influence emboldens the individual to do the same (Allen & Levine, 1969; Morris & Miller, 1975; Nemeth & Chiles, 1988).

The difficulty of being the lone dissenter is apparent even in the U.S. Supreme Court. After hearing a case, the nine justices first determine, informally, whether they are unanimous or split in their decision. Some justices then write drafts and others decide which draft they will sign. There are informal attempts at influence, and eventually all make a decision. A content analysis of all the Supreme Court decisions from 1953 to 2001 (4,178 decisions, involving 29 different justices) indicated that the most common decision was the 9–0, unanimous one (35% of all decisions). And the least common decision? The one that required one justice to disagree with all of his or her colleagues, the 8–1 split, which accounted for only 10% of decisions over 48 years (Granberg & Bartels, 2005).

When the Group's Culture is Collectivistic "In America, the squeaky wheel gets the grease. In Japan, the nail that stands out gets pounded down" (Markus & Kitayama, 1991, p. 224). Is it true that the society in which one is raised affects the frequency of normative social influence? Perhaps not surprisingly, the answer is yes. Stanley Milgram (1961, 1977) replicated the Asch studies in Norway and France and found that the Norwegian participants conformed to a greater degree than the French participants did. Milgram (1961, p. 51) describes Norwegian society as "highly cohesive," with "a deep feeling of group identification," while French society, in comparison, shows "far

Idiosyncrasy Credits

The tolerance a person earns, over time, by conforming to group norms; if enough idiosyncrasy credits are earned, the person can, on occasion, behave deviantly without retribution from the group

TRY IT! Fashion: Normative Social Influence in Action

You can observe social impact theory in action by focusing on fashion—specifically, the clothes and accessories that you and your group of friends wear, as well as the look of other groups on campus. You can also observe what happens when you break those normative rules for fashion.

When you are with a group of friends and acquaintances, note carefully how everyone is dressed. Pretend that you are from another culture and not acquainted with the norms of this group; this will help you notice details that you might otherwise overlook. For example, what kinds of pants, shoes, shirts, jewelry, and other items are worn by this group? Are there similarities in their haircuts? Can you discover their fashion "rules"?

Next, spend some time on campus "people-watching," specifically observing what other groups of people are wearing. Can you discern different subgroups on your campus, defined by their style of dress? If so, there are different types of normative conformity operating on your campus; groups of friends are dressing according to the rules of their subgroup and not according to the rules of the campus as a whole.

Finally, if you are brave enough, break some normative fashion rules and see what happens. You can do this subtly or you can be very obvious. (But do be sensible; don't get yourself arrested!) For example, try wearing a suit and tie or a formal dress to the dining hall one day. Wear pajamas to class or to your professor's office hours. Wear a garbage bag (with holes cut out for your head and arms) over regular clothing. In any of these cases, just walk around as usual, seeming unaware that you are doing or wearing anything strange at all. How do people react to you? What will your friends say? Strangers will stare at you, but will they also avoid you?

Your group of friends (as well as the students at your school in general) may well have the qualities that social impact theory discusses: The group is important to you, the group is large, and the group is unanimous (which would be the case if your group of friends or your college student body has definite fashion norms). If you stop conforming to this normative social influence, the other group members will likely feel uncomfortable and exert some kind of pressure on you, trying to get you to return to a state of conformity.

less consensus in both social and political life." In another cross-cultural study of normative social influence, people in Lebanon, Hong Kong, and Brazil conformed to a similar extent (both to each other and to the American sample), whereas participants from the Bantu tribe of Zimbabwe conformed to a much greater degree (Whittaker & Meade, 1967). As the researchers point out, conformity has a very high social value in Bantu culture.

The extent to which conformity is valued varies across cultures. In the Opening Ceremony of the 2008 Beijing Olympics, a worldwide television audience was mesmerized by the sight of 2,008 drummers performing in perfect synchronization.

Although Japanese culture is more highly conforming than our own in many areas, two Asch-type studies found that when the group unanimously gave the incorrect answer, Japanese students were less conformist in general than North Americans (Frager, 1970; Williams & Sogon, 1984). In Japan, cooperation and loyalty are directed to the groups to which one belongs and with which one identifies; there is little expectation that one should conform to the behavior of strangers, especially in such an artificial setting as a psychology experiment. Similarly, conformity was much higher in a British sample when the participants thought the other group members were psychology majors like themselves rather than art history majors (Abrams et al., 1990). Similarly, German research participants have shown less conformity in the Asch experiment than North Americans (Timaeus, 1968); in Germany, conformity to strangers is less valued than conformity to a few well-defined groups (Moghaddam, Taylor, & Wright, 1993).

A more systematic review of the role of culture in conformity is provided by a meta-analysis of 133 Asch line-judgment studies conducted in 17 countries: United States, Canada, Britain, France, the Netherlands, Belgium, Germany, Portugal, Japan, Hong Kong, Fiji, Zimbabwe, Congo, Ghana, Brazil, Kuwait, and Lebanon (Bond & Smith, 1996). Participants from collectivistic cultures showed higher rates of conformity on the line task than participants from individualistic cultures. In collectivistic cultures, conformity is seen as a valued trait, not as a somewhat negative one, as in the United States. Agreeing with others is not viewed as an act of submission or cowardice in collectivist cultures, but an act of tact and sensitivity (Hodges & Geyer, 2006; Smith & Bond, 1999). Because the emphasis is on the group and not the individual, people in collectivistic cultures value normative social influence because it promotes harmony and supportive relationships in the group (Guisinger & Blatt, 1994; Kim et al., 1994; Markus et al., 1996; Zhang et al., 2007).

J. W. Berry (1967; Kim & Berry, 1993) explored the issue of conformity as a cultural value by comparing two cultures that had very different strategies for accumulating food. He hypothesized that societies that relied on hunting or fishing would value independence, assertiveness, and adventurousness—traits that were needed to find and bring home food. He also postulated that societies that were primarily agricultural would value cooperativeness, conformity, and acquiescence—traits that made close living and interdependent farming more successful. Berry used an Asch-type conformity task to compare the Inuit people of Baffin Island in Canada, a hunting and fishing society, to the Temne of Sierra Leone in Africa, a farming society. Consistent with Berry's hypothesis, the Temne showed a significant tendency to accept the suggestions of fellow group members in the study, while the Inuit almost completely disregarded them. As one Temne put it, "When the Temne people choose a thing, we must all agree with the decision—this is what we call cooperation"; in contrast, the few times the Inuit did conform to the group's wrong answer, they did so with "a quiet, knowing smile" (Berry, 1967, p. 417).

Minority Influence: When the Few Influence the Many

We shouldn't leave our discussion of normative social influence with the impression that groups affect individuals but the individual never has an effect on the group. As Serge Moscovici (1985, 1994; Moscovici, Mucchi-Faina, & Maass, 1994) says, if groups always succeeded in silencing nonconformists, rejecting deviants, and persuading everyone to go along with the majority point of view, how could change ever be introduced into the system? We would all be like little robots, marching along with everyone else in monotonous synchrony, never able to adapt to changing reality. Clearly, this is not the case (Imhoff & Erb, 2009).

People create social conditions, and people can change them.

—Tess Onwueme

Instead, the individual, or the minority of group members, can influence the behavior or beliefs of the majority (Moscovici, 1985, 1994; Mucchi-Faina & Pagliaro, 2008; Sinaceur et al., 2010). This is called **minority influence**. The key is consistency: People with minority views must express the same view over time, and different members of the minority must agree with one another. If a person in the minority wavers

Minority Influence

The case where a minority of group members influences the behavior or beliefs of the majority between two different viewpoints or if two individuals express different minority views, the majority will dismiss them as people who have peculiar and groundless opinions. If, however, the minority expresses a consistent, unwavering view, the majority is more likely to take notice and even adopt the minority view (Moscovici & Nemeth, 1974). For example, in the 1970s, a minority of scientists began to call attention to evidence of human-caused climate change. Today, the majority is paying attention, and political leaders from the industrialized nations have met to discuss possible worldwide solutions. As another example, in the 1960s, a minority of feminists began to address women as Ms. instead of Miss or Mrs. Today, Ms. is the standard form of address in the workplace and many other contexts (Zimmer, 2009).

In a meta-analysis of nearly 1 hundred studies, Wendy Wood and her colleagues describe how minority influence operates (Wood et al., 1994). People in the majority can cause other group members to conform through normative influence. As in the Asch experiments, the conformity that occurs may be a case of public compliance without private acceptance. People in the minority can rarely influence others through normative means. In fact, majority group members may be hesitant to agree publicly with the minority; they don't want anyone to think that they side with those unusual, strange views. Minorities therefore exert their influence on the group via the other principal method: informational social influence. The minority can introduce new and unexpected information to the group and cause the group to examine the issues more carefully. Such careful examination may cause the majority to realize that the minority view has merit, leading the group to adopt all or part of the minority's view. In short, majorities often obtain public compliance because of normative social influence, whereas minorities are more likely to achieve private acceptance because of informational social influence (De Dreu & De Vries, 2001; Levine, Moreland, & Choi, 2001; Wood et al., 1996.)

Never let anyone keep you contained, and never let anyone keep your voice silent.

—Adam Clayton Powell

CONNECTIONS

The Power of Propaganda

One extraordinary example of social influence is propaganda, especially as perfected by the Nazi regime in the 1930s. Propaganda is defined as "the deliberate, systematic attempt to shape perceptions, manipulate cognitions, and direct behavior to achieve a response that furthers the desired intent of the propagandist" (Jowett & O'Donnell, 1999, p. 6).

Adolf Hitler was well aware of the power of propaganda as a tool of the state. In *Mein Kampf* (1925), written before he came to power, Hitler stated, "Its task is not to make an objective study of the truth . . . and then set it out before the masses with academic fairness; its task is to serve our right, always and unflinchingly" (pp. 182–183). In 1933, Hitler appointed Joseph Goebbels as head of the newly created Nazi Ministry of Popular Enlightenment and Propaganda. It was a highly efficient agency that permeated every aspect of Germans' lives. Nazis controlled all forms of the media, including newspapers, films, and radio. They also disseminated Nazi ideology through the extensive use of posters and "spectacles"—lavish public rallies that aroused powerful emotions of loyalty and patriotism among massive crowds (Jowett & O'Donnell, 1999; Zeman, 1995). Nazi propaganda was taught in schools and further promoted in Hitler Youth groups. The propaganda always presented a consistent, dogmatic message: The German people must take action to protect their racial purity and to increase their *Lebensraum* (living space) through conquest (Staub, 1989).

The concerns with *Lebensraum* led to World War II; the concerns with racial purity led to the Holocaust. How could the German people have acquiesced to the destruction of European Jewry? A major factor was prejudice (which we will discuss further in Chapter 13). Anti-Semitism was not a new or a Nazi idea. It had existed in Germany and in many other parts of Europe for hundreds of years. Propaganda is most successful when it taps into an audience's

Nazi propaganda permeated all facets of German life in the 1930s and 1940s. Here, huge crowds attend the 1934 Nuremberg rally. Such large public gatherings were a technique frequently used by Goebbels and Hitler to promote loyalty and conformity to the Nazi party.

preexisting beliefs. Thus, the German people's anti-Semitism could be quite easily strengthened and expanded by Goebbels's ministry. Jews were described in the Nazi propaganda as destroyers of Aryan racial purity and thus a threat to German survival. They were "pests, parasites, bloodsuckers" (Staub, 1989, p. 103) and were compared to "a plague of rats that needed to be exterminated" (Jowett & O'Donnell, 1999, p. 242); however, anti-Semitism is not a sufficient cause in and of itself for the extermination of Jews. Germany was initially no more prejudiced against Jews than its neighboring countries (or even the United States) in the 1930s, but none of these other countries came up with the concept of a "final solution" as Germany did (Tindale et al., 2002).

Although prejudice was an important precursor, more is needed to explain the Holocaust. Clearly, the propaganda operated as persuasive messages leading to attitude change, as we discussed in Chapter 7. But the propaganda also initiated social influence processes. In a totalitarian, fascist regime, the state is the "expert"—always present, always right, and always to be obeyed. Propaganda would persuade many Germans through informational conformity. They learned new "facts" (which were really lies) about the Jews and learned new solutions to what the Nazis had defined as the "Jewish question." The propaganda did an excellent job of convincing Germans that the Jews were a threat. As we saw earlier, people experiencing a crisis—in this case, runaway inflation and economic collapse in Germany—are more likely to conform to information delivered by an expert.

But surely, you are thinking, there must have been Germans who did not agree with the Nazi propaganda. Yes, there were, but it certainly wasn't easy. Just think about the position they were in. The Nazi ideology so permeated daily life that children and teenagers in Hitler Youth groups were encouraged to spy on their own parents and report them to the Gestapo if they were not "good" Nazis (Staub, 1989). Neighbors, coworkers, salespeople in shops, or passersby on the street—they could all turn you in if you said or did something that indicated you were disloyal. This situation is ripe for normative conformity, where public compliance occurs without, necessarily, private acceptance. Rejection, ostracism, even torture or death were strong motivators for normative conformity, and many ordinary Germans conformed to Nazi propaganda. Whether they did so for informational or normative reasons, their conformity permitted the Holocaust to occur. In the early years of the Third Reich, Hitler was very concerned about public resistance to his ideas (Staub, 1989). Unfortunately, because of social influence processes, prejudice, and the totalitarian system, public resistance never arose with sufficient strength to challenge Hitler's regime.

> *To swallow and follow, whether old doctrine or new propaganda, is a weakness still dominating the human mind.*
>
> —Charlotte Perkins Gilman

Using Social Influence to Promote Beneficial Behavior

We have seen how informational and normative conformity occurs. Even in a highly individualistic culture such as the United States, conformity of both types is common. Is there a way that we can use this tendency to conform to change people's behavior for the common good? Robert Cialdini, Raymond Reno, and Carl Kallgren have developed a model of normative conduct in which social norms (the rules that a society has for acceptable behaviors, values, and beliefs) can be used to subtly induce people to conform to correct, socially approved behavior (Cialdini, Kallgren, & Reno, 1991; Jacobson, Mortensen, & Cialdini, 2011; Kallgren, Reno, & Cialdini, 2000; Schultz et al., 2007).

For example, we all know that littering is wrong. But when we've finished enjoying a snack at the beach or in a park, what determines whether we toss the wrapper on the ground or carry it with us until we come to a trash can? Let's say we wanted to decrease littering or increase voter participation or encourage people to donate blood. How would we go about doing it?

Cialdini and his colleagues (1991) suggest that first we need to focus on what kind of norm is operating in the situation. Only then can we invoke a form of social influence that will encourage people to conform in socially beneficial ways. A culture's social norms are of two types. **Injunctive norms** have to do with what we think other people approve or disapprove of. Injunctive norms motivate behavior by promising rewards (or punishments) for normative (or nonnormative) behavior. For example, an injunctive norm in our culture is that littering is wrong and that donating blood is a good thing to do. **Descriptive norms** concern our perceptions of the way people actually behave in a given situation, regardless of whether the behavior is approved or disapproved of by others. Descriptive norms motivate behavior by informing people about what is effective or adaptive behavior. For example, while we all know that littering is wrong (an injunctive norm), we also all know that there are times and situations when people are likely to do it (a descriptive norm)—for example, dropping peanut shells on the ground at a baseball game or leaving your trash behind at your seat in a movie theater. Descriptive norms also tell us that relatively few people donate blood and that only a small percentage of registered voters actually vote. In sum, an injunctive norm relates to what most people in a culture approve or disapprove of; a descriptive norm relates to what people actually do (Kallgren et al., 2000; White et al., 2009).

Injunctive Norms
People's perceptions of what behaviors are approved or disapproved of by others

Descriptive Norms
People's perceptions of how people actually behave in given situations, regardless of whether the behavior is approved or disapproved of by others

The Role of Injunctive and Descriptive Norms

In a series of studies, Cialdini and colleagues have explored how injunctive and descriptive norms affect people's likelihood to litter. For example, in one field experiment, patrons of a city library were returning to their cars in the parking lot when a confederate approached them (Reno, Cialdini, & Kallgren, 1993). In the control group, the confederate just walked by. In the *descriptive norm condition*, the confederate was carrying an empty bag from a fast-food restaurant and dropped the bag on the ground before passing the participant. By littering, the confederate was subtly communicating, "this is what people do in this situation." In the *injunctive norm condition*, the confederate was not carrying anything but instead picked up a littered fast-food bag from the ground before passing the participant. By picking up someone else's litter, the confederate was subtly communicating that "littering is wrong." These three conditions occurred in one of two environments: Either the parking lot was heavily littered (by the experimenters, using paper cups, candy wrappers, and so on), or the area was clean and unlittered (cleaned up by the experimenters).

At this point, research participants have been exposed to one of two types of norms about littering or to no norm at all (the control group). And all this has happened in a littered or a clean environment. How were participants' own littering tendencies affected in these environments? When they got back to their cars, they found a large handbill slipped under the driver's side of the windshield. The handbill appeared on all the other cars too (not surprising, since the experimenters put them there). The participant had two choices at this point: throw the handbill on the ground, littering, or bring the handbill inside their car to dispose of it later. What did they do? Who refrained from littering?

Invoking conformity to social norms can be used in the effort to address societal problems such as littering.

The control group tells us the baseline of what percentage of people typically litter in this situation. As you can see in Figure 8.7, the researchers found that slightly more than one-third of people threw the handbill on the ground; it didn't matter if the area was already littered or if it was clean. In the descriptive norm condition, the confederate's littering communicated two different messages, depending on the condition of the parking lot. In the littered parking lot, the confederate's behavior reminded participants that people often litter here—the confederate served as just one salient example of the type of behavior that had led to such a messy parking lot in the first place. In the clean parking lot, however, the confederate's behavior communicated a different message. Now, the behavior stood out as unusual—it reminded participants that most people don't litter in this area, which is why it looked so clean otherwise. Hence, we would expect the confederate's littering behavior to remind participants of a descriptive norm against littering more in the clean environment than in the littered one, and this is what the researchers found (see Figure 8.7). Finally, what about the injunctive norm condition? This kind of norm was less context-dependent: Seeing the confederate picking up someone else's litter invokes the injunctive norm that littering is wrong in both the clean and the littered environments, thereby leading to the lowest amount of littering in the study (see Figure 8.7; Reno et al., 1993).

In light of studies such as this one, researchers have concluded that injunctive norms are more powerful than descriptive norms in producing desirable behavior (Cialdini, 2003; Kallgren et al., 2000). This should not surprise you, because injunctive norms tap into normative conformity—we conform (for example, refraining from littering) because someone's behavior reminds us that our society disapproves of littering. We will look like selfish slobs if we litter, and we will feel embarrassed if other people see us litter. While norms are always present to some extent—we *know* that littering is bad—they are not always *salient* to us (Jonas et al., 2008; Kallgren et al., 2000). To promote socially beneficial behavior, something in the situation needs to draw our attention to the relevant norm. Thus, anything that highlights *injunctive norms*—what society approves and disapproves of—can be used to create positive behavioral change.

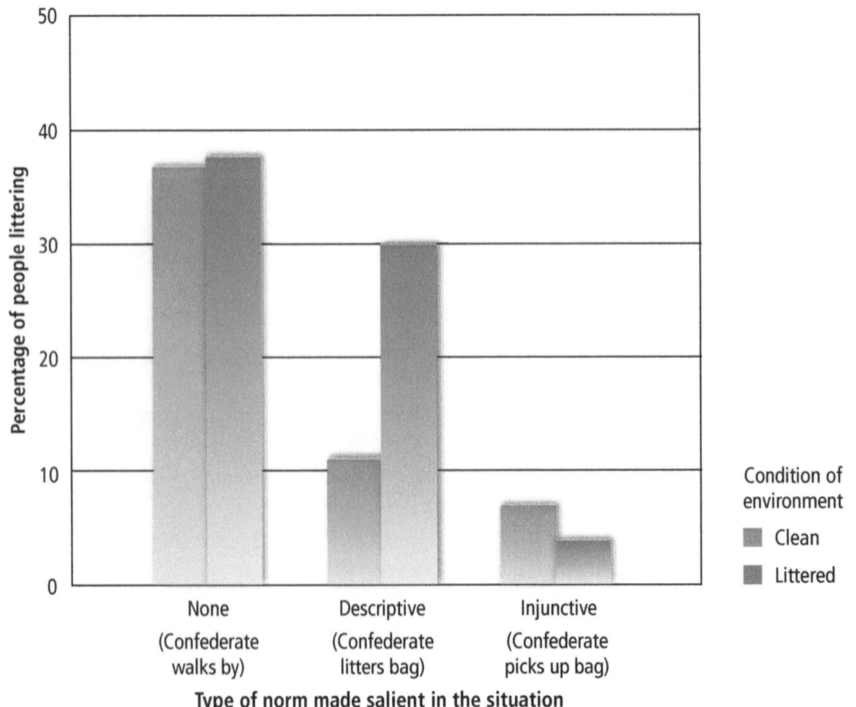

FIGURE 8.7

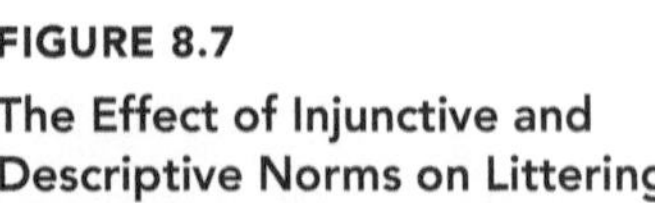

The Effect of Injunctive and Descriptive Norms on Littering

The data for the control group (left) indicate that 37% to 38% of people litter a handbill found on their car windshield whether the environment (a parking lot) is littered or clean. When a descriptive norm is made salient, littering decreases significantly only in the clean environment (middle). When an injunctive norm is made salient, littering decreases significantly in both types of environment, indicating that injunctive norms are more consistently effective at changing behavior.

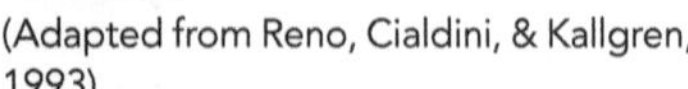

(Adapted from Reno, Cialdini, & Kallgren, 1993)

Using Norms to Change Behavior: Beware the "Boomerang Effect"

In recent years, university administrators have tried a new technique for decreasing alcohol binge drinking on their campuses. The idea is that students typically overestimate how much their peers drink each week (Berkowitz, 2004; Lewis et al., 2007; Perkins, 2007). Thus, telling them, "Students at your school, on average, consume only X number of drinks a week" should lead them to decrease their own alcohol intake as they conform to this lower level. However, researchers have noted a major problem with this approach: Sometimes, it backfires, or "boomerangs." That is, for students who already drink very little (or not at all), finding out that the average student on campus drinks more than they do leads them to *increase* their own alcohol intake to be more like everyone else! In short, the public service message meant to decrease alcohol consumption can actually have the effect of increasing it (Perkins, Haines, & Rice, 2005; Wechsler et al., 2003). Accordingly, your efforts to change others' behavior through processes of conformity must consider that there are different types of people receiving your message: Those performing the undesirable behavior at an *above-average* level (whom you want to convince to decrease their behavior) and those who are performing the undesirable behavior at a *below-average* level (who you want to continue doing what they're already doing rather than to "boomerang" by increasing the undesirable behavior).

P. Wesley Shultz and colleagues tested this idea by focusing on a desirable behavior we've already discussed in this chapter: conserving electrical energy in the home (Shultz et al., 2007). Residents of a California neighborhood agreed to take part in the study. Their baseline energy usage was measured, and they were divided into two groups: those whose energy consumption was above the average for their neighborhood and those whose energy consumption was below the average. The households were then randomly assigned to receive one of two kinds of feedback about their energy usage over several weeks. In the *descriptive norm condition*, they were told how much energy they had used that week, told how much energy the average household in their neighborhood had used (the descriptive norm information), and given suggestions for how to conserve energy. In the *descriptive norm plus injunctive norm condition*, they received all of the above information plus one subtle, but important, addition: If they had consumed less energy than the average household, the researcher drew a smiley face next to the information. If they had consumed more energy than the average household, the researcher drew a sad face instead. The happy or sad face communicated the *injunctive* part of the message—the recipients were receiving either approval or disapproval for the amount of energy they had used.

Weeks later, researchers measured energy usage again. Did the messages help convince people to conserve energy? Did those who already used low amounts stray from the path of conservation righteousness and "boomerang," deciding that it would not be so bad for them to be a little less efficient just like their wasteful neighbors? First, the results indicated that the descriptive norm message had a positive effect on those who consumed more energy than average; they cut back and conserved. However, the descriptive norm message had a boomerang effect on those who consumed less energy than average. Once they learned what their neighbors were doing (using electricity like crazy), they felt liberated to increase their own usage!

On the other hand, the "descriptive norm plus injunctive norm" message was uniformly successful. Those whose consumption was more than average decreased their usage when they received this message. Most importantly, those whose consumption was below average to begin with did not boomerang when they received this message—they maintained their low level of energy use, the same level as before the study started. Thus, the smiley face reminded them that they were doing the right thing, and they kept on doing it (Schultz et al., 2007).

This study has had a major impact on energy conservation strategies in the United States. The use of smiley and sad faces to give injunctive norm feedback, combined with descriptive norm energy-usage information, is now being used by utility companies in various major metropolitan areas, including Boston, Chicago, Sacramento, and Seattle (Kaufman, 2009).

Obedience to Authority

We are socialized, beginning as children, to obey authority figures who we perceive as legitimate (Blass, 2000; Staub, 1989). We internalize the social norm of obedience such that we usually obey rules and laws even when the authority figure isn't present—you stop at red lights even if the cops aren't parked at the corner. However, obedience can have extremely serious and even tragic consequences as well. People will obey the orders of an authority figure to hurt or even kill other human beings.

As with many eras, the past century was marked by repeated atrocities and genocides—in Germany and the rest of Europe, Armenia, the Ukraine, Rwanda, Cambodia, Bosnia, Sudan, and elsewhere. One of the most important questions facing the world's inhabitants, therefore, becomes, where does obedience end and personal responsibility begin? The philosopher Hannah Arendt (1965) was particularly interested in understanding the causes of the Holocaust. How could Hitler's Nazi regime in Germany accomplish the murder of 6 million European Jews and millions of others, based on ethnicity, sexual orientation, or political beliefs? Arendt argued that most participants in the Holocaust were not sadists or psychopaths who enjoyed the mass murder of innocent people, but rather ordinary citizens subjected to complex and powerful social pressures. As a journalist, she covered the trial of Adolf Eichmann, the Nazi official responsible for the transportation of Jews to the death camps, and concluded that he was not the bloodthirsty monster that many people made him out to be, but a commonplace bureaucrat who did what he was told without questioning his orders (Miller, 1995).

Our point is not that Eichmann—or the soldiers at My Lai or the Khmer Rouge in Cambodia or the Serbs in Bosnia—should be excused for the crimes they committed. The point is that it is too easy to explain their behavior as the acts of madmen. It is more fruitful—and more frightening—to view their behavior as the acts of ordinary people exposed to extraordinary social influence. But how can we be sure that these atrocities were not caused solely by evil, psychopathic people, but rather by powerful social forces operating on people of all types? The way to find out is to study social pressure in the laboratory under controlled conditions. We could take a sample of ordinary citizens, subject them to various kinds of social influence, and see to what extent they will conform and obey. Can an experimenter influence ordinary people to commit immoral acts, such as inflicting severe pain on an innocent bystander? Stanley Milgram (1963, 1974, 1976) decided to find out, in what has become the most famous series of studies in social psychology.

Imagine that you were a participant in one of Milgram's studies. You answer an ad in the newspaper, asking for participants in a study on memory and learning. When you arrive at the laboratory, you meet another participant, a 47-year-old, somewhat overweight, pleasant-looking fellow. The experimenter, wearing a white lab coat, explains that one of you will play the role of a teacher and the other the role of a learner. You draw a slip of paper out of a hat and discover that you will be the teacher. It turns out that your job is to read to the other participant a list of word pairs (e.g., *blue–box*, *nice–day*) and then test him on the list. The experimenter instructs you to deliver an electric shock to the learner whenever he makes a mistake, because the purpose of the study is to examine the effects of punishment on learning.

Victims of the Holocaust from the Bergen-Belsen concentration camp, 1945.

You watch as the other participant—the learner—is strapped into a chair in an adjacent room and electrodes are attached to his arm. You are seated in front of a shock generator whose 30 switches deliver varying levels of shock in 15-volt increments, from 15 to 450 volts. There are labels accompanying these switches, from "Slight Shock" to "Danger: Severe Shock" to an ominous "XXX" next to the highest levels (see the photos on page 226). The experimenter tells you that the first time the learner makes a mistake, you should give him a shock of 15 volts—the smallest amount—and then increase the amount by

15 volts for each subsequent mistake he makes. So that you will know what the shocks are like, the experimenter gives you a sample shock of 45 volts, which is rather painful.

You read the list of word pairs to the learner and then begin the testing phase. After announcing the first word of each pair, you give four possible answers; the learner responds by pressing one of four switches, illuminating a light on the answer box in front of you. Everything begins smoothly as the learner gets the first few right. Then he gets some wrong, and as instructed, you deliver a shock each time. At this point, you are probably getting concerned about the number and severity of the shocks you will have to give. When you get to the 75-volt level, the learner, whom you can hear over an intercom, emits a painful "Ugh!" Perhaps you pause and ask the experimenter what you should do. "Please continue," he responds without hesitation. As the learner continues to make mistakes, you deliver a few more shocks. The learner protests, shouting, "Ugh! Experimenter! That's all! Get me out of here!" You look at the experimenter with concern. He tells you calmly, "It is absolutely essential that you continue." (See Figure 8.8.)

Learner's Protests

75 volts: Ugh!

90 volts: Ugh!

105 volts: Ugh! (louder)

120 volts: Ugh! Hey this really hurts.

135 volts: Ugh!!

150 volts: Ugh!!! Experimenter! That's all. Get me out of here. I told you I had heart trouble. My heart's starting to bother me now. Get me out of here, please. My heart's starting to bother me. I refuse to go on. Let me out.

165 volts: Ugh! Let me out! (shouting)

180 volts: Ugh! I can't stand the pain. Let me out of here! (shouting)

195 volts: Ugh! Let me out of here. Let me out of here. My heart's bothering me. Let me out of here! You have no right to keep me here! Let me out! Let me out of here! Let me out! Let me out of here! My heart's bothering me. Let me out! Let me out!

210 volts: Ugh! Experimenter! Get me out of here. I've had enough. I won't be in the experiment anymore.

225 volts: Ugh!

240 volts: Ugh!

255 volts: Ugh! Get me out of here.

270 volts: Ugh! (agonized scream) Let me out of here. Let me out of here. Let me out of here. Let me out. Do you hear? Let me out of here.

285 volts: Ugh! (agonized scream)

300 volts: Ugh! (agonized scream) I absolutely refuse to answer anymore. Get me out of here. You can't hold me here. Get me out. Get me out of here.

315 volts: Ugh! (intensely agonized scream) I told you I refuse to answer. I'm no longer part of this experiment.

330 volts: Ugh! (intense and prolonged agonized scream) Let me out of here. Let me out of here. My heart's bothering me. Let me out, I tell you. (hysterically) Let me out of here. Let me out of here. You have no right to hold me here. Let me out! Let me out! Let me out of here! Let me out!

Instructions Used by the Experimenter to Achieve Obedience

Prod 1: Please continue *or* Please go on.

Prod 2: The experiment requires that you continue.

Prod 3: It is absolutely essential that you continue.

Prod 4: You have no other choice; you must go on.

The prods were always made in sequence: Only if prod 1 had been unsuccessful could prod 2 be used. If the subject refused to obey the experimenter after prod 4, the experiment was terminated. The experimenter's tone of voice was at all times firm but not impolite. The sequence was begun anew on each occasion that the subject balked or showed reluctance to follow orders.

Special prods. If the subject asked whether the learner was likely to suffer permanent physical injury, the experimenter said:

Although the shocks may be painful, there is no permanent tissue damage, so please go on. [Followed by prods 2, 3, and 4 if necessary.]

If the subject said that the learner did not want to go on, the experimenter replied: Whether the learner likes it or not, you must go on until he has learned all the word pairs correctly. So please go on. [Followed by prods 2, 3, and 4 if necessary.]

FIGURE 8.8

Transcript of the learner's protests in Milgram's obedience study and of the prods used by the experimenter to compel people to continue giving shocks.

(Adapted from Milgram, 1963, 1974)

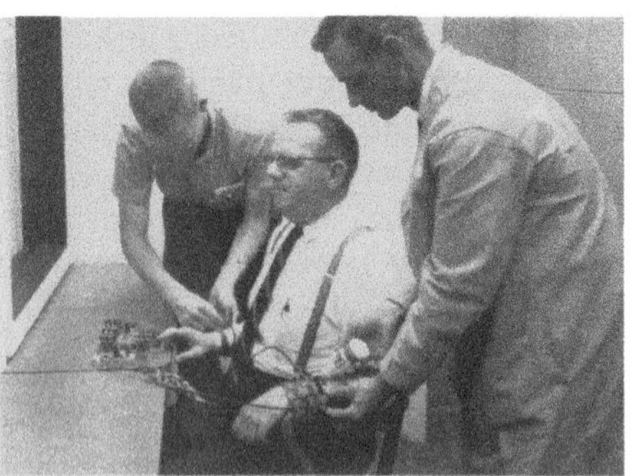

Left: The shock generator used in Milgram's research. *Right:* The learner (an accomplice of the experimenter) is strapped into the chair, and electrodes are attached to his arm.

(Adapted from Milgram, 1974)

What would you do? How many people do you think would continue to obey the experimenter, increasing the levels of shock all the way up the shock panel until they had delivered the maximum amount of 450 volts?

When this question was posed to psychology majors at Yale University, they estimated that only about 1% of the population would go to this extreme. A sample of middle-class adults and a panel of psychiatrists made similar predictions. Based on our discussion of conformity thus far, however, perhaps you are not so optimistic. Indeed, most of Milgram's participants succumbed to the pressure of an authority figure. The average maximum shock delivered was 360 volts, and 62.5% of the participants went all the way to the end of the panel, delivering the 450-volt shock. A full 80% of the participants continued giving the shocks even after the learner, who earlier had mentioned that he had a heart condition, screamed, "Let me out of here! Let me out of here! My heart's bothering me. Let me out of here! ... Get me out of here! I've had enough. I won't be in the experiment any more" (Milgram, 1974, p. 56).

It is important to note that the learner was actually an accomplice of the experimenter who was acting rather than suffering—he did not receive any actual shocks. It is equally important to note that the study was very convincingly done so that people believed they really were shocking the learner. Here is Milgram's description of one participant's response to the teacher role:

> I observed a mature and initially poised businessman enter the laboratory smiling and confident. Within 20 minutes he was reduced to a twitching, stuttering wreck, who was rapidly approaching a point of nervous collapse. He constantly pulled on his earlobe, and twisted his hands. At one point he pushed his fist into his forehead and muttered, "Oh God, let's stop it." And yet he continued to respond to every word of the experimenter, and obeyed to the end. (Milgram, 1963, p. 377)

Why did so many research participants (who ranged in age from the twenties to the fifties and included blue-collar, white-collar, and professional workers) conform to the wishes of the experimenter, to the point where they genuinely believed they were inflicting great pain on another human being? Why were the college students, middle-class adults, and psychiatrists so wrong in their predictions about what people would do? In a dangerous way, each of the reasons that explain why people conform combined to cause Milgram's participants to obey—just as many Germans did during the Holocaust and soldiers have done during recent atrocities in Iraq and Afghanistan. Let's take a close look at how this played out in Milgram's research.

Watch on **MyPsychLab**
To learn more, watch the MyPsychLab video ***Classic Footage of Milgram's Obedience Study***.

The Role of Normative Social Influence

First, it is clear that normative pressures made it difficult for people in Milgram's studies to refuse to continue. As we have seen, if someone really wants us to do something, it can be difficult to say no. This is particularly true when the person is in a position of authority over us. Milgram's participants probably believed that if they refused to continue, the experimenter would be disappointed, hurt, or maybe even angry—all of which put pressure on them to continue. It is important to note that this study, unlike the Asch study, was set up so that the experimenter actively attempted to get people to conform, giving commands such as "It is absolutely essential that you continue." When an authority figure is so insistent that we obey, it is difficult to say no (Blass, 1991, 2000, 2003; Hamilton, Sanders, & McKearney, 1995; Meeus & Raaijmakers, 1995; Miller, 1986).

The fact that normative pressures were present in the Milgram study is clear from a variation that he conducted. This time, there were three teachers, two of whom were confederates. One confederate was instructed to read the list of word pairs; the other, to tell the learner whether his response was correct. The (real) participant's job was to deliver the shocks, increasing their severity with each error, as in the original study. At 150 volts, when the learner gave his first vehement protest, the first confederate refused to continue, despite the experimenter's command that he do so. At 210 volts, the second confederate refused to continue. The result? Seeing their peers disobey made it much easier for the actual participants to disobey too. Only 10% of the participants gave the maximum level of shock in this version of the study (see Figure 8.9). This result is similar to Asch's finding that people did not conform nearly as much when one accomplice bucked the majority.

The Role of Informational Social Influence

Despite the power of the normative pressures in Milgram's original study, they are not the sole reason people complied. The experimenter was authoritative and insistent, but he was hardly pointing a gun at participants and telling them to "conform or else"; the participants were free to get up and leave anytime they wanted to. Why didn't they, especially when the experimenter was a stranger they had never met before and probably would never see again?

As we saw earlier, when people are in a confusing situation and unsure of what they should do, they use other people to help define the situation. Informational social influence is especially powerful when the situation is ambiguous, when it is a crisis, and when the other people in the situation have some expertise. All three of these characteristics describe the situation Milgram's participants faced. The scenario—a study of the effects of punishment on learning—seemed straightforward enough when the experimenter explained it, but then it turned into something else altogether. The learner cried out in pain, but the experimenter told the participant that the shocks did not cause any permanent damage. The participant didn't want to hurt anyone, but he or she had agreed to be in the study and to follow the directions. When in such a state of conflict, it was only natural for the participants to use an expert—the experimenter in the scientific-looking white lab coat—to help them decide what was the right thing to do (Hamilton et al., 1995; Krakow & Blass, 1995; Miller, 1986; Miller, Collins, & Brief, 1995).

Another version of Milgram's study supports the idea that informational influence was operative. This version was identical to the original one except for three critical changes: First, the experimenter never said which shock levels were to be given, leaving this decision up to the participant. Second, before the study began, the experimenter received a telephone call and had to leave the room, telling the participant to continue without him. Third, there was a confederate playing the role of an additional teacher, whose job was to record how long it took the learner to respond to each word pair. When the experimenter left, this other "teacher" said that he had just thought of a good system: How about if they increased the level of shock each time the learner made a mistake? He insisted that the real participant follow this procedure.

Note that in this situation the expertise of the person giving the commands is nonexistent: He was just a regular person, no more knowledgeable than the participants themselves. Because he lacked expertise, people were much less likely to use him as a source of information about how they should respond. As seen in Figure 8.9, in this version, full compliance dropped from 62.5%, to only 20%. (The fact that 20% still gave the maximum shock suggests that some people were so uncertain about what to do that they used even a nonexpert as a guide.)

An additional variation conducted by Milgram underscores the importance of authority figures as experts in eliciting such

When you think of the long and gloomy history of man, you will find more hideous crimes have been committed in the name of obedience than in the name of rebellion.

—C. P. Snow

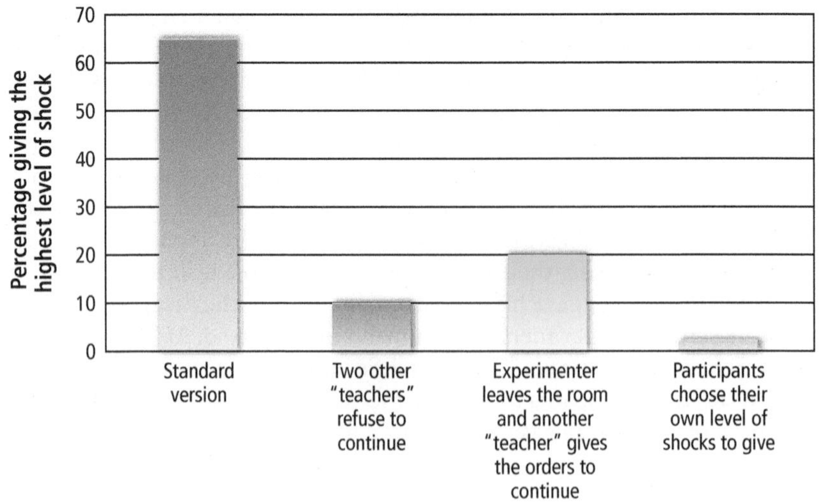

FIGURE 8.9

Results of Different Versions of the Milgram Study

Obedience is highest in the standard version, where the participant is ordered to deliver increasing levels of shock to another person (left panel). Obedience drops when other participants model disobedience or when the authority figure is not present (two middle panels). Finally, when no orders are given to increase the shocks, almost no participants do so (right panel). The contrast in behavior between the far-left and far-right panels indicates just how powerful a tendency obedience is.

(Adapted from Milgram, 1974)

obedience. In this variation, two experimenters gave the real participants their orders. At 150 volts, when the learner first cried out that he wanted to stop, the two experimenters began to disagree about whether they should continue the study. At this point, 100% of the participant-teachers stopped responding. Note that nothing the victim ever did caused all the participants to stop obeying; however, when the authorities' definition of the situation became unclear, the participants broke out of their conforming role.

Other Reasons Why We Obey

Both normative and informational social influences were very strong in Milgram's research; however, these reasons for complying still fall short of fully explaining why people acted in a manner that seems so inhumane. They seem to account for why people initially complied with the experimenter's instructions, but after it became increasingly obvious what was happening to the learner, why didn't participants realize that what they were doing was terribly wrong and stop? Just as the fast-food restaurant managers continued to abuse their employees long after the demands of the "policeman" on the phone shifted from bizarre to illegal, many of Milgram's participants pressed the shock levers time after time after time, despite the cries of anguish from a fellow human being.

Conforming to the Wrong Norm To understand this continued compliance, we need to consider additional aspects of the situation. We don't mean to imply that Milgram's participants were completely mindless or unaware of what they were doing. All were terribly concerned about the plight of the victim. The problem was that they were caught in a web of conflicting norms, and it was difficult to determine which ones to follow. At the beginning of the study, it was perfectly reasonable to heed the norm that says, "Obey expert, legitimate authority figures." The experimenter was confident and knowledgeable, and the study seemed as if it was a reasonable test of an interesting hypothesis. So why not cooperate and do as you are told?

But, gradually, the rules of the game changed, and this "obey authority" norm was no longer appropriate. The experimenter, who seemed so reasonable before, was now asking people to inflict great pain on their fellow participant. But once people are following one norm, it can be difficult to switch midstream or to realize that this norm is no longer appropriate and that another norm, "Do not inflict needless harm on a fellow human being," should be followed. For example, suppose the experimenter had explained, at the outset, that he would like people to deliver possibly fatal shocks to the other participant. How many people would have agreed? Very few, we suspect, because it would have been clear that this violated an important social and personal norm about inflicting harm on others. Instead, the experimenter pulled a kind of "bait and switch" routine, whereby he first made it look like an "obey authority" norm was appropriate and then gradually violated this norm (Collins & Brief, 1995).

It was particularly difficult for people to abandon the "obey authority" norm in the Milgram study because of three key aspects of the situation. First, the study was fast paced, preventing the participants from reflecting on what they were doing. They were busy recording the learner's responses, keeping track of the word pairs, and determining whether the learner's responses were right or wrong. Given that they had to attend carefully to these details and move along at a fast pace, it was difficult for them to realize that the norm that was guiding their behavior—cooperating with the authority figure—was, after a while, no longer appropriate (Conway & Schaller, 2005; Modigliani & Rochat, 1995). We suspect that if, halfway through the study, Milgram's participants had been told to take a break or had been left in the room by themselves for a period of time, many more would have successfully redefined the situation and refused to continue.

Self-justification A second important aspect of the situation in the Milgram study is that, as alluded to above, the experimenter asked people to increase the shocks in very small increments. The participants did not go from giving a small shock to giving a potentially lethal one. Instead, at any given point, they only faced a smaller decision about whether to increase by a meager 15 volts the amount of shock they had just given. As we saw in Chapter 6, every time a person makes an important or difficult decision, dissonance is produced, with resultant pressures to reduce it. An effective way of reducing dissonance produced by a difficult decision is to decide that the decision was fully justified. But because reducing dissonance provides a justification for the preceding action, in some situations it makes a person vulnerable to further escalating the previously chosen activity.

Thus, in the Milgram study, the participants' initial agreement to administer the first shock created internal pressure on them to continue to obey. As the participants administered each successive level of shock, they had to justify it in their own minds. After they had justified a particular shock level, it became very difficult for them to decide on a place where they should draw the line and stop. How could they say, in effect, "OK, I gave him 200 volts, but not 215—never 215!" Each succeeding shock and its justification laid the groundwork for the next shock and would have been dissonant with quitting; 215 volts is not *that* different from 200, and 230 is not *that* different from 215. Those who did break off the series did so against enormous internal pressure to continue (Darley, 1992; Gilbert, 1981; Miller et al., 1995).

The Loss of Personal Responsibility The third reason why it was difficult for participants to abandon the "obey authority" norm in the Milgram studies is a particularly troubling one. When you are the research participant (or the employee) and the other person is a legitimate authority figure (the experimenter, the boss, the military commander, the police officer), you are the "puppet" and they are pulling the strings. They define what it is you are supposed to do, and they are responsible for the end results—after all, it was their idea and you were "just following orders." Milgram (1974) stressed that the loss of a sense of personal responsibility for one's actions was a critical component explaining the results of the obedience studies.

A particularly disturbing job is that of prison guards who must carry out a capital punishment sentence. How do these guards respond to a job where they are told to kill another person? Clearly, they need to reduce their cognitive dissonance. Taking a life is a supremely problematic and disturbing act, so they very much need to engage in self-justification in order to do it. Michael Osofsky, Albert Bandura, and Philip Zimbardo (2005) studied guards on the execution teams of three southern state prisons and compared them to their fellow guards who did not conduct executions. All the guards responded anonymously to a questionnaire that asked them to rate their level of agreement with statements such as "Because of the nature of their crime, murderers have lost the right to live" and "Those who carry out state executions should not be criticized for following society's wishes."

The researchers found a highly significant difference in the attitudes of the two types of guards. The execution-team guards demonstrated much more "moral disengagement" from their work than did the other guards. The execution-team guards denied all personal responsibility for the executions. They felt they were just following orders—in this case, those of a judge and jury. They also engaged in high levels of justification in other areas. As compared to the regular prison guards, they dehumanized the prisoners more, seeing them as lacking important human qualities. They perceived the prisoners as more of a threat to society, such that it was necessary that they be killed. All these attitudes helped the execution guards reduce their qualms about the morality of what they did at work. As one guard put it, "I had a job to do, that's what we did. Our job was to execute this man and we were going to do it in a professional manner" (Osofsky, Bandura, & Zimbardo, 2005, p. 386).

The Obedience Studies, Then and Now

Stanley Milgram's study of obedience is widely considered to be one of the most important contributions to the field of psychology (Benjamin & Simpson, 2009). His work, conducted in the early 1960s, was replicated in the following years by researchers in 11 countries, involving approximately 3,000 research participants (Blass, 2009). However, Milgram's research paradigm also ignited a storm of protest (and soul-searching) in the research community over the ethical treatment of research participants.

Milgram's research was criticized by some as unethical for several reasons. First, the study involved *deception*. For example, participants were told it was a study on memory and learning, when of course it was not; participants were told the electric shocks were real, when of course they were not. Second, there was no true *informed consent* on the part of participants. When they agreed to be in the study, they were not informed as to its true nature, and thus they never really consented to take part in the scenario they eventually experienced. Third, their role as teacher caused them *psychological distress* during the course of the study; for many participants, this occurred at a high level. Fourth, it was not made clear to participants that they had the *right to withdraw* from the study at any time; in fact, the experimenter stated the exact opposite—for example, that they "had to continue." Fifth, the participants experienced *inflicted insight*. When the study ended, some of them had learned unpleasant things about themselves that they had not agreed to beforehand (Baumrind, 1964, 1985; Milgram, 1964; Miller, 2009).

Although the ethical issues surrounding Milgram's study were not, as is often suggested, the reason formal ethical guidelines for research participants were created in the United States in 1966 (they were primarily created to protect participants in medical research), these new guidelines made conducting obedience research such as Milgram's increasingly problematic (Benjamin & Simpson, 2009). Indeed, decades would pass without researchers conducting follow-up studies of obedience using Milgram's procedure (Blass, 2009), and many students learned in their psychology courses that such studies could never be run again. But that all changed in 2006.

That year, Jerry M. Burger (2009) conducted the first obedience study in the United States in 30 years. Much had changed in the country over these decades. Had the likelihood of being obedient, even to the point of inflicting harm, changed as well? In order to conduct this study under modern ethical guidelines, Burger (2009) had to make a number of changes to the procedure. First, he reduced the psychological distress experienced by participants by stopping the study after 150 volts, when the learner is first heard yelling that he wants out and refuses to go on. Analysis of data from eight of Milgram's study versions indicated that when disobedience occurred, it was most likely to happen at this point in the study; most previous participants who passed the 150-volt mark tended to go all the way to end of the shock panel (Packer, 2008). Thus, Burger could compare obedience versus disobedience up to this critical 150-volt juncture and then end the study without further subjecting participants to the many, many levels of shock (and stress) that remained. Second, participants were prescreened by a clinical psychologist, and those who were identified as even slightly likely to have a negative reaction to the experience were excluded from the study (38% were excluded). Finally, Burger (2009) explicitly and repeatedly told his participants that they could leave the study at any time, as could the learner.

In most respects, though, Burger's (2009) study was like the original. His experimenter used the same four "prods" that Milgram's used (e.g., "It is absolutely essential that you continue") to order participants to continue when they began to waver. Burger's participants, like Milgram's, were adult residents recruited through newspaper advertisements and flyers. Their age range of 20 to 81 years was broader than Milgram's, though their average age of about 43 years was similar. They were ethnically more diverse than Milgram's participants, and they were also more highly educated: Forty percent of Burger's sample had college degrees, and another 20% had master's degrees. Both men and women participated as teachers in Burger's study; Milgram had female participants in only one of his many study versions. Finally, because the Milgram obedience studies are quite well known, Burger excluded participants who had taken more than two college-level psychology courses.

What did Burger (2009) find? Are people more disobedient today than they were in Milgram's time 45 years ago? After all, during the intervening decades, as large numbers of Americans took part in the civil rights movement and various antiwar movements, they had accepted the injunctive norm that questioning authority was the right thing to do. Americans had also grown less complacent and accepting of their government at both the state and federal level (Cohen, 2008). Did these cultural experiences translate into a newly empowered, disobedient participant? Sadly, the answer is no; they did not. Burger (2009) found no significant difference in obedience rates between his participants and Milgram's. After the critical 150-volt shock had been delivered (and the learner cried out to be released), 70% of Burger's participants had obeyed and were ready to continue (at which point, Burger ended the study). At this same point in the comparable Milgram study, 82.5% were obedient and continued; the difference between 70% and 82.5% is not statistically significant. Similarly, Burger (2009) found no significant difference in obedience between his male and female participants, which was also the case in Milgram's research.

Note that Burger's ethically necessary changes in methodology also complicate a direct comparison to Milgram's results (Miller, 2009). Some of Burger's changes may have decreased the likelihood of obedience; others may have increased its likelihood. For example, perhaps repeated reminders beforehand that they could withdraw from the study at any time made it easier for participants to ultimately disobey. But the most profound change that Burger made was stopping the study after 150 volts. While this makes the procedure more ethical, it means we have no idea how many participants, today, would go all the way to the 450-volt shock (Twenge, 2009). Much of the extraordinary power of the Milgram obedience studies came from participants' choices after 150 volts, as they continued step by small step to the last switch on the shock generator. It is during this part of the study that participants felt the most conflicted and anxious. It is here that they revealed their response to a pressing moral conflict (Miller, 2009). This information is lost in the present replication. And as such, it reminds us that scientific inquiry has two, sometimes competing aims: to discover new knowledge, and to do no harm.

Simulate on **MyPsychLab**
To learn more, try the MyPsychLab ***Closer Look Simulation: Social Psychology.***

It's not About Aggression Before leaving our discussion of Milgram's research, we should mention one other possible interpretation of his results: Did the participants act so inhumanely because there is an inherently evil side to human nature, lurking just below the surface, ready to be expressed with the flimsiest excuse? To test this hypothesis, Milgram conducted another version of his study. Everything was the same except that the experimenter told the participants that they could choose any level of shock they wished to give the learner when he made a mistake. Milgram gave people permission to use the highest levels, telling them that there was a lot to be learned from all levels of shock. This instruction should have allowed any aggressive urges to be expressed unchecked. Instead, the participants chose to give very mild shocks (see Figure 8.9 on page 228). Only 2.5% of the participants gave the maximum shock. Thus, the Milgram studies do not show that all people have an evil streak that shines through when the surface is scratched (Reeder, Monroe, & Pryor, 2008). Instead, these studies demonstrate that social pressures can combine in insidious ways to make humane people act in an inhumane manner. Let us conclude this chapter with the words of Stanley Milgram:

> Even Eichmann was sickened when he toured the concentration camps, but in order to participate in mass murder he had only to sit at a desk and shuffle papers. At the same time the man in the camp who actually dropped [the poison] into the gas chambers is able to justify his behavior on the grounds that he is only following orders from above. Thus there is fragmentation of the total human act; no one man decides to carry out the evil act and is confronted with its consequences. The person who assumes full responsibility for the act has evaporated. Perhaps this is the most common characteristic of socially organized evil in modern society.
>
> (1976, pp. 183–184)

USE IT!

The topics of conformity and obedience bring to mind the great opening sentence in Charles Dickens's novel *A Tale of Two Cities*: "It was the best of times, it was the worst of times." These types of social influence are incredibly useful in maintaining social order. Without them, life would be chaotic, even dangerous. However, they have their "dark side" as well, even to the point of promoting and enabling genocide. What can you do to protect yourself from the potentially negative effects of social influence? Probably the most difficult is informational conformity; by definition, you conform to others because you don't know what's going on. Therefore, it is very difficult to know if they're wrong. Typically, it's best to rely on an expert instead of a nonexpert, but even this advice can be tricky. Resisting normative conformity is more straightforward. You'll know what the right thing to do is, but will you be able to withstand the disapproval of others? Remember that having an ally will help you to stand up to group pressure. Obedience also presents a fairly straightforward scenario. You'll know when you've been given an order that goes against your ethical or moral beliefs. As with normative conformity, it will be a matter of whether or not you are willing and able to withstand the repercussions of your disobedience. Luckily, learning about these types of social influence will make you more aware in the future of when it is appropriate to agree with the group and when it is not.

Summary

What is conformity and why does it occur?

- **Conformity: When and Why** Conformity occurs when people change their behavior due to the real (or imagined) influence of others. There are two main reasons people conform: informational and normative social influences.

How does informational social influence motivate people to conform?

- **Informational Social Influence: The Need to Know What's "Right"** Informational social influence occurs when people do not know what is the correct (or best) thing to do or say. They look to the behavior of others as an important and needed source of information, and they use it to choose appropriate courses of action for themselves. Informational social influence usually results in private acceptance, in which people genuinely believe in what other people are doing or saying.
    - **Importance of Being Accurate** In situations where it is important to be accurate, the tendency to conform to other people through informational social influence increases.
    - **When Informational Conformity Backfires** Using other people as a source of information can backfire when they are wrong about what's going on. Contagion occurs when emotions and behaviors spread rapidly throughout a group; one example is **mass psychogenic illness**.
    - **When Will People Conform to Informational Social Influence?** People are more likely to conform to informational social influence when the situation is ambiguous, when they are in a crisis, or if experts are present.

How does normative social influence motivate people to conform?

- **Normative Social Influence: The Need to Be Accepted** **Normative social influence** occurs when we change our behavior to match that of others because we want to remain a member of the group in good standing and continue to gain the advantages of group membership. We conform to the group's **social norms**, implicit or explicit rules for acceptable behaviors, values, and attitudes. Normative social influence usually results in **public compliance**, but not private acceptance of other people's ideas and behaviors.
  - **Conformity and Social Approval: The Asch Line-Judgment Studies** In a series of classic studies, Solomon Asch found that people would conform, at least some of the time, to the obviously wrong answer of the group.
  - **The Importance of Being Accurate, Revisited** When it is important to be accurate, people are more likely to resist normative social influence and go against the group, giving the right answer.
  - **The Consequences of Resisting Normative Social Influence** Resisting normative social influence can lead to ridicule, ostracism, and rejection by the group.
  - **Normative Social Influence in Everyday Life** Normative social influence operates on many levels in social life: It influences our eating habits, hobbies, fashion, body image, and so on, and it promotes polite behavior in society.
  - **When Will People Conform to Normative Social Influence?** **Social impact theory** specifies when normative social influence is most likely to occur by referring to the strength, immediacy, and size of the group. We are more likely to conform when the group is one we care about, when the group members are unanimous in their thoughts or behaviors, when the group has three or more members, and when we are members of collectivist cultures. Past conformity gives people **idiosyncrasy credits**, allowing them to deviate from the group without serious consequences.
  - **Minority Influence: When the Few Influence the Many** Under certain conditions, an individual (or small number of people) can influence the majority. The key is consistency in the presentation of the minority viewpoint.

How can we use our knowledge of social influence for positive purposes?

- **Using Social Influence to Promote Beneficial Behavior** Social influence techniques can be used to promote socially beneficial behavior in others. Communicating **injunctive norms** is a more powerful way to create change than communicating **descriptive norms.** In addition, one must be careful that descriptive norms do not create a "boomerang effect."
  - **The Role of Injunctive and Descriptive Norms**

What have studies demonstrated about people's willingness to obey someone in a position of authority?

- **Obedience to Authority** In the most famous series of studies in social psychology, Stanley Milgram examined obedience to authority figures. He found chilling levels of obedience, to the point where a majority of participants administered what they thought were potentially lethal shocks to a fellow human being.
  - **The Role of Normative Social Influence** Normative pressures make it difficult for people to stop obeying authority figures. They want to please the authority figure by doing a good job.
  - **The Role of Informational Social Influence** The obedience studies created a confusing situation for participants, with competing, ambiguous demands. Unclear about how to define what was going on, they followed the orders of the expert.
  - **Other Reasons We Obey** Participants conformed to the wrong norm: They continued to follow the "obey authority" norm when it was no longer appropriate. It was difficult for them to abandon this norm for three reasons: the fast-paced nature of the study, the fact that the shock levels increased in small increments, and their loss of a feeling of personal responsibility.
  - **The Obedience Studies, Then and Now** Milgram's research design was criticized on ethical grounds, involving deception, informed consent, psychological distress, the right to withdraw, and inflicted insight. A recent U.S. replication of the Milgram study found that the level of obedience in 2006 was not significantly different from that found in the classic study in the 1960s. Similarly, there was no difference in obedience between men and women participants in either time period.

Chapter 8 Test

Study and Review on MyPsychLab

1. All of the following are examples of informational social influence *except*
   a. you are running a race, but because you are unsure of the route, you wait to check which of two roads the other runners follow.
   b. you've just started work at a new job, and a fire alarm goes off; you watch your coworkers to see what to do.
   c. when you get to college you change the way you dress so that you "fit in" better—that is, so that people will like you more.
   d. you ask your adviser which classes you should take next semester.
   e. mass psychogenic illness.

2. Which of the following is true, according to social impact theory?
   a. People conform more to others who are physically close than to others who are physically distant.
   b. People conform more if the others are important to them.

c. People conform more to three or more people than to one or two people.
d. All of the above are true.
e. Only (a) and (b) are true.

3. In Asch's line studies, participants who were alone when asked to report the length of the lines gave the correct answer 98% of the time. When they were with the confederates, however (i.e., all of whom gave the wrong answer on some trials), 76% of participants gave the wrong answer at least once. This suggests that Asch's studies are an illustration of
   a. public compliance with private acceptance.
   b. the fundamental attribution error.
   c. public compliance without private acceptance.
   d. informational influence.
   e. private compliance.

4. Which of the following situations demonstrates mass psychogenic illness?
   a. You share the happiness a close friend experiences when she learns that she's won the state lottery.
   b. During the past week, complaints of dizziness and fainting spells spread throughout the dorm though no physical cause can be identified.
   c. After looking through a medical dictionary, you fear that you have three separate illnesses.
   d. Panic spreads throughout a crowd when someone yells, "Killer bees!"

5. Whereas ________________ may be the mechanism by which women learn what kind of body type is considered attractive, ________________ explains their attempts to obtain such a shape through dieting and other means.
   a. contagion influence, minority influence
   b. minority influence, contagion influence
   c. informational social influence, normative social influence
   d. normative social influence, informational social influence

6. Which of the following is most true about informational social influence?
   a. When deciding whether to conform, people should ask themselves whether the other people know more about what is going on than they do.
   b. People should always try to resist it.
   c. People are most likely to conform when other people have the same level of expertise as they do.
   d. Often, people publicly conform but do not privately accept this kind of influence.

7. Brandon knows that society considers underage drinking to be wrong; he also knows, however, that on a Saturday night at his university many of his friends will engage in this behavior. His belief that most of the public would disapprove of underage drinking is ________________, while his perception that many teenagers drink under certain circumstances is ________________.
   a. an injunctive norm, a descriptive norm
   b. a descriptive norm, an injunctive norm
   c. a descriptive norm, conformity
   d. an injunctive norm, conformity

8. Tom is a new student at his university. During the first week of classes, he notices a fellow student from one of his classes getting on a bus. Tom decides to follow the student and discovers that this bus takes him right to the building where his class meets. This best illustrates what kind of conformity?
  a. Obedience to authority
  b. Informational social influence
  c. Public compliance
  d. Normative social influence
  e. Mindless conformity

9. Which of the following best describes an example of normative social influence?
  a. Sarah is studying with a group of friends. When comparing answers on the practice test, she discovers that they all answered the question differently than she had. Instead of speaking up and telling them she thinks the answer is something else, she agrees with their answer, because she figures they must be right.
  b. Sarah is supposed to bring a bottle of wine to a dinner party she is attending. She doesn't drink wine herself but figures she can just ask the store clerk for advice on what kind to buy.
  c. Sarah is out to lunch with her boss and coworkers. Her boss tells a joke that makes fun of a certain ethnic group and everyone else laughs. Sarah doesn't think the joke is funny but laughs anyway.
  d. Sarah is flying on an airplane for the first time. She is worried when she hears the engine make a strange noise but feels better after she looks at the flight attendants and sees that they are not alarmed.

10. Which of the following had the least influence on participants' willingness to keep giving shocks in the Milgram studies?
  a. Normative social influence
  b. Activation of the "obey authority" norm
  c. Self-justification
  d. Informational social influence
  e. Participants' aggression

Answer Key

1-c, 2-d, 3-c, 4-b, 5-c,
6-a, 7-a, 8-b, 9-d, 10-e

Group Processes

Influence in Social Groups

On March 19, 2003, an unseasonably cool spring day in Washington, D.C., President George W. Bush convened a meeting with his top advisers in the Situation Room, the nerve center in the basement of the White House. Months of planning had come down to this moment—final approval of the invasion of Iraq. The president first asked whether any of his advisers had any last thoughts or recommendations. When none did, he asked the staff to establish a secure video link with General Tommy Franks, the commander of all U.S. armed forces in the Middle East. Franks and his senior field commanders, who were at Prince Sultan Air Force Base in Saudi Arabia, gave President Bush a final briefing, after which General Franks concluded, "The force is ready to go, Mr. President." President Bush then gave a prepared statement: "For the peace of the world and the benefit and freedom of the Iraqi people, I hereby give the order to execute Operation Iraqi Freedom. May God bless the troops" (Woodward, 2004, p. 379).

With these words, President Bush set in motion a controversial war that will undoubtedly be debated by historians for decades to come. For social psychologists, a fascinating question is how the decision to invade Iraq was made—indeed, how important decisions of any kind are made. Do groups of experts make better decisions, for example, than do individuals? The American government has at its disposal a huge number of talented people with expertise in world affairs, national security, human rights, and military intelligence, and it might seem that drawing upon and combining this expertise would lead to the best decisions. Groups don't always make good decisions, however—especially when they are blinded by the desire to maintain cohesiveness or to please a dominant leader. In this chapter, we will focus on questions about the nature of groups and how they influence people's behavior, which are some of the oldest topics in social psychology (Forsyth & Burnette, 2010; Hackman & Katz, 2010; Kerr & Tindale, 2004; Wittenbaum & Moreland, 2008).

- What are groups and why do people join them?
- In what ways do people act differently when other people are around? What are the key variables that determine what the effects of others will be on individual performance?
- When people make decisions, are two (or more) heads better than one? Why or why not?
- When individuals or groups are in conflict, what determines the likelihood that this conflict will escalate or that it will be resolved?

What Is a Group?

Six students studying at a table in the library are not a group. But if they meet to study for their psychology final together, they are. A **group** consists of three or more people who interact and are interdependent in the sense that their needs and goals cause them to influence each other (Cartwright & Zander, 1968; Lewin, 1948). (Two people are generally considered to be a dyad rather than a group; Moreland, 2010). Like a president's advisers working together to reach a foreign policy decision, citizens meeting to solve a community problem, or people who have gathered to blow off steam at a party, groups consist of people who have assembled for some common purpose.

Group
Three or more people who interact and are interdependent in the sense that their needs and goals cause them to influence each other.

Think for a moment of the number of groups to which you belong. Don't forget to include your family, campus groups (such as clubs or political organizations), community groups (such as churches or synagogues), sports teams, and more-temporary groups (such as your classmates in a small seminar). All

Groups have a number of benefits. They are an important part of our identity, helping us define who we are, and are a source of social norms, the explicit or implicit rules defining what is acceptable behavior.

of these count as groups because you interact with the other members and you are interdependent: You influence them, and they influence you.

Why Do People Join Groups?

Forming relationships with other people fulfills a number of basic human needs—so basic, in fact, that there may be an innate need to belong to groups. Some researchers argue that in our evolutionary past there was a substantial survival advantage to establishing bonds with other people (Baumeister & Leary, 1995; DeWall & Richman, 2011). People who bonded together were better able to hunt for and grow food, find mates, and care for children. Consequently, they argue, the need to belong has become innate and is present in all societies. Consistent with this view, people in all cultures are motivated to form relationships with other people and to resist the dissolution of these relationships (Gardner, Pickett, & Brewer, 2000; Manstead, 1997). People monitor their status in groups and look for any sign that they might be rejected (Blackhart et al., 2009; Kerr & Levine, 2008; Leary & Baumeister, 2000; Pickett & Gardner, 2005). One study found that people who were asked to recall a time when they had been rejected by other people estimated that the temperature of the room was 5 degrees lower than did people who were asked to recall a time when they were accepted by other people (IJzerman & Semin, 2010; Zhong & Leonardelli, 2008). Social rejection is, literally, chilling.

Not only do people have a strong need to belong to social groups, but they also have a need to feel distinctive from those who do *not* belong to the same groups. If you go to a large state university, you might have a sense of belonging, but being a member of such a large collective is unlikely to make you feel distinctive from others. Groups that are relatively small can fulfill both functions, by giving us a sense of belonging with our fellow group members and also making us feel special and distinctive. This helps explain why people are attracted to smaller groups at their college universities, such as fraternities or sororities (Brewer, 1991, 2007; Tasdemir, 2011).

Watch on **MyPsychLab**
To learn more about the effects of belonging to a group, watch the MyPsychLab video ***Group Learning.***

Another important function of groups is that they help us define who we are. As we saw in Chapter 8, other people can be an important source of information, helping us resolve ambiguity about the nature of the social world (Darley, 2004). All groups make assumptions about the nature of the social world and thus provide a lens through which we can understand the world and our place in it (Hogg, Hohman, & Rivera, 2008). So groups become an important part of our identity—witness the number of times people wear shirts emblazoned with the name of one of their groups (e.g., a campus organization). Groups also help establish social norms, the explicit or implicit rules defining what is acceptable behavior.

The Composition and Functions of Groups

The groups to which you belong probably vary in size from a few members to several dozen members. Most groups, however, have three to six members (Desportes & Lemaine, 1988; Levine & Moreland, 1998; McPherson, 1983). If groups become too large, you cannot interact with all the members; for example, the college or university that you attend is not a group, because you are unlikely to meet and interact with every other student.

Another important feature of groups is that the members tend to be alike in age, sex, beliefs, and opinions (George, 1990; Levine & Moreland, 1998; Magaro & Ashbrook, 1985). There are two reasons for the homogeneity of groups. First, many groups tend to attract people who are already similar before they join (Alter & Darley, 2009; Feld, 1982). As we'll see in Chapter 10, people are attracted to others who share their attitudes and thus are likely to recruit fellow group members who are similar to them. Second, groups tend to operate in ways that encourage similarity in the members (Moreland, 1987). This can happen in a number of important ways, some of which we discussed in Chapter 8.

Social Roles
Shared expectations in a group about how particular people are supposed to behave.

Social Norms As we saw in Chapter 8, *social norms* are a powerful determinant of our behavior (Hogg, 2010; Kameda, Takezawa, & Hastie, 2005). All societies have norms about which behaviors are acceptable, some of which all members are expected to obey (e.g., we should be quiet in libraries) and some of which vary from group to group (e.g., rules about what to wear to weddings and funerals). If you belong to a fraternity or sorority, you can probably think of social norms that govern behavior in your group, such as whether alcoholic beverages are consumed and how you are supposed to feel about rival fraternities or sororities. It is unlikely that other groups to which you belong share these norms. The power of norms to shape behavior becomes clear when we violate them too often: We are shunned by other group members and, in extreme cases, pressured to leave the group (Marques, Abrams, & Serodio, 2001; Schachter, 1951).

Social Roles Most groups have a number of well-defined **social roles**, which are shared expectations in a group about how particular people are supposed to behave (Hare, 2003). Whereas norms specify how all group members should act, roles specify how people who occupy certain positions in the group should behave. A boss and an employee in a business occupy different roles and are expected to act in different ways in that setting. Like social norms, roles can be very helpful, because people know what to expect from each other. When members of a group follow a set of clearly defined roles, they tend to be satisfied and perform well (Barley & Bechky, 1994; Bettencourt & Sheldon, 2001).

There are, however, potential costs to social roles. People can get so far into a role that their personal identities and personalities get lost. Suppose that you agreed to take part in a 2-week psychology experiment in which you were randomly assigned to play the role of a prison guard or a prisoner in a simulated prison. You might think that the role you were assigned to play would not be very important; after all, everyone knows that it is only an experiment and that people are just pretending to be guards or prisoners. Philip Zimbardo and his colleagues, however, had a different hypothesis. They believed that social roles can be so powerful that they overwhelm our personal identities to the point that we become the role we are playing.

To see if this is true, Zimbardo and colleagues conducted an unusual study. They built a mock prison in the basement of the psychology department at Stanford University and paid students to play the role of guard or prisoner (Haney, Banks, & Zimbardo, 1973; Zimbardo, 2007). The role students played was determined by the flip of a coin. The guards were outfitted with a uniform of khaki shirts and pants, a whistle, a police nightstick, and reflecting sunglasses, and the prisoners with a loose-fitting smock with an identification number stamped on it, rubber sandals, a cap made from a nylon stocking, and a locked chain attached to one ankle.

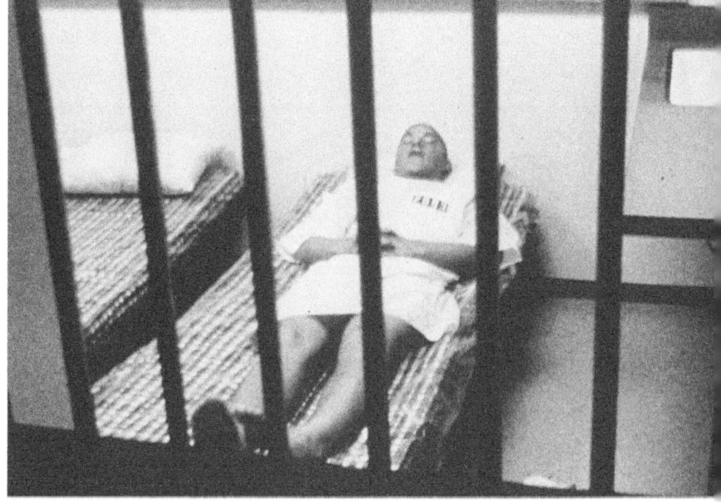

Philip Zimbardo and his colleagues randomly assigned students to play the role of prisoner or guard in a mock prison. The students assumed these roles all too well.

The researchers planned to observe the students for 2 weeks to see whether they began to act like real prison guards and prisoners. As it turned out, the students quickly assumed these roles—so much so that the researchers ended the experiment after only 6 days. Many of the guards became quite abusive, thinking of creative ways of verbally harassing and humiliating the prisoners. The prisoners became passive, helpless, and withdrawn. Some prisoners, in fact, became so anxious and depressed that they had to be released from the study earlier than the others. Remember, everyone knew that they were in a psychology experiment and that the prison was only make-believe. The roles of guard and prisoner were so compelling and powerful, however, that this simple truth was often overlooked. People got so far into their roles that their personal identities and sense of decency somehow got lost.

Prison Abuse at Abu Ghraib Does this sound familiar? In 2004, it came to light that American military guards had been abusing prisoners in Abu Ghraib, a prison in Iraq (Hersch, 2004). A report written by U.S. Major General Taguba, who investigated the claims of abuse, documented numerous cases of physical beatings, sexual abuse, and psychological humiliation. The American public was shocked by pictures of U.S. soldiers smiling as they stood in front of naked Iraqi prisoners, as if they were posing in front of local landmarks for the folks back home.

Did a few bad apples happen to end up in the unit guarding the prisoners? Not according to Phillip Zimbardo (2007), who has analyzed the similarities between the abuse at Abu Ghraib and the prison study he conducted 30 years earlier. "What's bad is the barrel," Zimbardo argued. "The barrel is the barrel I created by my prison—and we put good boys in, just as in this Iraqi prison. And the barrel corrupts. It's the barrel of the evil of prisons—with secrecy, with no accountability—which gives people permission to do things they ordinarily would not" (quoted in O'Brien, 2004). The military guards at Abu Ghraib were under tremendous stress, had received scant training, had little supervision, and were asked to set their own rules for interrogation. It was easy to dehumanize the prisoners, given that the guards didn't speak their language and that many of the prisoners were naked (due to a shortage of prison suits). "You start looking at these people as less than human," said one guard, "and you start doing things to 'em that you would never dream of" (Zimbardo, 2007, p. 352).

Watch on **MyPsychLab**
To learn more about the Stanford prison experiment, watch the MyPsychLab video ***The Power of the Situation: Phil Zimbardo.***

This is not to say that the soldiers should be excused for their actions. The abuse came to light when 24-year-old Joe Darby, an Army Reservist at Abu Ghraib, reported what was happening, and, as in Zimbardo's study, there were some guards who treated the prisoners well. Thus, not everyone was caught in the web of their social roles, unable to resist. But as much as we would like to think that we would be one of these heroes, the lesson from the Zimbardo prison study—and Milgram's studies of obedience, discussed in Chapter 8—is that most of us would not resist the social influences in these powerful situations and would perhaps perform acts we thought we were incapable of.

Social roles can be very helpful, because people know what to expect from each other. However, people can get too far into a role that their personal identities and personalities get lost, sometimes with tragic consequences. Some people think that the abuse at the Abu Ghraib prison in Iraq was due to soldiers getting too far into their roles as prison guards.

Gender Roles Of course, not all social roles involve such extreme behavior. But even in everyday life, roles can be problematic when they are arbitrary or unfair. All societies, for example, have expectations about how people who occupy the roles of women and men should behave. In many cultures, women are expected to assume the role of wife and mother and have limited opportunities to pursue other careers. In the United States and other countries, these expectations are changing, and women have more opportunities than ever before. Conflict can result, however, when expectations change for some roles but not for others assumed by the same person. In India, for example, women were traditionally permitted to take only the roles of wife, mother, agricultural laborer, and domestic worker. As their rights have improved, women are increasingly working at other professions. At home, though, many husbands still expect their wives to assume the traditional role of child rearer and household manager, even if their wives have other careers. Conflict results, because many women are expected to "do it all"—maintain a career, raise the children, clean the house, and attend to their husband's needs (Brislin, 1993; Wax, 2008). Such conflicts are not limited to India; many American readers will find this kind of role conflict all too familiar (Eagly & Diekman, 2003; Kite, Deaux, & Haines, 2008; Marks, Lam, & McHale, 2009; Rudman, 1998).

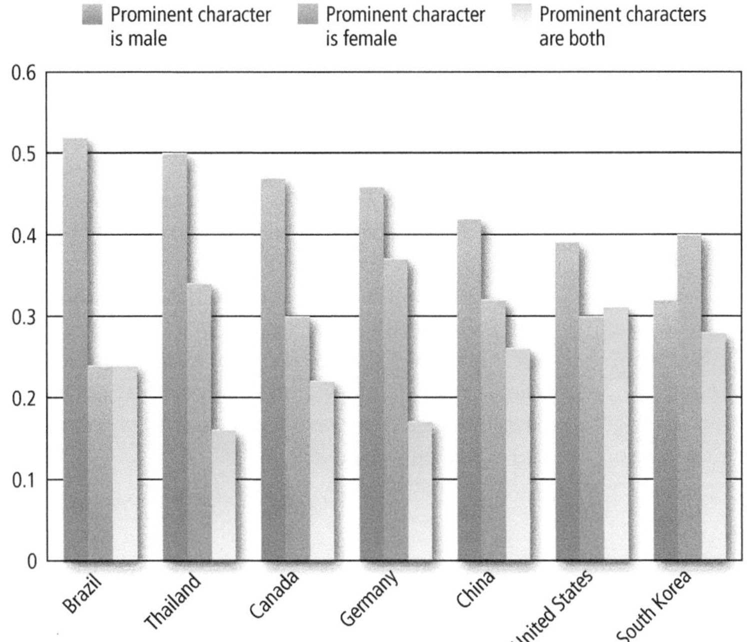

FIGURE 9.1

Percentage of Prominent Characters in Television Commercials Who Were Men, Women, or Both Men and Women

Researchers examined television commercials that were broadcast in seven countries and coded the gender of the prominent characters (the ones who were in the foreground demonstrating or commenting on the product being advertised). This figure shows, for each country, the percentage of the prominent characters who were men, women, or both men and women.

(Based on data in Paek, Nelson, & Vilela, 2011)

Gender roles vary from country to country and change over time within countries. To look at cultural differences in gender roles, researchers examined the content of over 2,600 television commercials that were broadcast in the year 2002 in seven countries: Brazil, Canada, China, Germany, South Korea, Thailand, and the United States (Paek, Nelson, & Vilela, 2011). They coded the gender of the prominent characters in the commercials, namely the people who were in the foreground demonstrating or commenting on the product being advertised. As seen in Figure 9.1, the gender of the main characters in commercials varied widely by country. In Brazil, the prominent characters were much more likely to be male than female, whereas in the United States and South Korea, there was much less of a gender difference. South Korea was the only country in which women were more likely than men to be the prominent character. The authors of the study point out that South Korean women have made substantial economic advances in recent years; however, they also note that even when women are shown prominently in South Korean television ads, they are much more likely than men to be shown in the role of homemaker.

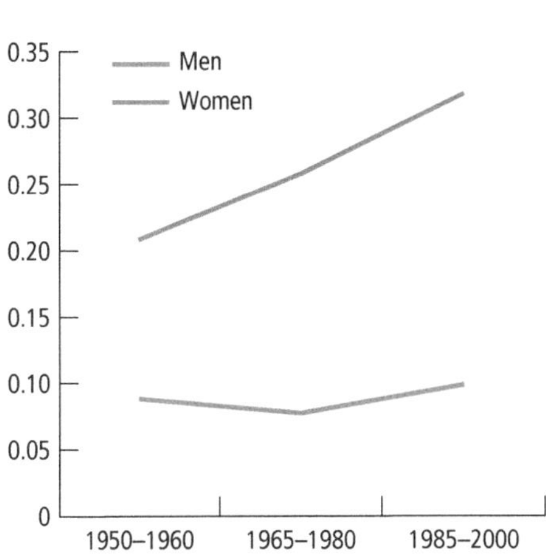

FIGURE 9.2

Percentage of Ads Showing Women Versus Men in a Subordinate Role, by Time Period

Researchers analyzed advertisements that appeared in U.S. magazines from 1950 to 2000 and coded the percentage of ads in each year that showed women in a subordinate role versus men in a subordinate role (such as showing deference to someone or receiving guidance from another person). This figure shows the percentage of ads in each category for three different time periods.

(Based on data in Mager & Helgeson, 2011)

In the United States, gender roles have changed a lot over the past several decades. Women did not achieve the right to vote until 1920. In 1950, about a third of women had a job outside the home; by 1998, 60% did. In 1965, the United States Supreme Court struck down the last state law that prohibited the use of contraceptives by married couples. In 1976, Nebraska was the first state to pass a law making it illegal for a man to rape his wife. In 2009, women held about half of the nation's jobs (Rampell, 2009). But an analysis of magazine advertisements that appeared in U.S. magazines from 1950 to 2000 suggests that we have a ways to go (Mager & Helgeson, 2011). These researchers coded the percentage of ads in each year that showed women in a subordinate role versus men in a subordinate role, such as showing deference to someone or receiving guidance from another person. As seen in Figure 9.2, women were far more likely than men to be shown in a subordinate role. Perhaps more surprisingly, the percentage of times that women were shown this way has actually increased over time. Advertisements are but one small peek into a culture, of course, and as we noted, there are many ways in which women have made advances in the United States. But the content analysis of advertisements does suggest that women continue to be portrayed in more-subordinate roles than are men.

TRY IT! What Happens When You Violate a Role?

Pick a behavior that is part of the role for your gender in your culture, and deliberately violate it. For example, if you are male in the United States, you might decide to put on makeup or carry a purse to your next class. If you are female, you might wear a jacket and tie to a party. Keep a journal describing how others react to you. More than likely, you will encounter a good deal of social disapproval, such as people staring at you or questioning your behavior. For this reason, you want to avoid role violations that are too extreme.

The social pressure that is brought to bear on people who do not conform to their roles explains why it can be so difficult to break out of the roles to which we are assigned, even when they are arbitrary. Of course, there is safety in numbers; when enough people violate role expectations, others do not act nearly as negatively, and the roles begin to change. For example, it is now much more acceptable for men to wear earrings than it was 20 years ago. To illustrate this safety in numbers, enlist the help of several same-sex friends and violate the same role expectation together. Again, note carefully how people react to you. Did you encounter more or less social disapproval in the group than you did as an individual?

Does all of this matter, psychologically speaking? Well, one study found that the status of women in American society was related to how assertive women considered themselves to be (Twenge, 2001). During the period of 1931 to 1945, women's status increased; they earned college degrees and worked outside the home in increasing numbers. During this same time period, women's ratings of their own assertiveness increased. Between the years 1946 and 1967, however, the stay-at-home mom became the norm. Women increasingly dropped out of the workforce and fewer women went to college. During this time period, women's ratings of their own assertiveness dropped. Between 1968 and 1993, women's status improved again as the feminist movement took hold in the United States; by the early 1990s, for example, women were again earning more college degrees than men. And wouldn't you know it, women's ratings of their own assertiveness reversed course during this time period, increasing again. This research suggests that the roles that people assume in groups, and in society at large, are powerful determinants of their feelings, behavior, and personality (Eagly & Steffen, 2000; Eagly, Diekman, Johannesen-Schmidt, & Koenig, 2004). The Try It! exercise on this page describes a way you can experience this for yourself.

Group Cohesiveness Another important aspect of group composition is how cohesive the group is. The qualities of a group that bind members together and promote mutual liking are known as **group cohesiveness** (Dion, 2000; Friedkin, 2004; Hogg, 1993; Holtz, 2004). If a group has formed primarily for social reasons, such as a group of friends who like to go to the movies together on weekends, then, the more cohesive the group is, the better. This is pretty obvious; would you rather spend your free time with a bunch of people who don't care much for each other or a tight-knit bunch of people who feel committed to you and the other members of the group? As might be expected, the more cohesive a group is, the more its members are likely to stay in the group, take part in group activities, and try to recruit new like-minded members (Levine & Moreland, 1998; Pickett, Silver, & Brewer, 2002; Sprink & Carron, 1994).

If the function of the group is to work together and solve problems, however—as it is for a military unit or sales team at a company—then the story is not quite so simple. Doing well on a task causes a group to become more cohesive (Mullen & Cooper, 1994), but is the reverse true? Does cohesiveness cause a group to perform well? It does if the task requires close cooperation between the group members, such as the case of a football team executing a difficult play or a military unit carrying out a complicated maneuver (Gully, Devine, & Whitney, 1995). Sometimes, however, cohesiveness can get in the way of optimal performance if maintaining good relations among group members becomes more important than finding good solutions to a problem. Is it possible, for example, that the cohesiveness felt by President Bush and his advisers got in the way of clear thinking about whether to invade Iraq? We will return to this question later in the chapter, when we discuss group decision making.

Group Cohesiveness
Qualities of a group that bind members together and promote liking between members.

Individual Behavior in a Group Setting

Do you act differently when other people are around? Simply being in the presence of other people can have a variety of interesting effects on our behavior. We will begin by looking at how a group affects your performance on something with which you are very familiar—taking a test in a class.

Social Facilitation: When the Presence of Others Energizes Us

Mere social contact begets . . . a stimulation of the animal spirit that heightens the efficiency of each individual workman.

—KARL MARX, *DAS KAPITAL*, 1867

It is time for the final exam in your psychology class. You have spent countless hours studying the material, and you feel ready. When you arrive, you see that the exam is scheduled in a tiny room already packed with students. You squeeze into an empty desk, elbow to elbow with your classmates. The professor arrives and says that if any students are bothered by the close quarters, they can take the test by themselves in one of several smaller rooms down the hall. What should you do?

The question is whether being with other people will affect your performance (Geen, 1989; Guerin, 1993; Zajonc, 1965). The presence of others can mean one of two things: (1) performing a task with coworkers who are doing the same thing you are or (2) performing a task in front of an audience that is not doing anything but observing you. Note that the question is a basic one about the mere presence of other people, even if they are not part of a group that is interacting. Does the simple fact that other people are around make a difference, even if you never speak or interact with them in any way?

To answer this question, we need to talk about insects—cockroaches, in fact. Believe it or not, a classic study using cockroaches as research participants suggests an answer to the question of how you should take your psychology test. Robert Zajonc and his colleagues (Zajonc, Heingartner, & Herman, 1969) built a contraption to see how a cockroach's behavior was influenced by the presence of its peers. The researchers placed a bright light (which cockroaches dislike) at the end of a runway and timed how long it took a roach to escape the light by running to the other end, where it could scurry into a darkened box (see the left side of Figure 9.3). The question was, did roaches perform this simple feat faster when they were by themselves or when they were in the presence of other cockroaches?

You might be wondering how the researchers managed to persuade other cockroaches to be spectators. They simply placed other roaches in clear plastic boxes next to the runway. These roaches were in the bleachers, so to speak, observing the solitary cockroach do its thing (see Figure 9.3). As predicted, the individual cockroaches performed the task faster when other roaches were there than when they were by themselves.

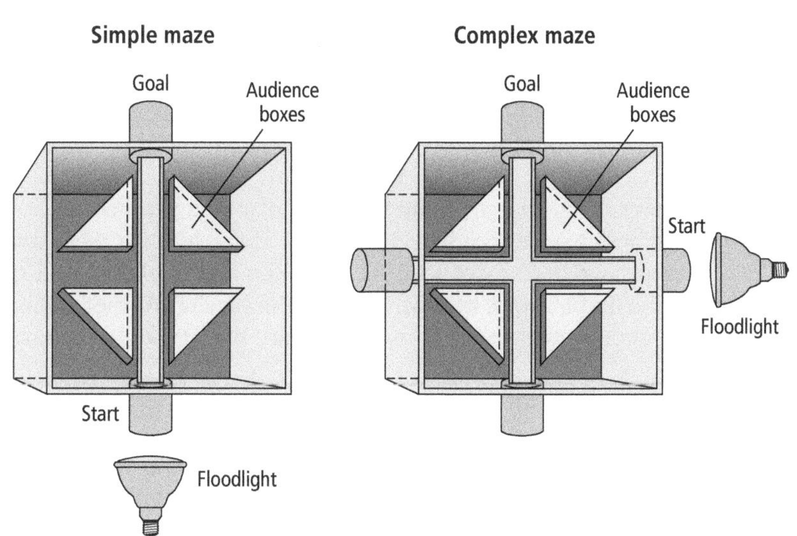

FIGURE 9.3

Cockroaches and Social Facilitation

In the maze on the left, cockroaches had a simple task: to go from the starting point down the runway to the darkened box. They performed this feat faster when other roaches were watching than when they were alone. In the maze on the right, the cockroaches had a more difficult task. It took them longer to solve this maze when other roaches were watching than when they were alone.

(Based on data in Zajonc, Heingartner, & Herman, 1969)

Research on social facilitation finds that people do better on a well-learned task when in the presence of others than when they are alone. If students have studied hard and know the material well, they might be better off taking an exam in a room with lots of other people.

We would not give advice on how you should take your psychology test based on one study that used cockroaches. But the story does not end here. Dozens of studies have been done on the effects of the mere presence of other people, involving human beings as well as other species such as ants and birds (e.g., Aiello & Douthitt, 2001; Rajecki, Kidd, & Ivins, 1976; Sharma et al., 2010). The findings of these studies are remarkably consistent: As long as the task is a relatively simple, well-learned one—as escaping a light is for cockroaches—the mere presence of others improves performance.

Simple Versus Difficult Tasks Before concluding that you should stay in the crowded classroom to take your exam, we need to consider a different set of findings. Remember that we said the presence of others enhances performance on *simple, well-learned* tasks, as escaping a light is for a cockroach. What happens when we give people a more difficult task to do and place them in the presence of others? To find out, Zajonc and his colleagues (1969) included another condition in the cockroach experiment. This time, the cockroaches had to solve a maze that had several runways, only one of which led to the darkened box (see the right side of Figure 9.3). When working on this more difficult task, the opposite pattern of results occurred: The roaches took *longer* to solve it when other roaches were present than when they were alone. Many other studies have also found that people and animals do worse in the presence of others when the task is difficult (e.g., Bond & Titus, 1983; Geen, 1989).

Arousal and the Dominant Response In an influential article, Robert Zajonc (1965) offered an elegant theoretical explanation for why the presence of others facilitates a well-learned response but inhibits a less practiced or new response. The presence of others increases physiological arousal (i.e., our bodies become more energized). When such arousal exists, it is easier to perform a dominant response (e.g., something we're good at) but harder to do something complex or learn something new. Consider, for example, a behavior that is second nature to you, such as riding a bicycle or writing your name. Arousal caused by the presence of other people watching you should make it even easier to perform these well-learned tasks. But let's say you have to do something more complex, such as learning a new sport or working on a difficult math problem. Now arousal will lead you to feel flustered and do less well than if you were alone (Schmitt et al., 1986). This phenomenon became known as **social facilitation**, which is the tendency for people to do better on simple tasks and worse on complex tasks when they are in the presence of others and their individual performance can be evaluated.

Why the Presence of Others Causes Arousal Why does the presence of others lead to arousal? Researchers have developed three theories to explain the role of arousal in social facilitation: Other people cause us to become particularly alert and vigilant, they make us apprehensive about how we're being evaluated, and they distract us from the task at hand.

The first explanation suggests that the presence of other people makes us more alert. When we are by ourselves reading a book, we don't have to pay attention to anything but the book; we don't have to worry that the lamp will ask us a question. When someone else is in the room, however, we have to be alert to the possibility that he or she will do something that requires us to respond. Because other people are less predictable than lamps, we are in a state of greater alertness in their presence. This alertness, or vigilance, causes mild arousal. The beauty of this explanation (the one preferred by Zajonc, 1980) is that it explains both the animal and the human studies. A solitary cockroach need not worry about what the cockroach in the next room is doing; however, it needs to be alert when in the presence of another member of its species—and the same goes for human beings.

Social Facilitation

The tendency for people to do better on simple tasks and worse on complex tasks when they are in the presence of others and their individual performance can be evaluated.

The second explanation focuses on the fact that people are not cockroaches and are often concerned about how other people are evaluating them. When other people can see how you are doing, the stakes are raised: You feel as if the other people are evaluating you and will feel embarrassed if you do poorly and pleased if you do well. This concern about being judged, called *evaluation apprehension*, can cause mild arousal. According to this view, then, it is not the mere presence of others but the presence of others who are evaluating us that causes arousal and subsequent social facilitation (Blascovich et al., 1999; Bond, Atoum, & Van Leeuwen, 1996; Muller & Butera, 2007; Seta & Seta, 1995).

The third explanation centers on how distracting other people can be (Baron, 1986; Muller, Atzeni, & Fabrizio, 2004). It is similar to Robert Zajonc's (1980) notion that we need to be alert when in the presence of others, except that it focuses on the idea that any source of distraction—be it the presence of other people or noise from the party going on in the apartment upstairs—will put us in a state of conflict because it is difficult to pay attention to two things at the same time. This divided attention produces arousal, as any parent knows who has ever tried to read the newspaper while his or her 2-year-old clamors for attention. Consistent with this interpretation, nonsocial sources of distraction, such as a flashing light, cause the same kinds of social facilitation effects as the presence of other people (Baron, 1986).

We have summarized research on social facilitation in the top half of Figure 9.4 (we will discuss the bottom half in a moment). This figure illustrates that there is more than one reason why the presence of other people is arousing. The consequences of this arousal, however, are the same: When people are around other people, they do better on tasks that are simple and well learned, but they do worse on tasks that are complex and require them to learn something new.

Where, then, should you take your psychology exam? We recommend that you stay with your classmates, assuming you know the material well, so that it is relatively simple for you to recall it. The arousal produced by being elbow to elbow with your classmates should improve your performance. But when you study for an exam—that is, when

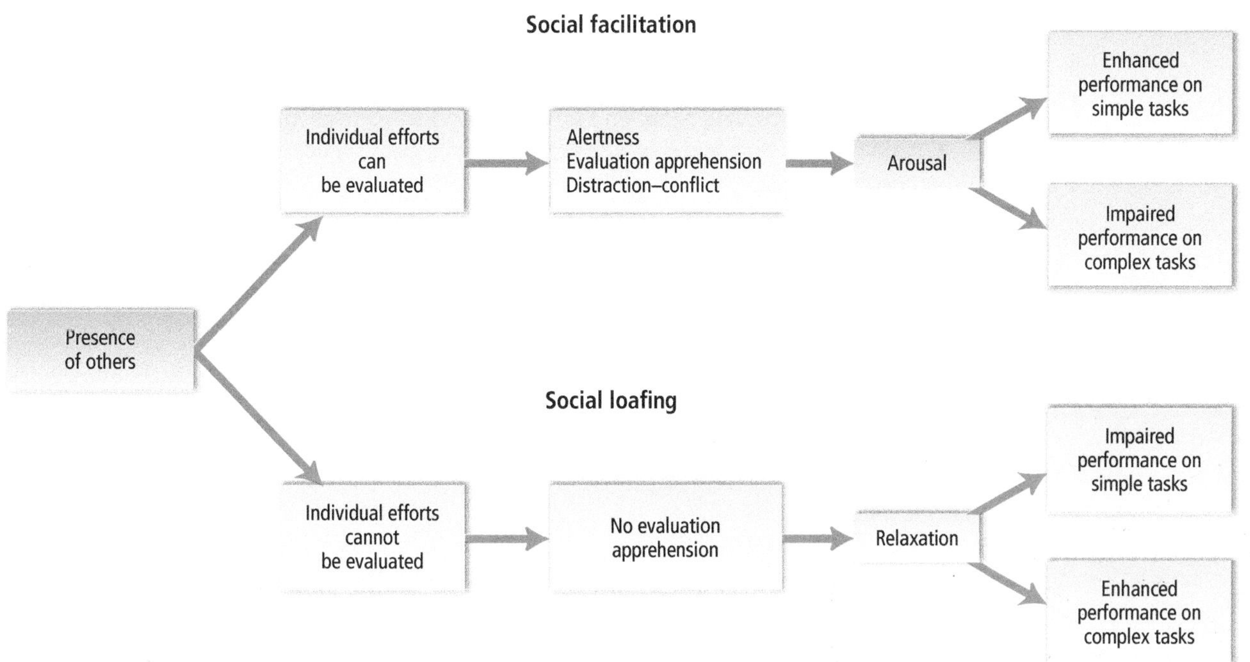

FIGURE 9.4

Social Facilitation and Social Loafing

The presence of others can lead to social facilitation or social loafing. The important variables that distinguish the two are evaluation, arousal, and the complexity of the tasks.

you learn new material—you should do so by yourself, away from other people. In this situation, the arousal caused by others will make it more difficult to concentrate. And, oh yes, it is not only the presence of real people who can influence our behavior—so can the presence of our favorite TV characters. In a recent study, college students performed a simple or complex task while a picture of their favorite TV character or some other TV character was displayed on a computer screen. When the TV character was people's favorite—such as George from *Grey's Anatomy*—it was as if a real person was in the room: People did better on the simple task but worse on the complex task. When the TV character wasn't people's favorite, their performance was unaffected (Gardner & Knowles, 2008).

Simulate on **MyPsychLab**
To learn more about how the presence of others affects performance, try the MyPsychLab simulation ***Social Facilitation.***

Social Loafing: When the Presence of Others Relaxes Us

When you take your psychology exam, your individual efforts will be evaluated (you will be graded on the test). This is typical of the condition for research on social facilitation we have reviewed: People are working on something (either alone or in the presence of others), and their individual efforts are easily observed and evaluated. Often when people are in the presence of others, however, their individual efforts cannot be distinguished from those of the people around them. Such is the case when you clap after a concert (no one can tell how loudly you are clapping) or when you play an instrument in a marching band (your instrument blends in with all the others).

Which of us . . . is to do the hard and dirty work for the rest—and for what pay?

—John Ruskin

These situations are the opposite of the kinds of social facilitation settings we have just considered. In social facilitation, the presence of others puts the spotlight on you, making you aroused. But if being with other people means we can merge into a group, becoming less noticeable than when we are alone, we should become relaxed. Because no one can tell how well we are doing, we should feel less evaluation apprehension and thus be less willing to try our hardest. What happens then? Will this relaxation produced by becoming lost in the crowd lead to better or worse performance? Again, the answer depends on whether we are working on a simple or a complex task.

Let's first consider simple tasks, such as trying to pull as hard as you can on a rope. The question of how working with others would influence performance on such a task was first studied in the 1880s by a French agricultural engineer, Max Ringelmann (1913). He found that when a group of men pulled on a rope, each individual exerted less effort than when he did it alone. A century later, social psychologists Bibb Latané, Kipling Williams, and Stephen Harkins (1979) called this **social loafing**, which is the tendency for people to relax when they are in the presence of others and their individual performance cannot be evaluated, such that they do worse on simple tasks but better on complex tasks. Social loafing in groups has since been found on a variety of simple tasks, such as clapping your hands, cheering loudly, and thinking of as many uses for an object as you can (Karau & Williams, 2001; Shepperd & Taylor, 1999).

What about complex tasks? Recall that when performance in a group cannot be identified, people become more relaxed. Recall also our earlier discussion of the effects of arousal on performance: Arousal enhances performance on simple tasks but impairs performance on complex tasks. By the same reasoning, becoming relaxed impairs performance on simple tasks—as we have just seen—but improves performance on complex tasks (Jackson & Williams, 1985). This process is illustrated on the bottom part of Figure 9.4.

Social Loafing

The tendency for people to relax when they are in the presence of others and their individual performance cannot be evaluated, such that they do worse on simple tasks but better on complex tasks.

Gender and Cultural Differences in Social Loafing: Who Slacks Off the Most?

Jane and John are working with several classmates on a class project, and no one can assess their individual contributions. Who is more likely to slack off and let the other do most of the work: John or Jane? If you said John, you are probably right. In a review of more than 150 studies of social loafing, the tendency to loaf was found to be stronger in men than in women (Karau & Williams, 1993). As discussed in Chapter 5, women tend to be higher than men in *relational interdependence*, which is the tendency to focus on and care about personal relationships with other individuals. Perhaps it is this focus that makes women less likely to engage in social loafing when in groups (Eagly, 1987; Wood, 1987).

Research has also found that the tendency to loaf is stronger in Western cultures than Asian cultures, which may be due to the different self-definitions prevalent in these cultures (Karau & Williams, 1993). Asians are more likely to have an *interdependent view of the self*, which is a way of defining oneself in terms of relationships to other people (see Chapter 5). This self-definition may reduce the tendency toward social loafing when in groups. We should not, however, exaggerate these gender and cultural differences. Women and members of Asian cultures do engage in social loafing when in groups; they are just less likely to do so than men or members of Western cultures (Chang & Chen, 1995; Hong, Wyer, & Fong, 2008).

The robes and hoods of the Ku Klux Klan cloak its members in anonymity; their violent behavior is consistent with research on deindividuation.

To summarize, you need to know two things to predict whether the presence of others will help or hinder your performance: whether your individual efforts can be evaluated and whether the task is simple or complex. If your performance can be evaluated, the presence of others will make you alert and aroused. This will lead to social facilitation effects, where people do better on simple tasks but worse on complex tasks (see the top of Figure 9.4). If your efforts cannot be evaluated (i.e., you are one cog in a machine), you are likely to become more relaxed. This leads to social loafing effects, where people do worse on simple tasks but better on complex ones (see the bottom of Figure 9.4).

These findings have numerous implications for the way in which groups should be organized. On the one hand, if you are a manager who wants your employees to work on a relatively simple problem, a little evaluation apprehension is not such a bad thing—it should improve performance. You shouldn't place your employees in groups where their individual performance cannot be observed, because social loafing (lowered performance on simple tasks) is likely to result. On the other hand, if you want your employees to work on a difficult, complex task, then lowering their evaluation apprehension—by placing them in groups in which their individual performance cannot be observed—is likely to result in better performance.

Deindividuation: Getting Lost in the Crowd

If you are going to make people more anonymous, you should be aware of other consequences of being a face in the crowd. So far, we have discussed the ways in which a group affects how hard people work and how successfully they learn new things. Being in a group can also cause **deindividuation**, which is the loosening of normal constraints on behavior when people can't be identified (such as when they are in a crowd; Lea, Spears, & de Groot, 2001). In other words, getting lost in a crowd can lead to an unleashing of behaviors that we would never dream of doing by ourselves. Throughout history, there have been many examples of groups of people committing horrendous acts that no individual would do on his or her own. The massacre at My Lai during the Vietnam War, when a group of American soldiers systematically murdered hundreds of defenseless women, children, and elderly men (see Chapter 8), was one such instance. In the summer of 2011, mobs of people throughout England committed acts of looting, arson, and violence. In the United States, hysterical fans at rock concerts have trampled each other to death. And the United States has a shameful history of whites—often cloaked in the anonymity of white robes—lynching African Americans.

Deindividuation

The loosening of normal constraints on behavior when people can't be identified (such as when they are in a crowd).

Brian Mullen (1986) content-analyzed newspaper accounts of 60 lynchings committed in the United States between 1899 and 1946 and discovered an interesting fact: The more people there were in the mob, the greater the savagery and viciousness with which they killed their victims. Similarly, Robert Watson (1973) studied 24 cultures and found that warriors who hid their identities before going into battle—for example, by using face and body paint—were significantly more likely to kill, torture, or mutilate captive prisoners than were warriors who did not hide their identities.

Deindividuation Makes People Feel Less Accountable Why does deindividuation lead to impulsive (and often violent) acts? One reason is that people feel less accountable for their actions because it reduces the likelihood that any individual will be singled out and blamed (Diener, 1980; Postmes & Spears, 1998; Zimbardo, 1970). In Harper Lee's novel *To Kill a Mockingbird*, for example, a mob of white Southerners assembled to lynch Tom Robinson, a black man falsely accused of rape. Here is a classic case of deindividuation: It was night, the men were dressed alike, and it was difficult to tell one from another. But then Scout, the 8-year-old daughter of Robinson's attorney, Atticus, recognized one of the farmers and greeted him by name. She unwittingly performed a brilliant social psychological intervention by increasing the extent to which the mob felt like individuals who were accountable for their actions. And, indeed, the mob disbanded and went home at that point.

Deindividuation Increases Obedience to Group Norms In a meta-analysis of more than 60 studies, researchers found that becoming deindividuated also increases the extent to which people obey the group's norms (Postmes & Spears, 1998). Sometimes the norms of a specific group of which we are a member conflict with the norms of other groups or of society at large. When group members are together and deindividuated, they are more likely to act according to the group norms than the other norms. In *To Kill a Mockingbird*, for example, the norms of the lynch mob were to take the law into their own hands, but clearly these norms conflicted with other rules and laws (e.g., "Thou shalt not kill"). Because of the conditions promoting deindividuation, they were about to act on the group's norms and ignore the others until Scout stepped in and reminded them that they were individuals. Thus, it is not just that deindividuation reduces the likelihood that one person will stand out and be blamed, but also that it increases adherence to the specific group's norms.

If you can keep your head when all about you are losing theirs . . .

—Rudyard Kipling, "If," 1909

Consequently, deindividuation does not always lead to aggressive or antisocial behavior—it depends on what the norm of the group is. Imagine that you are at a rowdy college party at which everyone is dancing wildly to very loud music. To the extent that you feel deindividuated—it is dark, and you are dressed similarly to other people—you are more likely to join the group and let loose on the dance floor. Thus, it is the specific norm of the group that determines whether deindividuation will lead to positive or negative behaviors (Gergen, Gergen, & Barton, 1973; Johnson & Downing, 1979). If the group is angry and the norm is to act violently, deindividuation will make people in the group act aggressively. If we are at a party and the norm is to eat a lot, being deindividuated will increase the likelihood that we will eat the entire bowl of guacamole.

Deindividuation in Cyberspace Have you ever participated in an Internet forum in which people post anonymous comments about some issue or event? If so, you have probably witnessed deindividuation at work, whereby people feel less inhibited about what they write because of their anonymity. In January 2006, the *Washington Post* had to temporarily shut down the blog on its Web site after the site was deluged with postings from angry readers, many of whom wrote obscene or insulting comments.

Before blogs and Internet forums became popular, angry readers could have written letters to the editor or vented their feelings to their coworkers at the watercooler. In both cases, their discourse would have likely been more civil, free of the profanities used by many of the people who posted comments on the *Post*'s blog—in no small part because people are not anonymous in these settings (most newspapers require people to sign letters to the editor). The Internet has provided new ways in which people can communicate with each other anonymously, and just as research on deindividuation predicts, in these settings people often feel free to say things they would never dream of saying if they could be identified (Lee, 2004). There are advantages, of course, to free and open discussion of difficult topics, but the cost seems to be a reduction in common civility, as the editors of the *Post*'s blog discovered.

Group Decisions: Are Two (or More) Heads Better Than One?

Nor is the people's judgement always true: The most may err as grossly as the few.
—John Dryden, *Absalom and Achitophel*, 1682

We have just seen that the presence of other people influences individual behavior in a number of interesting ways. We turn now to one of the major functions of groups: to make decisions. Most important decisions in the world today are made by groups, because it is assumed that groups make better decisions than individuals do. In the American judicial system, many verdicts are determined by groups of individuals (juries), not single individuals (for a discussion of jury decision making, see Social Psychology in Action 3, "Social Psychology and the Law"). The United States Supreme Court is made up of nine justices, not just one member of the judiciary. Similarly, governmental and corporate decisions are often made by groups of people who meet to discuss the issues, and U.S. presidents have a cabinet and the National Security Council to advise them.

Is it true that two (or more) heads are better than one? Most of us assume the answer is yes. A lone individual may be subject to all sorts of whims and biases, whereas several people together can exchange ideas, catch each other's errors, and reach better decisions. We have all taken part in group decisions in which we listened to someone else and thought to ourselves, "Hmm, that's a really good point—I never would have thought of that." In general, groups do better than individuals if they rely on the person with the most expertise and if people are motivated to search for the answer that is best for the entire group and not just for themselves (De Dreu, Nijstad, & van Knippenberg, 2008). Sometimes, though, two or more heads are not better than one—or at least no better than two heads working alone (Hackman & Katz, 2010; Kerr & Tindale, 2004). Several factors can cause groups to make worse decisions than would individuals.

Process Loss: When Group Interactions Inhibit Good Problem Solving

One problem is that a group will do well only if the most talented member can convince the others that he or she is right—which is not always easy, given that many of us bear a strong resemblance to mules when it comes to admitting we are wrong. You undoubtedly know what it's like to try to convince a group to follow your idea, be faced with opposition and disbelief, and then have to sit there and watch the group make the wrong decision. This is called **process loss**, which is any aspect of group interaction that inhibits good problem solving (Hurley & Allen, 2007; Steiner, 1972). Process loss can occur for a number of reasons. Groups might not try hard enough to find out who the most competent member is and instead rely on someone who really doesn't know what he or she is talking about. The most competent member might find it difficult to disagree with everyone else in the group (recall our discussion of normative social pressures in Chapter 8). Other causes of process loss involve communication problems within the group: In some groups, people don't listen to each other; in others, one person is allowed to dominate the discussion while the others tune out (Sorkin, Hays, & West, 2001; Watson et al., 1998).

Failure to Share Unique Information Suppose you are meeting with three other people to decide whether to support a particular candidate for Student Council president. You all know some of the same things about the candidate, such as the fact that she was president of her sophomore class and is an economics major. But each of you has unique information as well. Maybe you are the only one who knows that she was punished for underage drinking in her first-year dorm, whereas one of the other group members is the only one who knows that she volunteers every week at a local homeless shelter. Obviously, the four of you will make the best decision if you share with each other everything you know about the candidate.

But there is a funny thing about groups: They tend to focus on the information they share and ignore facts known to only some members of the group (Stasser & Titus,

Process Loss
Any aspect of group interaction that inhibits good problem solving.

1985; Toma & Butera, 2009; Wittenbaum & Park, 2001). One study, for example, used a situation similar to the one we have just described, in which students decided who among several candidates was most qualified to be Student Council president (Stasser & Titus, 1985). In the shared information condition, groups of four participants were given the same packet of information to read, which indicated that Candidate A was the best choice for office. Not surprisingly, when the groups met to discuss the candidates, almost all of the members chose Candidate A. In the unshared information condition, each participant in the group received a different packet of information. All participants learned that Candidate A had the same four negative qualities, but each learned that Candidate A also had two unique positive qualities—that is, positive qualities that were different from those listed in other participants' packets. Thus, if the four participants shared with each other the information that was in their packets, they would learn that Candidate A had a total of eight positive qualities and four negative qualities. Instead, most of the groups in the unshared information condition never realized that Candidate A had more good than bad qualities, because when they met they focused on the information they shared rather than on the information they did not. As a result, few of these groups chose Candidate A.

Subsequent research has focused on ways to get groups to focus more on unshared information (Campbell & Stasser, 2006; Scholten et al., 2007; Stasser & Birchmeier, 2003). Unshared information is more likely to be brought up later in the discussion, suggesting that group discussions should last long enough to get beyond what everyone already knows (Fraidin, 2004; Larson et al., 1998). It also helps to tell group members not to share what their initial preferences are at the outset of the discussion; if they do, they will focus less on unique, unshared information (Mojzisch & Schulz-Hardt, 2010). Another approach is to assign different group members to specific areas of expertise so that they know that they alone are responsible for certain types of information (Stasser, Stewart, & Wittenbaum, 1995; Stewart & Stasser, 1995).

The only sin which we never forgive in each other is difference of opinion.

—Ralph Waldo Emerson, *Society and Solitude*, 1870

This last lesson has been learned by many couples, who know to rely on each other's memories for different kinds of information. One member of a couple might be responsible for remembering the times of social engagements, whereas the other might be responsible for remembering when to pay the bills (Wegner, Erber, & Raymond, 1991). The combined memory of two people that is more efficient than the memory of either individual is called **transactive memory** (Peltokorpi, 2008; Rajaram & Pereira-Pasarin, 2010; Wegner, 1995). By learning to specialize their memories and knowing what their partner is responsible for, couples often do quite well in remembering important information. The same can be true of groups, if they develop a system whereby different people are responsible for remembering different parts of a task (Ellis, Porter, & Wolverton, 2008; Lewis et al., 2007; Moreland, 1999). In sum, the tendency for groups to fail to share important information known to only some of the members can be overcome if people learn who is responsible for what kinds of information and take the time to discuss these unshared data (Stasser, 2000).

Groupthink: Many Heads, One Mind Earlier we mentioned that group cohesiveness can get in the way of clear thinking and good decision making. Using real-world events, Irving Janis (1972, 1982) developed an influential theory of group decision making that he called **groupthink**, a kind of thinking in which maintaining group cohesiveness and solidarity is more important than considering the facts in a realistic manner. According to Janis's theory, groupthink is most likely to occur when certain preconditions are met, such as when the group is highly cohesive, isolated from contrary opinions, and ruled by a directive leader who makes his or her wishes known. One of his examples was the decision by President John F. Kennedy and his advisers to invade Cuba in 1961. This was during the Cold War, when there were many tensions between the Soviet Union and the United States, and the Communist revolution in Cuba (with the support of the Soviet Union) was seen as an enormous threat. The idea was to land a small force of CIA-trained Cuban exiles on the Cuban coast, who would then instigate and lead a mass uprising against Fidel Castro, the Cuban leader. What looked good on paper to Kennedy and his advisers turned out to be a fiasco. Soon after the invasion was

Transactive Memory

The combined memory of two people that is more efficient than the memory of either individual.

Groupthink

A kind of thinking in which maintaining group cohesiveness and solidarity is more important than considering the facts in a realistic manner.

launched, Castro's forces captured or killed nearly all the U.S.-backed forces. Friendly Latin American countries were outraged that the United States had invaded one of their neighbors, and Cuba became even more closely allied with the Soviet Union. Later, President Kennedy would ask, "How could we have been so stupid?" (Sorenson, 1966).

The reason, according to Janis (1982), was that the decision met many of the symptoms of groupthink. Kennedy and his team were riding high on their close victory in the 1960 election and were a tight-knit, homogeneous group. Because they had not yet made any major policy decisions, they lacked well-developed methods for discussing the issues. Moreover, Kennedy made it clear that he favored the invasion, and he asked the group to consider only details of how it should be executed instead of questioning whether it should proceed at all.

"All those in favor say 'Aye.'" *"Aye."* *"Aye."* *"Aye."* *"Aye."* *"Aye."*

Henry Martin/The New Yorker Collection/ www.cartoonbank.com

When these preconditions of groupthink are met, several symptoms appear (see Figure 9.5). The group begins to feel that it is invulnerable and can do no wrong. People do not voice contrary views (they exercise self-censorship), because they are afraid of ruining the group's high morale or because they fear being criticized by the others. For example, Arthur Schlesinger, one of Kennedy's advisers, reported that he had severe doubts about the Bay of Pigs invasion but did not express these concerns during the discussions, out of a fear that "others would regard it as presumptuous of him, a college professor, to take issue with august heads of major government institutions" (Janis, 1982, p. 32). If anyone does voice a contrary viewpoint, the rest of the group is quick to criticize, pressuring the person to conform to the majority view. This kind of behavior creates an

Antecedents of groupthink	Symptoms of groupthink	Defective decision making
The group is highly cohesive: The group is valued and attractive, and people very much want to be members. **Group isolation:** The group is isolated, protected from hearing alternative viewpoints. **A directive leader:** The leader controls the discussion and makes his or her wishes known. **High stress:** The members perceive threats to the group. **Poor decision-making procedures:** No standard methods to consider alternative viewpoints.	**Illusion of invulnerability:** The group feels it is invincible and can do no wrong. **Belief in the moral correctness of the group:** "God is on our side." **Stereotyped views of out-group:** Opposing sides are viewed in a simplistic, stereotyped manner. **Self-censorship:** People decide not to voice contrary opinions so as not to "rock the boat." **Direct pressure on dissenters to conform:** If people do voice contrary opinions, they are pressured by others to conform to the majority. **Illusion of unanimity:** An illusion is created that everyone agrees—for example, by not calling on people known to disagree. **Mindguards:** Group members protect the leader from contrary viewpoints.	**Incomplete survey of alternatives** **Failure to examine risks of the favored alternative** **Poor information search** **Failure to develop contingency plans**

FIGURE 9.5

Groupthink: Antecedents, Symptoms, and Consequences

Under some conditions, maintaining group cohesiveness and solidarity is more important to a group than considering the facts in a realistic manner (see "Antecedents"). When this happens, certain symptoms of groupthink occur, such as the illusion of invulnerability (see "Symptoms"). These symptoms lead to defective decision making.

(Based on data in Janis & Mann, 1977.)

illusion of unanimity, where it looks as if everyone agrees. On the day the group voted on whether to invade, President Kennedy asked all those present for their opinion—except Arthur Schlesinger.

The perilous state of groupthink causes people to implement an inferior decision-making process. As seen at the far right in Figure 9.5, for example, the group does not consider the full range of alternatives, does not develop contingency plans, and does not adequately consider the risks of its preferred choice. Can you think of other governmental decisions that were plagued by groupthink? Some have suggested that President Bush's decision to invade Iraq in 2003 was such a case. President Bush's former press secretary, Scott McClelland, for example, wrote that once the president made his view known "it was rarely questioned," because "that is what Bush expected and made known to his top advisers" (McClelland, 2008, p. 128). On the other hand, President Bush was not known as a highly directive leader who dominated group discussions. We leave it to future historians to decide whether this important decision resulted from sound decision-making processes or from symptoms of groupthink.

A lot of water has gone over the dam since the theory of groupthink was first proposed, and a number of researchers have put it to the test (Packer, 2009; Tetlock et al., 1992; Turner et al., 2006; Turner, Pratkanis, & Struckman, 2007). The upshot of this research is that defective group decision making may be more common than the original theory assumed. The groupthink theory held that a specific set of conditions had to be met in order for groupthink to occur—namely the antecedents listed on the left side of Figure 9.5 (e.g., the group has to be highly cohesive). It now appears that groupthink can occur even when some of these antecedents are missing. It may be enough for people to identify strongly with the group, have clear norms about what the group is supposed to do, and have low confidence that the group can solve the problem (Baron, 2005; Henningsen et al., 2006). Research has also found, however, that some people are particularly likely to challenge a group decision that is wrong. One study, for example, examined the extent to which bicultural individuals—those who have two cultural backgrounds, as is the case with many first-generation Asian Americans—were willing to challenge a group decision that was incorrect. The study found that the bicultural individuals who identified strongly with one or the other of their cultures were the most likely to conform to the group, even when it was wrong. Interestingly, it was the bicultural individuals who felt the most torn about their identity—who had a foot in two different cultures—that were the *least* likely to conform (i.e., most likely to challenge the group when it was wrong). Having experience with two different cultures, and identifying with both, may make people more immune to group pressure (Mok & Morris, 2010).

Watch on **MyPsychLab**
To learn more about decision making and groupthink, watch the MyPsychLab video ***IT Video: Group Thinking.***

Avoiding the Groupthink Trap A wise leader can take several steps to ensure that his or her group is immune to the groupthink style of decision making (Flowers, 1977; McCauley, 1989; Zimbardo & Andersen, 1993).

- **Remain impartial.** The leader should not take a directive role, but should remain impartial.
- **Seek outside opinions.** The leader should invite outside opinions from people who are not members of the group and who are thus less concerned with maintaining group cohesiveness.
- **Create subgroups.** The leader should divide the group into subgroups that first meet separately and then meet together to discuss their different recommendations.
- **Seek anonymous opinions.** The leader might also take a secret ballot or ask group members to write down their opinions anonymously; doing so would ensure that people give their true opinions, uncensored by a fear of recrimination from the group.

Fortunately, President Kennedy learned from his mistakes with the Bay of Pigs decision, and when he encountered his next major foreign policy decision, the Cuban missile crisis, he took many of these steps to avoid groupthink. When his advisers met to decide what to do about the discovery that the Soviet Union had placed nuclear-tipped missiles in Cuba, pointed towards the United States, Kennedy often absented himself from the group so as not to inhibit discussion. He also brought in outside experts (e.g., Adlai Stevenson) who were not members of the in-group. That Kennedy successfully negotiated the removal of the Soviet missiles was almost certainly due to the improved methods of group decision making he adopted.

CONNECTIONS

Was the Financial Crisis of 2007 a Result of Groupthink?

The concept of groupthink has become widely known in the general culture, and writers and pundits alike have blamed it for many bad decisions. A *New York Times* article, for example, claimed that experts on the Federal Reserve Board should have predicted the financial crisis of 2007, but didn't because they exhibited symptoms of groupthink (Shiller, 2008).

By way of background, the financial crisis that began in 2007 in the United States was so severe that it has been called the Great Recession. Before that point, housing prices were skyrocketing; between 1996 and 2007, the average price of a house in the United States more than doubled. But then interest rates began to rise and home prices started to fall. More and more people couldn't afford to pay their mortgages, and banks foreclosed their properties. Banks themselves began to fail at an alarming rate. Between October of 2007 and March of 2009, the stock market lost over half of its value. Many people lost their jobs; in January of 2007, the unemployment rate was 4.6%, but by October of 2009, it was more than double that.

Why didn't financial experts see all of this coming? Well, according to the article in the *New York Times*, some did, but their voices weren't heeded: "Lots of people were worried about the housing boom and its potential for creating economic disaster. It's just that the Fed did not take them very seriously" (Shiller, 2008, p. BU5). The author suggests that some experts fell prey to groupthink, by buckling under the pressure of majority opinion and not voicing their concerns loudly enough due to self-censorship. He suggests that the chair of the Federal Reserve Board, Alan Greenspan, like other leaders before him, may have underestimated how much dissent there was among his experts because of groupthink processes. Does this claim hold up, based on what we know from research in social psychology?

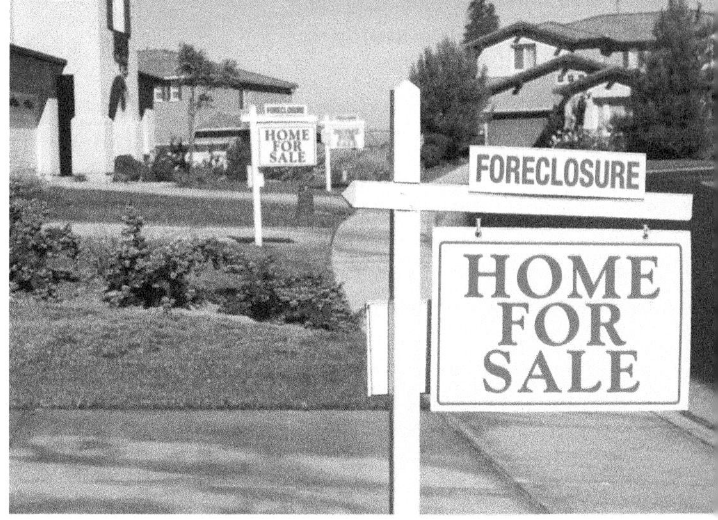

Some have argued that the financial crisis of 2007 was triggered by groupthink among financial experts. Based on what you have read about groupthink, do you think this is true?

Yes and no. To the extent that experts on the Federal Reserve Board failed to voice their concerns and that there was an illusion of unanimity on the Board, some of the symptoms of groupthink were present (see Figure 9.5). But the term *groupthink* is usually reserved for members of highly cohesive groups that exert direct pressure on each other to conform and believe in the moral correctness of the group. Furthermore, the Federal Reserve Board was not solely responsible for the financial crisis. In January of 2011, the Financial Crisis Inquiry Commission concluded that, yes, the Federal Reserve Board deserved some of the blame, but that the crisis was also caused by "dramatic breakdowns of corporate governance, profound lapses in regulatory oversight, and near fatal flaws in our financial system" (Financial Crisis Inquiry Report, 2011, pp. xxvii–xxviii). Thus, there may have been some elements of groupthink leading up to the crisis, but we can't blame it for the entire economic downturn.

Group Polarization: Going to Extremes

Maybe you are willing to grant that groups sometimes make poor decisions. Surely, though, groups will usually make less-risky decisions than a lone individual will. One individual might be willing to bet the ranch on a risky proposition, but if others help make the decision, they will interject reason and moderation. Or will they? The question of whether groups or individuals make more-risky decisions has been examined in numerous studies. Participants are typically given the Choice Dilemmas Questionnaire (CDQ), a series of stories that presents a dilemma for the main character and asks the reader to choose how much probability of success there would have to be before the reader would recommend the risky alternative (Kogan & Wallach, 1964). An example of a CDQ item about a chess player appears in the following Try It! exercise. People choose their answers alone and then meet in a group to discuss the options, arriving at a unanimous group decision for each dilemma.

Many of the initial studies found, surprisingly, that groups make riskier decisions than individuals do. For example, when deciding alone, people said that the chess player should make the risky gambit only if there were at least a 30% chance of success. But after discussing the problem with others in a group, people said that the chess player should go for it even if there were only a 10% chance of success (Wallach, Kogan, & Bem, 1962). Findings such as these have become known as the *risky shift*. But further research has made clear that such shifts are not the full story. It turns out that groups tend to make decisions that are more extreme, in the same direction as the individual's initial predispositions, which happened to be risky in the case of the chess problem. What would happen if people were initially inclined to be conservative? In cases such as these, groups tend to make even more-conservative decisions than individuals do.

Consider this problem: Roger, a young married man with two children, has a secure but low-paying job and no savings. Someone gives him a tip about a stock that will triple in value if the company's new product is successful, but will plummet if the new product fails. Should Roger sell his life insurance policy and invest in the company? Most people recommend a safe course of action here: Roger should buy the stock only if the new product is very certain to succeed. When they talk it over in a group, they become even more conservative, deciding that the new product would have to have a nearly 100% chance of success before they would recommend that Roger buy stock in the company.

The tendency for groups to make decisions that are more extreme than the initial inclination of its members—toward greater risk if people's initial tendency is to be risky

TRY IT! Choice Dilemmas Questionnaire

You'll need four or five friends for this exercise. First, copy the following questionnaire and give it to each of your friends to complete individually, without talking to anyone else. Then bring them all together and ask them to discuss the dilemma and arrive at a unanimous decision. They should try to reach a consensus such that every member of the group agrees at least partly with the final decision. Finally, compare people's initial decisions (made alone) with the group decision. Who made the riskier decisions on average: people deciding by themselves or the group?

The Choice Dilemmas Questionnaire

A low-ranked participant in a national chess tournament, playing an early match against a highly favored opponent, has the choice of attempting or not attempting a deceptive but risky maneuver that might lead to quick victory if it is successful or almost certain defeat if it fails. Indicate the lowest probability of success that you would accept before recommending that the chess player employ the risky move.

_________ 1 chance in 10 of succeeding

_________ 3 chances in 10 of succeeding

_________ 5 chances in 10 of succeeding

_________ 7 chances in 10 of succeeding

_________ 9 chances in 10 of succeeding

_________ I would not recommend taking the chance.

Remember, groups tend to make riskier decisions than individuals on problems such as these. Did you find the same thing? Why or why not? If the group did make a riskier decision, was it due more to the persuasive arguments interpretation discussed in the text, the social comparison interpretation, or both?

(Adapted from Wallach, Kogan, & Bem, 1962)

and toward greater caution if people's initial tendency is to be cautious—is known as **group polarization** (Brown, 1965; Palmer & Loveland, 2008; Rodrigo & Ato, 2002; Teger & Pruitt, 1967).

Group polarization occurs for two main reasons. According to the persuasive arguments interpretation, all individuals bring to the group a set of arguments, some of which other individuals have not considered, supporting their initial recommendation. For example, one person might stress that cashing in the life insurance policy is an unfair risk to Roger's children should he die prematurely. Another person might not have considered this possibility; thus, he or she becomes more conservative as well. A series of studies supports this interpretation of group polarization, whereby each member presents arguments that other members have not considered (Burnstein & Sentis, 1981; Burnstein & Vinokur, 1977).

According to the social comparison interpretation, when people discuss an issue in a group, they first check out how everyone else feels. What does the group value: being risky or being cautious? To be liked, many people then take a position that is similar to everyone else's but a little more extreme. In this way, the individual supports the group's values and also presents himself or herself in a positive light—a person in the vanguard, an impressive thinker. Both the persuasive arguments and the social comparison interpretations of group polarization have received research support (Blaskovich, Ginsburg, & Veach, 1975; Brown, 1986; Isenberg, 1986; Zuber, Crott, & Werner, 1992).

Group Polarization
The tendency for groups to make decisions that are more extreme than the initial inclinations of its members.

Great Person Theory
The idea that certain key personality traits make a person a good leader, regardless of the situation.

Transactional Leaders
Leaders who set clear, short-term goals and reward people who meet them.

Transformational Leaders
Leaders who inspire followers to focus on common, long-term goals.

Leadership in Groups

> *There is properly no history, only biography.*
> —Ralph Waldo Emerson, *Essays, History*, 1841

A critical question we have not yet considered is the role of the leader in group decision making. The question of what makes a great leader has intrigued psychologists, historians, and political scientists for some time (Bass, 1990; Chemers, 2000; Fiedler, 1967; Hogg, 2010; Hollander, 1985; Klenke, 1996; Simonton, 1987). One of the best-known answers to this question is the **great person theory**, which maintains that certain key personality traits make a person a good leader, regardless of the nature of the situation the leader faces.

If the great person theory is true, we ought to be able to isolate the key aspects of personality that make someone a great leader. Is it a combination of intelligence, charisma, and courage? Is it better to be introverted or extroverted? Should we add a dollop of ruthlessness to the mix as well, as Niccolò Machiavelli suggested in 1513 in his famous treatise on leadership, *The Prince*? Or do highly moral people make the best leaders?

Leadership and Personality Numerous studies have found weak relationships between personality and leadership abilities. Compared to nonleaders, for example, leaders tend to be slightly more intelligent, extroverted, driven by the desire for power, charismatic, socially skilled, open to new experiences, confident in their leadership abilities, less neurotic, and have a moderate degree of assertiveness (Ames & Flynn, 2007; Chemers, Watson, & May, 2000; Judge et al., 2002; Van Vugt, 2006). What is most telling, however, is the absence of strong relationships. Surprisingly few personality characteristics correlate strongly with leadership effectiveness, and the relationships that have been found tend to be modest (Avolio, Walumbwa, & Weber, 2009; von Wittich & Antonakis, 2011). For example, Dean Simonton (1987, 2001) gathered information about one hundred personal attributes of all U.S. presidents, such as their family backgrounds, educational experiences, occupations, and personalities. Only three of these variables—height, family size, and the number of books a president published before taking office—correlated with how effective the presidents were in office. Tall presidents, those from small families, and those who have published books are most likely to become effective leaders, as rated by historians. The other 97 characteristics, including personality traits, were not related to leadership effectiveness at all.

What determines whether someone, such as Martin Luther King, Jr., is a great leader? Is it a certain constellation of personality traits, or is it necessary to have the right person in the right situation at the right time?

Leadership Styles Although great leaders may not have specific kinds of personalities, they do appear to adopt specific kinds of leadership styles. **Transactional leaders** set clear, short-term goals and reward people who meet them. **Transformational leaders**, on the other hand, inspire followers to focus on common, long-term goals (Bass, 1998; Burns, 1978). Transactional leaders do a good job of making sure the needs of the organization are met and that things run smoothly. It is transformational leaders, however, who think outside the box, identify important long-term goals, and inspire their followers to exert themselves to meet these goals.

Interestingly, these leadership styles are not closely linked with personality traits; it is not as if people are "born to be" one or the other type of leader (Judge, Colbert, & Ilies, 2004; Nielsen & Cleal, 2011). Further, these styles are not mutually exclusive; in fact, the most effective leader is one who adopts both styles (Judge & Piccolo, 2004). If no one was minding the day-to-day operation of an organization, and people were not being rewarded for meeting short-term objectives, the organization would suffer. At the same time, it is important as well to have a charismatic leader who inspires people to think about long-term objectives.

The Right Person in the Right Situation As you know by now, one of the most important tenets of social psychology is that, to understand social behavior, it is not enough to consider personality traits alone—we must take the social situation into account as well. The inadequacy of the great person theory does not mean that personal characteristics are irrelevant to good leadership. Instead, being good social psychologists, we should consider both the nature of the leader and the situation in which the leading takes place.

A business leader, for example, can be highly successful in some situations but not in others. Consider the late Steve Jobs, who, at age 21, founded the Apple Computer Company with Stephen Wozniak. Jobs was anything but an MBA type of corporate leader. A product of the 1960s' counterculture, he turned to computers only after experimenting with LSD, traveling to India, and living on a communal fruit farm. In the days when there were no personal computers, Jobs's offbeat style was well suited to starting a new industry. Within 5 years, he was the leader of a billion-dollar company. But Jobs's unorthodox style was ill suited to managing a large corporation in a competitive market. Apple's earnings began to suffer, and in 1985 Jobs was forced out. Undeterred, Jobs co-founded Pixar in 1986, the first major company to make computer-generated animation, and sold it to the Disney Company in 2006 for $7.4 billion. And in the 1990s, the Apple company faced some of the same technological challenges it did at its inception, having to revamp the operating system for its Macintosh computers and regain market share. Whom did Apple hire to lead this new challenge? Steve Jobs, of course.

A comprehensive theory of leadership thus needs to focus on the characteristics of the leader, the followers, and the situation. The best-known theory of this type is the **contingency theory of leadership**, which argues that leadership effectiveness depends both on how task-oriented or relationship-oriented the leader is and on the amount of control and influence the leader has over the group (Fiedler, 1967, 1978). There are basically two kinds of leaders, the theory argues: those who are **task-oriented**, concerned more with getting the job done than with workers' feelings and relationships, and those who are **relationship-oriented**, concerned more with workers' feelings and relationships. Task-oriented leaders do well in *high-control work situations*, when the leader has excellent interpersonal relationships with subordinates, his or her position in the company is clearly perceived as powerful, and the work needing to be done by the group is structured and well defined. They also do well in *low-control work situations*, when the leader has poor relationships with subordinates and the work needing to be done is not clearly defined. What about relationship-oriented leaders? They are most effective in *moderate-control work situations*. Under these conditions, the wheels are turning fairly smoothly, but some attention is needed to the squeakiness caused by poor relationships and hurt feelings. The leader who can soothe such feelings will be most successful (see Figure 9.6). The contingency theory of leadership has been supported in studies of numerous types of leaders, including business managers, college administrators, military commanders, and postmasters (Ayman, 2002; Chemers, 2000; Schriesheim, Tepper, & Tetrault, 1994; Van Vugt & DeCremer, 1999).

Contingency Theory of Leadership

The idea that leadership effectiveness depends both on how task-oriented or relationship-oriented the leader is and on the amount of control and influence the leader has over the group.

Task-Oriented Leader

A leader who is concerned more with getting the job done than with workers' feelings and relationships.

Relationship-Oriented Leader

A leader who is concerned more with workers' feelings and relationships.

Gender and Leadership If you've seen an episode of the television show *Mad Men*, which is about an advertising agency in the 1960s, you know that it was not that long ago that businessmen were exactly that: men. Since that time, women started working outside the home in increasing numbers, and, as we noted earlier, the workforce in the United States is now about half women. But are women as likely as men to become leaders in business, politics, and other organizations? Barriers to

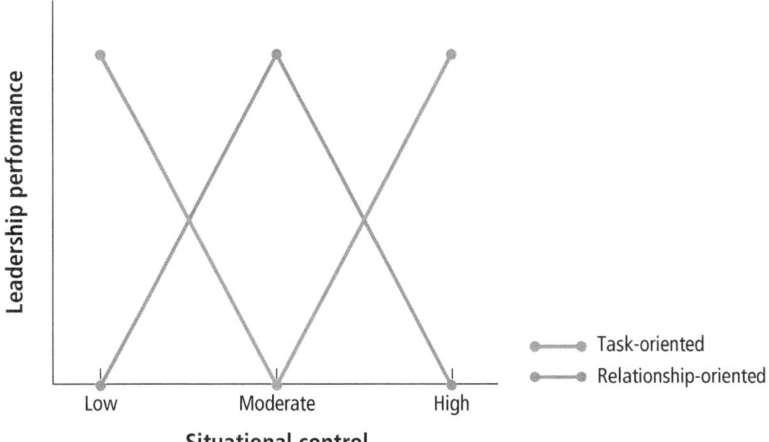

FIGURE 9.6

Fiedler's Contingency Theory of Leadership

According to Fiedler, task-oriented leaders perform best when situational control is high or low, whereas relationship-oriented leaders perform best when situational control is moderate.

advancement by women are breaking down; in 2008, for example, a woman (Hillary Clinton) came close to winning the Democratic nomination for president, and another woman (Sarah Palin) ran for vice president on the Republican ticket for the first time. In 2009, a woman (Nancy Pelosi) became the first female Speaker of the House of Representatives. Unfortunately, the barriers have not completely disappeared. In 2011, only 12 of the CEOs of Fortune 500 companies were women, and the boards of directors of U.S. companies included only 16% women (Catalyst, 2011). Things are not much different elsewhere. That 16% figure is actually among the highest in the world, except for Scandinavian countries (Norway has the highest percentage of women on boards of directors at 40%).

Leadership cannot really be taught. It can only be learned.

—Harold Geneen, 1984

One reason that it is difficult for women to achieve leadership positions is because many people believe that good leaders have *agentic* traits (assertive, controlling, dominant, independent, self-confident), which are traditionally associated with men. In contrast, women are expected to be more *communal* (concerned with the welfare of others, warm, helpful, kind, affectionate). Thus, if women behave in the way they are "supposed" to behave, they are often viewed as having less leadership potential. But if women succeed in attaining a leadership position and act in ways that leaders are expected to act—namely, in agentic, forceful ways—they are criticized for not "acting like a woman should" (Brescoll, Dawson, & Uhlmann, 2010; Eagly, Johannesen-Schmidt, & van Engen, 2003; Eagly & Karau, 2002; Koenig et al., 2011).

Here's another danger that women leaders face: Because they are perceived as being more communal, they are often thought to be better at managing crises, particularly ones that involve interpersonal problems, such as a conflict between high-level managers. That might seem like a good thing—trusting women leaders to solve problems—but it has a downside in which women are more likely to be put in precarious, high-risk positions where it is difficult to succeed. Michelle Ryan and her colleagues have called this a "glass cliff" (Ryan et al. 2008, 2011). Even when women have broken through the "glass ceiling" into top leadership positions, they are more likely than men to be put in charge of units that are in crisis and in which the risk of failure is high. Ryan and her colleagues found this to be true in studies of hiring in real-world companies, as well as in controlled laboratory studies in which people read descriptions of companies and recommended people for leadership positions. Participants were more likely to recommend a woman when an organizational unit was in crisis and a man when the unit was running smoothly—which makes it more likely that women will fail in their leadership positions.

If women seeking leadership roles conform to society's expectations about how they ought to behave, by being warm and communal, they are often perceived as having low leadership potential. If they become leaders and act in ways that leaders are expected to act—namely, in agentic, forceful ways—they are often perceived negatively for not "acting like a woman should."

The better news is that prejudice toward women leaders appears to be lessening over time. In a Gallup poll conducted in 1953, 66% of people said that they preferred a man

I wonder men dare trust themselves with men.
—William Shakespeare, *The Life of Timon of Athens*

as a boss, and only 5% preferred a woman (25% had no preference). In a similar poll conducted in 2011, 32% preferred a man as a boss, 22% preferred a woman, and 46% had no preference. Further, there is some evidence that people are becoming more accepting of women who act in stereotypical "male" ways (Twenge, 1997) and that there is a growing recognition that effective leaders must be able to act in stereotypical female (communal) ways as well as stereotypical male (agentic) ways (Eagly & Karau, 2002).

Culture and Leadership Most research on leadership has been conducted in Western countries; thus, the question arises as to how much the results apply to leadership in other cultures. For this reason, researchers have turned their attention to the kinds of traits people value in leaders, and actual leadership styles, in different cultures (Ayman & Korabik, 2010; Eagly & Chin, 2010; Gelfand, Erez, & Aycan, 2007). One ambitious study examined leadership practices and attitudes toward leaders in 62 different countries. The researchers gave questionnaires to 17,000 managers in 951 organizations in those countries, conducted extensive interviews, convened group discussions, and analyzed the content of media in each country. Not surprisingly, different cultures valued different traits in leaders. For example, autonomous leadership, defined as being independent of one's superiors and keeping one's distance from subordinates and to spend a lot of time working alone, was valued more in most Eastern European countries than it was in most Latin American countries. But there was universal agreement about the value of two leadership qualities: charisma and being team-oriented (House et al., 2004). Questions about cultural differences in leadership are receiving increasing attention, because in a global economy work groups are becoming more diverse and managers from different cultures have increasingly frequent contact.

Conflict and Cooperation

We have already examined how people work together to make decisions; in these situations, group members have a common goal. Often, however, people have incompatible goals, placing them in conflict with each other. This can be true of two individuals, such as romantic partners who disagree about who should clean the kitchen, or two groups, such as a labor union and company management who disagree over wages and working conditions. It can also be true of nations, such as in the long-standing conflict between Israel and its Arab neighbors or between the Shiites, Sunnis, and Kurds in Iraq. The opportunity for interpersonal conflict exists whenever two or more people interact. Sigmund Freud (1930) went so far as to argue that conflict is an inevitable by-product of civilization because the goals and needs of individuals often clash with the goals and needs of their fellow human beings. The nature of conflict, and how it can be resolved, has been the topic of a great deal of social psychological research (Cohen & Insko, 2008; De Dreu, 2010; Deutsch, 1973; Thibaut & Kelley, 1959).

Sometimes people are able to resolve conflicts peacefully, such as a couple that has an amicable divorce. At other times conflicts escalate into rancor and violence. Social psychologists have performed experiments to test ways in which conflict resolution is most likely to occur.

Many conflicts are resolved peacefully, with little rancor. Couples can find a way to resolve their differences in a mutually acceptable manner, and labor disputes are sometimes settled with a handshake. All too often, however, conflict erupts into open hostilities. The divorce rate in the United States is distressingly high. People sometimes resort to violence to resolve their differences, as shown by the high rate of murders in the United States, which has been called "the murder capital of the civilized world." Warfare between nations remains an all-too-common solution to international disputes. Obviously, it is of great importance to find ways of resolving conflicts peacefully.

Social Dilemmas

What is best for an individual is not always best for the group as a whole. Consider a publishing venture by the novelist Stephen King. He wrote two installments of a novel called *The Plant* and posted them on the Internet, asking readers to pay $1 per installment. The deal he offered was simple: If at least 75% of the people who downloaded the installments paid the fee, he would keep writing and posting new installments. If fewer than 75% of the people paid, he would stop writing and people would never get the rest of the novel.

King had devised a classic **social dilemma**, a conflict in which the most beneficial action for an individual will, if chosen by most people, be harmful to everyone (Weber, Kopelman, & Messick, 2004). It was to any individual's financial advantage to download King's novel free of charge and let other people pay. However, if too many people took this approach, everyone would lose, because King said he would stop writing the novel. At first, people acted for the good of all; more than 75% paid for the first installment. As with many other social dilemmas, however, people eventually acted in their own self-interest, to the detriment of all. The number of people who paid for their later installments dropped below 75%, and King stopped posting new ones, saying on his Web site that the novel was "on hiatus."

The Panera restaurant chain has had more success with this approach. In 2010 they began opening Panera Cares restaurants, which look and operate like other Paneras except for one thing: People aren't required to pay anything if they don't want to. There are suggested prices for all menu items, but customers are allowed to pay whatever they want. The CEO and founder of the restaurant chain, Ronald Shaich, had a vision in which people in real need could come get a good meal and pay whatever they could afford; the costs would be offset, he hoped, by customers who could afford to pay more than the suggested prices. So far it's working. At the first three Panera Cares restaurants to open—in St. Louis, Detroit, and Portland—about three in five people pay the suggested prices, one in five pays less, and one in five pays more. Those who pay less are usually people who couldn't otherwise afford to eat out, such as a teacher who was laid off after 25 years and low-income families who come in to celebrate a birthday. True, some people take advantage of the system, such as three college students who paid $3 for a $40 meal. But enough people pay more than the suggested price to offset those who pay less, and the three stores are self-sustaining (Salter, 2011). What determines how people respond in social dilemmas such as these? Social psychologists have attempted to find out by studying these conflicts experimentally, testing both their causes and resolutions in the laboratory.

One of the most common ways of studying social dilemmas in the laboratory is with a game called "the prisoner's dilemma." In each trial, two players have to choose one of two options without knowing what the other player will choose. The number of points they win depends on the options chosen by both people. Suppose that you were playing the game with a friend. As shown in the following Try It! exercise, you have to choose Option X or Option Y without knowing which option your friend will choose. Your payoff—the amount of money you win or lose—depends on the choices of both you and your friend. For example, if both you and your friend choose Option X, you both win $3. If, however, you choose Option Y and your friend chooses Option X, you win $6 and your friend loses $6. Which option would you choose?

Many people begin by choosing Option Y. At worst you will lose $1, and at best you will win the highest possible amount, $6. Choosing Option X raises the possibility that both sides will win some money, but this is also a risky choice. If your partner chooses Y while you choose X, you stand to lose a great deal. Because people often do not know how much they can trust their partners, Option Y frequently seems like the safest choice (Rapoport & Chammah, 1965). The rub is that both players will probably think this way, ensuring that both sides lose (see the lower right-hand corner of the table in the Try It! exercise).

People's actions in these games seem to mirror many conflicts in everyday life. To find a solution desirable to both parties, people must trust each other. Often they do not, and this lack of trust leads to an escalating series of competitive moves so that in the end no one wins (Insko & Schopler, 1998; Kelley & Thibaut, 1978; Lount et al., 2008). Two countries locked in an arms race, for example, may feel that they cannot afford to disarm, out of fear that the other side will take advantage of their weakened position. The result is that both sides add furiously to their stockpile of weapons, neither gaining superiority over the other and both spending money they could use to solve domestic problems (Deutsch, 1973). Such an escalation of conflict is also seen all too often among couples who are divorcing. Sometimes the goal seems more to hurt the other person than to further one's own needs (or the children's). In the end, both suffer because, metaphorically speaking, they both choose Option Y too often.

Social Dilemma

A conflict in which the most beneficial action for an individual will, if chosen by most people, have harmful effects on everyone.

TRY IT! The Prisoner's Dilemma

YOUR FRIEND'S OPTIONS	Your Options: OPTION X	OPTION Y
Option X	You win $3 Your friend wins $3	You win $6 Your friend loses $6
Option Y	You lose $6 Your friend wins $6	You lose $1 Your friend loses $1

Play this version of the prisoner's dilemma game with a friend. First, show the table to the friend, and explain how the game works: On each trial of the game, you and your friend can choose Option X or Option Y, without knowing what the other will choose. You should each write your choice on folded pieces of paper that are opened at the same time. The numbers in the table represent imaginary money that you and your friend win or lose on each trial. For example, if you choose Option X on the first trial and your friend chooses Option Y, you lose an imaginary $6 and your friend wins an imaginary $6. If both of you choose Option Y, you both lose an imaginary $1. Play the game for 10 trials, and keep track of how much each of you wins or loses. Did you and your friend choose the cooperative option (Option X) or the competitive option (Option Y) more often? Why? Did a pattern of trust or mistrust develop over the course of the game?

Increasing Cooperation in the Prisoner's Dilemma Such escalating conflict, though common, is not inevitable. Many studies have found that when people play the prisoner's dilemma game, they will, under certain conditions, adopt the more cooperative response (Option X), ensuring that both sides end up with a positive outcome. Not surprisingly, if people are playing the game with a friend or if they expect to interact with their partner in the future, they are more likely to adopt a cooperative strategy that maximizes both their profits and their partner's (Cohen & Insko, 2008). Also, subtly changing the norms about what kind of behavior is expected can have large effects on how cooperative people are. One study found that simply changing the name of a game from the "Wall Street Game" to the "Community Game" increased the percentage of people who cooperated from 33% to 71% (Liberman, Samuels, & Ross, 2004). Another, conducted with Chinese college students in Hong Kong, found that showing people symbols of Chinese culture before the game (e.g., a Chinese dragon) made people more cooperative, whereas showing people symbols of American culture (e.g., an American flag) made them more competitive (Wong & Hong, 2005).

To increase cooperation, you can also try the **tit-for-tat strategy**, which is a way of encouraging cooperation by at first acting cooperatively but then always responding the way your opponent did (cooperatively or competitively) in the previous trial. This strategy communicates a willingness to cooperate and an unwillingness to sit back and be exploited if the partner does not cooperate. The tit-for-tat strategy is usually successful in getting the other person to respond with the cooperative, trusting response (Axelrod, 1984; Klapwijk & Van Lange, 2009; Leite, 2011; Messick & Liebrand, 1995; Wubben, De Cremer, & van Dijk, 2009). Using this tactic in the arms race would mean matching not only any military buildup made by an unfriendly nation, but also any conciliatory gesture, such as a ban on nuclear testing.

Another proven strategy is to allow individuals rather than opposing groups to resolve a conflict, because two individuals who play the prisoner's dilemma are more likely to cooperate than two groups who play the same game (Schopler & Insko, 1999). The reason for this is that people are more likely to assume that another individual is cooperative at heart and can be trusted, but that most groups of individuals will, given the opportunity, stab us in the back. Does this mean that world leaders would be more cooperative when negotiating one-on-one than when groups of advisers from the two nations meet? Possibly. In 1985, Ronald Reagan and Mikhail Gorbachev, then leaders of the United States and the Soviet Union, met for the first time, in Switzerland, to discuss arms reduction. After formal meetings between the leaders and their aides stalled, Reagan and Gorbachev took a walk to a boathouse, accompanied only by translators. According to some reports, the two men came close to agreeing to dismantle all of their nuclear missiles—until their aides got wind of this "preposterous" idea and squelched it (Korda, 1997).

Tit-for-Tat Strategy

A means of encouraging cooperation by at first acting cooperatively but then always responding the way your opponent did (cooperatively or competitively) on the previous trial.

Using Threats to Resolve Conflict

When involved in a conflict, many of us are tempted to use threats to get the other party to cave in to our wishes, believing that we should, in the words of Teddy Roosevelt, "speak softly and carry a big stick." Parents commonly use threats to get their children to behave, and teachers often threaten their students with demerits or a visit to the principal. More alarming is the increasing number of youths in the United States who carry weapons and use them to resolve conflicts that used to be settled with a playground scuffle. Threats are commonly used on an international scale as well, to further the interests of one nation over another (Turner & Horvitz, 2001).

A classic series of studies by Morton Deutsch and Robert Krauss (1960, 1962) indicates that threats are not an effective means of reducing conflict. These researchers developed a game in which two participants imagined that they were in charge of trucking companies named Acme and Bolt. The goal of each company was to transport merchandise as quickly as possible to a destination. The participants were paid 60 cents for each "trip" but had 1 cent subtracted for every second it took them to make the trip. The most direct route for each company was over a one-lane road on which only one truck could travel at a time. This placed the two companies in direct conflict, as seen in Figure 9.7. If Acme and Bolt both tried to take the one-lane road, neither truck could pass, and both would lose money. Each company could take an alternate route, but this was much longer, guaranteeing that they would lose at least 10 cents in each trial.

After a while, most participants worked out a solution that allowed both trucks to make a modest amount of money. They took turns waiting until the other party crossed the one-lane road; then they would take that route as well. In another version of the study, the researchers gave Acme a gate that could be lowered over the one-lane road, thereby blocking Bolt from using that route. You might think that using force—the gate—would increase Acme's profits, because all Acme had to do was to threaten Bolt to "stay off the one-lane road or else." In fact, quite the opposite happened. When one side had the gate, both participants lost more than when neither side had the gate—as seen in the left panel of Figure 9.8. This figure shows the total amount earned or lost by both sides. (Acme won slightly more than Bolt when it had the gate, but won substantially more when neither side had a gate.) Bolt did not like to be threatened and often retaliated by parking its truck on the one-lane road, blocking the other truck's progress. Meanwhile, the seconds ticked away and both sides lost money.

> *My own belief is that Russian and Chinese behavior is as much influenced by suspicion of our intentions as ours is by suspicion of theirs. This would mean that we have great influence over their behavior—that, by treating them as hostile, we assure their hostility.*
>
> —J. William Fulbright, April 4, 1971

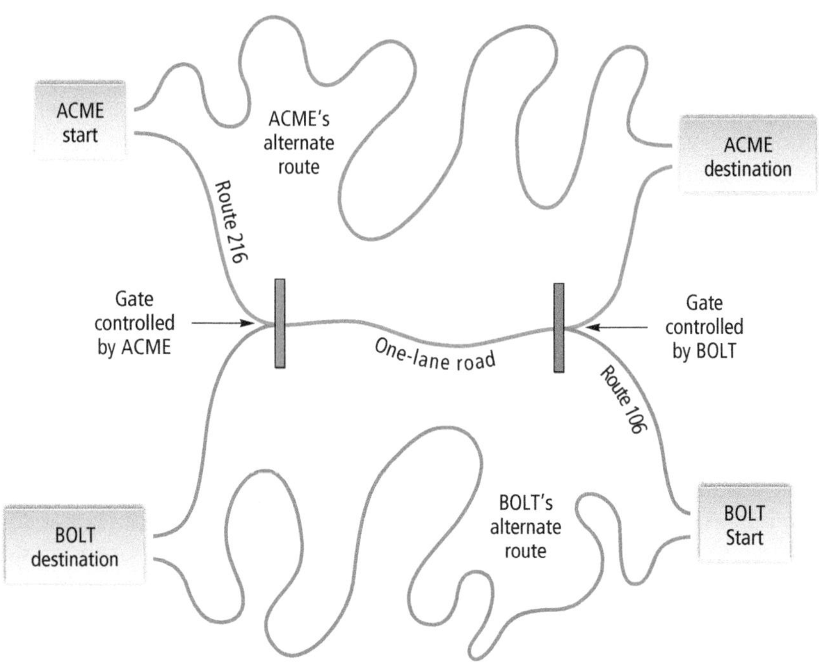

FIGURE 9.7

The Trucking Game

Participants play the role of the head of either Acme or Bolt Trucking Company. In order to earn money, they have to drive their truck from the starting point to their destination as quickly as possible. The quickest route is the one-lane road, but both trucks cannot travel on this road at the same time. In some versions of the studies, participants were given gates that they used to block the other's progress on the one-lane road.

(From Deutsch & Krauss, 1962.)

FIGURE 9.8

Results of the Trucking-Game Studies

The left-hand panel shows the amount of money the participants made (summed over Acme and Bolt) when they could not communicate. When threats were introduced by giving one ("unilateral threat") or both sides ("bilateral threat") a gate, both sides lost more money. The right-hand panel shows the amount of money the participants made when they were required to communicate in every trial. Once again, giving them gates reduced their winnings.

(Based on data in Deutsch & Krauss, 1962.)

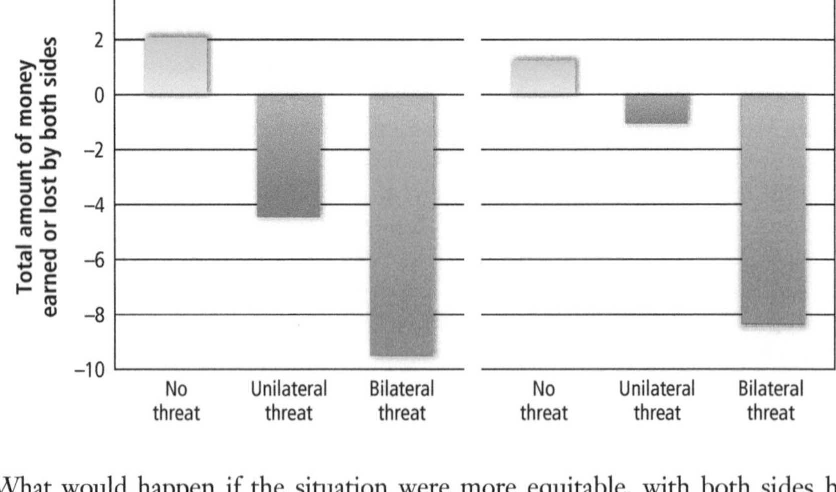

What would happen if the situation were more equitable, with both sides having gates? Surely they would learn to cooperate very quickly, recognizing the stalemate that would ensue if both of them used their gates—right? To the contrary (as you can see in the left panel of Figure 9.8), both sides lost more money in the bilateral threat condition than in any of the others. The owners of the trucking companies both threatened to use their gates and did so with great frequency.

Effects of Communication

There is a way in which the Deutsch and Krauss trucking game does not approximate real life: The two sides were not allowed to communicate with each other. Would the two adversaries work out their differences if they could talk them over? To find out, Deutsch and Krauss ran a version of their study in which the participants were required to communicate on every trial. Surely if people talked to each other, they would cooperate more. But as seen in the right panel of Figure 9.8, no dramatic increase in profits occurred. Making people communicate reduced losses somewhat when Acme alone had the gate (the unilateral threat condition) but failed to increase cooperation in either of the two other conditions (no threat, bilateral threat). Overall, requiring people to communicate did not raise profits dramatically. Why not?

The problem with the communication in the trucking studies is that it did not foster trust. In fact, people used the intercom to threaten each other. Krauss and Deutsch demonstrated this fact in a later version of their trucking study in which they specifically instructed people on how to communicate, telling them to work out a solution that was fair to both parties—that they would be willing to accept if they were in the other person's shoes. Under these conditions, verbal communication increased the amount of money both sides won, because it fostered trust instead of adding fuel to the competitive fires (Deutsch, 1973, 1990; Krauss & Deutsch, 1966; Pruitt, 1998).

Watch on MyPsychLab To learn more about conflict resolution in groups, watch the MyPsychLab video ***In the Real World: Resolving Conflict.***

Negotiation and Bargaining

In the laboratory games we have discussed so far, people's options are limited. They have to choose Option X or Y in the prisoner's dilemma, and they have only a couple of ways of getting their truck to its destination in the trucking game. In everyday life, we often have a wide array of options. Consider two people haggling over the price of a car. Both the buyer and the seller can give in to all of the other's demands, to some of them, or to none of them. Either party can walk away from the deal at any time. Given that there is considerable latitude in how people can resolve the conflict, communication between the parties is all the more important. By talking, bargaining, and negotiating, people can arrive at a satisfactory settlement. **Negotiation** is a form of communication between opposing sides in a conflict in which offers and counteroffers are made and a solution occurs only when both parties agree (De Dreu, 2010; Galinsky, Mussweiler, & Medvec, 2002; Thompson, Wang, & Gunia, 2010). How successful are people at negotiating mutually beneficial solutions?

Negotiation

A form of communication between opposing sides in a conflict in which offers and counteroffers are made and a solution occurs only when both parties agree.

Neutral mediators often help solve labor disputes, legal battles, and divorce proceedings. Mediators can be in a better position to recognize that there are mutually agreeable solutions to a conflict.

One limit to successful negotiation is that people often assume that they are locked in a conflict in which only one party can come out ahead. They don't realize that a solution favorable to both parties is available. A couple getting a divorce, for example, might lock horns and find it impossible to reach a financial settlement, until they realize that they have different priorities. Perhaps it is most important to one person to keep the furniture and the season tickets to the orchestra, whereas the other wants the china and the vintage collection of vinyl records. This type of compromise, called an **integrative solution**, is an outcome to a conflict whereby the parties make trade-offs on issues according to their different interests; each side concedes the most on issues that are unimportant to it but are important to the other side.

It might seem that such integrative solutions would be relatively easy to achieve. After all, the two parties simply have to sit down and figure out which issues are the most important to each. However, people often find it difficult to identify integrative solutions (Moran & Ritov, 2007; Thompson, 1997). For example, the more people have at stake in a negotiation, the more biased their perceptions of their opponent. They will tend to distrust proposals made by the other side and to overlook interests they have in common (O'Connor & Carnevale, 1997; Ross & Ward, 1995, 1996). This is one reason why people often use neutral mediators to solve labor disputes, legal battles, and divorce proceedings: Mediators are often in a better position to recognize that there are mutually agreeable solutions to a conflict (Carnevale, 1986; Kressel & Pruitt, 1989; Ross & LaCroix, 1996).

Yet there remains another wall. This wall constitutes a psychological barrier between us, ... [a] barrier of distorted and eroded interpretation of every event and statement. . . . I ask, why don't we stretch our hands with faith and sincerity so that together we might destroy this barrier?

—Former Egyptian president Anwar al-Sadat, speaking before the Israeli Knesset, 1977

What about the role of communication in negotiation? As we saw earlier, communication is only helpful if it allows parties to develop trust. It appears that this is easier in old-fashioned face-to-face negotiations than in electronic communications such as e-mail, instant messaging, text messaging, and video conferencing. The modern techniques have many advantages, of course, but a disadvantage is that it is harder to get to know people and learn to trust them. A meta-analysis of several studies found that negotiations conducted over electronic media were more hostile, and resulted in lower profits, than face-to-face negotiations (Stuhlmacher & Citera, 2005).

The bottom line? When you are negotiating with someone, it is important to keep in mind that integrative solutions are often available. Try to gain the other side's trust, communicate your own interests in an open manner (ideally in person or with the help of a mediator), and try taking the other person's perspective (Trötschel et al., 2011). Remember that the way you construe the situation is not necessarily the same as the way the other party construes it. You may well discover that the other side communicates its interests more freely as a result, increasing the likelihood that you will find a solution beneficial to both parties.

Integrative Solution

A solution to a conflict whereby the parties make trade-offs on issues according to their different interests; each side concedes the most on issues that are unimportant to it but important to the other side.

USE IT!

Chances are you will soon find yourself in a group that needs to make a decision. Perhaps you are an officer in a student organization that is making budget decisions, part of a team of students deciding how to proceed on a class project, or a member of a fraternity or sorority deciding whom to admit. Based on what you have learned in this chapter, will you act any differently to make sure that your group makes the best decision? What kinds of *process loss* should you be alert to, for example, that might impede good decision making? (See page 249.) How can you make sure that people share information that others don't have? (See page 249.) Is it possible that you and your friends will be subject to *groupthink*, and, if so, how can you prevent it? (See page 250.) Lastly, can you predict who is likely to become the leader in your groups and how effective they will be? What should you do to increase the chances that you will be chosen as the leader? (See pages 255–258.) Good luck!

Summary

What are groups and why do people join them?

- **What Is a Group?** A **group** consists of three or more people who interact with each other and are interdependent.
  - **Why Do People Join Groups?** The *need to belong* to groups may be innate. Groups also serve as a source of information about the social world and are an important part of our social identities. People are very sensitive to rejection from groups and do what they can to avoid it. Groups also make people feel distinctive from members of other groups.
  - **The Composition and Functions of Groups** Groups tend to consist of homogeneous members, in part because groups have *social norms* that people are expected to obey. Groups also have well-defined social roles, shared expectations about how people are supposed to behave. People can get so far into a social role that their personal identities and personalities get lost. Social roles are shaped by our culture. Gender roles have changed a lot over the past several decades in the United States, although studies of advertisements indicate that women are still portrayed in subordinate roles more often than men are. Group cohesiveness, qualities of a group that bind members together and promote liking between members, is another important property of groups that influences the group's performance.

In what ways do people act differently when other people are around? What are the key variables that determine what the effects of others will be on individual performance?

- **Individual Behavior in a Group Setting** Research has compared the performance of people who are by themselves versus in groups.
  - **Social Facilitation: When the Presence of Others Energizes Us** When people's individual efforts on a task can be evaluated, the mere presence of others leads to social facilitation: Their performance is enhanced on simple tasks but impaired on complex tasks.
  - **Social Loafing: When the Presence of Others Relaxes Us** When people's individual efforts *cannot* be evaluated, the mere presence of others leads to relaxation and social loafing: Performance is impaired on simple tasks but enhanced on complex tasks.
  - **Gender and Cultural Differences in Social Loafing: Who Slacks Off the Most?** Social loafing is more prevalent among men than women, and more prevalent in Western than Asian cultures.
  - **Deindividuation: Getting Lost in the Crowd** The mere presence of others can also lead to deindividuation, which is the loosening of normal constraints on behavior when people are in crowds.

When people make decisions, are two (or more) heads better than one? Why or why not?

- **Group Decisions: Are Two (or More) Heads Better Than One?** Research has compared how people make decisions when they are by themselves versus in groups.
  - **Process Loss: When Group Interactions Inhibit Good Problem Solving** Groups make better decisions than individuals if they are good at pooling ideas and listening to the expert members of the group. Often, however, process loss occurs, which is any aspect of group interaction that inhibits good decision making. For example, groups often focus on the information they have in common and fail to share unique information. Tightly knit, cohesive groups are also prone to groupthink, which occurs when maintaining group cohesiveness and solidarity becomes more important than considering the facts in a realistic manner.
  - **Group Polarization: Going to Extremes** Group polarization causes groups to make more extreme decisions in the direction toward which its members were initially leaning; these group decisions can be more risky or more cautious, depending on which attitude is valued in the group.
  - **Leadership in Groups** There is little support for the great person theory, which argues that good leadership is a matter of having the right personality traits. Leaders do adopt specific kinds of leadership styles, such as transactional or transformational. Leadership effectiveness is a function of both the kind of person a leader is and the nature of the work situation. Although strides have been made, women are still underrepresented in leadership positions. Women who become leaders often face a "glass cliff" whereby they are put in charge of work units that are in crisis and in which the risk of failure is high. Further, there is a double bind for women leaders: If they conform to societal expectations about how they ought to behave, by being warm and communal, they are often perceived as having low leadership potential. If they succeed in attaining a leadership position and act in ways that leaders are expected to act—namely, in agentic, forceful ways—they are often perceived negatively for not "acting like a woman should."

When individuals or groups are in conflict, what determines the likelihood that this conflict will escalate or that it will be resolved?

- **Conflict and Cooperation** Research has examined how people resolve conflicts when they have incompatible goals.
  - **Social Dilemmas** These occur when the most beneficial action for an individual will, if chosen by most people, have harmful effects on everyone. A commonly studied social dilemma is the prisoner's dilemma, in which two people must decide whether to look out for only their own interests or for their partner's interests as well. Creating trust is crucial in solving this kind of conflict.
  - **Using Threats to Resolve Conflict** Research has found that using threats tends to escalate rather than resolve conflicts.
  - **Effects of Communication** Communication resolves conflict only when it promotes trust.
  - **Negotiation and Bargaining** When two sides are negotiating and bargaining it is important to look for an integrative solution, whereby each side concedes the most on issues that are unimportant to it but are very important to its adversary.

Chapter 9 Test

Study and Review on MyPsychLab

1. Why are groups homogeneous (alike in age, sex, beliefs, and opinions)?
   a. People who are already similar to each tend to join the same group.
   b. Evolutionary pressures caused people with similar genes to join groups.
   c. Groups encourage similarity in their members.
   d. (a) and (c)
   e. (a), (b), and (c)

2. Group cohesiveness is best defined as
   a. shared expectations in a group about how people are supposed to behave.
   b. qualities that bind members together and promote liking between members.
   c. expectations about the roles and behaviors of men and women.
   d. the tendency for people to do better on simple tasks and worse on complex tasks in the presence of others.

3. You are trying to decide whether to take a test in a lecture hall where you will be surrounded by lots of other people or in a room by yourself. Assuming that you have studied for the test and know the material, you should take the test in the __________ because it will result in __________.
   a. hallway, social loafing
   b. hallway, social facilitation
   c. classroom, social loafing
   d. hallway, deindividuation
   e. classroom, social facilitation

4. The tendency to engage in social loafing is stronger in __________ than __________; it is also stronger in __________ than __________.
   a. men, women; Asian cultures, Western cultures
   b. women, men; Asian cultures, Western cultures
   c. men, women; Western cultures, Asian cultures
   d. women, men; Western cultures, Asian cultures

5. On his way back from class, Matt encounters an angry mob ready to storm the dining hall to demand better food. Matt likes the food as it is and wants to stop the mob. What would be the most effective solution?
   a. Increasing group cohesiveness by inviting the entire mob to his house for tea.
   b. Passing out blue shirts for everyone to wear.
   c. Reducing process loss in the group by making sure that its most expert members have the most influence.
   d. Finding a friend in the group, calling out her name, and talking to her loudly about an upcoming test.

6. Four psychology students working on a group project together are trying to figure out how they should avoid groupthink when making decisions about their project. Which of these ideas would be the *least* helpful?
   a. Bonding by going to see a movie together before starting the project.
   b. Assigning each group member to be responsible for a different chapter in their textbook so that they cover all the details.
   c. Having a student not in their group review the project.
   d. Designating a leader to oversee the project, one who is nondirective and encourages people to give honest feedback.

7. Bill and Pam, a married couple, are buying a house and have narrowed their choice down to two options. Bill remembers that one house had a beautiful kitchen; Pam, however, remembers that there were roaches in the broom closet. By sharing this information with each other, Pam and Bill are using __________ to avoid __________.
   a. mindguards, groupthink
   b. social roles, deindividuation
   c. transactive memory, process loss
   d. subgroups, group polarization

8. Which of the following is *least likely* to lead to process loss in a group?
   a. A group leader has high charisma but very little expertise.
   b. The group members have never met before.
   c. Group members do not share information that others lack.
   d. Some members in the group do not listen to each other.
   e. The most competent member doesn't feel free to speak up.

9. Which of the following is true about research on leadership?
   a. Female leaders are more likely than male leaders to be put in precarious, high-risk positions where it is difficult to succeed.
   b. The best leaders are born that way.
   c. People in all cultures value the same traits in leaders.
   d. If a woman succeeds in becoming a leader of an organization and acts in an agentic way, she is evaluated in the same way that male leaders are.

10. When is communication most effective for resolving conflict?
    a. When people communicate through electronic means (e.g., over e-mail).
    b. When it is required.
    c. When the stakes are high for people on both sides of a conflict.
    d. When a mediator is used.

Answer Key

1-d, 2-b, 3-e, 4-c, 5-d,
6-a, 7-c, 8-b, 9-a, 10-d

10 Interpersonal Attraction

From First Impressions to Close Relationships

LAURA AND DENNY ALLEN HAVE AN AWFUL LOT IN COMMON. Born in the same hospital in Oregon nearly 70 years ago, they both grew up in the Portland area and attended Oregon State University. They both dedicated their careers to fields in which they could better the lives of those around them; for Laura it was educational consulting for gifted children, for Denny it was working as an environmental health professional and food inspector (Willis, 2012).

Laura and Denny, now retired, both enjoy traveling overseas. They have a passion for volunteering. They love dogs, wine making, and hunting for wild mushrooms. In terms of politics and religion? You guessed it—their beliefs line up almost perfectly.

There's something pleasantly reassuring about stories of compatible soul mates who meet as youngsters and contentedly spend their lives together, isn't there? Except this description doesn't apply to the Allens.

Yes, the Allens are a happily married couple who live together in Wilsonville, Oregon, with their two pugs (named Georgia and Olive, in case you were wondering). But Laura and Denny have only been married for 5 years. Despite living in neighboring parts of the state for decades, the Allens didn't meet until recently—when they both signed up for the same Internet dating site.

Interpersonal attraction, like much of human nature, can be studied scientifically. And it's a good thing too, because many of our assumptions about falling in love turn out to be mistaken, as we'll discuss throughout this chapter. One such case is the belief that opposites attract: Research offers the clear conclusion that similarity is a stronger predictor of who we're drawn to (Heine, Foster, & Spina, 2009). And as to the idea that women are pickier than men in selecting mates, they often are, but not for the biologically based reasons you might assume (Finkel & Eastwick, 2009).

And what about the expectation that Internet dating is only for young people? By 2009, 22% of heterosexual couples reported meeting online, a number that rises to a whopping 61% for same-sex couples (Finkel et al., 2012). These numbers—as well as Web sites with names like seniormatch.com, seniorpeoplemeet.com, and silversingles.com—demonstrate that no longer do we live in a society in which only small subsets of the population are looking for relationships online.

In fact, social psychologists even study dating Web sites themselves, as explored in the final section of this chapter. For example, in 2012, Eli Finkel and colleagues reviewed data regarding online dating and concluded that although the practice has never been more popular than it is today, many of the promises made by these sites go unfulfilled. Specifically, the idea of mathematical algorithms that can point users toward ideally compatible mates has little in the way of empirical support. Sure, more Americans than ever are pairing up online, but the success rate for dates facilitated by Web site is no higher than the success rate for dates engineered through more old-fashioned routes, like meeting at a bar or getting fixed up by friends (Finkel et al., 2012).

The compatibility analyses of dating Web sites don't live up to their promises for a variety of reasons, according to Finkel and his colleagues. First, as you read about in Chapter 5, sometimes we don't have a good sense of why we do what we do or what will make us happy. By the same token, we aren't always accurate when it comes to predicting the mate characteristics that will lead to a satisfying relationship. Second, most dating Web site algorithms focus on matching people by personality traits or other stable characteristics. But many of the best predictors of relationship satisfaction—like communication style and sexual compatibility—can't be assessed until people actually get to know each other (Finkel et al., 2012).

FOCUS QUESTIONS

- How do humans decide whom they like and want to get to know better?
- What is love, and how do we form close relationships?
- What does research tell us about romantic breakups?
- How do new technologies influence how we form close relationships?

Propinquity Effect
The finding that the more we see and interact with people, the more likely they are to become our friends

Thus, even processes as basic to the human condition as falling in love and choosing a life partner show the effects of social psychology: the limitations of self-knowledge and the influence of the situation. As mystically romantic a view as many of us hold of love, the experience of falling for someone can still be studied using psychological theories and methods. In this chapter, we will explore what makes us feel attracted to other people, whether as friends or lovers, and how relationships develop and progress.

What Causes Attraction?

When social psychologist Ellen Berscheid asked people of various ages what made them happy, at or near the top of their lists were making friends and having positive, warm relationships (Berscheid, 1985; Berscheid & Peplau, 1983; Berscheid & Reis, 1998). The absence of meaningful relationships with other people makes people feel lonely, worthless, hopeless, helpless, and powerless (Baumeister & Leary, 1995; Cacioppo & Patrick, 2008; Hartup & Stevens, 1997; Stroebe & Stroebe, 1996). In fact, social psychologist Arthur Aron states that a central human motivation is "self-expansion." This is the desire to overlap or blend with another person, so that you have access to that person's knowledge, insights, and experience and thus broaden and deepen your own experience of life (Aron, Aron, & Norman, 2004; Aron, Mashuk, & Aron, 2004). We will begin this chapter by discussing the antecedents of attraction, from the initial liking of people meeting for the first time to the love that develops in close relationships.

The Person Next Door: The Propinquity Effect

One of the simplest determinants of interpersonal attraction is proximity (sometimes called *propinquity*). The people who, by chance, are the ones you see and interact with the most often are the most likely to become your friends and lovers (Berscheid & Reis, 1998).

Now, this might seem obvious. But the striking thing about proximity and attraction, or the **propinquity effect**, is that it works in a very narrow sense. For example, consider a classic study conducted in a housing complex for married students at MIT. Leon Festinger, Stanley Schachter, and Kurt Back (1950) tracked friendship formation among the couples in the various apartment buildings. One section of the complex, Westgate West, was composed of 17 two-story buildings, each having 10 apartments. Residents had been assigned to apartments at random, and nearly all were strangers when they moved in. The researchers asked residents to name their three closest friends in the complex. Just as the propinquity effect would predict, 65% of the friends mentioned lived in their same building, even though the other buildings were not far away.

Even more striking was the pattern of friendships within a building. Each Westgate West building was designed like the drawing in Figure 10.1: Most of the front doors were only 19 feet apart, and the greatest distance between apartment doors was only 89 feet. The researchers found that 41% of the next-door neighbors indicated that they

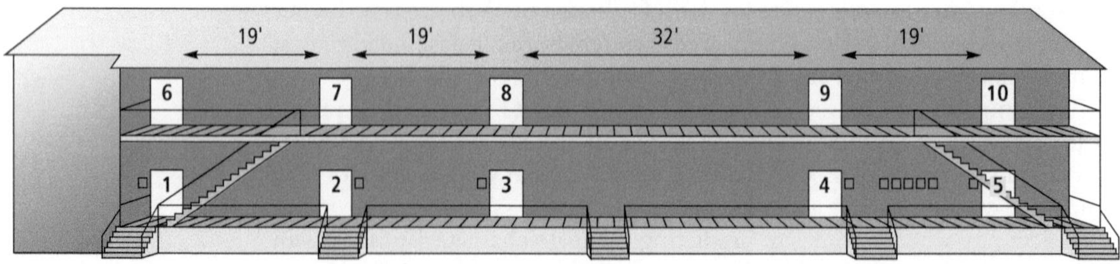

FIGURE 10.1
The Floor Plan of a Westgate West Building
All the buildings in the housing complex had the same floor plan.
(Adapted from Festinger, Schachter, & Back, 1950)

TRY IT! Mapping the Effect of Propinquity in Your Life

Try examining the relationship between your friends and acquaintances and the places where you spend time regularly. Does propinquity explain who your friends are?

First, pick a physical space to focus on. You could choose your dormitory, your apartment building, or the location where you work. (We'll use a dormitory for our example.) Draw a rough floor plan. Include the location of all the doors, stairs or elevators, bathrooms, common rooms, laundry rooms, and so on. Mark your room with a large X.

Second, think about your close friends on the floor or in the building. Mark their rooms with the number 1. Next, think about whom your not-as-close friends are; mark their rooms with a 2. Finally, think about your acquaintances—people you say hello to or chat with briefly now and then but aren't really close enough to be considered friends. Mark their rooms with a 3.

Now examine the pattern of friendships on your map. Are your friends clustered near your room in physical space? Are the rooms with the numbers 1 and 2 among the closest to your room in physical space? Are they physically closer to your room than the ones with number 3? And what about the dorm rooms that didn't get a number (meaning that you don't really know these people or interact with them)—are these rooms the farthest from yours, on average?

Finally, examine your propinquity map for the presence of functional distance. Do aspects of the architectural design of your dorm make you more likely to cross paths with some residents than others? For example, the location of the bathrooms, kitchen, living rooms, stairs, and mailboxes can play an important role in propinquity and friendship formation. These are all places where you go frequently; when walking there and back, you pass some people's rooms more than others'. Are you more likely to know the people who are located along your path? If so, propinquity has played an important role in determining your relationships!

were close friends, 22% of those who lived two doors apart said so, and only 10% of those who lived on opposite ends of the hall indicated that they were close friends.

Festinger and his colleagues (1950) demonstrated that attraction and propinquity rely not only on actual physical distance but also on "functional distance." Functional distance refers to aspects of architectural design that determine which people you cross paths with most often. For example, consider the friendship choices of the residents of apartments 1 and 5 in Figure 10.1. Living at the foot of the stairs or near the mailboxes meant that a couple saw a great deal of upstairs residents. Sure enough, apartment dwellers in apartments 1 and 5 throughout the complex had more friends upstairs than dwellers in the other first-floor apartments did. (You can map out propinquity effects in your own life with the preceding Try It! exercise.)

Propinquity works because of familiarity, or the **mere exposure effect**: The more exposure we have to a stimulus, the more apt we are to like it (Moreland & Topolinski, 2010; Zajonc, 1968). In reality, familiarity doesn't usually breed contempt; it breeds liking. We typically associate positive feelings with things that are familiar, like comfort food, songs we remember from childhood, certain corporate logos, and the sound of the local play-by-play announcer's voice. The same is true for the people we encounter. The more often we see certain people, and the more familiar they become, the more friendship blooms. However, there is one caveat: If the person in question is an obnoxious jerk, then, not surprisingly, the more exposure you have, the greater your dislike becomes (Norton, Frost, & Ariely, 2007). But in the absence of such negative qualities, familiarity breeds attraction and liking (Bornstein, 1989; Griffin & Sparks, 1990; Moreland & Beach, 1992; Lee, 2001).

> *Contrary to popular belief, I do not believe that friends are necessarily the people you like best; they are merely the people who got there first.*
>
> —Sir Peter Ustinov, *Dear Me*, 1977

A good example of the propinquity and mere exposure effects is your college classroom. All semester long, you see the same people. Does this increase your liking for them? Researchers tested this hypothesis with German students by randomly assigning them on the first day of class to permanent seats for the semester (Back, Schmukle, & Egloff, 2008). That first day, they had students rate each member of the class on likability and the extent to which they would like to get to know each other. These initial ratings indicated that students who sat in neighboring seats or in the same row had higher initial attraction scores than those seated far apart. A year later, they asked these students to rate the members of their original class again in terms of how much they liked them, how well

Mere Exposure Effect
The finding that the more exposure we have to a stimulus, the more apt we are to like it

Close friendships are often made in college, in part because of prolonged propinquity.

they knew them, and to what degree they were friends. Once again, those who had sat side by side or in the same row the prior semester were significantly more likely to be friends a year later than those who sat far apart. The propinquity effect means that some of our relationships develop simply because we were "at the right place, at the right time."

Similarity

As we saw, propinquity increases familiarity, which leads to liking, but something more is needed to fuel a growing friendship or a romantic relationship. (Otherwise, every pair of roommates would be best friends!) That "fuel" is often *similarity*—a match between our interests, attitudes, values, background, or personality and those of another person. As we discussed in Chapter 1, folk wisdom captures this idea in the expression "Birds of a feather flock together" (the concept of *similarity*). But folk wisdom also has another saying, "Opposites attract" (the concept of *complementarity*). Luckily, we don't have to remain forever confused by contradictory advice from old sayings; as mentioned in the opening to this chapter, research evidence demonstrates that it is overwhelmingly similarity and not complementarity that draws people together (AhYun, 2002; Berscheid & Reis, 1998; Byrne, 1997; Heine et al., 2009; McPherson, Smith-Lovin, & Cook, 2001).

Opinions and Personality A large body of research indicates that the more similar someone's opinions are to yours, the more you will like the person (e.g., Byrne & Nelson, 1965; Lutz-Zois et al., 2006). For example, in a classic study, Theodore Newcomb (1961) randomly assigned male students at the University of Michigan to be roommates in a particular dormitory at the start of the school year. Would similarity predict friendship formation? The answer was yes: Men became friends with those who were demographically similar (e.g., shared a rural background), as well as with those who were similar in attitudes and values (e.g., were also engineering majors or also held comparable political views). It's not just attitudes or demographics that are important. Similar personality characteristics also promote liking and attraction. For example, in a study of gay men's relationships, those who scored high on a test of stereotypical male traits desired a partner who was most of all logical—a stereotypical masculine trait. Gay men who scored high on a test of stereotypical female traits desired a partner who was most of all expressive—a stereotypical feminine trait (Boyden, Carroll, & Maier, 1984). Similar personality characteristics are important for heterosexual couples and for friends as well (Acitelli, Kenny, & Weiner, 2001; Caspi & Harbener, 1990; Gonzaga, Campos, & Bradbury, 2007; Klohnen & Luo, 2003; Weaver & Bosson, 2011).

Interests and Experiences The situations you choose to be in are usually populated by people who have chosen them for similar reasons. You're sitting in a social psychology class, surrounded by people who also chose to take social psychology this semester. You sign up for salsa dance lessons; the others in your class also want to learn Latin dancing. Thus, we choose to enter into certain social situations where we then find similar others. For example, in a study of the patterns of students' friendships that focused on the effects of "tracking" (grouping students by academic ability), researchers found that students were significantly more likely to choose friends from inside their track than from outside it (Kubitschek & Hallinan, 1998). Clearly, propinquity and initial similarity play a role in the formation of these friendships. However, the researchers add that similarity plays yet another role: Over time, students in the same academic track share many of the same experiences, which are different from the experiences of those in other tracks. Thus, new similarities are created and discovered, fueling the friendships. In short, shared experiences promote attraction (Pinel et al., 2006).

Appearance Finally, similarity also operates when it comes to more-superficial considerations. Sean Mackinnon, Christian Jordan, and Anne Wilson (2011) conducted a series of studies examining physical similarity and seating choice. In one study, they simply analyzed the seating arrangement of college students in a library computer lab, making observations multiple times over the course of several different days. Results indicated that students who wore glasses sat next to other students with glasses far more often than random chance alone would predict. A second study found the same pattern by hair color.

"I don't care if she is a tape dispenser. I love her."

Sam Gross/The New Yorker Collection/ www.cartoonbank.com.

In a third study, participants arrived at a psychology lab and were introduced to a partner who was already sitting. Handed a chair, they were told to have a seat, after which point the research team secretly measured how close to the partner's chair they put down their own chair. A separate set of researchers later evaluated photos of both the participant and the partner. Pairs judged as more physically similar had, on average, sat closer to each other. Without even realizing it, you are often drawn to those who look like you, to the point where people are even more likely to ask out on dates others who are similar to them in terms of attractiveness level (Taylor et al., 2011; Walster et al., 1966).

Some Final Comments about Similarity Here are two additional points about similarity. First, while similarity is very important in close relationships, it is important to make a distinction between "actual" (or real) similarity and "perceived" similarity (that is, the degree to which one *believes* oneself to be similar to another; Morry, 2007). In a recent meta-analysis, R. Matthew Montoya and his colleagues found that in long-term relationships, "perceived" similarity predicted liking and attraction better than "actual" similarity did. Thus, *feeling* similar to another is what's really important—so much so that we will create beliefs about the similarity between ourselves and intimate others even when they don't exist (Montoya, Horton, & Kirchner, 2008).

Second, a *lack* of similarity does appear to play an important role in one type of relationship. Sometimes when we begin a romantic relationship, we want a serious, committed relationship; but sometimes, we just want a "fling." David Amodio and Carolin Showers (2005) found that whether similarity or complementarity was important depended on the level of commitment that research participants felt toward their romantic partner. If participants wanted a committed relationship, they chose a similar partner; however, if they felt a low level of commitment to the relationship, they favored dissimilar partners. Thus, in low-commitment relationships, we may go out of our way to choose someone who is strikingly different from us. A relationship with this sort of person represents more of an adventure; however, as we'll see as we progress through this chapter, relationships based on differences, rather than similarities, can be difficult to maintain.

An administrator in the Housing Office of Barnard College sorts through roommate applications, placing them in piles according to their similar answers to questions about living habits and interests.

(Willie J. Allen Jr./*The New York Times*)

Reciprocal Liking

We like to be liked. In fact, just knowing that a person likes us fuels our attraction to that individual. Liking is so powerful that it can even make up for the absence of similarity. For example, in one experiment, when a young woman expressed interest in male research participants simply by maintaining eye contact, leaning toward them, and listening attentively, the men expressed great liking for her despite the fact that they knew she disagreed with them on important issues (Gold, Ryckman, & Mosley, 1984). Whether the clues are nonverbal or verbal, perhaps the most crucial determinant of whether we will like person A is the extent to which we believe person A likes us (Berscheid & Walster, 1978; Kenny, 1994b; Kenny & La Voie, 1982; Kubitschek & Hallinan, 1998; Montoya & Insko, 2008).

Life is to be fortified by many friendships. To love, and to be loved, is the greatest happiness of existence.
Love to faults is always blind, Always is to joy inclin'd.
—William Blake, *Love to Faults*

Just how powerful is reciprocal liking? According to recent research, it is powerful enough to neutralize our basic tendency to pay more attention to attractive faces. Nicolas Koranyi and Klaus Rothermund (2012) used a computer program to present a series of opposite-sex faces to German research participants. Each photo appeared for the same half-second duration, but its location in one of the four corners of the screen was determined at random. Immediately after each photo appeared, a geometrical shape was shown, once again randomly located in one of the four corners of the screen. Participants' task was to identify as quickly as possible whether the shape was a circle or a square. When the shape showed up in the same location as the previous photo, the task was easy: Participants were already looking in that vicinity and quickly identified the shape. When the shape appeared in a different area, however, the task was harder: With their eyesight still fixated on the spot where the face just was, participants had to shift their visual attention to find the shape. This shift proved particularly challenging when the previous photo was an attractive one, as we have a tendency to linger and look longer at good-looking faces.

But not all respondents showed this bias to stare a bit longer at attractive faces. Who was able to break the spell of the pretty face? It was the participants who had previously been asked to imagine that they had just learned that someone whom they had a crush on also had feelings for them. As the researchers suggest, it makes sense that this type of interest from someone else would disrupt our otherwise chronic focus on the attractive alternatives out there. Think about it: If our attention were repeatedly hijacked by *every* pretty face that passed by, we'd never get the chance to turn initial interactions into more-meaningful, sustained romantic relationships. Koranyi and Rothermund's (2012) results weren't limited to just imagining reciprocated liking, either. In a second study, the researchers created a heterosexual Internet dating site and asked participants to identify three opposite-sex students whom they'd be interested in dating. One week later, participants completed the same face/shape computer task; as expected, they were slower to identify shapes when preceded by attractive faces. But next they were told about one opposite-sex participant who had reciprocated their dating interest. When they then ran through the same face/shape task a second time, suddenly they showed no attentional bias for attractive faces. Basking in the glow of reciprocated liking is enough to stop a wandering eye and convince you, at least for a while, that the grass may not be greener on the other side.

Physical Attractiveness and Liking

Speaking of pretty faces, propinquity, similarity, and reciprocal liking are not the only determinants of whom we come to like. How important is physical appearance to our first impressions? In field experiments investigating actual behavior (rather than what they *say* they will do), people overwhelmingly go for physical attractiveness. For example, in a classic study, Elaine Walster Hatfield and her colleagues (Walster, et al., 1966) randomly matched 752 incoming students at the University of Minnesota for a blind date at a dance during freshman orientation week. Although the students had previously taken a battery of personality and aptitude tests, the researchers paired them up at random. On the night of the dance, the couples spent a few hours together dancing and chatting. They then evaluated their date and indicated the strength of their desire to see that person again. Of the many possible characteristics that could have determined whether they liked each other—such as their partner's intelligence, independence, sensitivity, or sincerity—the overriding determinant was physical attractiveness.

It is only shallow people who do not judge by appearances.
—Oscar Wilde, *The Picture of Dorian Gray*, 1891

What's more, there was no great difference between men and women on this count. This is an interesting point, for several studies have found that men and women pay equal attention to the physical attractiveness of others (Duck, 1994a, 1994b; Lynn & Shurgot, 1984; Speed & Gangestad, 1997; Woll, 1986), but other studies have reported that men value attractiveness more than women do (Buss, 1989; Buss & Barnes, 1986; Howard, Blumstein, & Schwartz, 1987). A meta-analysis of many studies found that while both sexes value attractiveness, men value it a bit more (Feingold, 1990); however, this gender difference was greater when men's and women's attitudes were being measured than when their actual behavior was being measured. Thus, it may be that men are more likely than women to *say* that physical attractiveness is important to them but that when it comes to actual behavior, the sexes are fairly similar in how they respond to the physical attractiveness of others. Indeed, across multiple studies, both genders rated physical attractiveness as the single most important characteristic that triggers sexual desire (Graziano et al., 1993; Regan & Berscheid, 1995, 1997).

Simulate on MyPsychLab
To learn more, try the MyPsychLab simulation ***Perceptions of Attractiveness.***

This powerful role of physical appearance in attraction is not limited to heterosexual relationships. When gay men participated in a "blind date" study like the one described earlier, they responded just as the heterosexual men and women had: The physical attractiveness of their dates was the strongest predictor of liking (Sergios & Cody, 1985).

What is Attractive? Is physical attractiveness "in the eye of the beholder," or do we all share the same notions of what is beautiful and handsome? From early childhood, the media tell us what is beautiful, and they tell us that beauty is associated with goodness. For example, illustrators of most traditional children's books, as well as the people who draw characters in Disney movies, have taught us that the heroines—as well as the princes who woo and win them—look alike. For example, the heroines all have regular features; small, pert noses; big eyes; shapely lips; blemish-free complexions; and slim, athletic bodies—rather like Barbie dolls.

Oh, what vileness human beauty is, corroding, corrupting everything it touches.
—Orestes, 408 B.C.

Bombarded as we are with media depictions of attractiveness, it is not surprising to learn that we share criteria for defining beauty (Fink & Penton-Voak, 2002; Tseëlon, 1995). Michael Cunningham (1986) designed a creative study to determine these standards of beauty. He asked college men to rate the attractiveness of 50 photographs of women, taken from a college yearbook and from an international beauty-pageant program. Cunningham then carefully measured the relative size of the facial features in each photograph. He found that high attractiveness ratings for female faces were associated with large eyes, a small nose, a small chin, prominent cheekbones, narrow cheeks, high eyebrows, large pupils, and a big smile. Researchers then examined women's ratings of male beauty in the same way (Cunningham, Barbee, & Pike, 1990). They found that men's faces with large eyes, prominent cheekbones, a large chin, and a big smile received higher attractiveness ratings.

She's beautiful and therefore to be woo'd.
—William Shakespeare

There is some overlap in the men's and women's ratings. Both sexes admire large eyes in the opposite sex; as mentioned in Chapter 4, these are considered a "baby face" feature, for newborn mammals have very large eyes relative to the size of their faces. Baby-face features are thought to be attractive because they elicit feelings of warmth and nurturance in perceivers—think of our typical response to infants, kittens, and puppies (e.g., Berry, 1995; Livingston & Pearce, 2009; Zebrowitz, 1997; Zebrowitz & Montepare, 1992). Both sexes also admire prominent cheekbones, an adult feature that is found only in the faces of those who are sexually mature. Note that the female face that is considered beautiful has more baby-face features (small nose, small chin) than the handsome male face, suggesting that beauty in the female is associated more with childlike qualities than male beauty is.

Photography models represent facial standards of beauty for men and women.

Cultural Standards of Beauty Are people's perceptions of what is beautiful or handsome similar across cultures? The answer is a surprising yes (Cunningham et al., 1995; Jones & Hill, 1993; McArthur & Berry, 1987; Rhodes et al., 2001). Even though racial and ethnic groups do vary in their specific facial features, people from a wide range of cultures agree on what is physically attractive in the human face. Researchers asked participants from various countries, ethnicities, and racial groups to rate the physical attractiveness of photographed faces of people who also represented various countries, ethnicities, and racial groups. Their ratings agreed to a remarkable extent. For example, one review of this literature found that the correlations between participants' ratings ranged from 0.66 to 0.93 (Langlois & Roggman, 1990), which are very strong correlations (see Chapter 2). A meta-analysis of several studies by Judith Langlois and her colleagues (2000) also found evidence for cross-cultural agreement in what constitutes a beautiful or handsome face. In short, perceivers think some faces are just better looking than others, regardless of cultural background (Berscheid & Reis, 1998).

Beauty is a greater recommendation than any letter of introduction.

—Aristotle, fourth century B.C.

How can we explain these results? Researchers have suggested that humans came to find certain dimensions of faces attractive during the course of our evolution (Langlois & Roggman, 1990; Langlois, Roggman, & Musselman, 1994). We know, for example, that even infants prefer photographs of attractive faces to unattractive ones, and infants prefer the same photographs that adults prefer (Langlois et al., 1991; Langlois, Roggman, & Rieser-Danner, 1990). One aspect of beauty that is preferred in both men and women is symmetry, where the size, shape, and location of the features on one side of the face match those on the other (Little et al., 2008; Langlois et al., 2000; Rhodes, 2006). Evolutionary psychologists suggest that we're attracted to symmetrical features because they serve as markers of good health and reproductive fitness—that is, facial symmetry is an indicator of "good genes" (Grammer & Thornhill, 1994).

A series of studies explored this preference by creating composite photographs of faces. Faces were morphed (i.e., combined digitally) to create a composite that was the mathematical average of the features of multiple faces; ultimately, 32 faces were combined into a single composite. When shown to research participants, composite photographs were judged as more attractive than were all the separate faces that had created them, and this held true for both male and female photographs (Langlois & Roggman, 1990; Langlois et al., 1994). The "averaged" composite face was more attractive because it had lost some of the atypical or asymmetrical variation that was present in the individual faces.

Does this mean that we find "average" faces the most attractive? Clearly not, for we respond to the physical appearance of movie stars and models because their looks are "above average" compared to most humans. David Perret and his colleagues made this point clear in the following study (Perret, May, & Yoshikawa, 1994). They created composite faces of two types: One composite was based on 60 photographs that had each been rated as average in attractiveness. The other composite was based on 60 photographs that had each been rated as highly attractive. Composites of these two types were made using photographs of Caucasian women, Caucasian men, Japanese women, and Japanese men. Research participants in Great Britain and Japan then rated all the composite faces for attractiveness.

The researchers found, first, that the composites of highly attractive faces were rated as significantly more attractive than the composites of average attractive faces. Second, Japanese and British participants showed the same pattern when judging the faces, reinforcing the idea that similar perceptions of facial attractiveness exist cross-culturally. Finally, what did those composites of highly attractive faces look like? Their

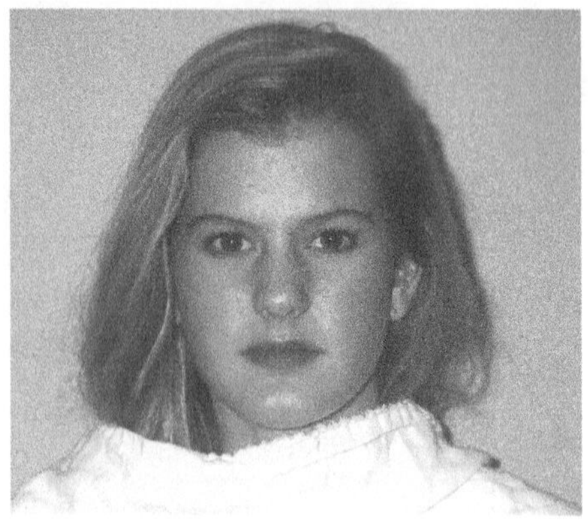
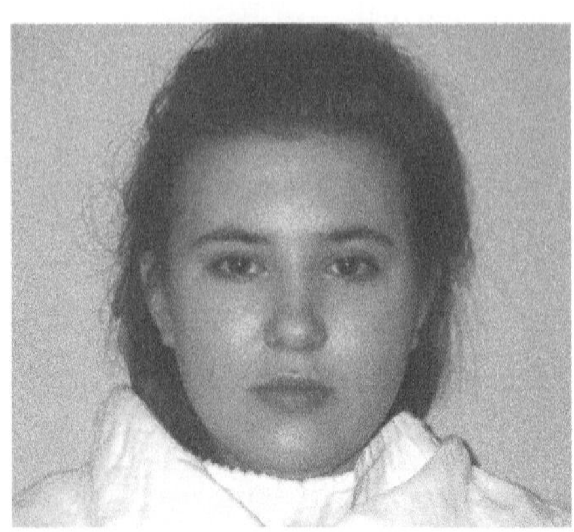
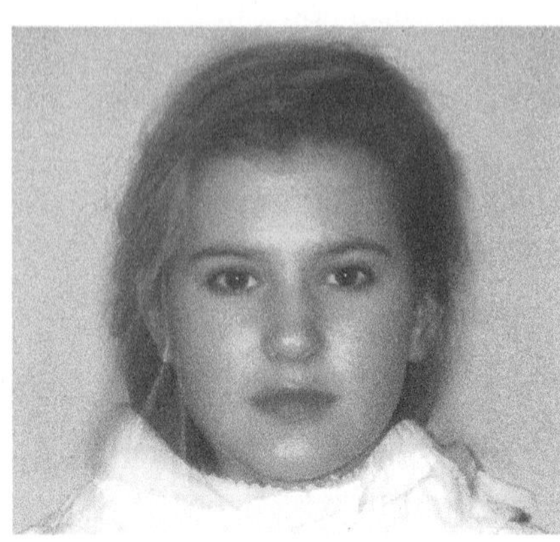

Physical attractiveness of composite faces. Langlois and Roggman (1990) created composites of faces using a computer. Pictured here is the first step in the process: The first two women's photos are merged to create the "composite person" at the far right. This composite person has facial features that are the mathematical average of the facial features of the two original women.

(From Langlois, Roggman, & Musselman, 1994)

facial shapes, whether Japanese or Caucasian, matched the descriptions that Michael Cunningham and his colleagues (Cunningham, 1986; Cunningham, Barbee, & Pike, 1990) found in their research. For example, the Japanese and Caucasian "highly attractive" female composites had higher cheekbones, a thinner jaw, and larger eyes than the "average attractive" composites did (Perrett et al., 1994).

The Power of Familiarity In the end, the crucial variable that explains interpersonal attraction may actually be familiarity (Berscheid & Reis, 1998). We've seen that "averaging" faces together produces one face that looks typical, familiar, and physically attractive (see also Halberstadt & Rhodes, 2000). Recent research has found evidence for an even more startling familiarity effect: When research participants rated the attractiveness of faces, they preferred the faces that most resembled their own! The researchers morphed a picture of each participant's face (without the participant's knowledge) into that of a person of the opposite sex. When presented with this photo of their opposite-sex "clone," participants gave it high ratings of attractiveness (Little & Perrett, 2002). This preference for the familiar appears to be shared by people in close relationships. Research participants who were members of the same family or close friends agreed much more with each other when they rated photographs of faces for attractiveness than they did with strangers (Bronstad & Russell, 2007).

Familiarity also underlies the other concepts we've discussed thus far: propinquity (people we see frequently become familiar through mere exposure), similarity (people who are similar to us will also seem familiar to us), and reciprocal liking (people who like each other get to know and become familiar with each other). All these attraction variables may be expressions of our "underlying preference for the familiar and safe over the unfamiliar and potentially dangerous" (Berscheid & Reis, 1998, p. 210).

Assumptions about Attractive People It's important to realize that beauty "matters"—even when it shouldn't. We're attracted to that which is beautiful, and that can lead to inequity in everyday life. A particularly chilling example of the unfair benefit of beauty was discovered by Lina Badr and Bahia Abdallah (2001), who rated the facial physical attractiveness and health status of premature infants born in hospitals in Beirut, Lebanon. They found that physical attractiveness significantly predicted the health outcomes of these infants above and beyond factors such as their medical condition. The more attractive the infant, the more quickly he or she gained weight and the shorter his or her stay in the hospital. The reason? Neonatal nurses responded more to the "prettier" infants and gave them better care.

Physical attractiveness confers other benefits as well. People of above-average looks tend to earn 10% to 15% more than those of below-average appearance (French, 2002; Hammermesh & Biddle, 1994; Judge, Hurst, & Simon, 2009; Mobius & Rosenblat, 2006). Attractiveness even helps win elections. Panu Poutvaara and his colleagues (2006) presented photographs of Finnish political candidates to research participants in many other countries (who would have no prior knowledge of these candidates) and asked them to rate the politicians on a variety of attributes including attractiveness. They found that the ratings of attractiveness were the best predictors of the actual number of votes each candidate had gotten in the real elections. A higher beauty rating predicted an increase of between 2.5 and 2.8 percentage points in the vote total for female candidates and between 1.5 and 2.1 percentage points for male candidates, amounts that could tip the balance of a close election (Poutvaara, Berggren, & Jordahl, 2006).

Many studies have found that physical attractiveness affects the attributions people make about others. Specifically, we tend to attribute to beautiful people positive qualities that have nothing to do with their looks. This is called the "what is beautiful is good" stereotype (Ashmore & Longo, 1995; Calvert, 1988; Dion, Berscheid, & Walster, 1972; Lemay, Clark, & Greenberg, 2010). Meta-analyses have revealed that physical attractiveness has the largest effect on both men's and women's attributions when they are judging social competence: The beautiful are thought to be more sociable, extroverted, and popular than the less attractive (Eagly et al., 1991; Feingold, 1992b). They are also seen as more sexual, happier, and more assertive.

TABLE 10.1 How Culture Affects the "What Is Beautiful Is Good" Stereotype

The "what is beautiful is good" stereotype has been explored in both individualistic cultures (e.g., North America) and collectivistic cultures (e.g., Asia). Male and female participants in the United States and Canada and in South Korea rated photographs of people with varying degrees of physical attractiveness. Responses indicated that some of the traits that make up the stereotype are the same across cultures, while other traits associated with the stereotype are different in the two cultures. In both cultures, the physically attractive are seen as having more of the characteristics that are valued in that culture than do the less physically attractive.

Traits Shared in the Korean, American, and Canadian Stereotype		
sociable	extraverted	likable
happy	popular	well-adjusted
friendly	mature	poised
sexually warm and responsive		
Additional Traits Present in the American and Canadian Stereotype		
strong	assertive	dominant
Additional Traits Present in the Korean Stereotype		
sensitive	empathic	generous
honest	trustworthy	

Sources: Eagly, Ashmore, Makhijani, & Longo (1991); Feingold (1992b); Wheeler & Kim (1997).

Do these stereotypes about the beautiful operate across cultures? The answer appears to be yes (Anderson, Adams, & Plaut, 2008; Chen, Shaffer, & Wu, 1997). For example, college students in South Korea were asked to rate a number of yearbook photographs (Wheeler & Kim, 1997). Both male and female participants thought the more physically attractive people would also be more socially skilled, friendly, and well adjusted—the same group of traits that North American participants thought went with physical attractiveness (see Table 10.1). But Korean and North American students differed in some of the other traits they assigned to the beautiful, highlighting differences in what is considered important in each culture (Markus et al., 1996; Triandis, 1995). For the American and Canadian students—who live in more-individualistic cultures that value independence, individuality, and self-reliance—the "beautiful" stereotype included traits of personal strength. These traits were not part of the Korean "beautiful" stereotype. Instead, for these students, who live in a more collectivistic culture that values harmonious group relations, the "beautiful" stereotype included integrity and concern for others (see Table 10.1).

Interestingly, the stereotype that the beautiful are particularly gifted in the area of social competence has some research support; highly attractive people *do* develop good social interaction skills and report having more-satisfying interactions with others than do less-attractive people (Feingold, 1992b; Langlois et al., 2000; Meier et al., 2010; Reis et al., 1982). Undoubtedly, this "kernel of truth" in the stereotype occurs because the beautiful, from a young age, receive a great deal of social attention that in turn helps them develop good social skills. You probably recognize the self-fulfilling prophecy at work here (see Chapter 3): The way we treat people affects how they behave and ultimately how they perceive themselves.

Can a "regular" person be made to act like a "beautiful" one through the self-fulfilling prophecy? To find out, researchers gave college men a photo and a packet of information about a woman with whom they were about to have a phone conversation (Snyder, Tanke, & Berscheid, 1977). But the photograph was rigged; at random, the men were either given a photo that a previous group of raters had judged to be attractive or one that a previous group had rated as unattractive. In both cases, this photo was *not* of the actual woman they were about to speak with. The experimental purpose of the photograph was to invoke the men's stereotype that "what is beautiful is good"—to test the possibility that the woman would be more likable, poised, and fun to talk to if her male conversation partner believed she was attractive than if he believed she was unattractive. Did the men's beliefs about appearance change the reality of how the women behaved?

In short, yes! The men who thought they were talking to an attractive woman responded to her in a warmer, more sociable manner than the men who thought they were talking to an unattractive woman. Not only that, but the men's behavior actually influenced how the women themselves behaved. When independent observers listened to a tape recording of only the woman's half of the conversation (without knowing anything about the photograph the men had seen), they rated the women whose male partners thought they were physically attractive as more confident, animated, and warm than they rated those women whose male partners thought they were unattractive. In other words, because the male partner thought he was talking to an attractive woman, he spoke to her in a way that brought out her best and most sparkling qualities. Subsequent studies have found similar results with the gender roles reversed (Andersen & Bem, 1981), reminding us that it is a myth that physical attractiveness only affects women's lives. Indeed, meta-analyses that have examined the effect of attractiveness across hundreds of studies have found that physical attractiveness is often as important a factor in men's lives as it is in women's (Eagly et al., 1991; Feingold, 1992b; Langlois et al., 2000).

Evolution and Mate Selection

The poet Robert Browning asked, "How do I love thee? Let me count the ways." For psychologists, the question is "*Why* do I love thee?" Some researchers believe that the answer lies in an **evolutionary approach to mate selection**. The basic tenet of evolutionary biology is that an animal's "fitness" is measured by its reproductive success (i.e, its capability to pass on its genes to the next generation). Reproductive success is not just part of the game; it *is* the game. This biological concept has been applied to social behavior by psychologists, who define **evolutionary psychology** as the attempt to explain social behavior in terms of genetic factors that have evolved over time according to the principles of natural selection. For example, as detailed above, one explanation for your tendency to find symmetrical faces more attractive is that symmetry indicates positive health and "good genes."

Evolution and Sex Differences Evolutionary psychology also makes some particularly interesting (and controversial) predictions regarding sex differences in mate preference. Specifically, evolutionary psychologists argue that men and women have very different agendas when it comes to mate selection, due to their differing roles in producing (and raising) offspring. For females, reproduction is costly in terms of time, energy, and effort: They must endure the discomforts and risks of pregnancy and birth, and, traditionally, theirs is the primary responsibility for caring for the infant until maturity. Reproducing, then, is serious business, so females, the theory goes, must consider carefully when and with whom to reproduce. In comparison, reproduction is a low-cost, short-term investment for males. The evolutionary approach to mate selection concludes that reproductive success for the two sexes translates into two very different behavior patterns: Throughout the animal world, males' reproductive success is measured by the *quantity* of their offspring. They pursue frequent pairings with many females in order to maximize their number of surviving progeny. In contrast, females' reproductive success lies in successfully raising each of their offspring to maturity. They pair less frequently and only with carefully chosen males, because the cost to them of raising and ensuring the survival of each offspring is so high (Berkow, 1989; Symons, 1979).

Now, what does all of this have to do with how people fall in love? David Buss and his colleagues argue that the evolutionary approach explains the different strategies and tendencies of men and women in romantic relationships (Buss, 1985, 1988a, 1996a, 1996b; Buss & Schmitt, 1993). Buss (1988b) explains that finding (and keeping) a mate requires one to display one's resources—the aspects of oneself that will appear attractive to potential mates. This approach argues that, across millennia, human beings have been selected through evolution to respond to certain external cues in the opposite sex. Women, facing high reproductive costs, will look for a man who can supply

Men seek to propagate widely, whereas women seek to propagate wisely.

—Robert Hinde

Evolutionary Approach to Mate Selection

A theory derived from evolutionary biology that holds that men and women are attracted to different characteristics in each other (men are attracted by women's appearance; women are attracted by men's resources) because this maximizes their chances of reproductive success

Evolutionary Psychology

The attempt to explain social behavior in terms of genetic factors that have evolved over time according to the principles of natural selection the resources and support she needs to raise a child. Men will look for a woman who appears capable of reproducing successfully. More precisely, men will respond to the physical appearance of women because age and health denote reproductive fitness, and women will respond to the economic and career achievements of men because these variables represent resources they and their offspring need (Buss, 1988b).

Many studies have provided support for these predictions. For example, Buss and colleagues (Buss, 1989; Buss et al., 1990) asked more than 9 thousand adults in 37 countries how desirable various characteristics were in a marriage partner. In general, women valued ambition, industriousness, and earning capacity in a potential mate more than the men did. The men valued physical attractiveness in a mate more than the women did. It should be noted, however, that the top characteristics on both men's and women's lists were the same—involving honesty, trustworthiness, and a pleasant personality (Buss & Barnes, 1986; Hatfield & Sprecher, 1995; Regan & Berscheid, 1997; Sprecher, Sullivan, & Hatfield, 1994). Other surveys have indicated that men prefer spouses who are younger than they are (youth indicating reproductive fitness), while women prefer spouses around their own age or older (Buss, 1989; Kenrick & Keefe, 1992).

Alternate Perspectives on Sex Differences The evolutionary approach to attraction and love has inspired its share of debate. For example, one could argue that evolutionary advantages to having multiple sexual partners should not be limited to men, but should also apply to women. With multiple partners, females would increase the odds of getting resources for their offspring, as well as benefit from genetic diversity. Females could choose an attractive male with "good genes" with whom to procreate and another male with whom to raise the offspring (Campbell, 2002; Gangestad & Simpson, 2000; Gangestad & Thornhill, 1998). It may also be the case that men value physical attractiveness in a partner, not because of evolved tendencies, but simply because they have been taught by society to value it—they have been conditioned by decades of advertising and media images to value beauty in women and to have a more recreational approach to sex than women do (Hatfield & Rapson, 1993). Similarly, research has found that in some situations, women value physical attractiveness just as much as men—specifically, when they are considering a potential sexual partner as opposed to a potential marriage partner (Regan & Berscheid, 1997; Simpson & Gangestad, 1992).

Other researchers offer additional arguments that the preference for different qualities in a mate can be explained without resorting to evolutionary principles: Around the world, women typically have less power, status, wealth, and other resources than men do. Therefore, in many societies women need to rely on men to achieve economic security, and they must consider this characteristic when choosing a husband (Rosenblatt, 1974). To test this hypothesis, Steven Gangestad (1993) correlated the extent to which women in several countries had access to financial resources and the extent to which women reported male physical attractiveness as an important variable in a mate. His results revealed that the more economic power women had in a given culture, the more highly women prioritized a man's physical attractiveness (Gangestad, 1993).

Watch on **MyPsychLab**
To learn more about evolutionary theories of mate selection, watch the MyPsychLab video ***Thinking Like a Psychologist: Evolutionary Psychology.***

As you can see, when discussing human mate preference, it is often difficult to disentangle "nature" (inborn preferences) from "nurture" (cultural norms and gender roles). When we hear about sex differences related to mate selection and attraction, our first instinct is often to turn to biological or evolutionary explanations (Conley et al., 2011). But a closer look often reveals that many of these differences are also attributable to situational factors. Take, for instance, the proposition that women are pickier than men when it comes to selecting a mate. Indeed, whether you look at online dating, speed-dating events, or old-fashioned face-to-face date requests, research indicates that women are significantly more discriminating in who they'll go out with than men are (Clark & Hatfield, 1989; Hitsch, Hortaçsu, & Ariely, 2010; Schützwohl et al., 2009; Penke, Fasolo, & Lenton, 2007). This makes sense from an evolutionary perspective. The argument would be that women *have* to be picky because they can't afford to make mistakes; unlike men, their fertility window is relatively narrow across the lifespan, and each decision to reproduce also requires more time and resources.

But consider the provocative results of a speed-dating study recently conducted by Eli Finkel and Paul Eastwick (2009). College students in this study had brief

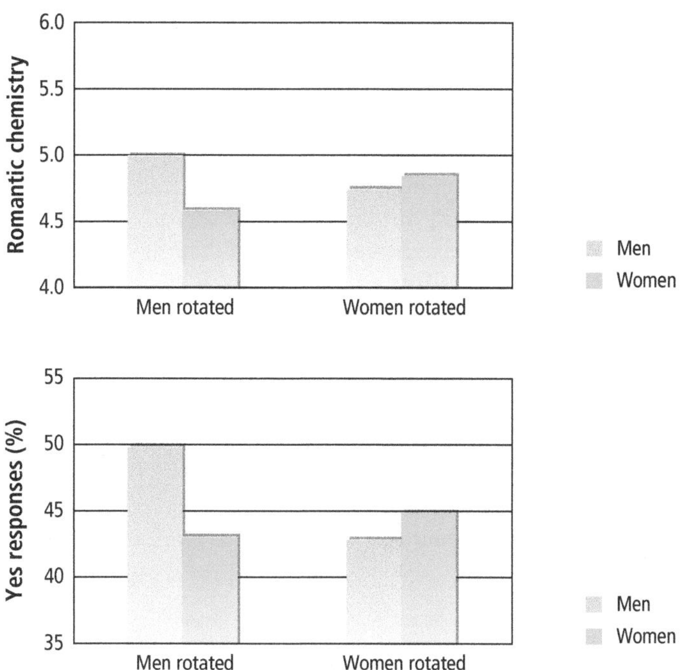

FIGURE 10.2

How Speed-Dating Rules Affect Attraction

In one version of Finkel and Eastwick's (2009) study, male college students rotated from one 4-minute speed date to the next as female students remained seated. As expected, the women were "pickier" than the men, perceiving less romantic chemistry and rating fewer of their speed-dating partners as people they'd like to get to know better. But changing the structure of the speed dates also changed these ratings: When the women rotated around and the men remained seated, women were no longer the pickier gender—if anything, now the *men* became slightly stingier when it came to perceptions of attraction.

(Adapted from Finkel & Eastwick, 2009)

conversations with a dozen different opposite-sex individuals. In these speed-dating sessions, the women remained seated while the men in attendance rotated in a circle, spending 4 minutes with each prospective dating partner before moving on to the next person. After each of the 12 women had been visited by each of the 12 men, all participants completed a questionnaire assessing their attraction to these potential mates (and later, from the comfort of their own homes, they recorded on the study Web site whether or not they'd be interested in seeing each person again). Once again, women were more selective than men, reporting lower levels of romantic desire and identifying fewer prospective mates that they'd like to get to know better (see Figure 10.2).

But an interesting thing happened when the researchers made a minor tweak to the speed-dating situation. In a second set of events, they had men and women swap roles. Now the men remained seated and the women rotated around—a simple modification, but one that stood regular dating protocol on its head. Instead of women sitting still while male suitors paraded in a circle, now the men remained stationary as women approached them. The "dates" themselves were still the same: 4-minute conversations after which both parties were asked for their impressions. But from a situational standpoint, this was traditional dating in reverse (Conley et al., 2011). And in this bizarro dating world where women did the approaching, women were no longer pickier than men. If anything, the female participants now reported more chemistry with their partners and identified more prospective mates that they wanted to see again.

Finkel and Eastwick's (2009) results suggest that the sex differences in mate selectivity do not simply reflect evolution or biology, but are also attributable to the established dating paradigm in most societies, in which men are the approachers and women the approachees. Being approached gives you control in the world of dating, regardless of sex or gender; being approached also means feeling in demand and having options. And so it is that, as with many aspects of human nature, we need both "nature" and "nurture" explanations to fully understand the psychology of attraction and mate selection.

Watch on **MyPsychLab**
To learn more about research on speed dating, watch the MyPsychLab video ***In The Real World: Speed Dating.***

Love and Close Relationships

By this point in the chapter, you have learned enough about attraction to make a favorable first impression the next time you meet someone. Suppose you want Claudia to like you. You should hang around her so that you become familiar, emphasize your similarity to her, and let her know you enjoy her company. But what if you want to do

This scene from the *Twilight* saga exemplifies the early stages of love.

more than make a good impression? What if you want to have a close friendship or a romantic relationship?

Until recently, social psychologists had little to say in answer to this question—research on attraction focused almost exclusively on first impressions. Why? Primarily because long-term relationships are much more difficult to study scientifically than first impressions. As we saw in Chapter 2, random assignment to different conditions is the hallmark of an experiment. When studying first impressions, a researcher can randomly assign you to a get-acquainted session with someone who is similar or dissimilar to you. But a researcher can't randomly assign you to the similar or dissimilar "lover" condition and make you have a relationship! In addition, the feelings and intimacy associated with close relationships can be difficult to measure. Psychologists face a daunting task when trying to analyze such complex feelings as love and passion.

Defining Love: Companionship and Passion

Love is or it ain't. Thin love ain't love at all.

—Toni Morrison

Despite the difficulties inherent to studying close relationships, social psychologists have made some interesting discoveries about the nature of love, how it develops, and how it flourishes. Let's begin with perhaps the most difficult question: What, exactly, is love? Early attempts to define love distinguished between liking and loving, showing that, as you might expect, love is something different from "lots of liking"—and not just in terms of sexual desire (Rubin, 1970).

For Shakespeare's Romeo and Juliet, love was passionate, turbulent, and full of longing; same goes for the Bella, Edward, and Jacob triangle of the *Twilight* series.

Love is something so divine, Description would but make it less; 'Tis what I feel, but can't define, 'Tis what I know, but can't express.

—Beilby Porteus

Your grandparents, if they've remained married for a long time, probably exemplify a calmer, more tranquil (and probably less supernatural) kind of love. We use the word *love* to describe all of these relationships, though each one seems to be of a different kind (Berscheid & Meyers, 1996, 1997; Fehr, 1994; Fehr & Russell, 1991; Vohs & Baumeister, 2004).

Social psychologists have recognized that a good definition of love must include the passionate, giddy feelings of romantic love as well as the deep, long-term devotion of married couples, lifelong friends, or siblings. In defining love, then, we generally distinguish between *companionate love* and *passionate love* (Hatfield, 1988; Hatfield & Rapson, 1993; Hatfield & Walster, 1978). **Companionate love** consists of feelings of intimacy and affection we have for someone that are not accompanied by passion or physiological arousal. People can experience companionate love in nonsexual close friendships, or in sexual relationships in which they experience great feelings of intimacy but not as much of the heat and passion as they once felt.

Companionate Love

The feelings of intimacy and affection we have for someone that are not accompanied by passion or physiological arousal

Passionate Love

An intense longing we feel for a person, accompanied by physiological arousal; when our love is reciprocated, we feel great fulfillment and ecstasy, but when it is not, we feel sadness and despair

Passionate love involves an intense longing for another person, characterized by the experience of physiological arousal—the feeling of shortness of breath and a thumping heart in someone's presence (Fisher, 2004; Regan & Berscheid, 1999). When things are going well (the other person loves us too), we feel great fulfillment and ecstasy. When things are not going well (our love is unrequited), we feel great sadness and despair. Cross-cultural research comparing an individualistic culture (the United States) and a collectivistic culture (China) indicates that American couples tend to value passionate love more than Chinese couples do, and Chinese couples tend to value companionate love more than American couples do (Gao, 1993; Jankowiak, 1995; Ting-Toomey & Chung, 1996). In comparison, the Taita of Kenya, in East Africa, value both equally; they conceptualize romantic love as a combination

TABLE 10.2 Cross-Cultural Evidence for Passionate Love Based on Anthropological Research in 166 Societies

Cultural Area	Passionate Love Present	Passionate Love Absent
Mediterranean	22 (95.7%)	1 (4.3%)
Sub-Saharan Africa	20 (76.9%)	6 (23.1%)
Eurasia	32 (97.0%)	1 (3.0%)
Insular Pacific	27 (93.1%)	2 (6.9%)
North America	24 (82.8%)	5 (17.2%)
South and Central America	22 (84.6%)	4 (15.4%)

Source: Data from Jankowiak & Fischer (1992).

of companionate and passionate love. The Taita consider this the best kind of love, and achieving it is a primary goal in their society (Bell, 1995). Reviewing the anthropological research on 166 societies, William Jankowiak and Edward Fischer (1992) found evidence for passionate love in 147 of them, as you can see in Table 10.2.

Try to reason about love, and you will lose your reason.
—French proverb

Elaine Hatfield and Susan Sprecher (1986) developed a questionnaire to measure passionate love. As measured by this scale, passionate love consists of strong, uncontrollable thoughts; intense feelings; and overt acts toward the target of one's affection. Find out if you are experiencing (or have experienced) passionate love by filling out the questionnaire in the following Try It! exercise.

TRY IT! Passionate Love Scale

These items ask you to describe how you feel when you are passionately in love. Think of the person whom you love most passionately right now. If you are not in love right now, think of the last person you loved passionately. If you have never been in love, think of the person you came closest to caring for in that way. Choose your answers as you remember how you felt when your feelings were the most intense.

For each of the 15 items, choose the number between 1 and 9 that most accurately describes your feelings. The answer scale ranges from 1 (not at all true) to 9 (definitely true). Write the number you choose next to each item.

1 2 3 4 5 6 7 8 9

↑ (1) Not at all true ↑ (5) Moderately true ↑ (9) Definitely true

1. I would feel deep despair if __________ left me.
2. Sometimes I feel I can't control my thoughts; they are obsessively on __________.
3. I feel happy when I am doing something to make __________ happy.
4. I would rather be with __________ than anyone else.
5. I'd get jealous if I thought __________ were falling in love with someone else.
6. I yearn to know all about __________.
7. I want __________—physically, emotionally, mentally.
8. I have an endless appetite for affection from __________.
9. For me, __________ is the perfect romantic partner.
10. I sense my body responding when __________ touches me.
11. __________ always seems to be on my mind.
12. I want __________ to know me—my thoughts, my fears, and my hopes.
13. I eagerly look for signs indicating ______'s desire for me.
14. I possess a powerful attraction for __________.
15. I get extremely depressed when things don't go right in my relationship with __________.

Scoring: Add up your scores for the 15 items. The total score can range from a minimum of 15 to a maximum of 135. The higher your score, the more your feelings for the person reflect passionate love; the items to which you gave a particularly high score reflect those components of passionate love that you experience most strongly.

(Adapted from Hatfield & Sprecher, 1986)

CONNECTIONS

This Is Your Brain . . . in Love

Falling in love is an extraordinary feeling—you are giddy, euphoric, full of energy, and more or less obsessed with your new beloved. These powerful emotions, experienced by people in many different cultures, suggest that romantic love may have evolved as a primary component of the human mating system. Is something special happening in our brains when we fall in love?

To find out, a team of researchers recruited college students in the greater New York area who described themselves as currently being "intensely in love" (Aron et al., 2005). They asked these research participants to bring two photographs to the experimental session: one of their beloved and one of an acquaintance of the same age and sex as their beloved. After filling out some questionnaires (including the Try It! Passionate Love Scale on page 281), the participants were ready for the main event. They slid into a functional MRI (fMRI) scanner, which records increases and decreases in blood flow in the brain, indicating which regions of the brain have neural activity at any given time. While the participant was in the scanner, the experimenters alternated projecting on a screen one photograph and then the other, interspersed with a mathematical distraction task.

The researchers found that two specific areas, deep within the brain, were activated when participants looked at the photograph of their romantic partner, but not when they looked at the photograph of their acquaintance (or engaged in the math task). Furthermore, those participants who self-reported higher levels of romantic love showed greater activation in these areas when looking at their beloved than those who reported lower levels (Aron et al., 2005). These two brain areas were the ventral tegmental area (VTA) and the caudate nucleus, which communicate with each other as part of a circuit. A great deal is already known about what causes these areas of the brain to fire and what kind of processing they do—and now, this knowledge can be applied to the experience of passionate love.

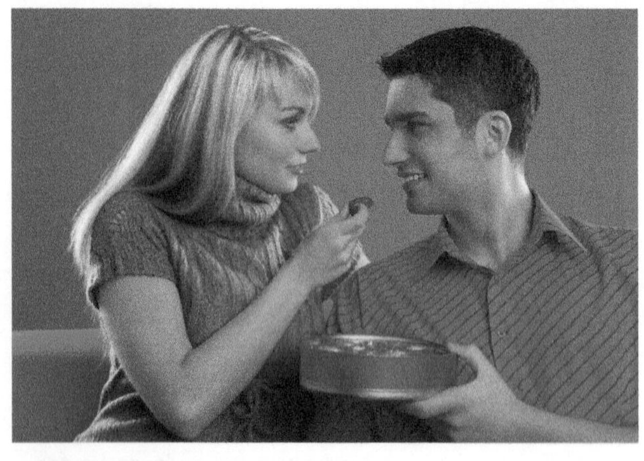

Falling in love activates a reward center in the brain that is also activated by eating chocolate.

Specifically, prior research has found that the VTA becomes active when people ingest cocaine—a drug that induces feelings of pleasure, euphoria, restlessness, sleeplessness, and loss of appetite (reactions that are also reminiscent of falling in love). The VTA, rich in the neurotransmitter dopamine, also fires when people eat chocolate. Thus, the VTA and the caudate nucleus constitute a major reward and motivation center of the brain. For example, fMRI studies of gamblers' brains as they gambled showed greatly increased activity in these dopamine-rich areas when they won—a rewarding and motivating event for them (Aron et al., 2005). Thus, when people say that falling in love is "addictive," "like a drug," or "like winning the lottery," they're right. All these experiences activate the same areas of the brain: dopamine-rich centers of pleasure, reward, and motivation (Bartels & Zeki, 2000, 2004; Fisher, 2004).

Culture and Love

As indicated above, the process of finding a romantic partner varies across the world. For example, in villages in Nepal, dating is forbidden, and even casual meetings between young men and women are considered inappropriate. Traditionally, one's future spouse is chosen by one's parents, who focus on the potential mate's social standing: family, caste, and economic resources. In these arranged marriages, the bride and groom often speak to each other for the first time on their wedding day. It is not unusual for the bride to cry during the ceremony and for the groom to look stunned and resigned (Goode, 1999). But despite what might seem an inauspicious beginning, many of these unions turn out to be very successful, especially when considered in light of the high divorce rate of unarranged marriages in the United States.

Beyond differences in custom and ceremony, cultures also differ with regard to how people think about, define, and experience love. As we have discussed throughout this book, Western and Eastern cultures vary with respect to how they conceptualize the needs of individuals and of the group or the society (Hofstede, 1984; Kim & Markus, 1999; Markus, Kitayama, & Heiman, 1996; Triandis, 1995). Social psychologists have noted that, while romantic love is an important, even crucial, basis for marriage in individualistic societies, it is less emphasized in collectivistic ones. In individualistic societies, romantic love is a heady, highly personal experience. One immerses oneself in the new partner, virtually ignoring friends and family for a while. The decision regarding whom to become involved with or marry is for the most part a personal one. In comparison, in collectivistic societies, the individual in love must consider the wishes of family and other group members, which sometimes includes agreeing to an arranged marriage (Dion & Dion, 1988, 1993; Fiske et al., 1998; Levine et al., 1995). Interestingly, though, in recent decades Western ways of finding a partner have begun to permeate collectivistic cultures through the media (Hatfield & Rapson, 2002). In Nepal, for example, prospective brides and grooms now write each other letters, getting to know each other a bit before the wedding (Goode, 1999).

Although people all over the world experience love, how love is defined varies across cultures.

How romantic love is defined varies across individualistic and collectivistic cultures. Researchers have found that Canadian college students have different attitudes about love, depending on their ethnocultural background: Asian (Chinese, Korean, Vietnamese, Indian, Pakistani), Anglo-Celtic (English, Irish, Scottish), or European (Scandinavian, Spanish, German, Polish). In comparison to their peers, Asian Canadian respondents are significantly more likely to identify with a companionable, friendship-based romantic love, a "style of love that would not disrupt a complex network of existing family relationships" (Dion & Dion, 1993, p. 465). Other researchers have found that in West African settings, relationships with one's parents, siblings, and other relatives are seen as more important and consequential than the more recent relationship one has formed with one's spouse. In many areas of West Africa, happily married couples do not live together in the same house, nor do they expect to sleep together every night. In stark contrast to the pattern of intimate relationships in individualistic cultures, their connection and obligation to their extended family members takes precedence over those to their spouse. In individualistic cultures, the opposite is typically true (Adams, Anderson, & Adonu, 2004). As another example of cross-cultural research, college students in 11 countries around the world were asked, "If a man (woman) had all the qualities you desired, would you marry this person if you were not in love with him (her)?" This study found that marrying for love was most important to participants in Westernized countries (e.g., the United States, Brazil, England, and Australia) and of least importance to participants in Asian countries (e.g., India, Pakistan, and Thailand; Levine et al., 1995).

The results of these studies indicate that the concept of romantic love is culturally specific (Dion & Dion, 1996; Gao & Gudykunst, 1995; Hatfield & Rapson, 2002; Hatfield & Sprecher, 1995; Sprecher, Aron et al., 1994). We all love, but we do not necessarily all love in the same way—or at least we don't describe it in the same way (Landis & O'Shea, 2000). For example, the Japanese use the word *amae* as an extremely positive emotional state in which one is a totally passive love object, indulged and taken care of by one's romantic partner, much like a mother-infant relationship. Amae has no equivalent word in English or in any other Western language; the closest is the word *dependency*, an emotional state that Western cultures consider unhealthy in adult relationships (Dion & Dion, 1993; Doi, 1988; Farrer, Tsuchiya, & Bagrowicz, 2008).

Similarly, the Chinese concept of *gan qing* differs from the Western view of romantic love. Gan qing is achieved by helping and working for another person; for example, a "romantic" act would be fixing someone's bicycle or helping someone learn new material (Gao, 1996). In Korea, a special kind of relationship is expressed by the concept of *jung*. Much more than "love," jung is what ties two people together. Couples in new relationships may feel strong love for each other, but they have not yet developed strong jung—that takes time and mutual experiences. Interestingly, jung can develop in negative relationships too—for example, between business rivals who dislike each other. Jung may unknowingly grow between them over time, with the result that they will feel that a strange connection exists between them (Lim & Choi, 1996; Kline, Horton, & Zhang, 2008).

Phillip Shaver and his colleagues (Shaver, Wu, & Schwartz, 1992) wondered if romantic or passionate love was associated with the same emotions in different cultures. They asked research participants in the United States, Italy, and China to sort emotional words into categories; their analysis indicated that love has similar and different meanings cross-culturally. The most striking difference was the presence of a "sad love" cluster in the Chinese sample. The Chinese had many love-related concepts that were sad, such as words for "sorrow-love," "tenderness-pity," and "sorrow-pity." Although this "sad love" cluster made a small appearance in the U.S. and Italian samples, it was not perceived as a major aspect of love in these Western societies.

Other researchers wondered what the lyrics of popular American and Chinese love songs would reveal about the experience of love in each culture (Rothbaum & Tsang, 1998). Finding that the Chinese love songs had significantly more references to suffering and to negative outcomes than the American love songs, the researchers looked to the Chinese concept of *yuan*. This is the belief that interpersonal relations are predestined. According to the traditional Buddhist belief in *karma*, fate determines what happens in a relationship. The romantic partners have little control over this process (Goodwin, 1999). If a relationship is not working, it cannot be saved; one must accept fate and the suffering that accompanies it (Rothbaum & Tsang, 1998). Although Chinese songs were sadder than American ones, there was no difference in the intensity with which love was described in the two countries. The researchers found that love in Chinese songs was as "passionate and erotic" as love expressed in American songs.

Thus, it appears that romantic love is nearly universal in the human species, but cultural rules alter how that emotional state is experienced, expressed, and remembered (Carillo, 2001; Farrer, 2002; Higgins et al., 2002; Jackson et al., 2006). As one final example, Shuangyue Zhang and Susan Kline (2009) found two major differences in American and Chinese dating couples' decisions to marry. When describing how they would decide whether or not to marry their partners, Chinese students placed a heavier emphasis on two concepts central to their collectivistic culture: *xiao* (the obedience and devotion shown by children to their parents) and *guanxi* (relationships as a network of connections). In contrast, American students placed importance on receiving support, care, and "living a better life." As Robert Moore (1998) noted in summarizing his research in the People's Republic of China, "Young Chinese do fall deeply in love and experience the same joys and sorrows of romance as young Westerners do. But they do so according to standards that require . . . the individual [to] sacrifice personal interests for the sake of the family . . . This means avoiding fleeting infatuations, casual sexual encounters, and a dating context [where] family concerns are forgotten" (p. 280).

Watch on **MyPsychLab**

For another cultural perspective on love, watch the MyPsychLab video ***Arranged Marriage: Rati and Subas, 20s.***

Attachment Styles in Intimate Relationships

Much as the culture in which we grow up shapes how we think about and experience love, so do our interactions in the early years of life with parents or caregivers. Specifically, one approach to examining intimate relationships among adults focuses on **attachment styles** and draws on the groundbreaking work of John Bowlby (1969, 1973, 1980) and Mary Ainsworth (Ainsworth et al., 1978) concerning how infants form bonds with their primary caregivers (usually their mothers or fathers).

Attachment Styles

The expectations people develop about relationships with others, based on the relationship they had with their primary caregiver when they were infants

Ainsworth and her colleagues (1978) identified three types of relationships between infants and their caregivers. Infants with a **secure attachment style** typically have caregivers who are responsive to their needs and who show positive emotions when interacting with them. These infants trust their caregivers, are not worried about abandonment, and come to view themselves as worthy and well liked. Infants with an **avoidant attachment style** typically have caregivers who are aloof and distant, rebuffing attempts to establish intimacy. These infants desire to be close to their caregiver but learn to suppress this need, as if they know that such attempts will be rejected. Infants with an **anxious/ambivalent attachment style** typically have caregivers who are inconsistent and overbearing in their affection. These infants are unusually anxious because they can never predict when and how their caregivers will respond to their needs.

Secure Attachment Style

An attachment style characterized by trust, a lack of concern with being abandoned, and the view that one is worthy and well liked

Avoidant Attachment Style

An attachment style characterized by a suppression of attachment needs because attempts to be intimate have been rebuffed; people with this style find it difficult to develop intimate relationships

Anxious/Ambivalent Attachment Style

An attachment style characterized by a concern that others will not reciprocate one's desire for intimacy, resulting in higher-than-average levels of anxiety

The key assumption of attachment theory is that the particular attachment style we learn in infancy becomes our working model or schema (as we discussed in Chapter 3) for what relationships are like. These early relationship schemas typically stay with us throughout life and generalize to adult relationships with other people (Fraley & Shaver, 2000; Hartup & Laursen, 1999; Mikulincer & Shaver, 2003, 2007; Mikulincer et al., 2009). Thus, people who as children had a secure relationship with their parents or caregivers are better able to develop mature, lasting relationships as adults; people who had avoidant relationships with their parents are less able to trust others and find it difficult to develop close, intimate relationships; and people who had anxious/ambivalent relationships with their parents want to become close to their adult partners but often worry that their partners will not return their affections (Collins & Feeney, 2000; 2004a; Rholes, Simpson & Friedman, 2006; Simpson et al., 2007). This has been borne out in numerous studies that measure adults' attachment styles with questionnaires and then correlate the styles with the quality of their romantic relationships (though, as we note below, it is *not* the case that attachment style is destiny—people who had less-happy relationships with their parents are *not* doomed to perpetually unhappy adult relationships).

In my very own self, I am part of my family.

—D. H. Lawrence

For example, researchers asked adults to choose one of the three statements shown in Table 10.3, according to how they typically feel in romantic relationships (Hazan & Shaver, 1987). Each statement was designed to capture one of the three kinds of attachment styles we described. The researchers also asked people questions about their current relationships. The results of this study were consistent with an attachment theory perspective (Feeney, Noller, & Roberts, 2000; Feeney, Cassidy, & Ramos-Marcuse, 2008; Hazan & Shaver, 1994a, 1994b; Simpson & Rholes, 1994).

Other researchers have reported similar findings: Securely attached individuals have the most enduring romantic relationships of the three attachment types. They experience the highest level of commitment to relationships as well as the highest level of satisfaction with their relationships. The anxious/ambivalently attached individuals have the most short-lived romantic relationships. They enter into relationships the most quickly, often before they know their partner well. For example, a study conducted at a marriage license bureau found that anxious men acquired marriage licenses after a shorter courtship than did either secure or avoidant men (Senchak & Leonard, 1992). They are also the most upset and angriest of the three types when their love is not reciprocated. The third category, avoidant individuals, are the least likely to enter into a relationship and the most likely to report never having been in love. They maintain their emotional distance and have the lowest level of commitment to their relationships of the three types (Campbell et al., 2005; Feeney & Noller, 1990; Keelan, Dion, & Dion, 1994).

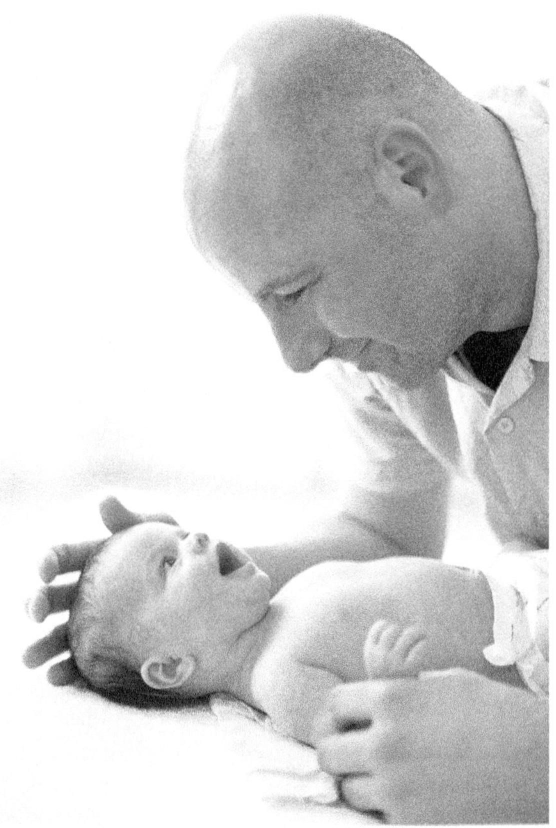

Attachment theory predicts that the attachment style we learn as infants and young children stays with us throughout life and generalizes to all of our relationships with other people.

TABLE 10.3 Measuring Attachment Styles

As part of a survey of attitudes toward love published in a newspaper, people were asked to choose the statement that best described their romantic relationships. The attachment style each statement was designed to measure and the percentage of people who chose each alternative are indicated.

Secure style	56%	"I find it relatively easy to get close to others and am comfortable depending on them and having them depend on me. I don't often worry about being abandoned or about someone getting too close."
Avoidant style	25%	"I am somewhat uncomfortable being close to others; I find it difficult to trust them completely, difficult to allow myself to depend on them. I am nervous when anyone gets close, and often love partners want me to be more intimate than I feel comfortable being."
Anxious style	19%	"I find that others are reluctant to get as close as I would like. I often worry that my partner doesn't really love me or won't stay with me. I want to merge completely with another person, and this desire sometimes scares people away."

Source: Adapted from Hazen & Shaver (1986).

Attachment in the Lab Attachment styles have also been found to affect men's and women's behavior in an experimental setting (Collins et al., 2006; Simpson, Rholes, & Nelligan, 1992). For example, researchers brought heterosexual dating couples into the lab and measured their attachment styles using a questionnaire (Collins & Feeney, 2004b). They then asked one member of each couple (the "speaker") to give a speech on the value of a college education, which would be videotaped and later judged for quality. The other member of the couple (the "waiter") was asked to sit in a waiting room while the speaker prepared and gave the speech. The couples were told that they would be allowed to communicate with each other, with the waiter sending a couple of notes to the speaker.

Unbeknownst to the participants, they had been randomly assigned to one of two conditions: The waiter would send either very supportive notes or less-supportive notes to the speaker. In fact, the experimenters had written the notes themselves, and they asked the waiters to copy the notes so they would be in their handwriting. The speakers received two notes, one while he or she prepared the speech and the other after he or she had given the speech. The supportive notes were: "Don't worry, just say how you feel and what you think and you'll do great," and "I liked your speech. That was a hard thing to do and you did a really good job." The two less supportive notes were: "Try not to say anything too embarrassing—especially since so many people will be watching your tape," and "Your speech was a little hard to follow, but I guess you did the best you could under the circumstances."

Now, how would you react to messages like these from your romantic partner? And how might your attachment style affect your perceptions? Collins and Feeney (2004b) found no differences between the participants in terms of their reactions to supportive notes; everyone felt supported by their partners, and there were no differences given their attachment styles. However, when participants received the less supportive notes, significant differences emerged. The first note, received while they were preparing their speech, was perceived the most negatively by highly avoidant participants. The second note, received after they'd given their speech, was perceived the most negatively by highly anxious participants. In both cases, these participants reported that the note was upsetting, was disappointing, and made them feel angry.

Thus, while securely attached participants reacted calmly to the less supportive messages, avoidant and anxious participants saw the same comments in a much more negative light. Avoidant individuals believe that people they are close to cannot be relied on for support or nurturance. Receiving the unsupportive note at a time when they needed support—preparing the speech—was particularly upsetting to them. Anxious individuals believe that people close to them are unpredictable and likely to reject them. Receiving the unsupportive note at a time when they needed positive feedback—after giving the speech—was particularly upsetting to them. In comparison, secure individuals took the somewhat unsupportive notes in stride, interpreting them as more neutral in tone than the avoidant or anxious participants did (Collins & Feeney, 2004b).

Attachment Style is not Destiny It is important to note, however, that attachment theory does not suggest that people who had unhappy relationships with their parents are doomed to repeat this same kind of unhappy relationship with everyone they ever meet (Simms, 2002). Some researchers have recontacted their research participants months or years after their original studies and asked them to take the attachment-style scale again. They have found that 25% to 30% of their participants have changed from one attachment style to another (Feeney & Noller, 1996; Kirkpatrick & Hazan, 1994). People can and do change; their experiences in relationships can help them learn new and healthier ways of relating to others than what they experienced as children (Baldwin & Fehr, 1995). Moreover, other research suggests that, at any given time, the attachment style that people display is the one that is called into play by their partner's behavior and the type of relationship that they've created as a couple. Thus, people may respond to situational variables in their relationships, displaying a more secure attachment style in one relationship and a more anxious one in another (Fraley, 2002; Hammond & Fletcher, 1991; Simpson et al., 2003).

Theories of Relationship Satisfaction: Social Exchange and Equity

So far, we've examined how cultural expectations and personal attachment styles predict the ways in which you define and experience love. But what aspects of your actual relationships influence relationship satisfaction? What factors determine how happy you are with your current mate or with your "love life" more generally? We turn now to theories of relationship satisfaction in the attempt to provide empirically based answers to these most intimate of questions.

Social Exchange Theory Many of the variables we discussed above as antecedents of attraction can be thought of as examples of social rewards. It is pleasing to have our attitudes validated; thus, the more similar a person's attitudes are to ours, the more rewarded we feel by spending time together. Likewise, it is rewarding to be around someone who likes us, particularly when that person is physically attractive. In other words, the more social rewards (and the fewer costs) a person provides us with, the more we like the person. The flip side of this equation is that if a relationship costs (e.g., in terms of emotional turmoil) far more than it gives (e.g., in terms of validation or praise), chances are that it will not last.

This simple notion that relationships operate on an economic model of costs and benefits, much like other marketplaces, has been expanded by researchers into complex theories of social exchange (Blau, 1964; Homans, 1961; Kelley & Thibaut, 1978; Secord & Backman, 1964; Thibaut & Kelley, 1959). **Social exchange theory** holds that how people feel about a relationship will depend on their perceptions of the rewards they receive from it, their perceptions of the costs they incur, and their beliefs regarding what kind of relationship they deserve (and the probability that they could find a better relationship with someone else). In essence, we "buy" the best relationship we can get—one that gives us the most value for our emotional dollar. The basic concepts of social exchange theory are reward, cost, outcome, and comparison level.

Rewards are the gratifying aspects of a relationship that make it worthwhile and reinforcing. They include the kinds of personal characteristics and behaviors of our relationship partner that we have already discussed, and our ability to acquire external resources by virtue of knowing this person (e.g., gaining access to money, status, activities, or other interesting people; Lott & Lott, 1974). For example, in Brazil, friendship

Love is often nothing but a favorable exchange between two people who get the most of what they can expect, considering their value on the personality market.
—Erich Fromm, *The Sane Society*, 1955

Friendship is a scheme for the mutual exchange of personal advantages and favors.
—François de La Rochefoucauld, *Maxims*, 1665

Social Exchange Theory
The idea that people's feelings about a relationship depend on their perceptions of the rewards and costs of the relationship, the kind of relationship they deserve, and their chances for having a better relationship with someone else

is openly used as an exchange value. Brazilians will readily admit that they need a *pistolão* (literally, a big, powerful handgun), meaning that they need a person who will use personal connections to help them get what they want (Rector & Neiva, 1996). Costs are, obviously, the other side of the coin, and all friendships and romantic relationships have some costs attached to them, such as putting up with those annoying habits and characteristics of the other person. The outcome of the relationship is a direct comparison of its rewards and costs; you can think of it as a mathematical formula where outcome equals rewards minus costs. If you come up with a negative number, your relationship is not in good shape.

Watch on MyPsychLab
To learn more about how we evaluate our relationships, watch the MyPsychLab video ***What's In It For Me? Attraction.***

In addition to rewards and costs, how satisfied you are with your relationship depends on another variable: your **comparison level**, or what you *expect* the outcome of your relationship to be in terms of costs and rewards (Kelley & Thibaut, 1978; Thibaut & Kelley, 1959). Over time, you have amassed a long history of relationships with other people, and this history has led you to have certain expectations as to what your current and future relationships should be like. Some people have a high comparison level, expecting lots of rewards and few costs in their relationships. If a given relationship doesn't match this expected comparison level, they quickly will grow unhappy and unsatisfied. In contrast, people who have a low comparison level would be happy in the same relationship because they expect their relationships to be difficult and costly.

Finally, your satisfaction with a relationship also depends on your perception of the likelihood that you could replace it with a better one—or your **comparison level for alternatives**. As the saying goes, there are plenty of fish in the sea. Could a relationship with a different person give you a better outcome (i.e., greater rewards and fewer costs) than your current one? People who have a high comparison level for alternatives—either because they believe the world is full of fabulous people dying to meet them or because they know of one particular fabulous person dying to meet them—are more likely to take the plunge and hit the market for a new friend or lover. People with a low comparison level for alternatives will be more likely to stay in a costly relationship, because, in their mind, what they have may not be great, but it's better than their expectation of what they could find elsewhere (Lehmiller & Agnew, 2006; Simpson, 1987).

What, after all, is our life but a great dance in which we are all trying to fix the best going rate of exchange?
—Malcolm Bradbury, 1992

Social exchange theory has received a great deal of empirical support. Friends and romantic couples do pay attention to the costs and rewards in their relationships, and these affect how positively people feel about the status of the relationship (Bui, Peplau, & Hill, 1996; Rusbult, 1983; Rusbult, Martz, & Agnew, 1998). Such findings have been observed for intimate relationships in cultures as different as Taiwan and the Netherlands (Lin & Rusbult, 1995; Le & Agnew, 2003; Rusbult & Van Lange, 1996; Van Lange et al., 1997). Generally speaking, when relationships are perceived as offering a lot of rewards, people report feeling happy and satisfied.

Comparison Level
People's expectations about the level of rewards and punishments they are likely to receive in a particular relationship

Comparison Level for Alternatives
People's expectations about the level of rewards and punishments they would receive in an alternative relationship

Investment Model
The theory that people's commitment to a relationship depends not only on their satisfaction with the relationship in terms of rewards, costs, and comparison level and their comparison level for alternatives, but also on how much they have invested in the relationship that would be lost by leaving it

However, many people do not leave their partners even when they are dissatisfied and their other alternatives look bright. Research indicates that we need to consider at least one additional factor to understand close relationships: a person's level of investment in the relationship (Impett, Beals, & Peplau, 2001–2002; Rusbult et al., 2001; Goodfriend & Agnew, 2008). In her **investment model** of close relationships, Caryl Rusbult (1983) defines *investment* as anything people have put into a relationship that will be lost if they leave it. Examples include tangible things, such as financial resources and possessions (e.g., a house), as well as intangible things, such as the emotional welfare of one's children, the time and emotional energy spent building the relationship, and the sense of personal integrity that will be lost if one gets divorced. As seen in Figure 10.3, the greater the investment individuals have in a relationship, the less likely they are to leave, even when satisfaction is low and other alternatives look promising. In short, to predict whether people will stay in an intimate relationship, we need to know (1) how satisfied they are with the relationship, (2) what they think of their alternatives, and (3) how great their investment in the relationship is.

To test this model, Rusbult (1983) asked college students involved in heterosexual dating relationships to fill out questionnaires for 7 months. Every 3 weeks, people answered questions about each of the components of the model shown in Figure 10.3.

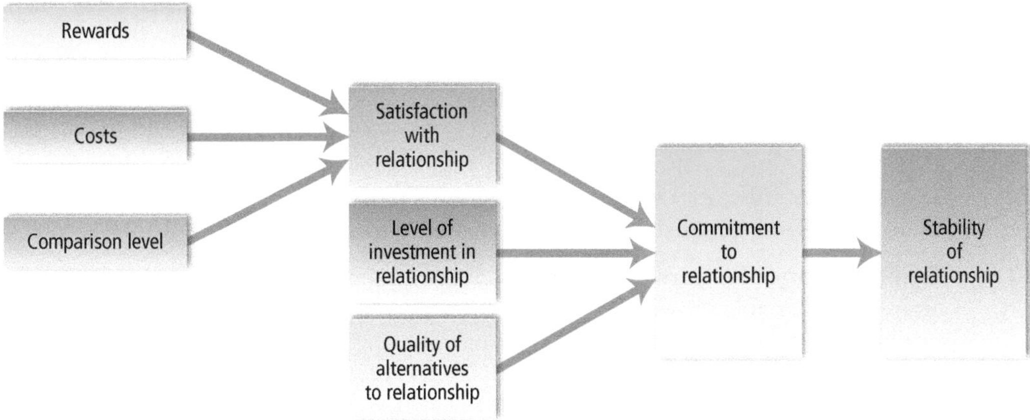

FIGURE 10.3

The Investment Model of Commitment

People's commitment to a relationship depends on several variables. First, their *satisfaction* with the relationship is based on their comparing their *rewards* to their *costs* and determining if the outcome exceeds their general expectation of what they should get in a relationship (or *comparison level*). Next, their *commitment* to the relationship depends on three variables: how *satisfied* they are, how much they feel they have *invested* in the relationship, and whether they have good *alternatives* to this relationship. These commitment variables in turn predict how *stable* the relationship will be. For example, a woman who feels her relationship has more costs and fewer rewards than she considers acceptable would have a low satisfaction. If she also felt she had little invested in the relationship and a very attractive person had just asked her for a date, she would have a low level of commitment. The end result is low stability; most likely, she will break up with her current partner.

(Adapted from Rusbult, 1983)

Rusbult also kept track of whether the students stayed in the relationships or broke up. As you can see in Figure 10.4, satisfaction, alternatives, and investments all predicted how committed people were to the relationship and whether it lasted. (The higher the number on the scale, the more each factor predicted the commitment to and length of the relationship.) Subsequent studies have found results similar to those shown in Figure 10.4 for married couples of diverse ages, lesbian and gay couples, nonsexual friendships, and residents of both the United States and Taiwan (Kurdek, 1992; Lin & Rusbult, 1995; Rusbult, 1991; Rusbult & Buunk, 1993).

Does the same model hold for destructive relationships? To find out, Rusbult and a colleague interviewed women who had sought refuge at a shelter for battered women,

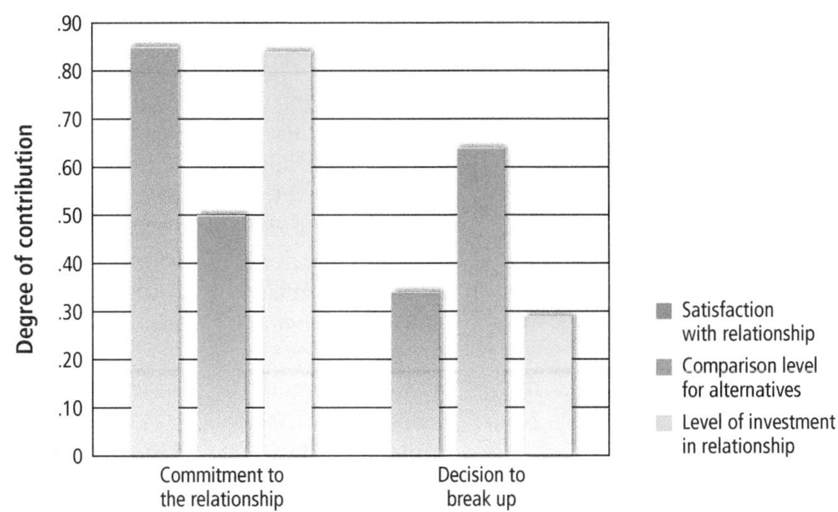

FIGURE 10.4

A Test of the Investment Model

This study examined the extent to which college students' satisfaction with a relationship, their comparison level for alternatives, and their investment in the relationship predicted their commitment to the relationship and their decision about whether to break up with their partner. The higher the number, the more each variable predicted commitment and breakup, independent of the two other variables. All three variables were good predictors of how committed people were and whether or not they broke up.

(Adapted from Rusbult, 1983)

Equity Theory
The idea that people are happiest with relationships in which the rewards and costs experienced and the contributions made by both parties are roughly equal

Exchange Relationships
Relationships governed by the need for equity (i.e., for an equal ratio of rewards and costs)

asking them about their abusive romantic relationships (Rusbult & Martz, 1995). Why had these women stayed in these relationships, even to the point where some of them returned to an abusive partner after leaving the shelter? As the theory predicts, feelings of commitment to the abusive relationship were greater among women who had poorer economic alternatives to the relationship or were more heavily invested in the relationship. In long-term relationships, then, commitment is based on more than just the amount of rewards and costs a partner elicits; it also depends on people's perceptions of their investments in, satisfaction with, and alternatives to the relationship.

Equity Theory Some researchers have criticized social exchange theory for ignoring an essential variable in relationships—the notion of fairness, or equity. Proponents of **equity theory** argue that people are not just out to get the most rewards for the least cost; we are also concerned about equity or the idea that the rewards and costs we experience (and the contributions we make to the relationship) should be roughly equal to those of the other person (Homans, 1961; Walster, Walster, & Berscheid, 1978). These theorists describe equitable relationships as the happiest and most stable (Kalmijn & Monden, 2012). In comparison, inequitable relationships result in one person feeling overbenefited (getting a lot of rewards, incurring few costs, having to devote little time or energy to the relationship) and the other feeling underbenefited (getting few rewards, incurring a lot of costs, having to devote a lot of time and energy to the relationship).

According to equity theory, both underbenefited and overbenefited partners should feel uneasy about this state of affairs, and both should be motivated to restore equity to the relationship. This makes sense for the underbenefited person—after all, who wants to feel miserable and unappreciated? But why should the overbenefited individual want to give up what social exchange theory indicates is a cushy deal: lots of rewards for little cost and little work? Theorists argue that equity is a powerful social norm and that people will eventually feel uncomfortable and guilty if they keep getting more than they deserve in a relationship. Still, being overbenefited isn't quite as bad as being underbenefited, and research has indicated that inequity is perceived as more of a problem by the underbenefited individual (Buunk & Schaufeli, 1999; Guerrero, La Valley, & Farinelli, 2008; Sprecher & Schwartz, 1994; Van Yperen & Buunk, 1990).

Of course, this whole notion of equity implies that partners in a relationship are keeping track of who is benefiting how much and who is getting shortchanged. Some might suggest that many people in happy relationships don't spend so much time and energy keeping tabs on contributions and benefits in this manner. Indeed, the more we get to know someone, the more reluctant we are to believe that we are simply exchanging favors or expecting immediate compensation for every kind gesture. Sure, in casual relationships, we trade "in kind"—you lend someone your class notes, she buys you lunch. But in intimate relationships, we're trading different types of resources, so even if we wanted to, determining whether or not equity has been achieved becomes difficult. Does "dinner at an expensive restaurant on Monday balance out three nights of neglect due to a heavy workload" (Hatfield & Rapson, 1993, p. 130)? In other words, long-term, intimate relationships may be governed by a looser give-and-take notion of equity rather than a rigid tit-for-tat strategy (Kollack, Blumstein, & Schwartz, 1994; Laursen & Hartup, 2002; Vaananen et al., 2005).

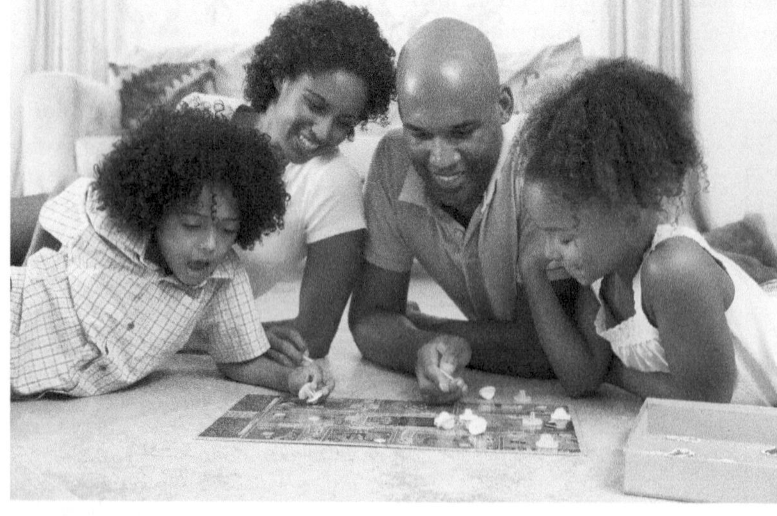

Close relationships can have either exchange or communal properties. Family relationships are typically communal.

According to Margaret Clark and Judson Mills (1993), interactions between new acquaintances are governed by equity concerns and are called **exchange relationships**. As you can see in Figure 10.5,

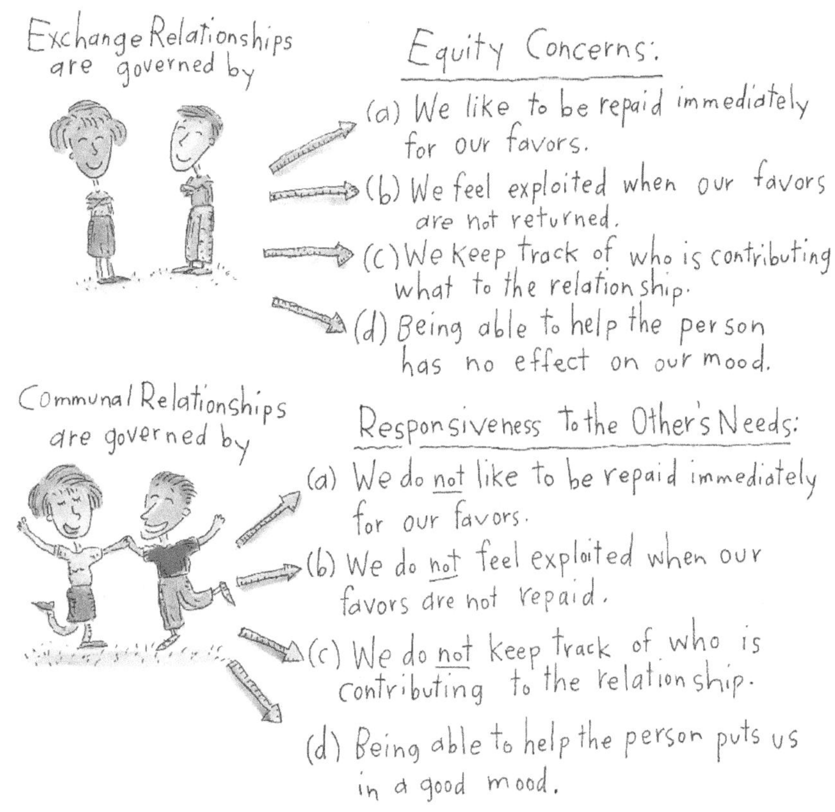

FIGURE 10.5
Exchange Versus Communal Relationships

in exchange relationships, people keep track of who is contributing what and feel taken advantage of when they feel they are putting more into the relationship than they are getting out of it. In comparison, longer-term interactions between close friends, family members, and romantic partners are governed less by an equity norm and more by a desire to help each other in times of need. In these **communal relationships**, people give in response to the other's needs, regardless of whether they get paid back (Clark, 1984, 1986; Clark & Mills, 1993; Mills & Clark, 1982, 1994, 2001; Vaananen et al., 2005). In this manner, communal interactions are the hallmark of long-term, intimate relationships. Research comparing heterosexual couples to same-sex couples has found that they are equally committed and communal in their relationships: if anything, gay men and lesbians report greater compatibility and less conflict than heterosexual couples do (Balsam et al., 2008; Roisman et al., 2008).

Are people in communal relationships completely unconcerned with equity? Not necessarily. As we saw earlier, people do feel distressed if they believe their intimate relationships are inequitable (Canary & Stafford, 2001; Walster et al., 1978); however, equity takes on a somewhat different form in communal relationships than it does in less-intimate ones. In communal relationships, the partners are more relaxed about what constitutes equity at any given time, believing that things will eventually balance out and a rough kind of equity will be achieved over the long run (Lemay & Clark, 2008; Lemay, Clark, & Feeney, 2007). If this doesn't happen—if they continue to feel that there is an imbalance—the relationship may ultimately end.

Ending Intimate Relationships

The American divorce rate is nearly 50% and has been for the past two decades (Thernstrom, 2003; National Center for Health Statistics, 2005). An examination of data from 58 societies, taken from the *Demographic Yearbook of the United Nations*, indicates that the majority of separations and divorces occur around the fourth year of

Communal Relationships
Relationships in which people's primary concern is being responsive to the other person's needs

Love is like war;.easy to begin but very hard to stop.
—H. L. Mencken

marriage (Fisher, 2004). And, of course, countless romantic relationships between unmarried individuals end every day. After many years of studying what love is and how it blooms, social psychologists are now beginning to explore the end of the story—how it dies.

The Process of Breaking Up

Ending a romantic relationship is one of life's more painful experiences. Researchers continue to examine what makes people end a relationship and the disengagement strategies they use to do so (Baxter, 1986; Femlee, Sprecher, & Bassin, 1990; Frazier & Cook, 1993; Helgeson, 1994; Rusbult & Zembrodt, 1983; Simpson, 1987). For example, Steve Duck (1982) reminds us that relationship dissolution is not a single event but a process with many steps (see Figure 10.6). Duck theorizes that four stages of dissolution exist, ranging from the intrapersonal (the individual thinks a lot about his or her dissatisfaction with the relationship) to the dyadic (the individual discusses the breakup with the partner) to the social (the breakup is announced to other people) and back to the intrapersonal (the individual recovers from the breakup and forms an internal account of how and why it happened). In terms of the last stage in the process, John Harvey and his colleagues (Harvey, 1995; Harvey, Flanary, & Morgan, 1986; Harvey, Orbuch, & Weber, 1992) have found that the honest version of "why the relationship ended" that we present to close friends can be very different from the official version that we present to coworkers or neighbors.

Why relationships end has been studied from several angles. One approach uses the investment model, which we discussed earlier (Bui et al., 1996; Drigotas & Rusbult, 1992). Caryl Rusbult has identified four types of behavior that occur in troubled relationships (Rusbult, 1987; Rusbult & Zembrodt, 1983). The first two types are destructive behaviors: actively harming the relationship (e.g., abusing the partner, threatening to break up, actually leaving) and passively allowing the relationship to deteriorate (e.g., refusing to deal with problems, ignoring the partner or spending less time together,

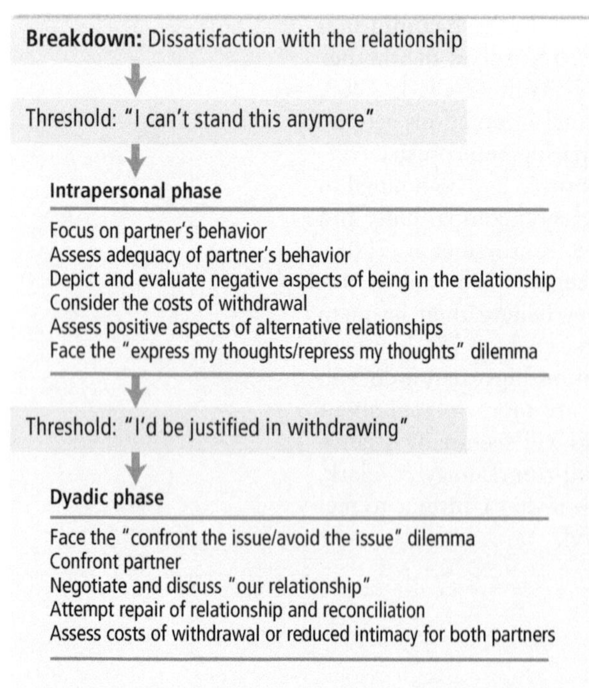

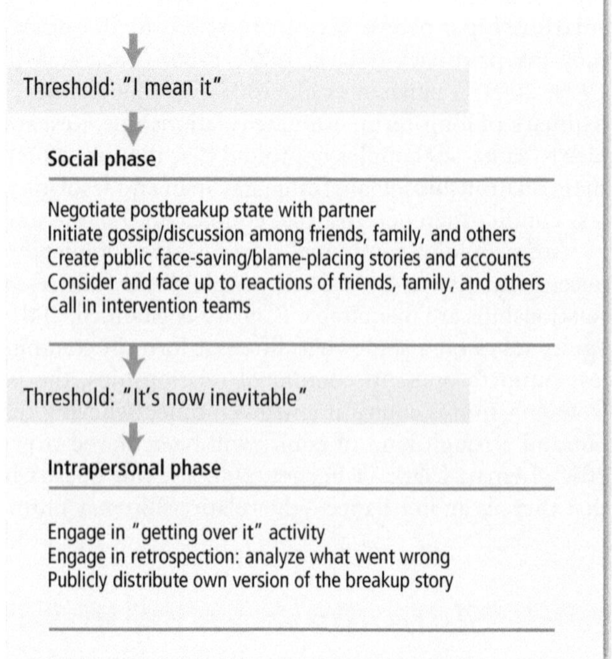

FIGURE 10.6

Steps in Dissolving Close Relationships

(Adapted from Duck, 1982)

Relationships can end for many reasons. For example, in "fatal attractions," the very qualities that once attracted you ("He's so mature and wise" / "She's so young and vivacious") can become the very reason you break up ("He's too old" / "She's too immature").

putting no energy into the relationship). The other two responses are positive, constructive behaviors: actively trying to improve the relationship (e.g., discussing problems, trying to change, going to a therapist) and passively remaining loyal to the relationship (e.g., waiting and hoping that the situation will improve, being supportive rather than fighting, remaining optimistic). Rusbult and her colleagues have found that destructive behaviors harm a relationship a lot more than constructive behaviors help it. When one partner acts destructively and the other partner responds constructively to save the relationship (the more common pattern), the relationship is likely to continue, but when both partners act destructively, the relationship typically ends (Rusbult, Johnson, & Morrow, 1986; Rusbult, Yovetich, & Verette, 1996).

Another approach to studying why relationships end considers what attracted the people to each other in the first place. For example, in one study, college men and women were asked to focus on a romantic relationship that had ended and to list the qualities that first attracted them to the person and the characteristics they ended up disliking the most about the person (Femlee, 1995, 1998a, 1988b). Thirty percent of these breakups were examples of "fatal attractions." The very qualities that were initially so attractive became the very reasons why the relationship ended. For example, "He's so unusual and different" became "He and I have nothing in common." "She's so exciting and unpredictable" became "I can never count on her." This type of breakup reminds us again of the importance of similarity between partners to successful relationships.

If a romantic relationship is in bad shape, can we predict who will end it? Much has been made about the tendency in heterosexual relationships for women to end relationships more often than men (Rubin, Peplau, & Hill, 1981). Research has found, however, that neither sex ends romantic relationships more frequently than the other (Akert, 1998; Hagestad & Smyer, 1982; Rusbult et al., 1986).

The Experience of Breaking Up

Can we predict the different ways people will feel when their relationship ends? One key is the role people play in the decision to end the relationship (Akert, 1998; Helgeson, 1994; Lloyd & Cate, 1985). For example, Robin Akert asked 344 college-age men and women to complete a questionnaire about their most important romantic relationship that had ended. One question asked to what extent they or their partner had been responsible for the decision to break up. Participants who indicated a high level of responsibility for the decision were labeled "breakers"; those who reported a low level of responsibility, "breakees"; and those who shared the decision making with their partners about equally, "mutuals."

"Somehow I remember this one differently."

Steve Duenes/The New Yorker Collection/ www.cartoonbank.com.

Akert found that the role people played in the decision to end the relationship was the single most powerful predictor of their breakup experiences. Not surprisingly, breakees were miserable; they reported high levels of loneliness, depression, and anger, and virtually all reported experiencing physical illness in the weeks after the breakup as well. Of the three groups, breakers found the end of the relationship the least upsetting, the least painful, and

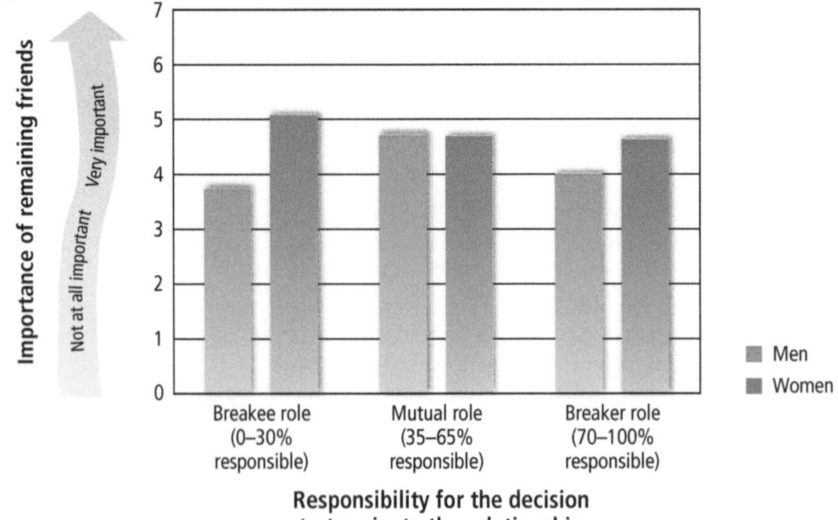

FIGURE 10.7

Importance of Remaining Friends After the Breakup

After ending a romantic relationship, do people want to remain friends with their ex-partner? It depends both on the role they played in the decision to break up and on their gender. Women are more interested than men in staying friends when they are in the breakee or breaker role; men and women are equally interested in staying friends when the relationship ends by mutual decision.

(Akert, 1998)

the least stressful. Although breakers did report feeling guilty and unhappy, they had the fewest negative physical symptoms (39%), such as headaches, stomachaches, and sleeping irregularities.

The mutual role, which carries with it a component of shared decision making, helped individuals evade some of the negative emotional and physical reactions to breaking up. Mutuals were not as upset or hurt as breakees, but they were not as unaffected as breakers. Some 60% of the mutuals reported physical symptoms, indicating that a mutual conclusion to a romantic relationship is a more stressful experience than simply deciding to end it on one's own. Finally, gender played a role in the emotional and physical responses of the respondents, with women reporting somewhat more negative reactions to breaking up than men.

Do people want to stay friends once they break up? It depends on the role played in the breakup as well as on gender. Akert (1998) found that men are not particularly interested in remaining friends with their ex-girlfriends when they are in either the breaker or the breakee role; women are more interested in remaining friends, especially when they are breakees (see Figure 10.7). Interestingly, the mutual role is the one where men's and women's interest in future friendship matches the most. These data suggest that when men experience either great control (breaker) or little control (breakee) over the end of a relationship, they tend to want to "cut their losses" and move on, severing ties with their ex-partner. In comparison, women tend to want to continue feeling connected to their ex-partner, hoping to reshape the intimate relationship into a platonic friendship. The mutual breakup is the one in which each partner effectively plays the breaker and breakee roles simultaneously, and this equality in roles appears to be important in producing an interest in future friendship among both men and women (see Figure 10.7).

Love in the Age of Technology

As this chapter details, psychologists have studied attraction and intimate relationships for decades now. And as is the case with any topic in social psychology, it is reasonable to ask whether research findings observed years and decades ago still apply to tendencies in the modern age. In particular, we now live in an era in which much of our social interaction is not of the face-to-face variety, but rather takes place via text, instant message, Internet chat room, Facebook, Twitter, interactive gaming, virtual reality, and probably even newer technologies developed since this sentence was typed. How do the principles, processes, and theories detailed in this chapter play out in this constantly evolving technological landscape? This final section provides some initial answers to this question, but clearly there is no shortage of interesting future research directions available to social psychologists interested in studying interpersonal attraction.

One question surrounding attraction is how tendencies regarding mate preference that have evolved over generations play out in the modern era of Internet dating, speed-dating events, and Facebook.

Attraction Revisited

One way to explore how our rapidly developing technological world affects the psychology of love is to revisit some of the classic findings reviewed above to see how factors like propinquity, similarity, and familiarity affect attraction in the Internet age. For example, consider how propinquity operates today, when physical distance no longer means what it once did and the Internet allows us to get to know people half a world away (Chan & Cheng, 2004; Dodds, Muhamad, & Watts, 2003). Jure Leskovec and Eric Horvitz conducted a study testing the concept that inspired the popular game "Six Degrees of Kevin Bacon." A "degree of separation" is a measure of social distance between people: You are one degree away from everyone you know, two degrees away from everyone they know, and so on. These researchers analyzed an instant-messaging network, looking at who sent messages to whom and calculating how many different people in a "chain" it would take, on average, to connect two random users to each other. After making calculations for 30 billion conversations among 240 million people, they found that the average length of a person chain was seven and that 90% of pairs could be connected in just eight "hops" (Leskovec & Horvitz, 2007). Thus, six (or seven) degrees of separation appear to explain quite well how interconnected people are in the modern era, regardless of their physical distance.

The effects of similarity have also been observed in technologically driven relationships. Earlier in this chapter, we discussed the tendency to be attracted to people of similar appearance, right down to your being attracted to others at the same level of physical attractiveness as you are. Recent research indicates that this tendency to try to date "in our own league" is little different when relationships go online. Lindsay Taylor (2011) and colleagues assessed the popularity of over 3 thousand heterosexual users of a dating Web site. They defined popularity as the number of opposite-sex individuals who sent unsolicited messages to a user. Because this measure did not include messages sent in response to contact initiated by the user or subsequent messages sent during an ongoing exchange, there was no way for the users in the study to increase their own popularity count once they posted their profile.

Taylor and colleagues (2011) found that high-popularity users of the site contacted other popular users at a rate greater than would be expected by chance—a finding that probably does not surprise you. After all, who wouldn't want to reach out to the popular potential mates? Well, the less popular users of the site, that's who. The researchers also found that users lower in popularity contacted other low-popularity users more often. A follow-up study with over 1 million users produced a comparable result: People tend to select (and be selected by) others with similar levels of popularity, and this tendency to try to "match up" with mates of comparable popularity was no different for men than for women. As the researchers concluded, "one reason that established couples tend to be similar is that matching is at play from the earliest stages of dating" (Taylor et al., 2011, p. 952).

What about familiarity? As you will recall, research has demonstrated that familiarity typically promotes attraction, to the point where even mere exposure to an object or person increases liking. But you may also recall that mere exposure works in the opposite direction when that additional exposure reveals negative characteristics of the object or person in question—a conclusion supported by another recent study of online dating. In this research, Michael Norton and colleagues (2007) gave a survey to participants both before and after going on a date. Pre-date, all that participants knew about their partner was what they had read on a Web site profile, so their ratings of how much knowledge they had about their partner increased post-date. But their ratings of how much they liked their partner *decreased* after the date, as did perceptions of how similar they were. Why? Because the more familiar participants became with their partner

"On the Internet, nobody knows you're a dog."

Peter Steiner/The New Yorker Collection/
www.cartoonbank.com

during the date, the more they realized that their initial impression (based on an ambiguous dating Web site profile) was not that accurate. As they obtained additional information during the date itself, they came to appreciate all the ways in which they were actually *dissimilar* to this person, which in turn decreased average liking ratings.

The Promise and Pitfalls of Online Dating

We began this chapter with the heartwarming story of Laura and Denny Allen, Oregon retirees whose shared love of international travel, volunteer work, wild mushrooms, and pugs has translated into a happy marriage. Despite their overlapping interests and social circles, Laura and Denny wouldn't be together today if not for the help of a dating Web site. The Allens are hardly alone. A recent review of online dating reports that "by 2005, 37% of single Internet users were dating online (a percentage that is almost certainly much higher today), and, by 2007–2009, more new romantic relationships had begun online than through any means other than meeting through friends" (Finkel et al., 2012, p. 11). Attitudes toward Internet dating have never been more positive than they are today. And this is for good reason, as dating Web sites advertise three primary services for users looking for love: (1) aggregating a large number of profiles for browsing, (2) providing opportunity for computer-mediated communication with potential mates, and (3) matching users based on analyses of compatibility (Finkel et al., 2012).

Clearly, dating Web sites have a lot to offer those who are looking for love, and there is no reason to expect their popularity to stop skyrocketing anytime soon. Still, some of the promise of online dating is tempered by other psychological research findings. For example, as discussed in the opening of this chapter, the dating Web site algorithms used to match potential mates by compatibility do not lead to higher relationship success rates than older, lower-tech methods of matching such as the fix-up among friends or getting to know someone through mutual activities. Furthermore, just how honest are people when they post profiles and photos on dating Web sites anyway? Norton et al. (2007) found that learning more about a partner during a date often makes you like that person less than you did when you had only seen a profile, suggesting that perhaps the profiles aren't too accurate to begin with.

Catalina Toma and Jeffrey Hancock have conducted a series of investigations to assess these questions regarding online dating profiles. Some of their research examines potential differences in how men and women describe themselves online. In one study, they interviewed 84 online daters, presenting them with a printout of their own dating profile and asking them how accurate they believed they were in describing their height, weight, and age (Toma, Hancock, & Ellison, 2008). Of course, the researchers were able to compare these self-assessments of accuracy to objective measures of participants' actual height, weight, and age. Results indicated that a full 81% of participants provided inaccurate information in their profile for at least one characteristic, with the most lies coming about weight, followed by age, then height. Interestingly, no gender differences emerged: Men and women were equally likely to try to stretch the truth. Participants' self-reported estimates of their profile accuracy were reasonably good predictors of actual accuracy, indicating that the discrepancies observed did not result from unconscious tendencies to view the self through rose-colored glasses, but rather intentional efforts to fudge facts.

A slightly different pattern emerges from analysis of photos used in dating profiles. Here, Hancock and Toma (2009) found that distortions are often less conscious, especially among women. Following a similar procedure to their previous study, the researchers interviewed online daters about how accurate they believed their profile photo to be. They then had a separate group of college students look at a series of two images side by side: (1) each participant's dating profile photo and (2) a photo taken of each participant during the recent interview. The college students were asked to evaluate how accurate a depiction the profile photograph was of the participant's current physical appearance. In total, 32% of profile photographs were judged to be deceptive or misleading, and females' photos were found to be less accurate than males'. Common inaccuracies included daters looking thinner in the profile photo than they currently do, having more hair in the profile photo than they do now, or using profile photos that were retouched or airbrushed. Unlike with written profiles, users' self-assessed accuracy ratings were not reliable predictors of the actual accuracy of their photo (as rated by the students), particularly among female daters.

In light of these inaccuracies—both intentional and unintentional—what's a lovelorn Internet dater to do? Luckily, the same research techniques that uncovered these inaccurate profiles and photos can also be used to identify which potential online mates are the most (and least) honest. Specifically, Toma and Hancock (2012) suggest three giveaways that the profile you're checking out online may not pass a reality check. First, deceptive profiles tend to have fewer first-person pronouns like *I* and *me*. The researchers explain that this is one way for those who lie or exaggerate to distance themselves psychologically from their half-truths. Second, deceptive profiles make more use of negations, or negative turns of phrase (e.g., "not judgmental" instead of "open-minded"; "not averse to taking risks" instead of "adventurous"). Third, deceptive profiles simply include fewer total words than accurate profiles. Stretching the truth is hard work and cognitively demanding; the fewer inaccurate statements you put in your profile, the fewer fabrications you have to remember later on when you meet someone in person.

Watch on **MyPsychLab**
Consider technology's effects on romance as you watch the MyPsychLab video ***IT Video: Rules for Dating.***

In short, online dating offers users a much larger pool of potential mates than do more-traditional methods that are constrained by personal contacts and physical geography. At the same time, in some important respects, dating Web sites fall short of the promises they make to daters. Nonetheless, it's clear that online dating is here to stay. And in addition to putting an interesting new twist on the human pursuit of love and intimacy, online dating provides contemporary social psychologists with a fascinating set of questions and methods for the experimental study of attraction and relationship formation.

USE IT!

If there was ever a chapter in a textbook that had something to say about your "real" life, this is probably it. Romantic relationships and friendships are an integral part of our lives, and, wonderful as they are, they are also frequently confusing and even upsetting. While the information in this chapter could help you when you're "falling in love," you'll probably be too distracted by your new partner to even think about research studies on attraction. However, when things go bad, this information can really be of help. Apply the various terms and theories to your predicament and ask yourself "Do they help shed some light on what is going on?" For example, are you and your friend or romantic partner seeing the relationship differently, perhaps one of you as an "exchange" and the other as "communal?" Does one or the other of you have an attachment style that is causing problems? Are the two of you dissimilar in areas that are important to you? Are there cultural differences that might explain what's going on? If your loved one is thinking of ending the relationship, is it because he or she has a viable "comparison level for alternatives"? Finally, if you're one of the millions of people turning to the Internet in your search for love, specific cues can help you determine which dating profiles are likely to be most accurate.

Summary

How do humans decide whom they like and want to get to know better?

- **What Causes Attraction?**
  - **The Person Next Door: The Propinquity Effect** In the first part of this chapter, we discussed the variables that cause initial attraction between two people. One such variable is physical proximity, or the **propinquity effect**: People who you come into contact with the most are the most likely to become your friends and lovers. This occurs because of the **mere exposure effect**: Exposure to any stimulus produces liking for it.
  - **Similarity** Similarity between people, whether in attitudes, values, demographic characteristics, or physical appearance is also a powerful cause of attraction and liking. Similarity is a more powerful predictor of attraction than complementarity, the idea that opposites attract.
  - **Reciprocal Liking** In general, we like others who behave as if they like us.
  - **Physical Attractiveness and Liking** Physical attractiveness also plays an important role in liking. People from different cultures perceive facial attractiveness quite similarly. The "what is beautiful is good" stereotype indicates that people assume that physical attractiveness is associated with other desirable traits.
  - **Evolution and Mate Selection Evolutionary psychology** explains love in terms of genetic factors that have evolved over time according to the principles of natural selection. According to this perspective, which is not without its critics, men and women are attracted to different characteristics because this maximizes their reproductive success.

What is love, and how do we form close relationships?

- **Love and Close Relationships**
  - **Defining Love: Companionship and Passion** One definition of love makes a distinction between **companionate love**, feelings of intimacy that are not accompanied by intense longing and arousal, and **passionate love**, feelings of intimacy that are accompanied by intense longing and arousal.
  - **Culture and Love** Although love is a universal emotion, cultural variations in the practice and definition of love do occur. Love has a somewhat different emphasis in collectivistic and individualistic cultures.
  - **Attachment Styles in Intimate Relationships** People's past relationships with their parents are a significant determinant of the quality of their close relationships as adults. There are three types of attachment relationships: **secure**, **avoidant**, and **anxious/ambivalent**.
  - **Theories of Relationship Satisfaction: Social Exchange and Equity Social exchange theory** states that how people feel about their relationship depends on their perception of the rewards they receive and the costs they incur. In order to determine whether people will stay in a relationship, we need to know their **comparison level** (expectations about the outcomes of their relationship), their **comparison level for alternatives** (expectations about how happy they would be in other relationships), as well as their **investment** in the relationship. **Equity theory** states that the most important determinant of satisfaction is that both parties feel comparably rewarded by the relationship. The equity of rewards and costs is different in **communal relationships** than in **exchange relationships**.

What does research tell us about romantic breakups?

- **Ending Intimate Relationships**
  - **The Process of Breaking Up** The breaking-up process is composed of stages. Strategies for responding to problems in a romantic relationship include both constructive and destructive behaviors. Fatal attractions occur when the qualities in a person that once were attractive become the very qualities that repel.
  - **The Experience of Breaking Up** A powerful variable that predicts how a person will weather the breakup is the role he or she plays in the decision to terminate the relationship.

How do new technologies influence how we form close relationships?

- **Love in the Age of Technology**
  - **Attraction Revisited** Basic determinants of attraction such as propinquity, similarity, and familiarity manifest themselves differently in the modern era of text messages, the Internet, and social media.
  - **The Promise and Pitfalls of Online Dating** Online dating expands your pool of potential mates, but carries its own risks; these include unproven compatibility algorithms and deceptive profile descriptions and photos.

Chapter 10 Test

Study and Review on MyPsychLab

1. Sam has his eye on Julie and wants her to like him. According to research in social psychology, which of the following is *least* likely to work? He should
   a. emphasize how similar their attitudes are.
   b. arrange to work with her on a class project so that he can spend time with her.
   c. emphasize that they have complementary personalities; after all, "opposites attract."
   d. make himself look as physically attractive as he can.

2. Rachel is considered physically attractive by her American classmates because of her large eyes and small nose—"baby face" characteristics. In another culture, she would most likely be considered
   a. unattractive because her features are not unique.
   b. unattractive because people's perceptions of beauty differ across cultures.
   c. attractive because people's perceptions of "baby face" attractiveness are similar across cultures.
   d. attractive because "baby face" characteristics appear exotic to people of other cultures.

3. Which of the following is *false?*
   a. People in communal relationships tend to keep track of who is contributing what to the relationship.
   b. People find "average" faces to be more attractive than unusual faces.
   c. People like others who like them.
   d. The more we see and interact with people, the more we will like them.

4. Kate and Jamie are dating. According to the *investment model of close relationships*, which of the following is *least* likely to influence their commitment to the relationship?
   a. Their satisfaction with the relationship
   b. Their level of investment in the relationship
   c. The availability and quality of alternative partners
   d. Their perception that what they are putting into the relationship is roughly the same as what they are getting out of it

5. ________ involves intense longing for another person, accompanied by physiological arousal, whereas ________ is the intimacy and affection we feel without arousal.
   a. passionate love, infatuation
   b. companionate love, passionate love
   c. infatuation, companionate love
   d. passionate love, companionate love

6. Which of the following statements regarding attachment style is true?
   a. Few if any individuals change their attachment style once they reach adulthood.
   b. A majority of adults have been found to exhibit an avoidant attachment style.
   c. The attachment style that adults display is shaped by their partner's behavior and the type of relationship they've created as a couple.
   d. Your attachment style as an infant typically has little to do with the attachment style you have in your adult relationships.

7. Matthew and Eric have been friends since the beginning of the school year. According to equity theory, their friendship will suffer if
   a. Eric is much more likely to help Matthew out when he needs it than Matthew is to help Eric.
   b. Eric has a "makeover" and becomes more attractive than Matthew.
   c. Eric and Matthew stop having similar interests.
   d. Eric and Matthew are romantically interested in the same person.

8. Elliot worries that his girlfriend doesn't really love him and smothers her with attention. According to attachment theory, Elliot probably has a(n) ________ attachment style, because when he was an infant, his caregivers were ________.
   a. avoidant, aloof and distant
   b. avoidant, inconsistent and overbearing
   c. anxious-ambivalent, aloof and distant
   d. anxious-ambivalent, inconsistent and overbearing
   e. secure, responsive to his needs

9. You are considering breaking up with your significant other after 1 month of being a couple. While the relationship gives you lots of rewards and has few costs, you have recently met someone new whom you anticipate will give you even more rewards for even fewer costs. Your dilemma stems from the fact that you have a ________ and a ________.
   a. low satisfaction level, high comparison level for alternatives
   b. high satisfaction level, high comparison level for alternatives
   c. low satisfaction level, low comparison level for alternatives
   d. low satisfaction level, high equity level
   e. high satisfaction level, low equity level

10. Research on the ability of dating Web sites to effectively match up mates using mathematical compatibility analyses indicates that
    a. the Web sites do a better job of matching up same-sex couples than opposite-sex couples.
    b. the Web sites produce a higher "hit rate" of happy relationships than do less-mathematical means of meeting a dating partner.
    c. the Web sites are no better at producing happy relationships than are more old-fashioned ways of meeting a dating partner, like being set up by friends.
    d. contrary to many assumptions, older individuals (e.g., senior citizens) are more likely to be successful finding love online than younger individuals (e.g., college students).

Answer Key

1-c, 2-c, 3-a, 4-d, 5-d,
6-c, 7-a, 8-d, 9-b, 10-c

11 Prosocial Behavior

Why Do People Help?

SEPTEMBER 11, 2001, WAS TRULY A DAY OF INFAMY IN AMERICAN HISTORY, WITH TERRIBLE LOSS OF LIFE AT THE WORLD TRADE CENTER, THE PENTAGON, AND THE FIELD IN PENNSYLVANIA WHERE UNITED AIRLINES FLIGHT 93 CRASHED. It was also a day of incredible courage and sacrifice by people who did not hesitate to help their fellow human beings. Many people lost their lives while helping others, including 403 New York firefighters and police officers who died trying to rescue people from the World Trade Center.

Many of the heroes of September 11 were ordinary citizens who found themselves in extraordinary circumstances. Imagine that you were working in the World Trade Center towers when they were hit by the planes and how strong the desire must have been to flee and seek personal safety. This is exactly what William Wik's wife urged him to do when he called her from the 92nd floor of the South Tower shortly after the attacks. "No, I can't do that; there are still people here," he replied (Lee, 2001, p. 28). Wik's body was found in the rubble of the South Tower after it collapsed; he was wearing work gloves and holding a flashlight.

Abe Zelmanowitz worked on the 27th floor of the North Tower and could easily have walked down the stairs to safety when the plane struck the floors above. Instead, he stayed behind with his friend Ed Beyea, a quadriplegic, waiting for help to carry him down the stairs. Both died when the tower collapsed.

Rick Rescorla was head of security for the Morgan Stanley brokerage firm. After the first plane hit the North Tower, Rescorla and the other employees in the South Tower were instructed to remain at their desks. Rescorla, who had spent years studying the security of the towers, had drilled his employees repeatedly on what to do in an emergency like this—find a partner, avoid the elevators, and evacuate the building. He invoked this plan immediately, and when the plane hit the South Tower, he was on the 44th floor supervising the evacuation, yelling instructions through a bullhorn. After most of the Morgan Stanley employees made it out of the building, Rescorla decided to do a final sweep of the offices to make sure no one was left behind, and he perished when the South Tower collapsed. Rescorla is credited with saving the lives of the 3,700 employees he guided to safety (Stewart, 2002).

And then there were the passengers on United flight 93. Based on phone calls made from the plane in the fateful minutes after it was hijacked, it appears that several passengers, including Todd Beamer, Jeremy Glick, and Thomas Burnett—all fathers of young children—stormed the cockpit and struggled with the terrorists. They could not prevent the plane from crashing, killing everyone on board, but they did prevent an even worse tragedy. The plane was headed for Washington, DC, with the White House or the U.S. Capitol the likely target.

FOCUS QUESTIONS

- What are the basic motives that determine whether people help others?
- What are some personal qualities that influence whether a given individual will help?
- In what situations are people more likely, or less likely, to help others?
- What can be done to promote prosocial behavior?

Basic Motives Underlying Prosocial Behavior: Why Do People Help?

How can we explain acts of great self-sacrifice and heroism when people are also capable of acting in uncaring, heartless ways? In this chapter, we will consider the major causes of **prosocial behavior**—any act performed with the goal of benefiting another person (Penner et al., 2005). We are particularly

Prosocial Behavior
Any act performed with the goal of benefiting another person

concerned with prosocial behavior that is motivated by **altruism**, which is the desire to help another person even if it involves a cost to the helper. Someone might act in a prosocial way out of self-interest, hoping to get something in return. Altruism is helping purely out of the desire to benefit someone else, with no benefit (and often a cost) to oneself; the heroes of September 11, who gave their lives while helping strangers, are a clear example of this.

We begin by considering the basic origins of prosocial behavior and altruism: Is the willingness to help a basic impulse with genetic roots? Must it be taught and nurtured in childhood? Is there a pure motive for helping? Or do people typically help only when there is something in it for them? Let's see how psychologists have addressed these centuries-old questions (McCullough & Tabak, 2010; Piliavin, 2009).

Evolutionary Psychology: Instincts and Genes

According to Charles Darwin's (1859) theory of evolution, natural selection favors genes that promote the survival of the individual (see Chapter 10). Any gene that furthers our survival and increases the probability that we will produce offspring is likely to be passed on from generation to generation. Genes that lower our chances of survival, such as those causing life-threatening diseases, reduce the chances that we will produce offspring and thus are less likely to be passed on. Evolutionary biologists such as E. O. Wilson (1975) and Richard Dawkins (1976) have used these principles of evolutionary theory to explain such social behaviors as aggression and altruism. Several psychologists have pursued these ideas, spawning the field of *evolutionary psychology*, which is the attempt to explain social behavior in terms of genetic factors that have evolved over time according to the principles of natural selection (Buss, 2005; Neuberg, Kenrick, & Schaller, 2010; Tooby & Cosmides, 2005). In Chapter 10, we discussed how evolutionary psychology attempts to explain love and attraction; here we discuss its explanation of prosocial behavior (Simpson & Beckes, 2010).

Altruism
The desire to help another person even if it involves a cost to the helper

Kin Selection
The idea that behaviors that help a genetic relative are favored by natural selection

Darwin realized early on that there was a problem with evolutionary theory: How can it explain altruism? If people's overriding goal is to ensure their own survival, why would they ever help others at a cost to themselves? It would seem that over the course of human evolution altruistic behavior would disappear, because people who acted that way would, by putting themselves at risk, produce fewer offspring than would people who acted selfishly. Genes promoting selfish behavior should be more likely to be passed on—or should they?

Kin Selection One way that evolutionary psychologists attempt to resolve this dilemma is with the notion of **kin selection**, the idea that behaviors that help a genetic relative are favored by natural selection (Hamilton, 1964; Vasey & VanderLaan, 2010; West & Gardner, 2010). People can increase the chances that their genes will be passed along not only by having their own children, but also by ensuring that their genetic relatives have children. Because a person's blood relatives share some of his or her genes, the more that person ensures their survival, the greater the chances that his or her genes will flourish in future generations. Thus, natural selection should favor altruistic acts directed toward genetic relatives.

According to evolutionary psychology, prosocial behavior occurs in part because of kin selection.

In one study, for example, people reported that they would be more likely to help genetic relatives than nonrelatives in life-and-death situations, such as a house fire. People did not report that they would be more likely to help genetic relatives when the situation was non-life-threatening, which supports the idea that people are most likely to help in ways that ensure the survival of their own genes. Interestingly, both males and females, and both American and Japanese participants, followed this rule of kin selection in life-threatening situations (Burnstein, Crandall, & Kitayama, 1994).

Of course, in this study people reported what they thought they would do; this doesn't prove that in a real fire they would indeed be more likely to save their sibling than their cousin. Anecdotal evidence from real emergencies, however, is consistent with these results. Survivors of a fire at a vacation complex reported that when they became aware that there was a fire, they were much more likely to search for family members before exiting the building than they were to search for friends (Sime, 1983).

Altruism based on kin selection is the enemy of civilization. If human beings are to a large extent guided to favor their own relatives and tribe, only a limited amount of global harmony is possible.

—E. O. Wilson, 1978

Evolutionary psychologists are not suggesting that people consciously weigh the biological importance of their behavior before deciding whether to help: We don't compute the likelihood that our genes will be passed on before deciding whether to help someone push his or her car out of a ditch. According to evolutionary theory, however, the genes of people who follow this "biological importance" rule are more likely to survive than the genes of people who do not. Over the millennia, kin selection may have become ingrained in human behavior (Vasey & VanderLaan, 2010; Bishop et al., 2009).

Watch on MyPsychLab
To learn more about how and why people help their own family members, watch the MyPsychLab video ***Successful Aging, Extended Family Maria, 68 Years Old.***

The Reciprocity Norm To explain altruism, evolutionary psychologists also point to the **norm of reciprocity**, which is the expectation that helping others will increase the likelihood that they will help us in the future. The idea is that as human beings were evolving, a group of completely selfish individuals, each living in his or her own cave, would have found it more difficult to survive than a group that had learned to cooperate. Of course, if people cooperated too readily, they might have been exploited by an adversary who never helped in return. Those who were most likely to survive, the argument goes, were people who developed an understanding with their neighbors about reciprocity: "I will help you now, with the agreement that when I need help, you will return the favor." Because of its survival value, such a norm of reciprocity may have become genetically based (Cosmides & Tooby, 1992; de Waal, 1996; Trivers, 1971; Zhang & Epley, 2009). Some researchers suggest that the emotion of *gratitude*—the positive feelings that are caused by the perception that one has been helped by others—evolved in order to regulate reciprocity (Bartlett & DeSteno, 2006; Grant & Gino, 2010; McCullough, Kimeldorf, & Cohen, 2008). That is, if someone helps us, we feel gratitude, which motivates us to return the favor in the future. The following Try It! describes how the reciprocity norm can work to increase helping in everyday life.

Group Selection Classic evolutionary theory argues that natural selection operates on individuals: People who have traits that make them more likely to survive are more likely to reproduce and pass those traits on to future generations. Some argue that natural selection also operates at the level of the group. Imagine two neighboring villages, for example, that are often at war with each other. Village A is made up entirely of selfish individuals who refuse to put themselves at risk to help the village. Village B, on the other hand, has selfless sentries who put their lives at risk by alerting their comrades of an invasion. Which *group* is more likely to win the war and pass on its

Norm of Reciprocity
The expectation that helping others will increase the likelihood that they will help us in the future

TRY IT! Does the Reciprocity Norm Increase Helping?

Have you ever gotten a fund-raising appeal from a charity that included a little gift, such as address labels with your name? If so, did the gift make you more inclined to donate money to the charity? If so, you were subject to the reciprocity norm; because the charity did something for you, you felt more obligated to do something for the charity. The same norm applies when stores offer free samples of a product they are selling. It can feel rude not to reciprocate by buying the product, even though these are strangers trying to sell us something, and not friends doing us a favor. What about in everyday life? Can you think of times when the reciprocity norm influenced how likely you were to help a friend? Have you found that doing a favor for a friend makes it more likely that your friend will do a favor for you? Give this a try and see if it works.

genes to later generations? The one with the selfless (altruistic) sentries, of course. Even though the *individual* sentries in Village B are at risk and likely to be captured and killed, their selfless behavior increases the likelihood that their *group* will survive—namely, the group that values altruism. Though the idea of group selection is controversial and not supported by all biologists, it is has prominent proponents (Wilson, Van Vugt, & O'Gorman, 2008; Wilson & Wilson, 2007).

In sum, evolutionary psychologists believe that people help others because of factors that have become ingrained in our genes. As we saw in Chapter 10, evolutionary psychology is a challenging and creative approach to understanding prosocial behavior, though it does have its critics (Batson, 1998; Buller, 2005; Caporael & Brewer, 2000; Confer et al., 2010; Panksepp & Panksepp, 2000; Wood & Eagly, 2002). How, for example, can evolutionary theory explain why complete strangers sometimes help each other, even when there is no reason for them to assume that they share some of the same genes or that their favor will ever be returned? It seems absurd to say that the heroes of September 11, who lost their lives while saving others, somehow calculated how genetically similar they were to the others before deciding to help. Further, just because people are more likely to save family members than strangers from a fire does not necessarily mean that they are genetically programmed to help genetic relatives. It may simply be that they cannot bear the thought of losing a loved one and therefore go to greater lengths to save the ones they love over people they have never met. We turn now to other possible motives behind prosocial behavior that do not necessarily originate in people's genes.

Let him who neglects to raise the fallen, fear lest, when he falls, no one will stretch out his hand to lift him up.
—Saadi, *The Orchard*, 1257

Study: Cavemen helped disabled

United Press International
NEW YORK—The skeleton of a dwarf who died about 12,000 years ago indicates that cave people cared for physically disabled members of their communities , a researcher said yesterday.

The skeleton of the 3-foot-high youth was initially discovered in 1963 in a cave in southern Italy but was lost to anthropologists until American researcher David W. Frayer reexamined the remains and reported his findings in the British journal Nature.

Frayer, a professor of anthropology at the University of Kansas at Lawrence, said in a telephone interview that the youth "couldn't have taken part in normal hunting of food or gathering activities so he was obviously cared for by others."

Archaeologists have found the remains of other handicapped individuals who lived during the same time period, but their disabilities occurred when they were adults, Frayer said.

"This is the first time we've found someone who was disabled since birth . . . .", Frayer said. He said there was no indication that the dwarf, who was about 17 at the time of his death, had suffered from malnutrition or neglect.

He was one of six individuals buried in the floor of a cave and was found in a dual grave in the arms of a woman, about 40 years old.

This touching story of early hominid prosocial behavior is intriguing to think about in terms of different theories of prosocial behavior. Evolutionary psychologists might argue that the caregivers helped the dwarf because he was a relative and that people are programmed to help those who share their genes (kin selection). Social exchange theory would maintain that the dwarf's caregivers received sufficient rewards from their actions to outweigh the costs of caring for him. The empathy-altruism hypothesis would hold that the caregivers helped out of strong feelings of empathy and compassion for him—an interpretation supported by the article's final paragraph.

Social Exchange: The Costs and Rewards of Helping

Although some social psychologists disagree with evolutionary approaches to prosocial behavior, they share the view that altruistic behavior can be based on self-interest. In fact, *social exchange theory* (see Chapter 10) argues that much of what we do stems from the desire to maximize our rewards and minimize our costs (Cook & Rice, 2003; Homans, 1961; Lawler & Thye, 1999; Thibaut & Kelley, 1959). The difference from evolutionary approaches is that social exchange theory doesn't trace this desire back to our evolutionary roots, nor does it assume that the desire is genetically based. Social exchange theorists assume that just as people in an economic marketplace try to maximize the ratio of their monetary profits to their monetary losses, people in their relationships with others try to maximize the ratio of social rewards to social costs.

Helping can be rewarding in a number of ways. As we saw with the norm of reciprocity, it can increase the likelihood that someone will help us in return. Helping someone is an investment in the future, the social exchange being that someday someone will help us when we need it. Helping can also relieve the personal distress of a bystander. Considerable evidence indicates that people are aroused and disturbed when they see another person suffer and that they help at least in part to relieve their own distress (Dovidio, 1984; Dovidio et al., 1991; Eisenberg & Fabes, 1991). By helping others, we can also gain such rewards as social approval from others and increased feelings of self-worth.

The other side of the coin, of course, is that helping can be costly. Helping decreases when the costs are high, such as when it would put us in physical danger, result in pain or embarrassment, or simply take too much time (Dovidio et al.,

1991; Piliavin et al., 1981; Piliavin, Piliavin, & Rodin, 1975). Perhaps Abe Zelmanowitz, who stayed behind with his friend Ed Beyea in the World Trade Center, found the prospect of walking away and letting his friend die too distressing. Basically, social exchange theory argues that true altruism, in which people help even when doing so is costly to them, does not exist. People help when the benefits outweigh the costs.

I once saw a man out of courtesy help a lame dog over a stile, and [the dog] for requital bit his fingers.
—William Chillingworth

What seems to be generosity is often no more than disguised ambition.
—François de La Rochefoucauld, *Maxims*, 1665

If you are like many of our students, you may think this is an overly cynical view of human nature. Is true altruism, motivated only by the desire to help someone else, really such a mythical act? Must we trace all prosocial behavior, such as large charitable gifts made by wealthy individuals, to the self-interest of the helper? Well, a social exchange theorist might reply, there are many ways in which people can obtain gratification, and we should be thankful that one way is by helping others. After all, wealthy people could decide to get their pleasure only from lavish vacations, expensive cars, and meals at fancy restaurants. We should applaud their decision to give money to the disadvantaged, even if, ultimately, it is just a way for them to feel good about themselves. Prosocial acts are doubly rewarding in that they help both the giver and the recipient of the aid. Thus, it is to everyone's advantage to promote and praise such acts.

Still, many people are dissatisfied with the argument that all helping stems from self-interest. How can it explain why people give up their lives for others, as many of the heroes of September 11 did? According to some social psychologists, some people do have hearts of gold and sometimes help only for the sake of helping.

Empathy and Altruism: The Pure Motive for Helping

C. Daniel Batson (1991) is the strongest proponent of the idea that people often help purely out of the goodness of their hearts. Batson acknowledges that people sometimes help others for selfish reasons, such as to relieve their own distress at seeing another person suffer. But he also argues that people's motives are sometimes purely altruistic, in that their only goal is to help the other person, even if doing so involves some cost to them. Pure altruism is likely to come into play, he maintains, when we feel **empathy** for the person in need of help, putting ourselves in the shoes of another person and experiencing events and emotions the way that person experiences them (Batson, 2011; Batson, Ahmad, & Stocks, 2011).

Empathy
The ability to put oneself in the shoes of another person and to experience events and emotions (e.g., joy and sadness) the way that person experiences them

Helping behavior is common in virtually all species of animals, and sometimes it even crosses species lines. In August 1996, a 3-year-old boy fell into a pit containing seven gorillas, at the Brookfield, Illinois, zoo. Binti, a 7-year-old gorilla, immediately picked up the boy. After cradling him in her arms, she placed the boy near a door where zookeepers could get to him. Why did she help? Evolutionary psychologists would argue that prosocial behavior is selected for and thus becomes part of the genetic makeup of the members of many species. Social exchange theorists would argue that Binti had been rewarded for helping in the past. In fact, because she had been rejected by her mother, she had received training in parenting skills from zookeepers, in which she was rewarded for caring for a doll (Bils & Singer, 1996).

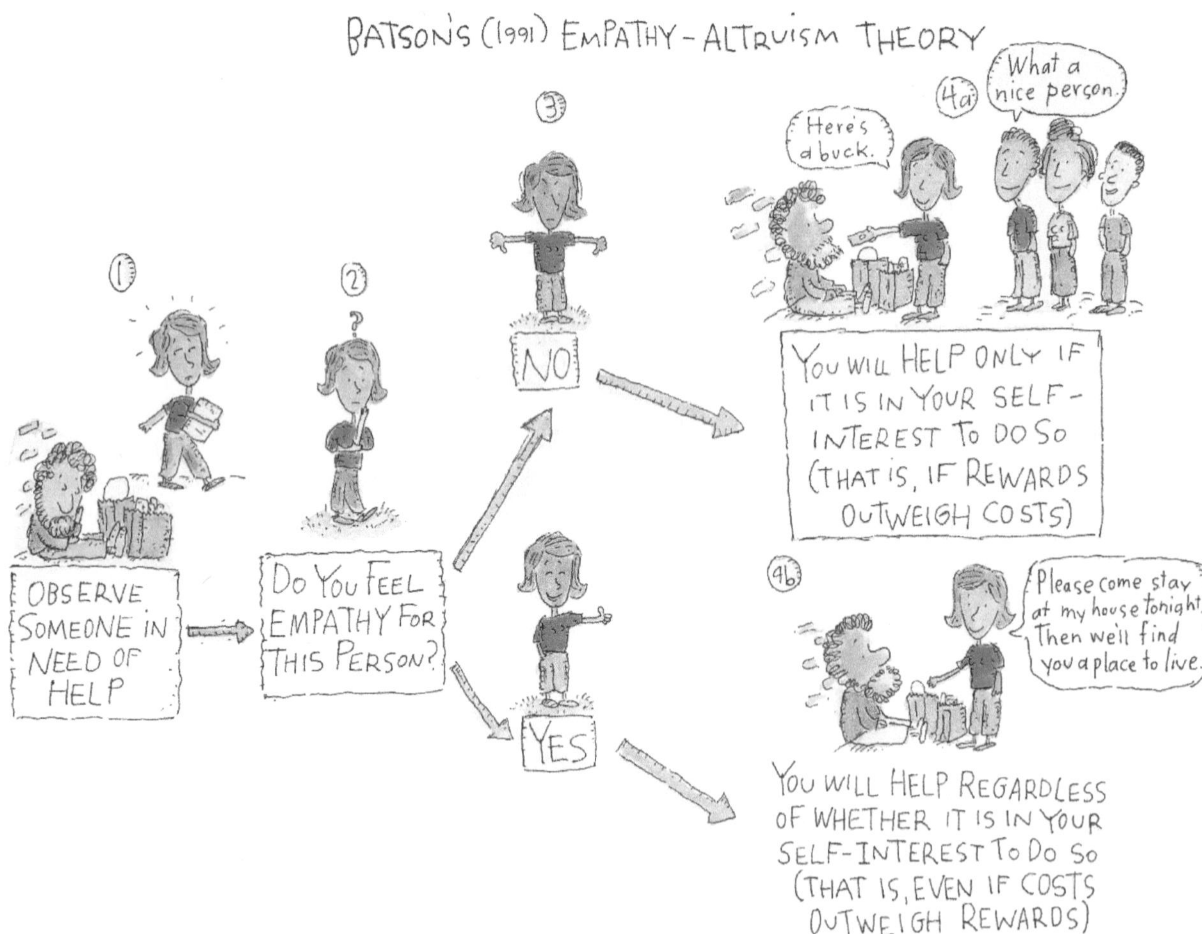

FIGURE 11.1
Empathy-Altruism Theory

Suppose that while you are food shopping, you see a man holding a baby and a bag full of diapers, toys, and rattles. As he reaches for a box of Wheat Chex, the man drops the bag, and everything spills onto the floor. Will you help him pick up his things? According to Batson, it depends first on whether you feel empathy for him. If you do, you will help, regardless of what you have to gain. Your goal will be to relieve the other person's distress, not to gain something for yourself. This is the crux of Batson's **empathy-altruism hypothesis**: When we feel empathy for another person, we will attempt to help that person for purely altruistic reasons, regardless of what we have to gain.

If you do not feel empathy, then, Batson says, social exchange concerns come into play. What's in it for you? If there is something to be gained, such as obtaining approval from the man or from onlookers, you will help the man pick up his things. If you will not profit from helping, you will go on your way without stopping. Batson's empathy-altruism hypothesis is summarized in Figure 11.1.

Batson and his colleagues would be the first to acknowledge that it can be very difficult to isolate the exact motives behind complex social behaviors. If you saw someone help the man pick up his possessions, how could you tell whether the person was acting out of empathic concern or to gain some sort of social reward? Consider a famous story about Abraham Lincoln. One day, while riding in a coach, Lincoln and a fellow passenger were debating the very question we are considering: Is helping ever truly altruistic? Lincoln argued that helping always stems from self-interest, whereas the other passenger took the view that true altruism exists. Suddenly, the men were interrupted by the screeching of a pig that was trying to save her piglets from drowning in a creek. Lincoln ordered the coach to stop, jumped out, ran down to the creek, and lifted the piglets to the safety of the bank. When he returned, his companion said, "Now, Abe, where does selfishness come in on this little episode?" "Why, bless your soul, Ed," Lincoln replied.

Empathy-Altruism Hypothesis

The idea that when we feel empathy for a person, we will attempt to help that person for purely altruistic reasons, regardless of what we have to gain

"That was the very essence of selfishness. I should have had no peace of mind all day had I gone on and left that suffering old sow worrying over those pigs. I did it to get peace of mind, don't you see?" (Sharp, 1928, p. 75).

As this example shows, an act that seems truly altruistic is sometimes motivated by self-interest. How, then, can we tell which is which? Batson and his colleagues have devised a series of clever experiments to unravel people's motives (Batson, Ahmad, & Stocks, 2004; Batson & Powell, 2003). Imagine that you were an introductory psychology student in one of these studies (Toi & Batson, 1982). You are asked to evaluate some tapes of new programs for the university radio station, one of which is called *News from the Personal Side.* There are lots of different pilot tapes for this program, and you are told that only one person will be listening to each tape. The one you hear is an interview with a student named Carol Marcy. She describes a bad automobile accident in which both of her legs were broken and talks about how hard it has been to keep up with her class work as a result of the accident, especially because she is still in a wheelchair. Carol says she is especially concerned about how far she has fallen behind in her Introductory Psychology class and mentions that she will have to drop the class unless she can find another student to tell her what she has missed.

> *It is one of the beautiful compensations of this life that no one can sincerely try to help another without helping himself.*
>
> —Charles Dudley Warner, 1873

After you listen to the tape, the experimenter hands you an envelope marked "To the student listening to the Carol Marcy pilot tape." The experimenter says she doesn't know what's in the envelope but was asked by the professor supervising the research to hand it out. You open the envelope and find a note from the professor, saying that he was wondering if the student who listened to Carol's tape would be willing to help her out with her psychology class. Carol was reluctant to ask for help, he says, but because she is so far behind in the class, she agreed to write a note to the person listening to her tape. The note asks if you could meet with her and share your Introductory Psychology lecture notes.

As you have probably guessed, the point of the study was to look at the conditions under which people agreed to help Carol. The researchers pitted two motives against each other: self-interest and empathy. They varied how much empathy people felt toward Carol by telling different participants to adopt different perspectives when listening to the tape. In the high-empathy condition, people were told to try to imagine how Carol felt about what had happened to her and how it had changed her life. In the low-empathy condition, people were told to try to be objective and not be concerned with how Carol felt. As expected, people in the high-empathy condition reported feeling more sympathy for Carol than people in the low-empathy condition did.

The researchers also varied how costly it would be *not* to help Carol. In one condition, participants learned that she would start coming back to class the following week and happened to be in the same psychology section as they were; thus, they would see her every time they went to class and would be reminded that she needed help. This was the high-cost condition because it would be unpleasant to refuse to help Carol and then run into her every week in class. In the low-cost condition, people learned that Carol would be studying at home and would not be coming to class; therefore, they would never have to face her in her wheelchair and feel guilty about not helping her.

When deciding whether to help Carol, did people take into account the costs involved? According to the empathy-altruism hypothesis, people should have been motivated purely by altruistic concerns and helped regardless of the costs—if empathy was high (see Figure 11.2). As you can see from the right side of Figure 11.2, this prediction was confirmed: In the high-empathy condition, about as many people agreed to help when they thought they would see Carol in class as when they thought they would not see her in class. This suggests that people had Carol's interests in mind and not their own. In the low-empathy condition, however, many more people agreed to help when they thought they would see Carol in class than when they thought they would not see her in class (see the left side of Figure 11.2). This suggests that when empathy was low, social exchange concerns came into play, in that people based their decision to help on the costs and benefits to themselves. They helped when it was in their interests to do so (i.e., when they would see Carol in her wheelchair and feel guilty for not helping), but not otherwise (i.e., when they thought they would never

FIGURE 11.2

Altruism Versus Self-Interest

Under what conditions did people agree to help Carol with the work she missed in her introductory psychology class? When empathy was high, people helped regardless of the costs and rewards (i.e., regardless of whether they would encounter her in their psychology class). When empathy was low, people were more concerned with the rewards and costs for themselves—they helped only if they would encounter Carol in their psychology class and thus feel guilty about not helping.

(Adapted from Toi & Batson, 1982)

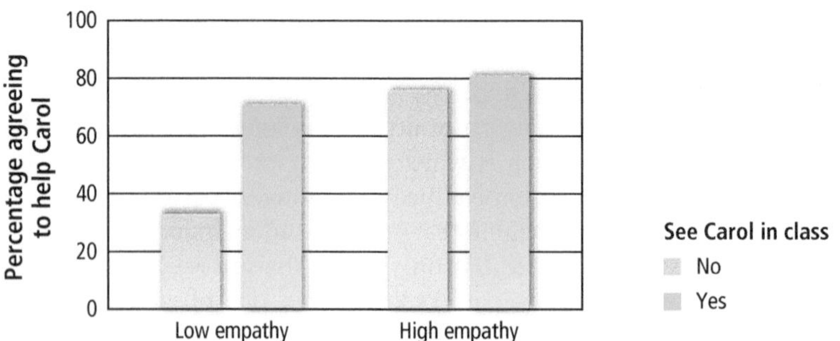

see her again). These results suggest that true altruism exists when people experience empathy toward the suffering of another.

To sum up, we've identified three basic motives underlying prosocial behavior:

1. Helping is an instinctive reaction to promote the welfare of those genetically similar to us (evolutionary psychology).
2. The rewards of helping often outweigh the costs, so helping is in our self-interest (social exchange theory).
3. Under some conditions, powerful feelings of empathy and compassion for the victim prompt selfless giving (the empathy-altruism hypothesis).

Each of these explanations has its supporters and critics.

Personal Qualities and Prosocial Behavior: Why Do Some People Help More Than Others?

On reflecting at dinner that he had done nothing to help anybody all day, he uttered these memorable and praiseworthy words: "Friends, I have lost a day."

—Suetonius, *Lives of the Twelve Caesars*, first century A.D.

If basic human motives are all there is to it, why are some people so much more helpful than others? Clearly, we need to consider the personal qualities that distinguish the helpful person from the selfish one.

Altruistic Personality

The qualities that cause an individual to help others in a wide variety of situations

Individual Differences: The Altruistic Personality

When you read the descriptions of the September 11 heroes at the beginning of this chapter, did you think about the personalities of the people we described? It is natural to assume that William Wik, Abe Zelmanowitz, Rick Rescorla, and the passengers of United flight 93 were cut from a different cloth—selfless, caring people who would never dream of ignoring someone's pleas for help. Psychologists have been interested in the nature of the **altruistic personality**, the qualities that cause an individual to help others in a wide variety of situations (Eisenberg, Spinrad, & Sadovsky, 2006; Mikulincer & Shaver, 2005; Penner & Orom, 2010).

Clearly, some people have more of an altruistic personality than do others, causing them to engage in more prosocial behavior. Personality, however, is not the whole story; the nature of the social situation also determines whether people help.

Although some people are obviously more helpful than others, personality alone does not determine behavior—the pressures of the situation matter as well (as we have seen throughout this book). Predicting how helpful people will be is no exception. Studies of both children and adults, for example, find that people with high scores on personality tests of altruism are not that much more likely to help than those with lower scores (Batson, 1998; Magoo & Khanna, 1991; Piliavin & Charng, 1990). Why not? We need to consider several other critical factors as well, such as the situational pressures that are affecting people, their gender, the culture in which they grew up, how religious they are, and even their current mood (Graziano et al., 2007).

Whereas men are more likely to perform chivalrous and heroic acts, women are more likely to be helpful in long-term relationships that involve greater commitment.

Gender Differences in Prosocial Behavior

Consider two scenarios. In one, someone performs a dramatic, heroic act, like storming the cockpit of United flight 93 to fight the terrorists. In the other, someone is involved in a long-term helping relationship, such as assisting a disabled neighbor with chores around the house. Are men or women more likely to help in each situation?

The answer is males in the first situation and females in the second (Eagly, 2009; Eagly & Crowley, 1986; Eagly & Koenig, 2006). In virtually all cultures, norms prescribe different traits and behaviors for males and females, learned as boys and girls are growing up. In Western cultures, the male sex role includes being chivalrous and heroic; females are expected to be nurturing and caring and to value close, long-term relationships. Indeed, of the 7000 people who received medals from the Carnegie Hero Fund Commission for risking their lives to save a stranger, 91% have been men. In contrast, women are more likely than men to provide social support to their friends and to engage in volunteer work that involves helping others (Eagly & Koenig, 2006; McGuire, 1994; Monin, Clark, & Lemay, 2008). Cross-cultural evidence suggests the same pattern. In a survey of adolescents in seven countries, more girls than boys reported doing volunteer work in their communities (Flanagan et al., 1998).

Cultural Differences in Prosocial Behavior

Suppose you find out that a student at your university needs help because she lost all of her possession in a fire at her apartment building. She has no insurance and very little money, so a call goes out to donate to a fund to help her buy clothes and other necessities. Would you donate money? Well, let's take this example a little further: Suppose that in one case the student was very similar to you; she is of the same race and has a similar background. Alternatively, suppose that she is a member of a different cultural group. Perhaps you grew up in the United States and she is an international student, or vice versa. Would this make a difference in your willingness to help her?

On the one hand, there is ample evidence that people often favor their **in-groups**, or the groups with which they identify as a member, and discriminate against members of **out-groups**, defined as groups with which they do not identify. Indeed, as we will see in Chapter 13, there is a long history of discrimination and prejudice against out-group members, including those of other races, cultures, and genders, as well as people with different sexual orientations. But on the other hand, people often go out of their way to help out-group members. People donate to charities that help disadvantaged strangers and rise to the occasion when an individual is in need, even if he or she belongs to a different group.

Recent research resolves this conundrum. It turns out that people often do help both in-group and out-group members, but for different reasons. We are more likely to feel empathy toward members of our in-groups who are in need. Thus, if the student who lost her possessions in the apartment fire is a member of your in-group, you will probably feel empathy for her, and the more empathy you feel, the more likely you are to help. We tend to help out-group members for a different reason—we do so, to put it bluntly, when there is something in it for us, such as making us feel good about ourselves or making a good impression on others. Sound familiar? Recall that Batson's empathy-altruism theory posits two routes to helping others: When we feel empathy, we help regardless of whether there is something in it for us, but when we don't feel empathy, we help only if there is something in it for us (see Figure 11.1). Research on intergroup helping suggests that we are more likely to take the first route when the

In-Group
The group with which an individual identifies as a member

Out-Group
Any group with which an individual does not identify

person in need is an in-group member, but more likely to take the second route when the person in need is an out-group member (van Leeuwen & Täuber, 2010; Stürmer & Snyder, 2010).

More generally, are there differences in cultural values that make people in one culture more likely to help than people in another culture? One such value is *simpatía*. Prominent in Spanish-speaking countries, simpatía refers to a range of social and emotional traits, including being friendly, polite, good-natured, pleasant, and helpful toward others (interestingly, it has no direct English translation). One study tested the hypothesis that helping would be higher in cultures that value simpatía than in cultures that do not (Levine, 2003; Levine, Norenzayan, & Philbrick, 2001). The researchers staged helping incidents in large cities in 23 countries and observed what people did. In one scenario, for example, a researcher posing as a blind person stopped at a busy intersection and observed whether pedestrians offered help in crossing or informed the researcher when the light turned green.

Watch on **MyPsychLab**

To learn more about factors that influence helping behavior, watch the MyPsychLab video ***Private Battles***.

If you look at Table 11.1, you'll see that the percentage of people who helped (averaged across the different incidents) in countries that value simpatía was higher than in countries that did not, 83% to 66%. The researchers noted that these results are only suggestive, because the five Latin American and Spanish countries differed from the others in ways other than the value they placed on simpatía. And some countries not known for their simpatía had high rates of helping. Nevertheless, if a culture strongly values friendliness and prosocial behavior, people may be more likely to help strangers on city streets (Janoff-Bulman & Leggatt, 2002).

TABLE 11.1 Helping in Twenty-Three Cities

In 23 cities around the world, researchers observed how many people helped in three situations: helping a person with a leg brace who dropped a pile of magazines, helping someone who did not notice that he or she had dropped a pen, and helping a blind person across a busy intersection. The percentages in the table are averaged across the three situations. The cities in boldface are in countries that have the cultural value of *simpatía*, which prizes friendliness, politeness, and helping others.

City	Percent Helping
Rio de Janeiro, Brazil	**93**
San José, Costa Rica	**91**
Lilongwe, Malawi	86
Calcutta, India	83
Vienna, Austria	81
Madrid, Spain	**79**
Copenhagen, Denmark	78
Shanghai, China	77
Mexico City, Mexico	**76**
San Salvador, El Salvador	**75**
Prague, Czech Republic	75
Stockholm, Sweden	72
Budapest, Hungary	71
Bucharest, Romania	69
Tel Aviv, Israel	68
Rome, Italy	63
Bangkok, Thailand	61
Taipei, Taiwan	59
Sofia, Bulgaria	57
Amsterdam, Netherlands	54
Singapore	48
New York, United States	45
Kuala Lumpur, Malaysia	40

(Adapted from Levine, Norenzayan, & Philbrick, 2001)

Religion and Prosocial Behavior

Most religions teach some version of the Golden Rule, urging us to do unto others as we would have others do unto us. Are religious people more likely to follow this advice than nonreligious people? That is, does religion foster prosocial behavior? The answer is yes in some ways but not all (Preston, Ritter, & Hernandez, 2010). People who attend religious services report on surveys that they give more money to charity and engage in more volunteer work than do people who do not attend religious services (Brooks, 2006). When it comes to what people actually do, however—not just what they report on surveys—the story is a little more complicated. Religious people are more likely to help (e.g., raising money for a sick child) in situations in which helping makes them look good to themselves or others. They are not more likely to help, however, in private situations in which no one will know that they helped (Batson, Schoenrade, & Ventis, 1993). In terms of Batson's empathy-altruism hypothesis, which we discussed earlier, religious people do not appear to feel more empathy toward others, though they are more likely to help when it is in their best interests to do so (Norenzayan & Shariff, 2008).

The Effects of Mood on Prosocial Behavior

Imagine that you are at your local shopping mall. As you walk from one store to another, a fellow in front of you drops a manila folder and papers go fluttering in all directions. He looks around in dismay, then bends down and starts picking up the papers. Would you stop and help him? The answer might depend on what your current mood happens to be.

Effects of Positive Moods: Feel Good, Do Good In a classic study, researchers wanted to see whether people's mood influenced shoppers' likelihood of helping a stranger, much like the example we just gave (Isen & Levin, 1972). To find out, they temporarily boosted some shoppers' moods in a clever way—they left dimes in the coin-return slot of a public telephone at the mall and then waited for someone to find the coins. (Note the year this study was done; there were no cell phones, so people relied on pay phones. Also, 10 cents then would be like finding 50 cents today.) As the lucky shoppers left the phone with their newly found dime, a research assistant played the role of the man with the manila folder. He intentionally dropped the folder a few feet in front of the shopper to see whether he or she would stop and help him pick up his papers. It turned out that finding the dime had a dramatic effect on helping. Only 4% of the people who did not find a dime helped the man pick up his papers, whereas a whopping 84% of the people who found a dime stopped to help.

This "feel good, do good" effect has been replicated many times with different ways of boosting people's moods (including doing well on a test, receiving a gift, thinking happy thoughts, and listening to pleasant music; North, Tarrant, & Hargreaves, 2004) and with many different kinds of helping (including contributing money to charity, helping someone find a lost contact lens, tutoring another student, donating blood, and helping coworkers on the job; Carlson, Charlin, & Miller, 1988; Isen, 1999; Kayser et al., 2010).

Being in a good mood can increase helping for three reasons. First, good moods make us look on the bright side of life. That is, when we're in a good mood, we tend to see the good side of other people, giving them the benefit of the doubt. A victim who might normally seem clumsy or annoying will, when we are feeling cheerful, seem like a decent, needy person who is worthy of our help (Carlson et al., 1988; Forgas & Bower, 1987). Second, helping other people is an excellent way of prolonging our good mood. If we see someone who needs help, then being a Good Samaritan spawns even more good feelings, and we can walk away feeling terrific. In comparison, not helping when we know we should is a surefire "downer," deflating our good mood (Clark & Isen, 1982; Isen, 1987; Lyubomirsky, Sheldon, & Schkade, 2005). (See the following Try It! for another example of how helping others improves our moods.) Finally, good moods increase the amount of attention we pay to ourselves, and this factor in turn makes us more likely to behave according to our values and ideals (see Chapter 3). Because most of us value altruism and because good moods increase our attention to this value, good

TRY IT! Do Good, Feel Good?

Suppose you found a $20 bill on the ground and could spend it on yourself (e.g., buy yourself a nice lunch) or on someone else (e.g., treat a friend to lunch). Which would you rather do? If your goal is to improve your mood, the answer might surprise you—spend it on your friend! Research by Dunn, Aknin, and Norton (2008) found that people who spent money on others were happier than people who spent money on themselves. Try this yourself the next time you have a little extra money. Rather than buying yourself a treat, try treating a friend or donating the money to charity. You might be surprised by how good you feel!

moods increase helping behavior (Berkowitz, 1987; Carlson et al., 1988; Salovey & Rodin, 1985).

Feel Bad, Do Good What about when we are in a bad mood? Suppose that when you saw the fellow in the mall drop his folder, you were feeling down. Would this influence the likelihood that you would help the man pick up his papers? One kind of bad mood clearly leads to an increase in helping: feeling guilty (Baumeister, Stillwell, & Heatherton, 1994; Estrada-Hollenbeck & Heatherton, 1998). People often act on the idea that good deeds cancel out bad deeds. When they have done something that has made them feel guilty, helping another person balances things out, reducing their guilty feelings. For example, one study found that Catholic churchgoers were more likely to donate money to charities before attending confession than afterward, presumably because confessing to a priest reduced their guilt (Harris, Benson, & Hall, 1975). Thus, if you just realized you had forgotten your best friend's birthday and you felt guilty about it, you would be more likely to help the fellow in the mall, to repair your guilty feelings.

If you want others to be happy, practice compassion. If you want to be happy, practice compassion.

—The Dalai Lama

But suppose you were feeling sad because you just had a fight with a friend or just found out you did poorly on a test. Given that feeling happy leads to greater helping, it might seem that feeling sad would decrease helping. Surprisingly, however, sadness can also lead to an increase in helping (Carlson & Miller, 1987; Kayser et al., 2010). When people are sad, they are motivated to engage in activities that make them feel better (Cialdini & Fultz, 1990; Cialdini et al., 1987; Wegener & Petty, 1994). To the extent that helping is rewarding, it can lift us out of the doldrums.

Situational Determinants of Prosocial Behavior: When Will People Help?

Personality, gender, culture, and mood all contribute a piece to the puzzle of why people help others, but they do not complete the picture. To understand more fully why people help, we also need to consider the social situation in which people find themselves.

Environment: Rural Versus Urban

Here's another helping scenario for you. Suppose you are walking down the street one day when you see a man suddenly fall down and cry out with pain. He rolls up his pants leg, revealing a bandaged shin that is bleeding heavily. What would you do? When this event was staged in small towns, about half the people who walked by stopped and offered to help the man. In large cities, only 15% of passersby stopped to help (Amato, 1983). Other studies have found that people in small towns are more likely to help when asked to find a lost child, give directions, and return a lost letter. Helping has been found to be more prevalent in small towns in several countries, including the United States, Canada, Israel, Australia, Turkey, Great Britain, and the Sudan (Hedge & Yousif, 1992; Steblay, 1987).

Do not wait for extraordinary circumstances to do good actions; try to use ordinary situations.

—John Paul Richter, 1763

People are less helpful in big cities than in small towns, not because of a difference in values, but because the stress of urban life causes them to keep to themselves.

Why are people more likely to help in small towns? One possibility is that people who grow up in a small town are more likely to internalize altruistic values. If this were the case, people who grew up in small towns would be more likely to help, even if they were visiting a big city. Alternatively, the immediate surroundings might be the key and not people's internalized values. Stanley Milgram (1970), for example, suggested that people living in cities are constantly bombarded with stimulation and that they keep to themselves in order to avoid being overwhelmed by it. According to this **urban overload hypothesis**, if you put urban dwellers in a calmer, less stimulating environment, they would be as likely as anyone else to reach out to others. Research has supported the urban overload hypothesis more than the idea that living in cities makes people less altruistic by nature. To predict whether people will help, it is more important to know whether they are currently in a rural or urban area than it is to know where they happened to grow up (Levine et al., 1994; Steblay, 1987).

Residential Mobility

In the United States, a man will carefully construct a home in which to spend his old age and sell it before the roof is on. . . . He will settle in one place only to go off elsewhere shortly afterwards with a new set of desires.

—Alexis de Tocqueville, 1835

It is not only where you live that matters, but how often you have moved from one place to another. In many areas of the world, it is common for people to move far away from where they were raised (Hochstadt, 1999). In the year 2000, for example, nearly one in five Americans (18%) were living in a different state than they were in 1995 ("Migration and Geographic Mobility," 2003), and in many urban areas, fewer than half of the residents were living in the same house as they were in 1995 (Oishi et al., 2007). As it turns out, people who have lived for a long time in one place are more likely to engage in prosocial behaviors that help the community. Residing in one place leads to a greater attachment to the community, more interdependence with one's neighbors, and a greater concern with one's reputation in the community (Baumeister, 1986; Oishi, 2010). For all these reasons, long-time residents are more likely to engage in prosocial behaviors. Shigehiro Oishi and colleagues (2007), for example, found that people who had lived for a long time in the Minneapolis-St. Paul area were more likely to purchase "critical habitat" license plates, compared to people who had recently moved to the area. (These license plates cost an extra $30 a year and provide funds for the state to purchase and manage natural habitats.)

Perhaps it is not surprising that people who have lived in one place for years feel more of a stake in their community. Oishi and his colleagues (2007) also found, though, that this increase in helping can arise quite quickly, even in a one-time laboratory setting. Imagine that you are in a study in which you are playing a trivia contest against four other students, where the winner will win a $10 gift certificate. The experimenter says that people in the group can help each other if they want, but that doing so might lower the helper's chances of winning the prize. As the game progresses, one of your

Urban Overload Hypothesis

The theory that people living in cities are constantly bombarded with stimulation and that they keep to themselves to avoid being overwhelmed by it fellow group members keeps sighing and commenting that he doesn't know the answers to the questions. Would you offer him some help or let him continue to struggle on his own?

The answer, it turns out, depends on how long you have been in the group with the struggling student. The study by Oishi and colleagues involved a total of four tasks; the trivia contest was the last one. Half of the participants remained together and worked on all the tasks throughout the study, whereas the other half switched to a new group after each task. Thus, in the former condition people had more of an opportunity to get to know each other and form a sense of community, whereas the latter group was more analogous to moving from one community to another. As the researchers predicted, people in the "stable community" condition were more likely to help their struggling companion than were people in the "transient" group condition. Another reason that people might be less helpful in big cities, then, is that residential mobility is higher in cities than in rural areas. People are more likely to have just moved to a city and thus feel less of a stake in the community.

The Number of Bystanders: The Bystander Effect

Remember Kitty Genovese? We have just seen one reason why her neighbors turned a deaf ear to her cries for help: The murder took place in New York City, one of the most densely populated areas in the world. Perhaps her neighbors had moved to the city recently, or maybe they were so overloaded with urban stimulation that they dismissed Genovese's cries as one small addition to the surrounding din. Although it is true that people help less in urban environments, that isn't the only reason Genovese's neighbors failed to help. Her desperate cries surely must have risen above the everyday noises of garbage trucks and car horns. And there have been cases where people ignored the pleas of their neighbors even in small towns. In Fredericksburg, Virginia, a convenience store clerk was beaten in front of customers, who did nothing to help, even after the assailant had fled and the clerk lay bleeding on the floor (Hsu, 1995). Fredericksburg and its surrounding county have only about 150,000 residents. Nor are such incidents limited to the United States, as we noted in Chapter 2. In October of 2011 in Southern China, a 2-year-old girl was hit by two different vans, minutes apart, and lay in the street dying. Neither van stopped, and a dozen people walked or rode past the girl without stopping to help her (Branigan, 2011).

Bibb Latané and John Darley (1970) are two social psychologists who taught at universities in New York at the time of the Genovese murder. As we discussed in Chapter 2, they too were unconvinced that the only reason her neighbors failed to help was the stresses and stimulation of urban life. They focused on the fact that so many people heard her cries. Paradoxically, they thought, it might be that the greater the number of bystanders who observe an emergency, the less likely any one of them is to help. As Latané (1987) put it, "We came up with the insight that perhaps what made the Genovese case so fascinating was itself what made it happen—namely, that not just one or two, but thirty-eight people had watched and done nothing" (p. 78). We should note that some of the details of the Kitty Genovese story have been questioned, such as whether there really were 38 people who heard her cries and whether no one helped (Manning, Levine, & Collins, 2007). That was the story of the murder at the time, however, and the account that inspired Latané and Darley's research.

In a series of now-classic experiments, Latané and Darley (1970) found that in terms of receiving help, there is no safety in numbers. Think back to the seizure experiment we discussed in Chapter 2. In that study, people sat in individual cubicles, participating in a group discussion of college life (over an intercom system) with students in other cubicles. One of the other students suddenly had a seizure, crying out for help, choking, and finally falling silent. There was actually only one real participant in the study. The other "participants," including the one who had the seizure, were prerecorded voices. The point of the study was to see whether the real participant would attempt to help the seizure victim by trying to find him or by summoning the experimenter or whether, like Kitty Genovese's neighbors, the person would simply sit there and do nothing.

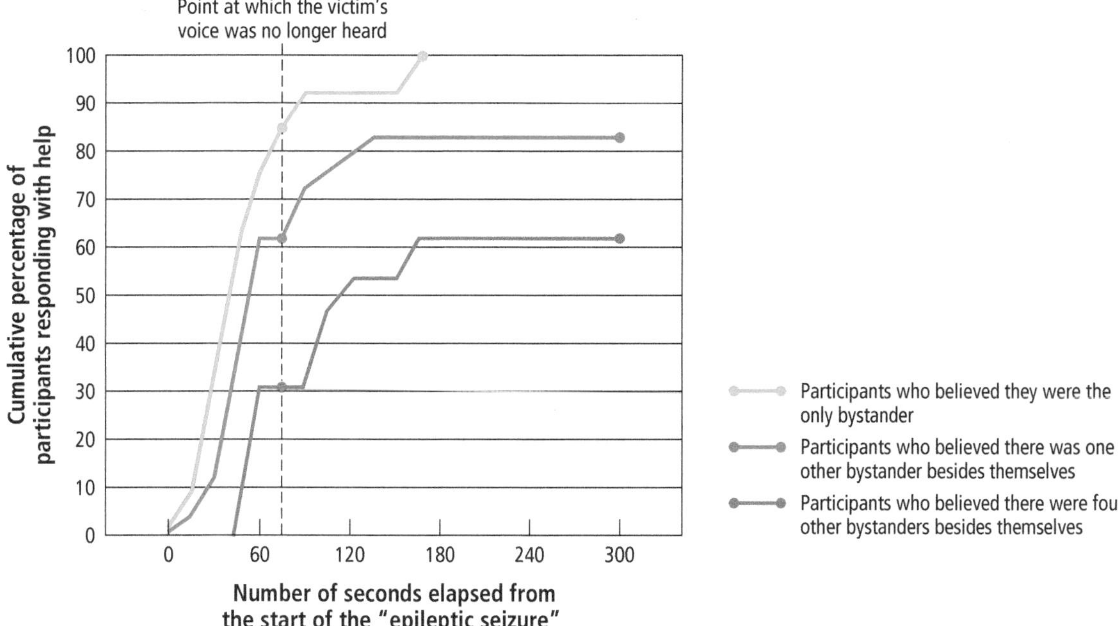

FIGURE 11.3

Bystander Intervention: The Presence of Bystanders Reduces Helping

When people believed they were the only one witnessing a student having a seizure, when they were the lone bystander, most of them helped him immediately, and all did so within a few minutes. When they believed that someone else was listening as well, that there were two bystanders, they were less likely to help and did so more slowly. And when they believed that four others were listening, that there were five bystanders, they were even less likely to help.

(Adapted from Darley & Latané, 1968)

As Latané and Darley anticipated, the answer depended on how many people the participant thought witnessed the emergency. When people believed they were the only ones listening to the student having the seizure, most of them (85%) helped within 60 seconds. By 2 1/2 minutes, 100% of the people who thought they were the only bystander had offered assistance (see Figure 11.3). In comparison, when the research participants believed there was one other student listening, fewer helped—only 62% within 60 seconds. As you can see in Figure 11.3, helping occurred more slowly when there were two bystanders and never reached 100%, even after 6 minutes, when the experiment was ended. Finally, when the participants believed there were four other students listening in addition to themselves, the percentage of people who helped dropped even more dramatically. Only 31% helped in the first 60 seconds, and after 6 minutes only 62% had offered help. Dozens of other studies, conducted in the laboratory and in the field, have found the same thing: The greater the number of bystanders who witness an emergency, the less likely any one of them is to help the victim—a phenomenon called the **bystander effect** (Fischer et al., 2011).

Why is it that people are less likely to help when others are present? Latané and Darley (1970) developed a five-step description of how people decide whether to intervene in an emergency (see Figure 11.4). Part of this description is an explanation of how the number of bystanders can make a difference. But let's begin with the first step—whether people notice that someone needs help.

Noticing an Event If you are hurrying down a crowded street, you might not notice that someone has collapsed in a doorway. Obviously, if people don't notice that an emergency situation exists, they will not intervene and offer to help. What determines whether people notice an emergency? John Darley and Daniel Batson (1973) demonstrated that something as seemingly trivial as how much of a hurry people are in can make more of a difference than what kind of people they are. These researchers conducted a study that mirrored the parable of the Good Samaritan, wherein many

Bystander Effect

The finding that the greater the number of bystanders who witness an emergency, the less likely any one of them is to help

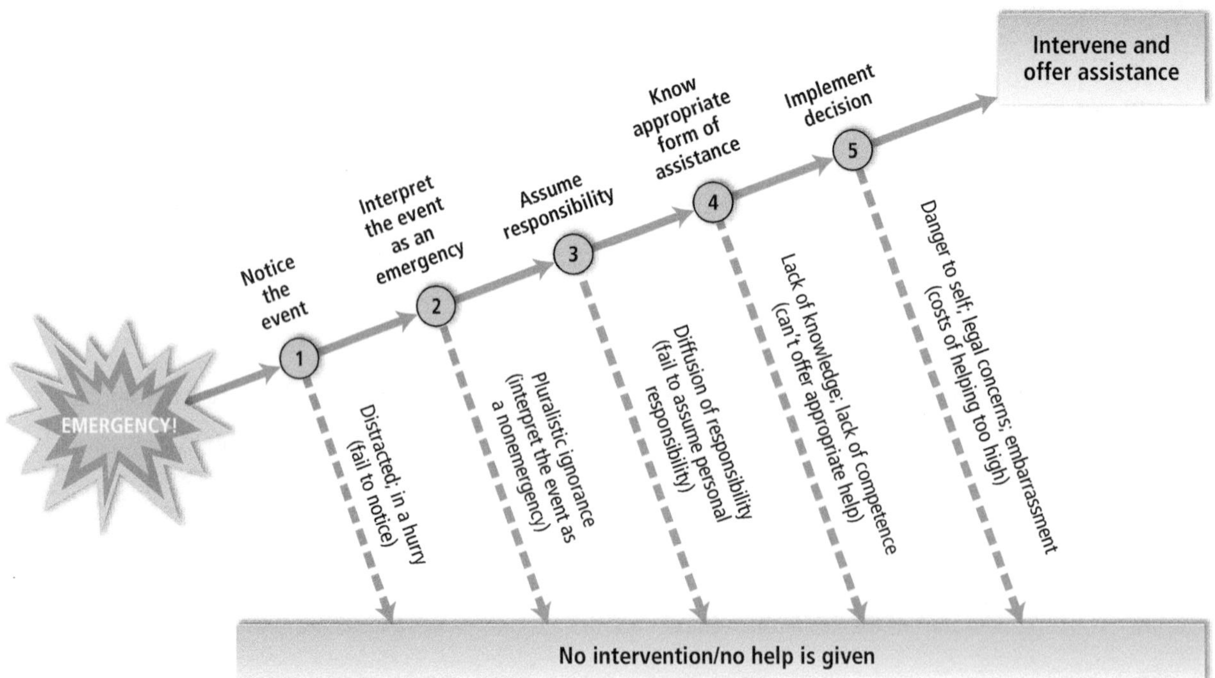

FIGURE 11.4

Bystander Intervention Decision Tree: Five Steps to Helping in an Emergency

Latané and Darley (1970) showed that people go through five decision-making steps before they help someone in an emergency. If bystanders fail to take any one of the five steps, they will not help. Each step is outlined here, along with the possible reasons why people decide not to intervene.

(Adapted from Latané & Darley, 1970)

passersby failed to stop to help a man lying unconscious at the side of the road. The research participants were people we might think would be extremely altruistic—seminary students preparing to devote their lives to the ministry. The students were asked to walk to another building, where the researchers would record them making a brief speech. Some were told that they were late and should hurry to keep their appointment. Others were told that there was no rush because the assistant in the other building was running a few minutes behind schedule. As they walked to the other building, each of the students passed a man who was slumped in a doorway. The man (an accomplice of the experimenters) coughed and groaned as each student walked by. Did the seminary students stop and offer to help him? If they were not in a hurry, most of them (63%) did. If they were hurrying to keep their appointment, however, only 10% stopped to help. Many of the students who were in a hurry did not even notice the man.

Surely if people were deeply religious, they would be less influenced by such a small matter as how hurried they were. Surprisingly, though, Darley and Batson (1973) found that the seminary students who were the most religious were no more likely to help than those who were the least religious. What about if they were thinking about helping people in need? The researchers also varied the topic of the speech they asked the students to give. Some were asked to discuss the kinds of jobs seminary students preferred; others were asked to discuss the parable of the Good Samaritan. You might think that seminary students who were thinking about the parable of the Good Samaritan would be especially likely to stop and help a man slumped in a doorway, given the similarity of this incident to the parable, but the topic of the speech made little difference in whether they helped. Students in a hurry were unlikely to help, even if they were very religious and about to give a speech about the Good Samaritan.

Interpreting the Event as an Emergency Even if people do notice someone slumped in a doorway, they might not stop and help. The next determinant of helping is whether the bystander interprets the event as an emergency—as a situation where help is needed (see Figure 11.4). Is the person in the doorway drunk or seriously ill? If we see white smoke coming out of a vent, is it something innocuous, such as mist from an air conditioner, or a sign that the building is on fire? Did that scream we just heard come from someone having a good time at a party, or is someone being attacked? If people assume that nothing is wrong when an emergency is taking place, they will not help.

When other bystanders are present, people are more likely to assume that an emergency is something innocuous. To understand why, think back to our discussion of informational social influence in Chapter 8. This type of social influence occurs when we use other people to help us define reality. When we are uncertain about what's going on, such as whether the smoke we see is a sign of a fire, one of the first things we do is look around to see how other people are responding. If other people look up, shrug, and go about their business, we are likely to assume that there is nothing to worry about. If other people look panic-stricken and yell, "Fire!" we immediately assume the building is indeed on fire. As we saw in Chapter 8, it's often a good strategy to use other people as a source of information when we are uncertain about what's going on. The danger is that sometimes no one is sure what is happening. Because an emergency is often a sudden and confusing event, bystanders tend to freeze, watching and listening with blank expressions as they try to figure out what is happening. When they glance at each other, they see an apparent lack of concern on the part of everyone else. This results in a state of **pluralistic ignorance**, wherein people think that everyone else is interpreting a situation in a certain way, when in fact they are not. When an emergency occurs, for example, bystanders often assume that nothing is wrong because no one else looks concerned—even though everyone is worried and concerned.

Consider another classic experiment by Latané and Darley (1970). You are participating in a study of people's attitudes toward the problems of urban life, and you arrive at the appointed time. A sign tells you to fill out a questionnaire while you're waiting for the study to begin, so you take a seat and get started. Then you notice something odd: White smoke is trickling into the room through a small vent in the wall. Before long, the room is so filled with smoke that you can barely see the questionnaire. What will you do?

In fact, there was no real danger—the experimenters were pumping smoke into the room to see how people would respond to this potential emergency. Not surprisingly, when people were alone, most of them took action. Within 2 minutes, 50% of the participants left the room and found the experimenter down the hall, reporting that there may have been a fire in the building; by 6 minutes, 75% of the participants had left the room to alert the experimenter.

But what would happen if people were not alone? Given that 75% of the participants who were by themselves reported the smoke, it would seem that the larger the group, the greater the likelihood that someone would report the smoke. In fact, this can be figured mathematically: If there is a 75% chance that any one person will report the smoke, then there is a 98% chance that at least one person in a three-person group will do so.

To find out if there really is safety in numbers, Latané and Darley (1970) included a condition in which three participants took part at the same time. Everything was identical except that three people sat in the room as the smoke began to seep in. Surprisingly, in only 12% of the three-person groups did someone report the smoke within 2 minutes, and in only 38% of the groups did someone report the smoke within 6 minutes. In the remaining groups, the participants sat there filling out questionnaires even when they had to wave away the smoke with their hands to see what they were writing. What went wrong?

Unsure whether the smoke signaled an emergency, participants used each other as a source of information. If the people next to you glance at the smoke and then continue filling out their questionnaires, you will feel reassured that nothing is wrong; otherwise, why would they be acting so unconcerned? The problem is that they are probably looking at you as well, and if you seem untroubled, they too are reassured that everything is OK. In short, each group member is reassured because they assume that

Pluralistic Ignorance
The case in which people think that everyone else is interpreting a situation in a certain way, when in fact they are not

Emergency situations can be confusing. Does this man need help? Have the bystanders failed to notice him, or has the behavior of the others led each of them to interpret the situation as a nonemergency—an example of pluralistic ignorance?

everyone else knows more about what's going on than they do. And when the event is ambiguous—as when smoke is coming from a vent—people in groups will convince each other that nothing is wrong (Clark & Word, 1972; Solomon, Solomon, & Stone, 1978).

Assuming Responsibility Sometimes it is obvious that an emergency is occurring, as when Kitty Genovese cried out, "Oh my God, he stabbed me! Please help me! Please help me!" (Rosenthal, 1964, p. 33). Genovese's neighbors must have believed that something terrible was happening and that she desperately needed help. That they did nothing indicates that even if we interpret an event as an emergency, we have to decide that it is *our* responsibility, not someone else's, to do something about it. Here again the number of bystanders is a crucial variable.

Think back to the Latané and Darley (1968) seizure experiment in which participants believed they were the only one listening to the student while he had a seizure. The responsibility was totally on their shoulders. If they didn't help, no one would, and the student might die. As a result, in this condition most people helped almost immediately, and all helped within a few minutes.

But what happens when there are many witnesses? A **diffusion of responsibility** occurs: Each bystander's sense of responsibility to help decreases as the number of witnesses increases. Because other people are present, no single bystander feels a strong personal responsibility to act. Recall from our earlier discussion that helping often entails costs: We might be putting ourselves in danger or end up looking foolish by overreacting or doing the wrong thing. Why should we risk these costs when many other people who can help are present? The problem is that everyone is likely to feel the same way, making all the bystanders less likely to help. This is particularly true if people cannot tell whether someone else has already intervened. When participants in the seizure experiment believed that other students were witnesses as well, they couldn't tell whether another student had already helped, because the intercom system allowed only the voice of the student having the seizure to be transmitted. Each student probably assumed that he or she did not have to help, thinking that surely someone else had already done so. Similarly, Kitty Genovese's neighbors had no way of knowing whether someone else had called the police. Most likely, they assumed that there was no need to do so, as someone else had already made the call. Tragically, everyone thought it was somebody else's responsibility to act, and Genovese was left to fight her assailant alone. The sad irony of Genovese's murder is that she probably would be alive today if fewer people had heard her cries for help.

Knowing How to Help Even if people have made it this far in the helping sequence, another condition must still be met (Step 4 in Figure 11.4): They must decide what kind of help is appropriate. Suppose that on a hot summer day you see a woman collapse in the street. No one else seems to be helping, so you decide it is up to you. But what should you do? Has the woman had a heart attack? Is she suffering from heatstroke? Should you call an ambulance, administer CPR, or try to get her out of the sun? If people don't know what form of assistance to give, obviously they will be unable to help.

Deciding to Implement the Help Finally, even if you know exactly what kind of help is appropriate, there are still reasons why you might decide not to intervene. For one thing, you might not be qualified to deliver the right kind of help. Even if the woman is complaining of chest pains, indicating a heart attack, you may not know how to give her CPR. Or you might be afraid of making a fool of yourself, of doing the wrong thing and making matters worse, or even of placing yourself in danger by trying to help. Consider the fate of three television network technicians who in 1982 saw a man beating a woman in a New York parking lot, tried to intervene, and were shot and killed by the assailant. Even when we know what kind of intervention is needed, we have to weigh the costs of trying to help.

Diffusion of Responsibility

The phenomenon wherein each bystander's sense of responsibility to help decreases as the number of witnesses increases

What about helping in situations that are not emergencies? The Latané and Darley model applies here as well. Consider an Internet chat room in which someone needs help figuring out how to use the software. Are people less likely to help each other as the number of people in the chat room increases? Researchers in one study entered chat groups on Yahoo! Chat where 2 to 19 people were discussing a wide variety of topics (Markey, 2000). The researchers posed as either a male or female participant and typed this request for help: "Can anyone tell me how to look at someone's profile?" (p. 185). The message was addressed either to the group as a whole or to one randomly selected person in the chat room. Then the researchers timed how long it took someone in the group to respond to the request for help.

When the request was addressed to the group as a whole, Latané and Darley's results were replicated closely: The more people there were in the chat room, the longer it took for anyone to respond to the request for help. But when the request was directed to a specific person, that person responded quickly, regardless of the size of the group. These results suggest that the diffusion of responsibility was operating. When a general request for help is made, a large group makes people feel that they do not have much responsibility to respond. When addressed by name, though, people are more likely to feel a responsibility to help, even when many others are present.

Even if people are by themselves, however, they can still experience a diffusion of responsibility. In a recent study, people who were asked to think about going out to dinner with 10 friends were less likely to donate money to charity or volunteer to help with another experiment than were people who were asked to think about going out to dinner with one friend (Garcia et al., 2002). Simply imagining ourselves in a group is enough to make us feel less responsible for helping others.

Simulate on **MyPsychLab**
To explore the bystander effect, try the MyPsychLab simulation ***Helping a Stranger***.

The Nature of the Relationship: Communal Versus Exchange Relationships

A great deal of research on prosocial behavior has looked at helping between strangers, such as Latané and Darley's research on bystander intervention. Although this research is very important, most helping in everyday life occurs between people who know each other well, such as family members and close friends. In Chapter 10, we distinguished between communal and exchange relationships. *Communal relationships* are those in which people's primary concern is the welfare of the other person (e.g., a child), whereas *exchange relationships* are governed by concerns about equity—that what you put into the relationship equals what you get out of it. How does helping occur in communal relationships?

Margaret Clark and Judson Mills (Clark & Mills, 2011) argue that people in communal relationships are concerned less with the benefits they will receive by helping and more with simply satisfying the needs of the other person. When parents are deciding whether to help their children, for example, they seldom think, "Well, what have they done for me lately?" Unlike in exchange relationships, where people are concerned with what they are getting in return from other people, in communal relationships people are more concerned with the welfare of the other person.

In communal relationships, such as those between parents and their children, people are concerned less with who gets what and more with how much help the other person needs.

Does this mean that people are more helpful toward friends than strangers? Yes—at least under most circumstances. We are more likely to have communal relationships with friends and are therefore more likely to help even when there is nothing in it for us. In fact, we like to help a partner in a communal relationship more than a partner in an exchange relationship (Williamson et al., 1996). There is, however, an interesting exception to this rule. Research by Abraham Tesser (1988) on self-esteem maintenance has shown that when a task is not important to us, we do indeed help friends more than strangers. But suppose that the most important thing in the world for you is to be a doctor, that you are struggling to pass a difficult premed physics course, and that two other people in the class—your best friend and a complete stranger—ask you to lend them your notes from a class they missed. According to Tesser's research, you will be more inclined to help the stranger than your friend (Tesser, 1991; Tesser & Smith, 1980). Why? Because it hurts to see a close friend do better than we do in an area of great importance to our self-esteem. Consequently, we are less likely to help a friend in these important areas than in areas we don't care as much about. To test hypotheses about helping behavior, see the Try It! on the next page.

Effects of the Media: Video Games and Music Lyrics

When we think about the effects of the media on behavior, we usually think about negative influences, such as whether violence on television or playing violent video games makes people more aggressive. There are indeed such negative effects, which we discuss in Chapter 12. But can the opposite also occur, such that seeing people act in prosocial ways or playing prosocial video games makes people more cooperative? Recent research suggests that it can.

Tobias Greitemeyer and his colleagues have conducted a number of studies that follow the same procedure: First, participants come into the lab and play a video game for about 10 minutes. Half are randomly assigned to play a game that involves prosocial acts, such as *Lemmings*, in which the goal is to care for a group of small beings and save them by helping them find the exit out of different worlds. The other half play a neutral video game such as *Tetris*, where the goal is to rotate falling geometric figures so that they cover the bottom of the screen. Participants then take part in what they think is an unrelated study, in which they are given the opportunity to help someone. The helping opportunities include relatively easy actions such as helping an experimenter pick up a cup of pencils that he or she accidentally knocked over, more time-consuming commitments such as volunteering to participate in future studies without compensation; and potentially dangerous actions such as helping a female experimenter when an ex-boyfriend enters the room and starts harassing her. As seen in Figure 11.5, people who had just played a prosocial video game were more likely to help in all of these ways than were people who had just played a neutral video game (Greitemeyer & Osswald, 2010).

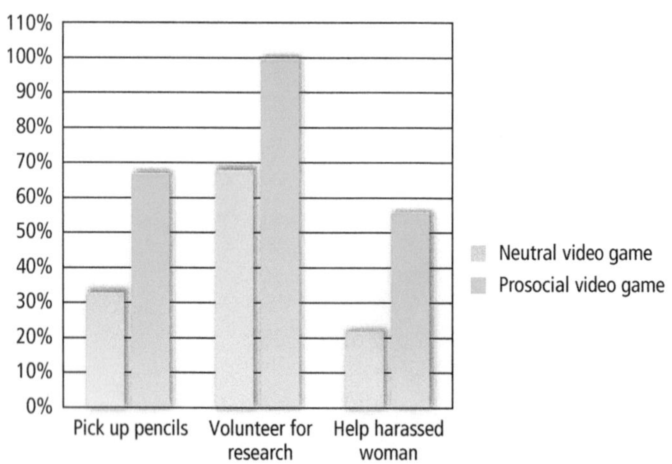

FIGURE 11.5

Effects of Playing Prosocial Video Games on the Likelihood of Helping

Participants played a prosocial video game (such as *Lemmings*) or a neutral video game (such as *Tetris*). Then, as part of what they thought was another study, they were given the opportunity to help in some way. In one study, an experimenter accidentally knocked over a jar of pencils and the researchers observed how many participants helped him or her pick them up. In another, participants were asked to volunteer to take part in future studies for no compensation. In a third, the researchers staged an event where the experimenter's ex-boyfriend charged into the room and tried to force her to leave with him. The researchers observed how many participants tried to help the experimenter in some way. As seen in the graph, playing a prosocial video game increased the likelihood that people helped in all of these situations.

(Adapted from Greitemeyer & Osswald, 2010)

It isn't just prosocial video games that can make people more helpful—listening to songs with prosocial lyrics works too. Studies have found that people who listen to such songs, such as Michael Jackson's *Heal the World* or the Beatles' *Help*, are more likely to help someone than people who listened to songs with neutral lyrics such as the Beatles' *Octopus's Garden* (Greitemeyer, 2009, 2011; North, Tarrant, & Hargreaves, 2004).

Why does playing a prosocial video game or listening to prosocial song lyrics make people more cooperative? It works in at least two ways: by increasing people's empathy toward someone in need of help and increasing the accessibility of thoughts about helping others (Greitemeyer,

TRY IT! The Lost-Letter Technique

Here's a simple technique you can use to test your own hypotheses about prosocial behavior. This procedure, called the "lost-letter technique," involves leaving stamped envelopes on the ground and seeing whether people pick them up and mail them. Stanley Milgram (1969), who first used this technique, found that people were more likely to mail letters addressed to organizations they supported. For example, 72% of letters addressed to "Medical Research Associates" were mailed, whereas only 25% of letters addressed to "Friends of the Nazi Party" were mailed (all were addressed to the same post office box so that Milgram could count how many were returned).

You can use the lost-letter technique to test some of the hypotheses about helping behavior that we have discussed in this chapter or hypotheses that you come up with on your own. Put your address on the letters so that you can count how many are returned, but vary where you put the letters or to whom they are addressed. For example, drop some letters in a small town and some in an urban area, to see whether people in small towns are more likely to mail them (be sure to mark the envelopes in some way that will let you know where they were dropped—e.g., put a little pencil mark on the back of the ones dropped in small towns). Did you replicate the finding of previous studies that people living in small towns are more likely to mail the letters (Bridges & Coady, 1996; Hansson & Slade, 1977)? Or you might vary the ethnicity of the name of the person on the address to see if people are more likely to help members of some ethnic groups more than others. Be creative!

After deciding what you want to vary (e.g., the ethnicity or gender of the addressee), be careful to place envelopes of both types (e.g., those addressed to males and females) in similar locations. It is best to use a fairly large number of letters (e.g., a minimum of 15 to 20 in each condition) to get reliable results. Obviously, you should not leave more than one letter in the same location. You might want to team up with some classmates on this project so that you can split the cost of the stamps.

Osswald, & Brauer, 2010). So, if you ever find yourself in need of help and see someone approaching who is listening to an MP3 player, hope that he or she is listening to music with prosocial lyrics!

What are the effects of playing prosocial video games (such as *Lemmings*) on people's behavior? Research shows that those who have just played a prosocial video game are more likely to help others than are people who have just played a neutral video game.

What about prosocial lyrics and romance? If you have your eye on someone special, consider this study, which took research on song lyrics one step further (Guéguen, Jacob, & Lamy, 2010). The study was conducted in France, and the participants were female college students who were not dating anyone. When a participant arrived for the study, she was ushered into a waiting room where music happened to be playing on a sound system. For half of the participants it was a romantic song called "Je l'aime à mourir" (which loosely translates as "I love her to death"), while for the others it was a song with neutral lyrics ("L'heure du thé," or "tea time"). After a few minutes, the participant was taken to another room where she performed a consumer taste test with another participant, who happened to be a male student of average attractiveness. During a break, the man asked for the woman's phone number. "I think you are very nice and I was wondering if you would give me your phone number," he said. "I'll phone you later and we can have a drink together somewhere next week" (Guéguen, Jacob, & Lamy, 2010, p. 305). Were the women who had just listened to the romantic song more likely to say yes? Indeed they were; 52% who had listened to "Je l'aime à mourir" gave the man their number, whereas only 30% of the women who had listened to "L'heure du thé" did so.

How Can Helping Be Increased?

We would all be better off if prosocial behavior were more common than it is. How can we get people, when faced with an emergency, to act more like Abe Zelmanowitz and less like Kitty Genovese's neighbors?

Before addressing this question, we should point out that people do not always want to be helped. Imagine that you are sitting at a computer terminal at the library and are struggling to learn a new e-mail system. You can't figure out how to send and receive mail and are becoming increasingly frustrated as the computer responds with messages such as "Invalid Command." A confident-looking guy whom you know only slightly walks over to you and looks over your shoulder for a few minutes. "You have a lot to learn," he says. "Let me show you how this baby works." How would you react? You might feel some gratitude, but you will probably also feel some resentment. His offer of help comes with a message: "You are too stupid to figure this out for yourself." Because receiving help can make people feel inadequate and dependent, they do not always react positively when someone offers them aid. People do not want to appear incompetent, so they often decide to suffer in silence, even if doing so lowers their chances of successfully completing a task (Alvarez & Van Leeuwen, 2011; Brown, Nesse, & Vinokur, 2003; Halabi & Nadler, 2010).

When death, the great reconciler, has come, it is never our tenderness that we repent of, but our severity.
—George Eliot (Marian Evans), *Adam Bede*, 1859

Nevertheless, the world would be a better place if more people helped those in need. How can we increase everyday acts of kindness, such as looking out for an elderly neighbor or volunteering to read to kids at the local school? The answer to this question lies in our discussion of the causes of prosocial behavior. For example, we saw that several personal characteristics of potential helpers are important, and promoting those factors can increase the likelihood that these people will help (Clary et al., 1994; Snyder, 1993). But even kind, altruistic people will fail to help if certain situational constraints are present, such as being in an urban environment or witnessing an emergency in the presence of numerous bystanders.

Why did this person help, even when several other bystanders witnessed the same emergency and didn't help? Perhaps this person learned about the barriers to bystander intervention in a social psychology class.

Increasing the Likelihood That Bystanders Will Intervene

There is evidence that simply being aware of the barriers to helping in an emergency can increase people's chances of overcoming those barriers. A few years ago at Cornell University, several students intervened to prevent another student from committing suicide. As is often the case with emergencies, the situation was very confusing, and at first the bystanders were not sure what was happening or what they should do. The student who led the intervention said that she was reminded of a lecture she had heard on bystander intervention in her introductory psychology class a few days before and realized that if she didn't act, no one would (Savitsky, 1998). Or consider an incident at Vassar College not long ago where students saw someone being attacked by a mugger. Like Kitty Genovese's neighbors, most of them did nothing, probably because they assumed that somebody else had already called the police. One of the students, however, immediately called the campus police because she was struck by how similar the situation was to the studies on bystander intervention she had read about in her social psychology course—even though she had taken the class more than a year earlier (Coats, 1998).

These are not controlled experiments, of course, and we cannot be certain that these helpful people were spurred on by what they had learned in their psychology classes. Fortunately, this question has been addressed experimentally (Beaman et al., 1978). The researchers randomly assigned students to listen to a lecture on Latané and Darley's (1970) bystander intervention research or a lecture on an unrelated topic. Two weeks later, all the students participated in what they thought was a completely unrelated sociology study, during which they encountered a student lying on the floor. Was he in need of help? Had he fallen and injured himself, or was he simply a student who had fallen asleep after pulling an all-nighter? As we have seen, when in an ambiguous situation such as this one, people look to see how other people are reacting. Because an accomplice of the experimenter (posing as another participant) intentionally acted unconcerned, the natural thing to do was to assume that nothing was wrong. This is exactly what most participants did if they had not heard the lecture about bystander intervention research; in this condition, only 25% of them stopped to help the student. However, if the participants had heard the lecture about bystander intervention, 43% stopped to help the student. Thus, knowing how we can be unwittingly influenced by others can by itself help overcome this type of social influence. We can only hope that knowing about other barriers to prosocial behavior will make them easier to overcome as well.

Positive Psychology and Prosocial Behavior

In recent years, a new field known as *positive psychology* has emerged (Seligman, 2002; Seligman, Steen, & Park, 2005; Sheldon, Kashdan, & Steger, 2011). Martin Seligman, an influential clinical psychologist, observed that much of psychology—particularly clinical psychology—had focused on mental disorders, largely ignoring how to define and nurture psychological health. Psychology should not just be the study of "disease, weakness, and damage," he argued, but the study of "strength and virtue" (2002, p. 4). Largely through Seligman's efforts, many psychologists are now focusing on such topics as the nature of healthy human functioning, how to define and categorize human strengths, and how to improve people's lives (Lopez & Snyder, 2009).

The positive psychology movement is a useful and necessary corrective to the emphasis on mental illness in clinical psychology and has led to many fascinating research programs. As we have seen in this book, though, social psychology has not concentrated solely on negative behaviors. For many years there have been active social psychological research programs on such topics as how people develop intrinsic interest in an activity (Chapter 5), how people maintain high self-esteem (Chapter 6), and how people form impressions of and lasting relationships with others (Chapter 10). To be sure, social psychology has documented many negative behaviors that can result from powerful social influences, such as obedience to authority and other kinds of conformity (Chapter 8). By studying the basic ways in which humans process information about themselves and their social worlds, however, it has been possible to understand both the bright and the dark side of human behavior, such as when people will help others and when they will not.

An excellent example of the social psychological approach is the topic of this chapter, the study of the conditions under which people help or fail to help their fellow humans. Is this the study of positive psychology or a focus on the dark side? Both, because social psychologists study the conditions under which people are likely to help (e.g., when people feel empathy toward another) and the conditions under which they are likely to fail to help (e.g., when they experience a diffusion of responsibility).

As noted earlier, Daniel Batson and his colleagues have been the strongest proponents of the idea that many people have a pure, unselfish motive for helping others and will do so when they feel empathy (Batson, 2011). In the experiment we reviewed earlier, for example, when people felt empathy toward a classmate who had been in an automobile accident, they were willing to help her regardless of whether there was a cost to them of doing so (see Figure 11.2). Research on empathy and prosocial behavior is an excellent example of the ways in which social psychologists have been interested in positive psychology, the study of people's strengths and virtues.

Watch on MyPsychLab
Think about the motivations for prosocial behavior as you watch the MyPsychLab video ***Friends, Family, and Strangers***.

CONNECTIONS

Increasing Volunteerism

There are many important kinds of prosocial behavior besides intervening in emergencies, including volunteerism and community service. Social psychologists have studied this kind of helping as well, wherein people commit to helping strangers on a more long-term basis (Mannino, Snyder, & Omoto, 2011; Penner, 2004; Piliavin, 2010).

Surveys of Western European and North American countries have found that many people engage in volunteer work, with the highest rate in the United States (47%; Ting & Piliavin, 2000). Of course, that means that even in the United States more than half of the population is not volunteering, raising the question of how to increase people's willingness to spend time helping others. Some institutions have responded by requiring their members to perform community service. Some high schools, colleges, and businesses, for example, require their students or employees to engage in volunteer work.

These programs have the benefit of increasing the pool of volunteers available to help community organizations such as homeless shelters, medical clinics, and day-care centers. But the question arises as to the effect of such "mandatory volunteerism" on the motivation of the people who do the helping. Many of these organizations assume that they are increasing the likelihood that their members will volunteer in the future, even after they leave the organizations. That is, making people volunteer is assumed to foster volunteerism by enlightening people about its benefits.

An increasing number of schools and businesses are requiring people to perform community service. These programs can actually lower interest in volunteering if people feel they are helping because of an external requirement. Encouraging people to volunteer while preserving the sense that they freely choose to do so is likely to increase people's intentions to volunteer again in the future.

As we discussed in Chapter 5, however, giving people strong external reasons for performing an activity can actually undermine their intrinsic interest in that activity. This is called the *overjustification effect*: People see their behavior as caused by compelling extrinsic reasons (e.g., being required to do volunteer work), making them underestimate the extent to which their behavior was caused by intrinsic reasons (e.g., that they like to do volunteer work). Consistent with this research, the more that people feel they are volunteering because of external requirements, the less likely they are to volunteer freely in the future (Batson et al., 1978; Bringle, 2005; Kunda & Schwartz, 1983; Stukas, Snyder, & Clary, 1999). The moral is that organizations should be careful about how heavy-handedly they impose requirements to volunteer. If people feel that they are complying only because they have to, they may actually become less likely to volunteer in the future. Encouraging people to volunteer while preserving the sense that they freely choose to do so has been shown to increase people's sense of well-being and their intentions to volunteer again in the future (Piliavin, 2008; Stukas et al., 1999).

USE IT!

We hope it never happens, but suppose you are injured in an accident in a public place and need help. Based on what you have learned in this chapter, how could you make sure that someone comes to your aid as soon as possible? As we saw in the section on the bystander effect, the trick is to make sure people notice that you need help, interpret it as an emergency, and assume that they (and not someone else) is responsible for helping. One way to avoid a diffusion of responsibility is to point to one person and ask for their help. That is, instead of shouting, "Will someone please help me?" single out one person—"Hey, you in the blue shirt and sunglasses, could you please call 911?" That makes one person feel responsible and also communicates to him or her how to help. Based on what you have read in this chapter, you should also know more about what to do if you witness an emergency—don't assume that someone else will help. By the way, you might be interested to know that, contrary to what happened in the final episode of the TV show *Seinfeld*, there are no laws in the United States obligating people to help a stranger in need. Many states do have Good Samaritan laws that make it hard for a victim to sue a bystander who tries to help but causes further injury. These laws don't give bystanders complete protection, but they are meant to increase the likelihood that people will come to each other's aid.

Summary

What are the basic motives that determine whether people help others?

- **Basic Motives Underlying Prosocial Behavior: Why Do People Help?** This chapter examined the causes of **prosocial behavior**, acts performed with the goal of benefiting another person. What are the basic origins of prosocial behavior?
  - **Evolutionary Psychology: Instincts and Genes** Evolutionary theory explains prosocial behavior in four ways. The first is **kin selection**, the idea that behaviors that help a genetic relative are favored by natural selection. The second is the **norm of reciprocity**, which is the expectation that helping others will increase the likelihood that they will help us in the future. The third is *group selection*, the idea that social groups with altruistic members are more likely to survive in competition with other groups.
  - **Social Exchange: The Costs and Rewards of Helping** Social exchange theory argues that prosocial behavior is not necessarily rooted in our genes. Instead, people help others in order to maximize social rewards and minimize social costs.
  - **Empathy and Altruism: The Pure Motive for Helping** People can be motivated by **altruism**, the desire to help another person even if it involves a cost to the helper. According to the **empathy-altruism hypothesis**, when people feel **empathy** toward another person (they experience events and emotions the other person experiences), they attempt to help that person purely for altruistic reasons.

What are some personal qualities that influence whether a given individual will help?

- **Personal Qualities and Prosocial Behavior: Why Do Some People Help More Than Others?** Basic motives are not all there is to understanding prosocial behavior—personal qualities matter as well.
  - **Individual Differences: The Altruistic Personality** Although some people have personalies that make them more likely than others to help, personality factors have not been shown to be strong predictors of who will help across a variety of social situations.
  - **Gender Differences in Prosocial Behavior** In many cultures, the male sex role includes helping in chivalrous and heroic ways, whereas the female sex role includes helping in close, long-term relationships.
  - **Cultural Differences in Prosocial Behavior** People are willing to help both **in-group** and **out-group** members, but for different reasons. People are more likely to feel empathy toward members of their in-groups who are in need, and the more empathy they feel, the more likely they are to help. People help out-group members for a different reason: They do so when they have something to gain, such as feeling good about themselves or making a good impression on others.
  - **Religion and Prosocial Behavior** People who are religious report on surveys that they help more than do people who are not religious, and they actually do help more in situations in which helping makes them look good to themselves or others. They are not more likely to help, however, in private situations in which no one will know that they helped.
  - **The Effects of Mood on Prosocial Behavior** People are more likely to help if they are in especially good moods, but also if they are in especially bad moods.

In what situations are people more likely, or less likely, to help others?

- **Situational Determinants of Prosocial Behavior: When Will People Help?** To understand why people help others, we also need to consider the nature of the social situation.
  - **Environment: Rural Versus Urban** People are less likely to help in dense, urban settings because of the **urban overload hypothesis**—the idea that people living in cities are constantly bombarded with stimulation and that they keep to themselves in order to avoid being overwhelmed by it.
  - **Residential Mobility** People who have lived for a long time in one place are more likely to engage in prosocial behaviors than are people who have recently moved to an area.
  - **The Number of Bystanders: The Bystander Effect** In order to help in an emergency, people must meet five conditions: They must notice the event, interpret it as an emergency, assume responsibility, know how to help, and implement their decision to help. As the number of bystanders who witness an emergency increases, the more difficult it is to meet two of these conditions—interpreting the event as an emergency and assuming responsibility. This produces the **bystander effect**: The larger the number of bystanders, the less likely any one of them is to help.
  - **The Nature of the Relationship: Communal Versus Exchange Relationships** People in *exchange relationships*—those governed by concerns about equity—are concerned primarily with the benefits they will receive by helping others. People in *communal relationships*—those in which the primary concern is the welfare of the other person—are less concerned with the benefits they will receive and more with simply satisfying the needs of the other person.
  - **Effects of the Media: Video Games and Music Lyrics** Playing a prosocial video game or listening to a song with prosocial lyrics makes people more likely to help others in a variety of ways.

What can be done to promote prosocial behavior?

- **How Can Helping Be Increased?** Prosocial behavior can be increased in a number of ways.
  - **Increasing the Likelihood That Bystanders Will Intervene** Research shows that teaching people about the barriers to bystander intervention increases the likelihood that they will help in emergencies.
  - **Positive Psychology and Prosocial Behavior** A new field called positive psychology has emerged that focuses on people's strengths and virtues instead of mental disease. The social psychological approach is to investigate the conditions under which people act in positive (e.g., helpful) and negative (e.g., unhelpful) ways. Many of these conditions were discussed in this chapter. For example, people will help at a cost to themselves when they feel empathy toward a person in need. When they do not feel empathy, they will help only when it is in their self-interest.

Chapter 11 Test

Study and Review on MyPsychLab

1. Which of the following is *not* a way in which evolutionary theory explains prosocial behavior?
   a. social exchange
   b. kin selection
   c. the reciprocity norm
   d. group selection

2. Amy is walking across campus and sees someone on her hands and knees looking for a ring that slipped off her finger. Which of the following is *false* according to the empathy-altruism hypothesis? Amy
   a. feels empathy toward the person, so she will probably stop and help the stranger look for the ring, regardless of whether it is in her self-interest to do so.
   b. feels empathy toward the person, but she doesn't think she has much to gain by helping, so she decides not to help the person look for the ring.
   c. doesn't feel empathy toward the person but recognizes her as a TA in her English class. Amy really wants to get a good grade in that class, so she will probably stop and help her TA look for the ring.
   d. doesn't feel empathy toward the person and doesn't think she has much to gain by helping, so she decides not to help the person look for the ring.

3. Which of the following is *not* a reason why being in a good mood tends to increase prosocial behavior?
   a. Good moods make us frame situations more positively, and thus we are more likely to give people the benefit of the doubt.
   b. Helping prolongs good moods.
   c. Good moods make us pay more attention to social norms, so we will be more aware of the altruism norm.
   d. Good moods increase how much attention we pay to ourselves, which makes us more likely to act according to our values.

4. Frank has recently graduated from college and moved from New York City back to the small town in Ohio where he grew up. He now finds that he is much more inclined to engage in prosocial behavior. What is the most likely reason for this change?
   a. Growing up in a small town caused him to internalize altruistic values.
   b. The change in his immediate surroundings changed his likelihood of helping.
   c. College students are less likely to help because they are more susceptible to the bystander effect.
   d. Frank is more likely to engage in negative-state relief when he is in the small town.

5. Luke listened to a lecture in his history class that he found very confusing, but at the end of the class when the professor asked whether there was anything students didn't understand, Luke didn't raise his hand. Because no other hands were raised, Luke assumed that other students had understood the material and that he just didn't pay enough attention. In fact, many students hadn't understood the material and were in the same situation as Luke. This is an example of
   a. jigsaw classroom.
   b. self-fulfilling prophecy.
   c. ultimate attribution error.
   d. pluralistic ignorance.
   e. normative conformity.

6. Research on prosocial behavior finds that religious people
   a. help others more than nonreligious people do in virtually all ways.
   b. report on surveys that they help the same amount as do nonreligious people.
   c. actually help more than nonreligious people, but only if it makes them look good to themselves or to others.
   d. actually help others less than do nonreligious people.

7. Which of the following is most true?
   a. Listening to song lyrics with prosocial lyrics makes people more helpful.
   b. If we want someone to say yes when we ask for a date, it doesn't really work to have him or her listen to a song with romantic lyrics.
   c. Playing prosocial video games has no effect on how helpful people will be.
   d. Playing violent video games makes people more helpful.

8. Meghan lives in a single room in a college dormitory. Late one night, she hears a scream coming from just outside her dorm. She is pretty sure that the person needs help because the person yelled, "Help me! I think I broke my leg!" Meghan goes back to sleep, only to find out the next day that the person was on the ground for 45 minutes before someone helped. Which of the following best explains why Meghan didn't help?
   a. Informational influence.
   b. A diffusion of responsibility.
   c. She didn't interpret it as an emergency.
   d. Pluralistic ignorance.

9. Which of the following is true about prosocial behavior?
   a. How often people have moved from one place to another influences how helpful they are.
   b. There is no effect of personality on prosocial behavior.
   c. Being in a bad mood decreases prosocial behavior.
   d. People are much more likely to help members of their in-group than members of an out-group.

10. Which of the following is *not* true about prosocial behavior?
   a. When people are put in a good mood, they are more likely to help.
   b. People in stable communities are more likely to help than people in communities with high residential mobility.
   c. When people are put in a bad mood, they are more likely to help.
   d. Having an altruistic personality is a strong predictor of helping behavior.

Answer Key

1-a, 2-b, 3-c, 4-b, 5-d,
6-c, 7-a, 8-b, 9-a, 10-d

12 Aggression

Why Do We Hurt Other People? Can We Prevent It?

On April 20, 1999, the corridors and classrooms of Columbine High School in Littleton, Colorado, reverberated with the sound of gunshots. Two students, Eric Harris and Dylan Klebold, armed with assault weapons and explosives, had gone on a rampage, killing a teacher and several of their fellow students. They then turned their guns on themselves. After the smoke cleared, 15 people lay dead (including the shooters) and 23 others were hospitalized, some with severe wounds.

As horrendous as it was, the toll could have been much higher. The two shooters made videotapes a few weeks before the massacre, and from these we have learned that they had prepared 95 explosive devices that failed to go off. Of these, one set was placed a few miles away, intended to explode first and distract police by keeping them busy at a distance from the school. A second set was intended to explode in the cafeteria, killing a large number of students and causing hundreds to evacuate the building in terror, with Harris and Klebold waiting to gun them down. They planted a third set of explosives in their own cars in the school parking lot, timed to explode after the police and paramedics had arrived on the scene, as a way of further increasing the number of casualties and creating even more chaos. The videotape shows the perpetrators gleefully predicting that, before the day was over, they would have killed 250 people.

The Columbine massacre was the deadliest of the 15 high school shootings that had taken place in the United States over a period of a few years. In the sad aftermath of Columbine, as always happens after a violent tragedy, the country needed someone or something to blame. Almost everyone wondered whether these youngsters were crazy. How could reasonably observant parents not know that their sons kept guns in their bedrooms and were manufacturing bombs in their garage? And where were the school authorities? Didn't the teachers notice behaviors that would have predicted such violence? Some people even wondered if schools should give students personality tests to identify the teenagers most likely to commit acts of this kind.

Certain observers quickly concluded that the major cause of such violence is the easy availability of guns. Others were quick to blame the Supreme Court for outlawing prayer in the schools: Wouldn't prayer prevent this sort of outrage? Still others pointed to the prevalence of violence in films, on TV, and in video games; Harris and Klebold were devoted to violent video games. If we could ban violent entertainment, wouldn't that make our schools safe again? And some people felt that these outrageous acts grew out of a general lack of respect among teenagers in our culture. One state legislature responded to the massacre by passing a law requiring students to call their teachers "sir" or "ma'am" as a way of showing respect, as if respect can be mandated (Aronson, 2000).

In this chapter, we will focus on aggression and try to understand what causes it. Are human beings innately aggressive? Can normal people be inspired to commit violence by watching violent characters on TV or in films or by the easy availability of weapons of destruction? Can a society, a school, or a parent do anything to reduce aggression? If so, specifically what? Needless to say, we don't have all the answers, but we do have some of them. By the time you get to the end of this chapter, we hope you will have gained some insight into those issues.

FOCUS QUESTIONS

- What is aggression? Is it innate, learned, or optional?
- What are some situational influences on aggression?
- What evidence is there that aggression is learned by observing and imitating others?
- How can aggression be reduced?

Aggression
Intentional behavior aimed at causing physical harm or psychological pain to another person.

Hostile Aggression
Aggression stemming from feelings of anger and aimed at inflicting pain or injury.

Instrumental Aggression
Aggression as a means to some goal other than causing pain.

What Is Aggression?

For social psychologists, **aggression** is defined as intentional behavior aimed at causing either physical or psychological pain. It should not be confused with assertiveness, even though most people loosely refer to others as "aggressive" if they stand up for their rights, write letters to the editor complaining about real or imagined injustices, or are supremely ambitious. Some people would say that a woman who speaks her mind or disagrees with a male coworker is being "aggressive." But true aggression involves the intent to harm another. The action might be physical or verbal; it might succeed in its goal or not. If someone throws a beer bottle at your head and you duck so that the bottle misses you, it was still an aggressive act. The important thing is the intention. By the same token, if a drunk driver unintentionally runs you down while you're attempting to cross the street, that is not an act of aggression, even though the damage would be far greater than that caused by the beer bottle that missed.

It is also useful to distinguish between types of aggression (Berkowitz, 1993). **Hostile aggression** is an act of aggression stemming from feelings of anger and is aimed at inflicting pain or injury. In **instrumental aggression**, there is an intention to hurt the other person, but the hurting takes place as a means to some goal other than causing pain. In a professional football game, a defensive lineman will usually do whatever it takes to thwart his opponent (the blocker) and tackle the ball carrier. This typically includes intentionally inflicting pain on his opponent if doing so is useful in helping him get the blocker out of the way so that he can get to the ball carrier. This is instrumental aggression. By contrast, if he believes his opponent has been playing dirty, he might become angry and go out of his way to hurt his opponent, even if doing so does not increase his chances of tackling the ball carrier. This is hostile aggression.

> *Man's inhumanity to man makes countless thousands mourn.*
>
> —Robert Burns

Today, social psychologists and other social scientists have made great strides in understanding the biological, social, cultural, and situational causes of aggressive behavior.

The Evolutionary Argument

Let's begin with the obvious fact that men are more physically aggressive than women, starting in childhood. In cultures all over the world—as diverse as the United States, Switzerland, and Ethiopia—little boys are far more likely than little girls to go in for "nonplayful" pushing, shoving, and hitting (Deaux & La France, 1998; Maccoby & Jacklin, 1974). In research conducted worldwide,, men are more violent than women and also more socially dominant (Buss, 2004, 2005). In one study, teenagers from 11 different countries, mostly in Europe and Asia, read stories involving conflict among people and were asked to write their own endings (Archer & McDaniel, 1995). In every one of the 11 countries, young men showed a greater tendency toward violent solutions to conflict than young women did.

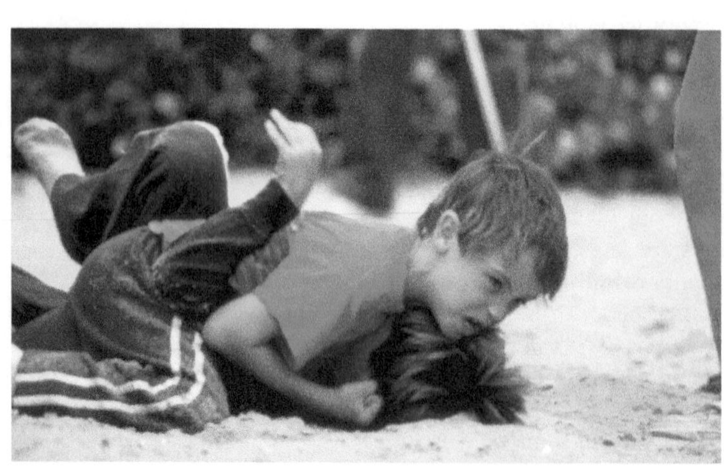

Boys are more likely than girls, the world over, to roughhouse and pummel each other. Is this evidence of hostile or instrumental aggression—or just of physical play?

Evolutionary psychologists argue that physical aggression is genetically programmed into men, because it enables them to defend their group and perpetuate their genes. (In previous chapters we have noted the evolutionary argument for prosocial behavior such as altruism and love.) Males are theorized to aggress for two reasons: first, to establish dominance over other males and secure the highest possible status. The idea here is that the female will choose the male who is most likely to provide the best genes and the greatest protection and resources for their offspring. Second, males aggress out of sexual jealousy, to ensure that their mate is not having sex with other men, thereby ensuring their paternity (Buss, 2004).

The hormone that fuels male aggression is testosterone, which both sexes have, although in higher proportion in males. Laboratory animals injected with testosterone become more aggressive (Moyer, 1983), and there is a parallel finding in humans: Naturally occurring testosterone levels are significantly higher among prisoners convicted of violent crimes than among those convicted of nonviolent crimes (Dabbs, 2000; Dabbs et al., 1995). Similarly, juvenile delinquents have higher testosterone levels than do college students (Banks & Dabbs, 1996). These studies, however, are correlational, and causality runs in both directions: That is, being in an aggressive, competitive, or sexual situation increases the production of testosterone (Thompson, Dabbs, & Frady, 1990; Mazur & Dabbs, 1992).

When people say that aggression is "natural," they often point to our primate relatives. Chimpanzees (top) are indeed pretty belligerent and aggressive, but bonobos (bottom) would rather make love than war.

Aggression in Other Animals To answer the "innate versus learned" question about aggressiveness, some scientists have turned to experiments with nonhuman species. Consider the common belief that cats will instinctively stalk and kill rats. Half a century ago, biologist Zing Yang Kuo (1961) performed a simple experiment: He raised a kitten in the same cage with a rat. Not only did the cat refrain from attacking the rat, but the two became close companions. Moreover, when given the opportunity, the cat refused either to chase or to kill other rats; thus, the benign behavior was not confined to this one buddy, but generalized to rats the cat had never met.

Although this experiment is charming, it fails to prove that aggressive behavior is not instinctive in cats; it merely demonstrates that early experience can override it. What if an organism grows up without any contact with other organisms? Will it or won't it show aggressive tendencies? It turns out that rats raised in isolation, without any experience in fighting other rats, will attack a fellow rat when one is introduced into the cage; moreover, the isolated rats use the same pattern of threat and attack that experienced rats use (Eibl-Eibesfeldt, 1963). So even though aggressive behavior can be modified by experience, as shown by Kuo's experiment, some kinds of aggressive behavior apparently do not need to be learned.

We can gain still greater insight into our own biological heritage by observing the behavior of those animals with whom we have the most genetic similarity. Our closest relatives in the animal kingdom are two primates: the chimpanzees and the bonobos. Both species have 98% of their DNA in common with human beings. The chimpanzee is known for its aggressive behavior; the females too can be pretty mean (Watts et al., 2006). It is the only nonhuman species in which groups of male members hunt and kill other members of their own kind—indeed, at about the same rate that humans in hunter-gatherer societies kill each other (Wrangham, Wilson, & Muller, 2006). Based on the research on chimps, we might conclude that humans, especially males, are genetically programmed for aggressive behavior.

However, living across the river from the chimpanzees and out of their reach are the bonobos, our equally close genetic relative. Unlike the chimp, the bonobo is known for its nonaggressive behavior. In fact, bonobos are often referred to as the "make love, not war" ape. Prior to engaging in activities that could otherwise lead to conflict, bonobos have sex, an activity that functions to diffuse potential conflict (De Waal, 1995). Thus, when the group arrives at a feeding ground, they first enjoy some sexual play and then proceed to eat peacefully. In contrast, when chimps arrive at a feeding ground, they compete aggressively for the food. Also, unlike the chimps, bonobos form female-dominated societies and are known for their sensitivity to others in their group (Parish & de Waal, 2000).

The bonobo way of life is a rare exception in the animal kingdom. The near universality of aggression strongly suggests that aggressiveness has evolved and has been maintained because it has survival value (Lore & Schultz, 1993; Buss, 2004). At the same time, nearly all organisms also seem to have evolved strong inhibitory mechanisms that enable them to suppress aggression when it is in their best interests to do so. Aggression is determined by the animal's previous social experiences as well as by the specific social context in which the animal finds itself.

The Cultural Argument

Most social psychologists, therefore, believe that aggression is an optional strategy: We humans may be born with the *capacity* for aggressive behavior, but how, whether, when, and where we express it is learned and depends on our circumstances and culture. Because of the complexity and importance of our social interactions, for human beings the social situation becomes even more important than hormones or genetic predispositions (Bandura, 1973; Berkowitz, 1993; Lysak, Rule, & Dobbs, 1989). For example, we seem to have an inborn tendency to respond to certain provocative stimuli by striking out against the perpetrator, but whether or not we actually do so depends on a complex interplay between these innate tendencies, a variety of learned inhibitory responses, and the precise nature of the social situation. You may be really, really angry if a police officer stops you for speeding, but it is likely that you will control your temper—and your behavior.

Thus, although it is true that many animals, from insects to apes, will usually attack another animal that invades their territory, we cannot conclude that human beings are likewise programmed to protect their territory and behave aggressively in response to specific stimuli. Three major lines of evidence support this view: studies of cultures across time, studies across cultures, and laboratory experiments.

Changes in Aggression Across Time Within a given culture, changing social conditions frequently lead to striking changes in aggressive behavior. Consider the Iroquois of North America. For hundreds of years, the Iroquois lived peacefully as a hunting nation, without fighting other tribes. But in the seventeenth century, barter with the newly arrived Europeans brought the Iroquois into direct competition with the neighboring Hurons over furs, which dramatically increased in value because they could now be traded for manufactured goods. A series of skirmishes with the Hurons ensued, and within a short time, the Iroquois developed into ferocious warriors. It would be hard to argue that they became ferocious warriors because of some innate aggressive instinct; rather, their aggressiveness almost certainly came about because a social change produced increases in competition (Hunt, 1940).

Differences in Aggression Across Cultures Human cultures vary widely in their degree of aggressiveness. European history, when condensed, consists of one major war after another. In contrast, cultures imbedded with cooperative, collectivist values have had lower levels of aggression than European societies (Bergeron & Schneider, 2005). Certain tribes, such as the Lepchas of Sikkim, the Pygmies of Central Africa, and the Arapesh of New Guinea, live in apparent peace and harmony, with acts of aggression being extremely rare (Baron & Richardson, 1994). In close-knit cultures that depend on cooperation for the group's survival, anger and aggression are considered dangerous and disruptive, and an offender will be ostracized or punished. But don't the men in these tribes have testosterone? Of course they do. But when men live in cultures that lack internal and external threats to their survival—and, admittedly, not many cultures are so blessed—they are not raised to be aggressive, sex differences are minimized, and cooperation is encouraged (Gilmore, 1990).

For example, the forest Teduray, a hunter-gatherer culture in the Philippine rain forest, have established institutions and norms specifically designed to prevent intragroup violence. In their societies, people are expected to pay special attention to the effect of their actions on the feelings of others. When a situation arises, such as adultery, in which there is significant risk that anger will lead to violence, specific members of a Teduray village work to placate the injured individuals. The Teduray believe that human beings are violent by nature but do all they can to reduce aggression within their group. They will, however, behave aggressively to protect themselves from aggression from outside groups (Schlegel, 1998).

Cultures of Honor and Aggression Perhaps the strongest evidence against the notion that "men are naturally aggressive because of their testosterone" comes from experiments showing how cultural norms and expectations literally "get inside" people, causing them to behave differently under similar provocation.

The early economies of the American South and West created a "culture of honor" in which a man was literally quick on the trigger if he thought another man was about to smear his reputation—or steal his cattle.

For example, in the United States there are some striking regional differences in aggressive behavior and in the kinds of events that trigger violence. Homicide rates for white southern males are substantially higher than those for white northern males, especially in rural areas. Richard Nisbett (1993) hypothesized that the higher rates of violence in the South derive from economic causes: The higher rates occur in cultures that were originally based on herding, in contrast to cultures based on agriculture. Why would this be so? People who depend economically on agriculture tend to develop cooperative strategies for survival. But people who depend on their herds are extremely vulnerable; their livelihoods can be lost in an instant by the theft of their animals. To reduce the likelihood of theft, Nisbett theorized, herders learn to be hyperalert to any threatening act (real or perceived) and respond to it immediately with force. This would explain why cattle rustling and horse thievery were capital crimes in the Old West, and why Mediterranean and Middle Eastern herding cultures even today place a high value on male aggressiveness. And indeed, when Nisbett looked at agricultural practices *within* the South, he found that homicide rates were more than twice as high in the hills and dry plains areas (where herding occurs) as in farming regions.

The emphasis on aggressiveness and vigilance in herding communities fosters, in turn, a *culture of honor* in which even small disputes put a man's reputation for toughness on the line, requiring him to respond with violence to restore his status (Cohen, 1998). Although the herding economy has become much less important in the South and West, the legacy of its culture of honor remains. These regions have rates of honor-related homicides (such as murder to avenge a perceived insult to one's family) that are five times higher than in other regions of the country. High school students in culture-of-honor states are far more likely than students from other states to bring a weapon to school and to use that weapon. These states have more than twice as many school shootings per capita than do other states (Brown, Osterman, & Barnes, 2009). Cultures of honor also have higher rates of domestic violence. Both sexes in such cultures believe it is appropriate for a man to physically assault a woman if he believes she is threatening his honor and reputation by being unfaithful or leaving him (Vandello & Cohen, 2008).

In a series of experiments with southern and northern students at the University of Michigan, Nisbett and his colleagues demonstrated how a culture of honor manifests itself in the cognitions, emotions, behaviors, and even physiological reactions of its young men. Each participant was "accidentally" bumped into by the experimenter's confederate, who then insulted him by calling him a denigrating name. Compared with northern white males, who tended to shrug off the insult, southerners were more likely to think their masculine reputation was threatened, became more upset (as shown by a rise in cortisol levels in their bloodstream), were more physiologically primed for aggression (as shown by a rise in testosterone levels in their bloodstream), became more cognitively primed for aggression, and were ultimately more likely to engage in aggressive and dominant behavior following the incident (Cohen et al., 1996).

The research on cultures of honor suggests that male aggression ("don't mess with me") fulfills a powerful part of the male role and identity. When "being a man" is defined by competitiveness and strength, men are constantly trying to "prove" their masculinity and status in displays of aggression (Bosson & Vandello, 2011).

Gender and Aggression

Nevertheless, the fact that men and boys are, on average, more *physically* aggressive does not mean that women are kinder than men or less willing to inflict harm on others. Women and girls tend to commit *relational aggression*, aggression that harms another person through the manipulation of relationships, usually in such covert acts as gossiping, backbiting, and spreading false rumors about the target person or shunning or excluding that person (Archer, 2004; Blakemore, Berenbaum, & Liben, 2009;

Males and females can be equally aggressive, when aggression is defined as intending to harm another person. But whereas men are more physically aggressive, women are more likely to indulge in "relational aggression"—backbiting, shunning, or spreading false rumors about their target.

Coie et al., 1999; Dodge & Schwartz, 1997; McFadyen-Ketchum et al., 1996; Matlin, 2012). In one sad example that went viral, Phoebe Prince, a 15-year-old Irish girl living in Massachusetts, was targeted by a group known as the "Mean Girls" after she had a brief relationship with a popular boy at her school. Seven girls and two boys began a relentless campaign against her of verbal assault (including calling her "Irish slut" and "whore" on Facebook and other social media) and threats of bodily harm. After 4 months of being slandered and harassed, Prince committed suicide.

Gender differences in physical versus relational aggression start early. In one study of 3- to 5-year-old children playing in groups of three, the kids were instructed to use a crayon to color in a picture on a white sheet of paper. Three crayons were provided, but only one was a color (orange), and the other two were white. Naturally, the children all wanted the orange crayon. The boys used physical aggression to get it, hitting or pushing the child who had the orange crayon. The girls used relational aggression, spreading rumors about the child with the orange crayon or ignoring her to make her cry (Ostrov et al., 2004).

Gender differences in physical aggression are most apparent when researchers study spontaneous, unprovoked acts, men being more likely to "pick a fight" (especially with a stranger), join in a flash mob, and commit crimes of violence (murder, aggravated assault, rape). But even in these studies, there is often great overlap between males and females. Indeed, in some studies that compared the sexes in levels of physical aggression, most of the boys and girls were similarly nonaggressive; the sex difference was primarily due to a small number of extremely aggressive boys (Archer, 2004).

Moreover, the sex difference vanishes when both sexes feel provoked (Matlin, 2012). Thus, one meta-analysis of 64 separate experiments found that although men are more aggressive than women under ordinary circumstances, the gender difference becomes much smaller when men and women are insulted and when women are given a chance to retaliate aggressively, especially when others are unaware of their gender (Bettencourt & Miller, 1996). Certainly adult women do not differ from men, on average, in their willingness to yell, be verbally abusive, humiliate or punish their children, and express aggression in similar ways (Archer, 2004).

Watch on **MyPsychLab**

To learn more, watch the MyPsychLab video ***Relational Aggression***.

Keep in mind too that just as male aggression is influenced by culture, so is female aggression. For example, in one international study women from Australia and New Zealand showed greater evidence of aggressiveness than men from Sweden and Korea (Archer & McDaniel, 1995). In a cultural community that admires physical aggression, both sexes may rely on violent tactics: Female teenage members of Mexican American gangs in Los Angeles carry any kind of weapon they can get hold of, from bats to guns, and told a researcher that they had joined not only for social support but for revenge (M. G. Harris, 1994). A study of all known female suicide bombers throughout the world since 1981 (including Afghanistan, Israel, Iraq, India, Lebanon, Pakistan, Russia, Somalia, Sri Lanka, and Turkey) found that "the main motives and circumstances that

TRY IT! Gender and Aggression

Interview several of your male friends and ask them to reflect on their childhood and adolescent experiences with physical fighting or being challenged to fight. Ask them what they think was at stake in the fight. How difficult was it to back down? Ask them to elaborate on their answers.

Now interview several of your female friends. Did any of them ever get into a physical fight with someone of the same or other sex? What experiences have they had with relational aggression, such as being shunned, gossiped about, or excluded? Did they ever treat other girls or women with those forms of aggression? If you have male and female friends of different ethnicities—or from different regions of the United States—you might ask them the same questions.

drive female suicide bombers are quite similar to those that drive men"—loyalty to their country or religion, anger at being occupied by a foreign military, and revenge for loved ones killed by the enemy (O'Rourke, 2008).

What is your own experience with gender and cultural differences in aggression? (See the Try It! on the previous page.)

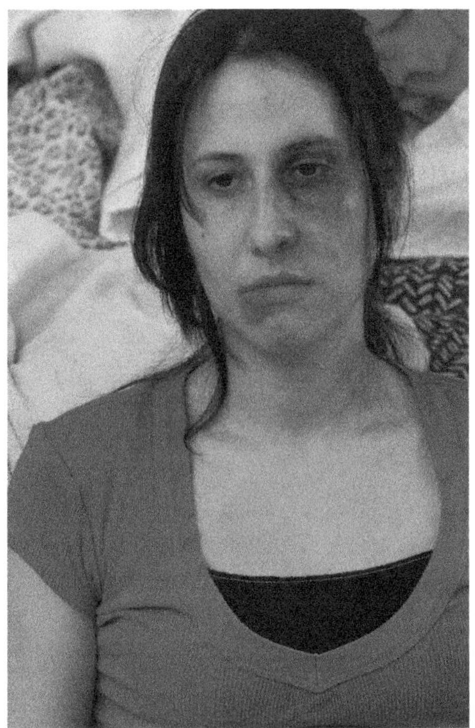

Why do some men physically abuse their partners?

Violence between Intimate Partners Finally, we must address the largest continuing gender difference in violence: that committed against intimate partners. According to the U.S. Department of Justice Statistics in 2011, of the 3.5 million violent crimes—primarily assault—committed against family members in a 5-year-period, 49% were crimes against spouses (the rest were assaults against children, parents, or other family members). Among victims of abuse by a spouse or other intimate partner, fully 84% were women. Eight in ten murderers who killed a family member were male.

Police statistics do not calculate other forms of aggression in intimate relationships. Numerous surveys in the United States and Canada report that some males begin to abuse girls as early as elementary school (with pushing, shoving, or slapping), and in high school this behavior can escalate into emotional abuse, such as publicly humiliating or degrading a girlfriend (Matlin, 2012). The rate of the physical abuse of women—beatings, stabbings, hitting, and rape—is high around the world, and highest in cultures that regard such abuse as a male prerogative (Levy, 2008). In some cultures of honor, men are legally permitted to kill their wives or daughters if they feel the women have "dishonored" them.

This gender difference in rates of domestic violence could be due, at least in part, to male physiology and men's greater average strength. Evolutionary psychologists argue that male jealousy and control of women originated as a way for men to make sure of their paternity and improve the survival chances of their progeny (Buss, 2004); other social scientists suggest that male violence against women is a means of asserting power and control (Eisenstat & Bancroft, 1999). Whatever the complex causes, however, they do not excuse violent behavior, nor do they mean that such behavior cannot be altered by a social intervention, as we shall see.

Some Physiological Influences on Aggression

It is hardly news that when people are drunk, hot, or in considerable pain, they are more likely to lash out at others, getting into fights and quarrels, than if they feel completely fine, sipping lemonade on a cool spring day. But why does the chance of aggression increase under these physical influences? Does it always?

Alcohol and Aggression As most college students know, alcohol is a social lubricant that lowers our inhibitions against acting in ways frowned on by society, including acts of aggression (Desmond, 1987; Taylor & Leonard, 1983). The link between alcohol and aggressive behavior has been well documented, and it appears even among people who have not been provoked and who do not usually behave aggressively when sober (Bailey & Taylor, 1991; Bushman & Cooper, 1990; Graham et al., 2006; Yudko et al., 1997). This might explain why fistfights frequently break out in bars and nightclubs and why family violence is often associated with alcohol abuse.

Why can alcohol increase aggressive behavior? Alcohol often serves as a disinhibitor: It reduces anxiety and lowers social inhibitions, making us less cautious than we usually are (MacDonald, Zanna, & Fong, 1996). But it is more than that. Alcohol also disrupts the way we usually process information, by impairing the part of the brain involved in planning and controlling behavior (Bushman, 1993, 1997; Bushman & Cooper, 1990; Hanson et al., 2011). This is why intoxicated people often respond to the earliest and most obvious aspects of a social situation and tend to miss the subtleties. If you are sober and someone steps on your toe, you would notice that the person didn't do it on purpose. But if you were drunk, you might miss the subtlety of the situation and respond as if that person had purposely stomped on your foot. If you and the

"Oh, that wasn't me talking, it was the alcohol."

Dana Fradon/The New Yorker Collection/ www.cartoonbank.com.

offender are males, you might slug him. This response is typical of the kinds of ambiguous situations that men tend to interpret as provocative, especially under the influence of alcohol. Laboratory experiments demonstrate that when individuals drink enough alcohol to make them legally drunk, they tend to respond more violently to provocations than do people who have ingested little or no alcohol (Bushman, 1993; Lipsey et al., 1997; Taylor & Leonard, 1983).

There is another way in which alcohol facilitates aggression, however, and this is through what has been called the "think-drink" effect: When people *expect* alcohol to have certain effects on them, it often does (Marlatt & Rohsenow, 1980). Indeed, when people expect that alcohol will "release" their aggressive impulses, they often do become more aggressive—even when they are drinking something nonalcoholic. In a study of 116 men ages 18 to 45, experimenters gave one-third of the men a nonalcoholic drink, one-third a drink targeting a modest blood alcohol level, and one-third a stronger drink targeting a high blood alcohol level. Within each of these three groups, the researchers manipulated the drinkers' expectancies of how much alcohol they were getting. They then measured the men's behavior toward a person (a research confederate) who had behaved aggressively toward them. Remarkably, the actual quantity of alcohol that the men drank was less related to their aggressive behavior than their *expectations* were. The more alcohol the men believed they were drinking, the more aggressively they behaved toward the confederate (Bègue et al., 2009). Of course, as we saw, alcohol does have potent physiological effects on cognition and behavior. But those effects interact with what people have learned about alcohol, such as whether it provides an excuse to behave aggressively (or sexually) and how they expect to feel after imbibing.

Pain, Heat, and Aggression If an animal is in pain and cannot flee the scene, it will almost invariably attack; this is true of rats, mice, hamsters, foxes, monkeys, crayfish, snakes, raccoons, alligators, and a host of other creatures (Azrin, 1967; Hutchinson, 1983). In those circumstances, animals will attack members of their own species, members of different species, or anything else in sight, including stuffed dolls and tennis balls. Do you think this is true of human beings as well? A moment's reflection might help you guess that it may very well be. Most of us feel a flash of irritation when we hit our thumb with a hammer and know the feeling of wanting to lash out at the nearest available target. Indeed, in a series of experiments, students who underwent the pain of having their hand immersed in very cold water were far more likely to act aggressively against other students than were those who had not suffered the pain (Berkowitz, 1983).

Other forms of bodily discomfort—such as heat, humidity, air pollution, crowds, and offensive odors—also lower the threshold for aggressive behavior (Stoff & Cairns, 1997). During the late 1960s and early 1970s, when tensions in the United States ran high over the war in Vietnam and the rise of the civil rights movement, national leaders worried about "the long, hot summer." The phrase was a code for the fear that the summer's heat would cause simmering tensions to explode. Their fears were justified. An analysis of disturbances in 79 cities between 1967 and 1971 found that riots were far more likely to occur on hot days than on cold ones (Carlsmith & Anderson, 1979) (see Figure 12.1).

Similarly, in major American cities from Houston, Texas, to Des Moines, Iowa, the hotter it is on a given day or a given average year, the greater the likelihood that violent crimes will occur (Anderson & Anderson, 1984; Anderson, Bushman, & Groom, 1997; Rotton & Cohn, 2004). Smaller "crimes" increase, too: In the desert city of Phoenix, Arizona, drivers in non-air-conditioned cars are more likely to honk their horns in traffic jams than drivers in air-conditioned cars (Kenrick & MacFarlane, 1986). Even on the baseball field, heat and hostility go together. In major league baseball games when the temperature rises above 90 degrees, significantly more batters are hit by pitched balls and pitchers are more likely to intentionally retaliate against a batter when the pitcher's teammates have been hit by the opposing team earlier in the game (Larrick et al., 2011).

As you know by now, one must be cautious about interpreting events that take place in natural settings outside the laboratory. The scientist in you might be tempted to ask whether increases in aggression are due to the temperature itself or merely to the fact that more people are apt to be outside (getting in one another's way) on hot days than on cold or rainy days. So how might we determine that it's the heat causing the aggression

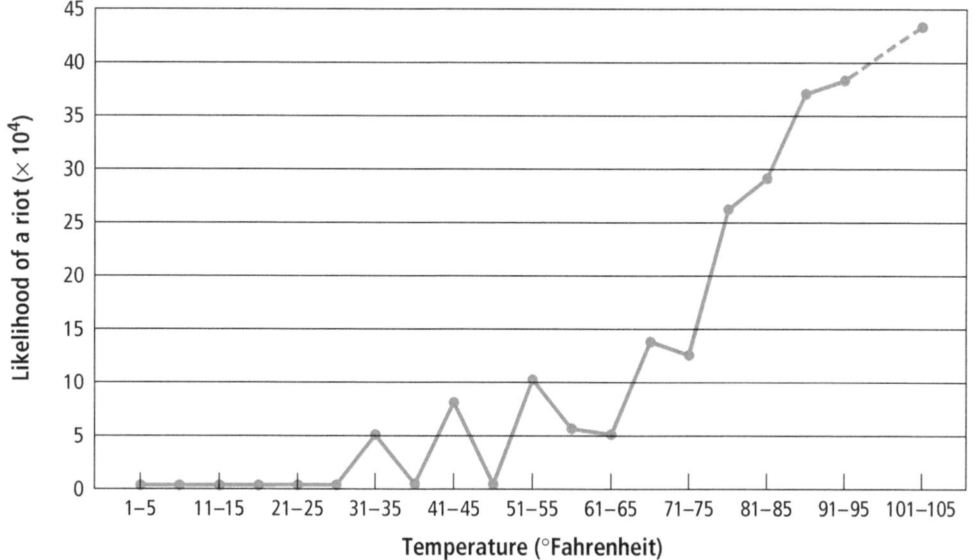

FIGURE 12.1

The Long, Hot Summer

Warm temperatures increase the likelihood that violent riots and other aggressive acts will occur.

(Adapted from Carlsmith & Anderson, 1979)

and not merely the greater opportunity for contact? We can bring the phenomenon into the laboratory; in fact, it is remarkably easy to do so. In one such experiment, students took the same test under different conditions: Some worked in a room at normal room temperature, while others worked in a room where the temperature reached 90 degrees (Griffitt & Veitch, 1971). The students in the hot room not only reported feeling more aggressive, but also expressed more hostility toward a stranger whom they were asked to describe and evaluate. Similar results have been reported by a number of investigators (Anderson, 2012; Anderson et al., 2000; Rule, Taylor, & Dobbs, 1987).

Watch on **MyPsychLab**
To learn more about physiological influences on aggression, watch the MyPsychLab video ***Heat Aggression***.

Most scientists agree that the climate will heat up due to the increase of greenhouse gasses in the atmosphere. Would you predict that global warming might have an effect on aggression as well? The answer appears to be yes. Craig Anderson (2012), the world's leading expert on the effects of climate and aggression, predicts that global warming is almost certain to produce a major increase in the rate of violent crime, for three reasons. One reason involves the effects of uncomfortable heat itself on irritability, aggression, and violence. A second involves the indirect effects global warming has on the economic and social factors known to put children and adolescents at risk for becoming violence-prone: poverty, poor prenatal and childhood nutrition, broken families, low IQ, growing up in violent neighborhoods, poor education, and living in a disorganized and unstable neighborhood. And a third involves the effects of rapid climate change on populations whose livelihoods and survival are at risk as a result of droughts, flooding, famine, and war.

Social Situations and Aggression

Imagine that your friend Sam is driving you to the airport so that you can fly home for the Christmas holidays. Sam has picked you up a bit later than you feel comfortable with; he accuses you of being overly anxious and assures you that he knows the route well and that you will arrive there with plenty of time to spare. Halfway to the airport, you are standing still in bumper-to-bumper traffic. Sam assures you that there is plenty of time, but this time he sounds less confident. After 10 more minutes, your palms are sweating. You open the car door and survey the road ahead: Not a car is moving as far ahead as you can see. You get back in the car, slam the door, and glare at Sam. He smiles lamely and says, "How was I supposed to know there would be so much traffic?" Should he be prepared to duck?

Frustration and Aggression

As this all-too-familiar story suggests, frustration is a major cause of aggression. Frustration occurs when a person is thwarted on the way to an expected goal or gratification. All of us have felt frustrated from time to time—at least three or four times a

Is road rage inevitably caused by frustration with drivers who get in the driver's way? If so, how come not every driver gets as angry as this guy?

week, if not three or four times a day! Research has shown that frustration can increase the probability of an aggressive response. This tendency is referred to as **frustration-aggression theory**, which holds that people's perception that they are being prevented from attaining a goal will increase the probability of an aggressive response (Dollard et al., 1939). This does not mean that frustration always leads to aggression, but it frequently does, especially when the frustration is decidedly unpleasant, unwelcome, and uncontrollable.

In a classic experiment, young children were led to a roomful of attractive toys that were kept out of their reach by a wire screen (Braker, Dembo, & Lewin, 1941). After a long wait, the children were finally allowed to play with the toys. In a control condition, a different group of children were allowed to play with the toys immediately, without first being frustrated. These children played joyfully with the toys, but the frustrated group, when finally given access to the toys, was extremely destructive: Many smashed the toys, threw them against the wall, stepped on them, and so forth.

Several things can increase frustration and, accordingly, will increase the probability that some form of aggression will occur. One such factor involves your closeness to the goal or the object of your desire. The closer the goal, the greater the expectation of pleasure that is thwarted; the greater the expectation, the more likely the aggression. This was demonstrated in a field experiment (Harris, 1974). A confederate cut in line in front of people who were waiting in a variety of places—for movie tickets, outside crowded restaurants, and at the checkout counter of a supermarket. On some occasions, the confederate cut in front of the second person in line; at other times, in front of the twelfth person. The results were clear: The people standing right behind the intruder were much more aggressive when the confederate cut into the second place in line.

Aggression also increases when the frustration is unexpected (Kulik & Brown, 1979). Experimenters hired students to telephone strangers and ask for donations to a charity. The students worked on a commission basis, receiving a small fraction of each dollar pledged. Some of the students were led to expect a high rate of contributions, others to expect far less success. The experiment was rigged so that none of the potential donors agreed to make a contribution. What happened? The callers with high expectations were more verbally aggressive toward the nondonors, speaking more harshly and slamming down the phone with more force, than were the callers with low expectations.

As we've said, frustration does not always produce aggression. Rather, it seems to produce anger or annoyance and a *readiness* to aggress if other things about the situation are conducive to aggressive behavior (Berkowitz, 1989, 1993; Gustafson, 1989). What are those other things? Well, an obvious one would be the size and strength of the person responsible for your frustration, as well as that person's ability to retaliate. It is undoubtedly easier to slam the phone down on a reluctant donor who is miles away and has no idea who you are than to take out your anger against your frustrator if he turned out to be the middle linebacker of the Green Bay Packers and was staring you right in the face. Similarly, if the frustration is understandable, legitimate, and unintentional, the tendency to aggress will be reduced. In one experiment, when a confederate "unwittingly" sabotaged his teammates' effort to solve a problem because his hearing aid had stopped working, the teammates' resulting frustration did not lead to a measurable degree of aggression (Burnstein & Worchel, 1962).

We want to make it clear that frustration is not the same as deprivation: Children who don't have toys do not aggress more than children who do. In the toy experiment, frustration and aggression occurred because the children had every reason to expect to play with the toys, and their reasonable expectation was thwarted; this thwarting was what caused the children to behave destructively.

Frustration-Aggression Theory

The theory that frustration—the perception that you are being prevented from attaining a goal—increases the probability of an aggressive response.

On a national scale also, thwarted expectations combined with frustration can produce riots and revolutions. Social scientists have found that it is often not *absolute* deprivation that creates anger and aggression, but *relative* deprivation, which occurs when people see a discrepancy between what they have and what they expect to have (Moore, 1978). For example, the nationwide race riots of 1967 and 1968 occurred in the middle of rising expectations and increased social spending to fight poverty. The most serious riots in that era occurred not in the geographic areas of greatest poverty, but in Los Angeles and Detroit, where things were not nearly as bad for African Americans as they were in most other large urban centers. But conditions were bad relative to the rioters' perception of how white people were doing and relative to the positive changes many African Americans had a right to expect.

A similar phenomenon occurred in Eastern Europe in 1991, when serious rebellion against the Soviet Union took place only after the government had loosened the chains controlling the population. And research on contemporary suicide bombers in the Middle East, including Mohamed Atta, who led the 9/11 attack on the World Trade Center, shows that they usually have no psychopathology and are often quite educated and affluent (Krueger, 2007; Sageman, 2008; Silke, 2003). But they were motivated by anger over the perceived discrepancy between what they had and what they felt their nation and religion were entitled to. Thus, an important cause of aggression is relative deprivation: the perception that you (or your group) have less than you deserve, less than what you have been led to expect, or less than what people similar to you have.

Evils which are patiently endured when they seem inevitable become intolerable when once the idea of escape from them is suggested.

—Alexis de Tocqueville

Provocation and Reciprocation

Suppose you are working at your part-time job behind the counter, flipping hamburgers in a crowded fast-food restaurant. Today, you are working harder than usual because the other short-order cook went home sick, and the customers are lining up at the counter, clamoring for their burgers. In your eagerness to speed up the process, you spin around too fast and knock over a large jar of pickles that smashes on the floor just as the boss enters the workplace. "Boy, are you clumsy!" he screams. "I'm gonna dock your pay $10 for that one; grab a broom and clean up, you moron! I'll take over here!" You glare at him. You'd love to tell him what he can do with this lousy job.

Nothing is more costly, nothing is more sterile, than revenge.

—Winston Churchill

Aggression frequently stems from the need to reciprocate after being provoked by aggressive behavior from another person. Although the Christian plea to "turn the other cheek" is wonderful advice, most people don't take it, as has been demonstrated in countless experiments in and out of the laboratory. Typical of this line of research is an experiment by Robert Baron (1988) in which participants prepared an advertisement for a new product; their ad was then evaluated and criticized by an accomplice of the experimenter. In one condition, the criticism, though strong, was done in a gentle and considerate manner ("I think there's a lot of room for improvement"); in the other condition, the criticism was given in an insulting manner ("I don't think you could be original if you tried"). When provided with an opportunity to retaliate, those people who were criticized harshly were far more likely to do so than those in the "gentle criticism" condition.

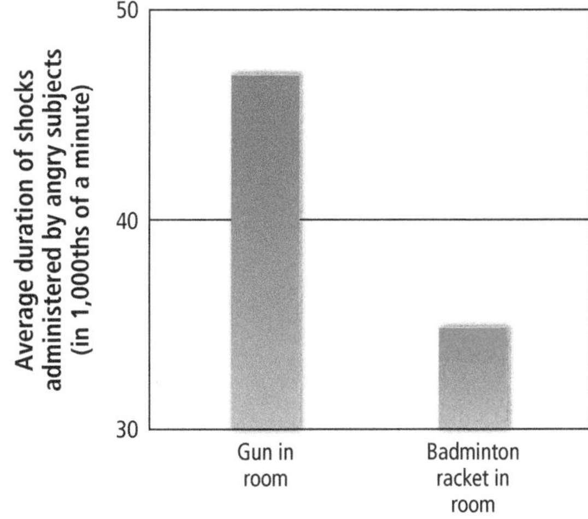

FIGURE 12.2

The Trigger Can Pull the Finger

Aggressive cues, such as weapons, tend to increase levels of aggression.

(Based on data in Berkowitz & Le Page, 1967)

But even when provoked, people do not always reciprocate. We ask ourselves, was the provocation intentional or not? When we are convinced it was unintentional, or if there are mitigating circumstances, most of us will not reciprocate (Kremer & Stephens, 1983). But to curtail an aggressive response, we must be aware of those mitigating circumstances at the time of the provocation (Johnson & Rule, 1986). In one study, students were insulted by the experimenter's assistant. Half of them were first told that the assistant was upset after receiving an unfair low grade on a chemistry exam; the other students received this information only after the insult was delivered. All subjects later had an opportunity to retaliate by choosing the level of unpleasant noise

TRY IT! Insults and Aggression

Think about the last time you felt insulted by another person, and note down your answers to these questions:

- Who insulted you?
- What were the circumstances?
- Did you take it personally or not?
- How did you respond?

Review your answers. How does your behavior relate to the material you have just finished reading?

with which to zap the assistant. Those students who knew about the mitigating circumstances before being insulted delivered weaker bursts of noise. Why the difference? At the time of the insult, the informed students simply did not take it personally and therefore felt no need to retaliate. This interpretation is bolstered by evidence of their physiological arousal: At the time of the insult, the heartbeat of the insulted students did not increase as rapidly if they knew about the assistant's unhappy state of mind beforehand.

Aggressive Objects as Cues

Certain stimuli seem to impel us to action. Is it conceivable that the mere presence of an **aggressive stimulus**—an object that is associated with aggressive responses—might increase the probability of aggression? (See the Try It! on this page.)

In a classic experiment, Leonard Berkowitz and Anthony Le Page (1967) purposely angered college students by insulting them. Some of the students were in a room in which a gun was left lying around (ostensibly from a previous experiment), and others in a room in which a neutral object (a badminton racket) was substituted for the gun. Participants were then given the opportunity to administer what they believed were electric shocks to a fellow college student. Those individuals who had been angered in the presence of the gun administered stronger electric shocks than those angered in the presence of the racket (see Figure 12.2 on the previous page). This provocative finding has been replicated many times in the United States and Europe (Frodi, 1975; Turner & Leyens, 1992; Turner et al., 1977). Male college students asked to interact with a gun for 15 minutes show higher testosterone levels than do students playing a children's game for the same amount of time (Klinesmith et al., 2006). Such findings point to a conclusion opposite to the familiar slogan often used by opponents of gun control, that "guns don't kill; people do." As Leonard Berkowitz (1981) put it, "The finger pulls the trigger, but the trigger may also be pulling the finger."

Violence, especially involving guns, is a major part of American society, so it is no wonder that it plays a major role in the expectations and fantasies of American youngsters. When teenagers from the United States and 10 other countries were asked to read stories involving conflict among people and to predict the outcome of the conflict, American teenagers were more likely than teenagers from other countries to anticipate a violent conclusion (Archer, 1994; Archer & McDaniel, 1995). Moreover, those conclusions were far more likely to be "lethal, gun-laden and merciless" (Archer, 1994, p. 19).

Aggressive Stimulus
An object that is associated with aggressive responses (e.g., a gun) and whose mere presence can increase the probability of aggression.

Social Learning Theory
The theory that people learn social behavior (e.g., aggression) in large part by observing others and imitating them.

Learning to Behave Aggressively

Most American children are immersed in images of violence in TV, movies, video games, pop and rap music, music videos, comics, and everywhere on the Internet. Immersed in it? They are marinated in it! They see an unending parade of murders, rapes, beatings, explosions, and bad guys committing brutal acts as well as good guys doing brutal things to catch them.

Social learning theory holds that we learn social behavior, from aggression to altruism, in large part by observing others and imitating them. Most people take their cues from others. If we want to know whether aggressive behavior is okay, we will look to see what others are doing or what others are saying about it. Thus, if a respected person or institution endorses aggression, it will have an impact on the attitudes and behavior of many people. Brad Bushman and his colleagues (2007) explored the impact of religiously sanctioned stories of violence and aggression. They found that when a violent story was attributed to the Bible and when, in that story, God sanctioned the violence, the reader was more likely to behave aggressively afterward. The effect held for nonreligious as well as religious participants.

When it comes to the imitation of aggression, the influence of others is not confined to prestigious institutions like religion. Almost anyone will do, and children are especially vulnerable to influence. Children frequently learn to solve conflicts aggressively by imitating adults and their peers, especially when they see that the aggression is rewarded. For example, in most sports the more aggressive players usually achieve the greatest fame and the highest salaries, and the more aggressive teams win more games. In sports, it usually doesn't pay to be a gentle soul. Famed baseball manager Leo Durocher once said, "Nice guys finish last," and the data bear him out. In professional hockey, those players most frequently sent to the penalty box for overly aggressive play also scored the most goals and earned the highest salaries (McCarthy & Kelly, 1978). To the extent that athletes serve as role models for children and adolescents, what is being modeled is that fame and fortune go hand in hand with excessive aggressiveness.

Similarly, if children watch their parents or other adults they admire yelling, kicking, and acting in other aggressive ways, that is the behavior they will copy. In a classic series of experiments, Albert Bandura and his associates demonstrated the power of social learning on children's aggressive behavior (Bandura, Ross, & Ross, 1961, 1963). Their basic procedure was to have an adult knock around a plastic, air-filled Bobo doll, the kind that bounces back after it's been knocked down. The adult would smack the doll around with the palm of a hand, strike it with a mallet, kick it, and yell aggressive things at it. The kids were then allowed to play with the doll. In these experiments, the children imitated the aggressive adults and treated the doll in almost exactly the same ways, as you can see in Figure 12.3. Some of them went beyond mere imitation, coming up with inventive new forms of beating up the doll. Children who did not see the aggressive adult in action almost never unleashed any aggression against the hapless doll. This research offers strong support for the social learning of aggressive behavior—the power of watching and imitating the behavior of others.

Children have never been very good at listening to their elders, but they have never failed to imitate them.

—James Baldwin, *Nobody Knows My Name*

Simulate on **MyPsychLab**
To learn more about the Bobo Doll studies, try the MyPsychLab simulation ***Aggression and Prosocial Behavior.***

Violence in the Media

If merely watching adults behave aggressively causes children to mistreat dolls, what does watching violence on television and in the movies do to them, or for that matter to all of us? What about violent video games in which children participate in the virtual destruction of cities and the lopping off of heads and limbs of characters?

For many people, it is as obvious as the Bobo doll study that children imitate the violence they see and are otherwise affected emotionally by all those exploding heads and guts. For just as many others, media violence consists of cartoon-like stories and images that everyone knows are not real. As one columnist wrote, "I grew up playing with toy guns and have never shot anybody (though I know plenty who deserve it)" (Simon, 2011). But if prosocial videos can increase helpful behavior in children who watch them (Gentile et al., 2009; Greitemeyer & Osswald, 2010; see Chapter 11), surely the far more common antisocial, violent videos can increase antisocial, violent behavior, right?

Television has brought murder back into the home—where it belongs.

—Alfred Hitchcock, 1965

In 2011, in a 7-to-2 decision, the Supreme Court overruled a California ban on the sale of violent video games to minors. The Court ruled that videos can be sold to minors no matter how violent the games are, including the popular *Mortal Kombat* and *Grand Theft Auto* series. Anthony Scalia, a conservative justice of the court, reasoned that fairy tales are also plenty violent. "Grimm's Fairy Tales are grim indeed," he wrote.

FIGURE 12.3

The Bobo Doll Experiment

Children learn aggressive behavior through imitation. In this classic study, the experimenter modeled some rather violent treatment of the doll—and the children imitated her perfectly.

"As her just deserts for trying to poison Snow White, the wicked queen is made to dance in red hot slippers until she fell dead on the floor."

Well, maybe Judge Scalia is right. But it seems reasonable to ask whether reading a fairy tale, even a violent one, is equivalent to blowing up the wicked queen yourself and watching her guts explode. How would you investigate this question, or any other effects of media violence? There are countless stories in the news that seem to provide a compelling answer. For example, several years ago, a man drove his truck through the window of a crowded cafeteria in Killeen, Texas, emerged from the cab, and began shooting people at random. He killed 22 people and then turned the gun on himself. In his pocket police found a ticket stub to *The Fisher King*, a film depicting a deranged man firing a shotgun into a crowded bar, killing several people. Dylan Klebold and Eric Harris, the Columbine killers, enjoyed the violent video game *Doom*, and the Columbine murders themselves spurred many acts of violence across the United States (Aronson, 2000). Two teenagers in Tennessee took their guns and went out sniping at passing cars on a freeway, killing one driver, because they wanted to act out their favorite video game, *Grand Theft Auto*. And then there is the case of a man who, having seen a movie showing women dancing on screen, became convinced that all women were immoral and deserved to die. He then committed four brutal rape-murders before he was caught. The film that set him off was *The Ten Commandments*.

Listen on **MyPsychLab**
To learn more, listen to the MyPsychLab audio ***Psychology in the News: Social Psychology—Aggression and Video Games***.

But social scientists know that anecdotes, no matter how interesting they may be, are not sufficient to answer the question of the effects of media violence. It's too easy to cherry-pick your examples to make a case either way; you could select examples of kids who play *Grand Theft Auto* and then go off to do their homework and take piano lessons. The beauty of the laboratory experiment is that it allows us to determine whether aggressive media have any impact at all on the behavior of a random sample of people (see Chapter 2). In such an experiment, the situation is completely controlled; every factor can be held constant except for exposure to violence; and the dependent variable, the participant's behavior, can likewise be carefully measured.

Experimental Studies of Media Violence Most of the experimental evidence demonstrates that watching violence does increase the frequency of aggressive behavior, angry emotions, and hostile thoughts (Anderson et al., 2003; Anderson et al., 2010; Cantor et al., 2001; Greitemeyer & McLatchie, 2011; Huesmann & Miller, 1994; Paik & Comstock,

1994; Wood, Wong, & Chachere, 1991). The research is not consistent, however, and two reviews of the experimental literature found minimal or no effects (Ferguson, 2007a, 2007b; Sherry, 2001). However, actively playing violent video games seems to have a stronger influence: Games that directly reward violence—for example, by awarding points or moving the player to the next level after a "kill"—are especially likely to increase feelings of hostility, aggressive thoughts, and aggressive acts (Carnagey & Anderson, 2005). Exposing children to a graphically violent video game has a direct and immediate impact on their aggressive thoughts and behavior, and this is true not only for American youngsters but also for those in other nations (Anderson et al., 2010).

Does watching violent movies make children numb to what violence really does?

In one early experiment, a group of children watched an extremely violent TV episode of a police drama. In a control condition, a similar group of children watched an exciting but nonviolent TV sporting event for the same length of time. Each child was then allowed to play in another room with a group of other children. Those who had watched the violent police drama later behaved far more aggressively with their playmates than did those who had watched the sporting event—the Bobo doll effect (Liebert & Baron, 1972).

Exposure to media violence has these effects for three reasons: It increases physiological arousal and excitement; it triggers an automatic tendency to imitate the hostile or violent characters; and it *primes* existing aggressive ideas and expectations (Anderson et al., 2003). Just as exposing young adults to rifles and other weapons left lying around the house or the laboratory has a tendency to increase the probability of an aggressive response when they are subsequently frustrated or hurt, exposing children to an endless stream of violence in films and on TV has a tendency to prime an aggressive response. Movies and games also prime our social **scripts**, approved ways of behaving socially that we learn implicitly from the culture. (Of course, scripts can prime thoughts of helping and being kind as well as being selfish and aggressive.)

The Numbing and Dehumanizing Effects of Media Violence Does watching violence have other effects? What is going on in people's heads when they are playing violent games or watching people being blown up, and with what results?

Repeated exposure to difficult or unpleasant events tends to have a numbing effect on our sensitivity to those events. In one experiment, researchers measured the physiological responses of young men while they were watching a rather brutal and bloody boxing match (Cline, Croft, & Courier, 1973). Those who had watched a lot of TV in their daily lives seemed relatively indifferent to the mayhem in the ring; that is, they showed little physiological evidence of excitement, anxiety, or other arousal. They were unmoved by the violence. But those who typically watched relatively little TV showed major physiological arousal; the violence really agitated them.

Viewing television violence can subsequently numb people's reactions when they face real-life aggression (Thomas et al., 1977). The researchers had their subjects watch either a violent police drama or an exciting but nonviolent volleyball game. After a short break, the subjects were allowed to observe a verbally and physically aggressive interaction between two preschoolers. Those who had watched the police show responded less emotionally than those who had watched the volleyball game. Viewing the initial violence seemed to have desensitized them to further acts of violence; they were not upset by an incident that by all rights should have upset them. Although such a reaction may psychologically protect us from feeling upset, it may also have the unintended effect of increasing our indifference to victims of violence and perhaps render us more accepting of violence as an aspect of life in the modern world.

This numbing effect may also make people more oblivious to the needs of others. In one field study, people who had just seen a violent movie took longer to come to the aid of a woman struggling to pick up her crutches than did people who had seen a nonviolent movie or people still waiting to see one of the two movies (Bushman & Anderson, 2009).

When you are playing a violent video game, you are likely to see yourself as the hero who is blasting those evil creatures out of existence. That's fun, as far as it goes, but some

Scripts

Ways of behaving socially that we learn implicitly from our culture.

Simulate on **MyPsychLab**

To learn more about how studies like these are conducted, try the MyPsychLab simulation ***Media Violence and Societal Aggression***.

research suggests it can go further: Once players get in the habit of dehumanizing the "enemy," that habit can be carried over into how players come to regard real people, not just robots and lifelike cartoons. In two experiments in England, researchers found that participants (male and female) who played a violent video game (*Lamers*) were later more likely to dehumanize immigrants to Britain, seeing them as somehow less human and deserving than native Britons, in contrast to the students who played a prosocial version of the game (*Lemmings*) or a neutral game (*Tetris*) (Greitemeyer & McLatchie, 2011).

Longitudinal Effects of Media Violence Taken together, these experiments show that under controlled conditions there is an impact of media violence on children and teenagers. The lab allows us to demonstrate that something of significance is happening, but it has a major limitation: Experiments cannot begin to capture the effects on a person who plays video games 20 or 30 hours a week and lives on a steady diet of action and horror films over weeks, months, and years.

To investigate that effect, we need to use longitudinal studies in which children are followed for a year or longer. The researcher has less control over the factors being studied, but it is a better way of determining the effects of what a child is *really* being exposed to. In addition, unlike most laboratory experiments that must use artificial measures of aggression (such as administering fake electric shocks or loud noises to the victim), longitudinal studies can examine seriously aggressive behavior such as assault. The disadvantage of this method is that people's lives are full of many other factors that can enhance or mitigate the effects of media violence.

Longitudinal research finds that the more violence children watch on TV, the more violence they exhibit later as teenagers and young adults (Anderson et al., 2003; Eron, 1987, 2001). For example, one study followed more than 700 families over a period of 17 years. The amount of time spent watching television during adolescence and early adulthood was strongly related to the likelihood of later committing violent acts against others, including assault. This association was significant regardless of parental education, family income, and extent of neighborhood violence (Johnson, 2002). Another, more recent study followed 430 elementary-age children in the third to fifth grades over the course of a school year. The investigators measured three types of aggression—verbal, relational, and physical—and exposure to violence in television, movies, and video games. They measured both aggressive and prosocial behaviors in the children twice during the year, interviewing the children's peers and teachers as well as observing the children directly. They found that the children's consumption of media violence early in the school year predicted higher rates of all three kinds of aggression (verbal, relational, and physical) and less prosocial behavior later in the year (Gentile, Coyne, & Walsh, 2011).

Longitudinal studies find another, unexpected consequence of watching a heavy dose of media violence: the magnification of danger. If I am watching all this murder and mayhem on the TV screen, wouldn't it be logical for me to conclude that it isn't safe to leave the house, especially after dark? That is precisely what many heavy TV viewers do conclude. Adolescents and adults who watch TV for more than 4 hours per day are more likely than light TV viewers (who watch less than 2 hours per day) to have an exaggerated view of the degree of violence taking place outside their own homes, and they have a much greater fear of being personally assaulted (Gerbner et al., 2002).

The Problem of Cause and Effect The greatest challenge involved in trying to interpret the data in most nonexperimental longitudinal studies and survey research is that of teasing apart cause and effect. The usual assumption has been that watching violence makes people more aggressive, but aggressive people are also drawn to watching violence. Moreover, another entirely independent factor may be causing both. Consider the survey research showing that people who watch a lot of TV also believe that the outside world is a dangerous place and that the crime rate is higher than it actually is. It is possible that watching TV violence made them fearful. But it is just as likely that they spend a lot of time indoors because they think there is danger in the streets; and being at home with nothing to do, they watch a lot of TV. Similarly, some children are born with a mental or emotional predisposition toward violence, or learn it as toddlers from the way they are treated by abusive parents or siblings, or in other ways develop aggressiveness as a personality trait. In turn, this trait or predisposition manifests itself in both their aggressive behavior *and* their liking for watching violence or playing aggressive games (Bushman, 1995).

Indeed, where violence in the media is concerned, causality is a two-way street. In one experiment, youngsters were exposed to either a film depicting a great deal of police violence or an exciting, nonviolent film about bike racing. The youngsters then played a game of floor hockey. Watching the violent film had the effect of increasing the number of aggressive acts committed during the hockey game, but primarily by the youngsters who had previously been rated as highly aggressive by their teachers. These kids hit others with their sticks, threw elbows, and yelled aggressive things at their opponents to a much greater extent than did either the kids rated as nonaggressive who had also watched the violent film or the kids rated as aggressive who had watched the nonviolent film (Josephson, 1987).

Does playing violent games, like paintball, make adults more prone to real violence?

Likewise, a few longitudinal studies have shown that exposure to violence in media or video games has the strongest relationship in children who are already predisposed to violence (Anderson & Dill, 2000). Thus, it may be that watching media violence merely serves to give them permission to express their aggressive inclinations (Ferguson & Kilburn, 2009). The same conclusions apply to the research on violent pornography. Meta-analyses repeatedly conclude that exposure to violent pornography has a strong effect on male viewers, increasing their hostility and aggressiveness toward women (Allen, D'Alessio, & Brezgel, 1995; Paik & Comstock, 1994). But the effects of watching violent pornography are strongest on men who already have high levels of hostility toward women and are predisposed to commit violence against them (see Chapter 2).

Does Violence Sell? Keep in mind that one reason that violence in the media is so prevalent is simply that it sells: People flock to action films with lots of killing and car chases, to horror films with lots of scary exploding body parts, and to video games that total up the kills. So it is understandable that advertisers would want to place their ads on TV shows that provide plenty of mayhem, assuming that viewers would be more inclined to see their ads and buy their products. Yet this logical assumption has an unexpected consequence. What if it turns out that certain kinds of shows produce so much mental turmoil that the sponsor's product is soon forgotten?

In one experiment, people watched TV shows that were either violent, sexually explicit, or neutral (Bushman & Bonacci, 2002). Each of the shows contained the same nine ads. Immediately after seeing the show, the viewers had to recall the brands and to pick them out from photos of supermarket shelves. Twenty-four hours later, the researchers telephoned the viewers and asked them to recall the brands they had seen during the viewing. The people who had seen the ads while watching a neutral (nonviolent, non–sexually explicit) show were able to recall the advertised brands better than did the people who saw the violent show or the sexually explicit show. This was true both immediately after viewing and 24 hours later, and was true for both men and women of all ages. It seems that watching media violence and sex impairs the memory of viewers, at least for ads that get in the way of the story! In terms of maximizing sales, advertisers might be well advised to sponsor nonviolent shows.

Conclusions: Putting Media Violence in Perspective Taking all this research together, we conclude that violent media does have an impact on average children and adolescents, but its impact is greatest on those who are already prone to violent behavior. Clearly, not all people, or even a sizable percentage of people, are motivated to commit violence as a result of watching it. People's interpretation of what they are watching, their personality dispositions, and the social context can all affect how they respond (Feshbach & Tangney, 2008). Children and teens watch many different programs and movies and have many models to observe besides those they see in the media, including parents and peers. But the fact that some people *are* influenced by violent entertainments, with tragic results, cannot be denied. As suggested throughout this discussion, there are at least five distinct reactions that explain why exposure to media violence might increase aggression in vulnerable viewers:

1. *If they can do it, so can I.* When people see characters behaving violently, it may weaken their previously learned inhibitions against violent behavior.
2. *Oh, so that's how you do it!* When people see characters behaving violently, it might trigger imitation, providing them with ideas as to how they might go about it.
3. *Those feelings I am having must be real anger rather than merely my reaction to a stressful day.* Watching violence may put people more in touch with their feelings of anger and make an aggressive response more likely through priming. Having recently viewed violence, someone might interpret his or her own feelings of mild irritation as intense anger and then be more likely to lash out.
4. *Ho-hum, another brutal beating. What's on the other channel?* Watching a lot of mayhem seems to reduce both our sense of horror about violence and our sympathy for the victims, making it easier for us to live with violence and perhaps easier for us to act aggressively.
5. *I had better get him before he gets me!* If watching a lot of TV makes people think the world is a dangerous place, they might be more apt to be hostile to a stranger who approaches them on the street.

Finally, however, let's put all of this research in larger perspective. The impact of the media pales in comparison to the biological, social, economic, and psychological factors that are far more powerful predictors of aggressive behavior: a child's genetic predispositions to violence, low feelings of self-control, being socially rejected by peers (which we will discuss further at the end of this chapter), criminal opportunity, being the victim of childhood physical abuse, and living in a violent community where aggression is a way of life (Crescioni & Baumeister, 2009; Ferguson & Kilburn, 2009).

Sexual Violence Against Women

A particularly troubling aspect of aggression is sexual violence. Why do men rape? Some men commit rape out of a desire to dominate, humiliate, or punish their victim. This motive is apparent among soldiers who rape captive women during war and then often kill them (Olujic, 1998), and among men who rape other men, usually by anal penetration (King & Woollett, 1997). The latter form of rape typically occurs in youth gangs, where the intention is to humiliate rival gang members, and in prison, where the motive, in addition to having a sexual outlet, is to conquer and degrade the victim. Far rarer are the men who commit gruesome serial rape-murders and who are mentally ill.

When most people think of a "rapist," they imagine a predatory stranger or a crazy serial killer. But the fact is that about 85% of all rapes or attempted rapes do not involve assaults by a stranger but are instances of acquaintance rape, in which the victim knows the assailant, or date rape, in which the victim may be having a relationship with the assailant (Koss, 2011). Acquaintance and date rape include direct assault: drugging the victim into a blackout with Rohypnol ("roofies"), sex with a victim who is drunk or otherwise incapacitated, and sex under physical coercion and threat.

Sexually aggressive males who commit these acts are often narcissistic, are unable to empathize with women, may feel hostility and contempt toward women, and feel entitled to have sexual relations with whatever woman they choose. (This may be why sexual violence is often committed by high-status men, including sports heroes, powerful politicians, and celebrities, who could easily find consenting sexual partners.) They misperceive women's behavior in social situations, equate feelings of power with sexuality, and accuse women of provoking them (Bushman et al., 2003; Malamuth et al., 1995; Zurbriggen, 2000). One interesting study compared men who had forcibly raped a woman with men who used manipulative techniques to have sex and with men who had had consensual sex only. The rapists were far more likely to have grown up in violent households, were more accepting of male violence, and were less likely to endorse love as a motive for sex than did the others (Lyden, White, & Kadlec, 2007).

But date rape can, unfortunately, also occur because of misunderstandings caused by the different roles that males and females play, which is why the sexes often disagree on whether or not a "rape" has occurred (Hamby & Koss, 2003). In a nationally representative survey of more than 3 thousand Americans ages 18 to 59, nearly one-fourth of the women said that a man, usually a husband or boyfriend, had forced them to do something sexually that they did not want to do, yet only about 3% of the men said they had ever forced a woman into a sexual act (Laumann et al., 1994). Conversely, however, some women are uncomfortable about or unwilling to admit that they have been raped, especially if they know their assailant (Koss, 2011). About half of all women who report a sexual assault that meets the legal definition of rape—being forced to engage in sexual acts against their will—do not label it as rape (McMullin & White, 2006; Ward & Lundberg-Love, 2006). College women tend to define rape as being forced into intercourse by an acquaintance or stranger, or as having been molested as a child. They are least likely to call their experience rape if they were sexually assaulted by a boyfriend, were drunk or otherwise drugged, or were forced to have oral sex (Kahn, 2004).

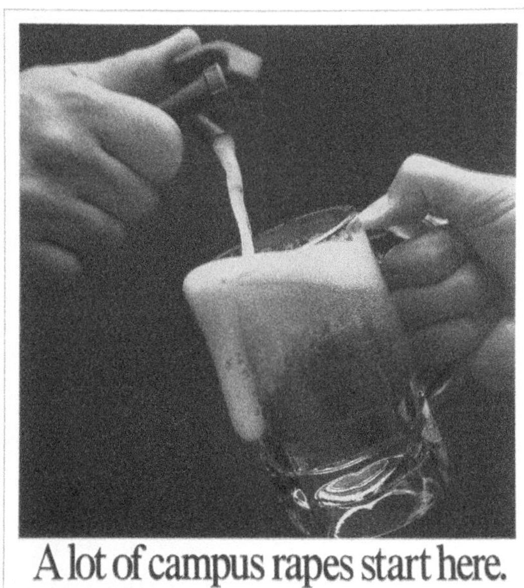

A lot of campus rapes start here.
Whenever there's drinking or drugs, things can get out of hand. So it's no surprise that many campus rapes involve alcohol.
But you should know that under any circumstances, sex without the other person's consent is considered rape. A felony, punishable by prison. And drinking is no excuse.
That's why, when you party, it's good to know what your limits are. You see, a little sobering thought now can save you from a big problem later.

A complicating factor in defining date rape stems from the different *sexual scripts* that adolescents learn as part of their gender roles in society (Gagnon & Simon, 1973; Laumann & Gagnon, 1995). Sexual scripts vary according to one's culture, sexual orientation, ethnicity, and geographic region, and they change over time. Nonetheless, one dominant script in America for young heterosexuals is that the female's role is to resist the male's sexual advances and the male's role is to be persistent. For example, an analysis of 25 primetime television shows that are most popular with teenagers found that male characters frequently act out the traditional male script by actively and aggressively pursuing sex; many female characters still play the part of "sex object" and are judged by their sexual conduct (Kim et al., 2007). (Sexual scripts for gay men and lesbians tend to be more flexible than heterosexual scripts because partners are not following traditional gender roles [Kurdek, 2005]).

The existence of scripts that dictate conventional sexual behavior may explain why there is so much confusion, anger, and joking over the meaning of the word *no*. The slogan of antirape groups—"What part of NO don't you understand?"—seems obvious. Yet, for men who are following traditional sexual scripts, "no" occasionally means "yes" or "in a little while," and many women, following their own scripts, agree with them. In one survey of high school students, although almost 100% of the males and females agreed that the man should stop his sexual advances as soon as the woman says no, nearly half of those same students also believed that when a woman says no she doesn't always mean it (Monson, Langhinrichsen-Rohling, & Binderup, 2002). The resulting confusion may also explain why some college women feel they need to be drunk in order to have sex (Cole, 2006; Howard, Griffin, & Boekeloo, 2008). After all, if they are drunk, they haven't said "yes," and if they haven't explicitly said "yes," no one can accuse them of being a slut (or one of the many other negative words often assigned to women who are sexually active). Such findings suggest that an important step toward reducing sexual aggression is for both sexes to make sure that they are following a script that is in the same play.

How to Reduce Aggression

"Stop hitting your brother!" "Turn off the TV and go to your room RIGHT NOW!" Most parents, trying to curb the aggressive behavior of their children, use some form of punishment. Some deny privileges; others shout, threaten, or use force, believing in the old saying, "Spare the rod and spoil the child." How well does punishment work? On the

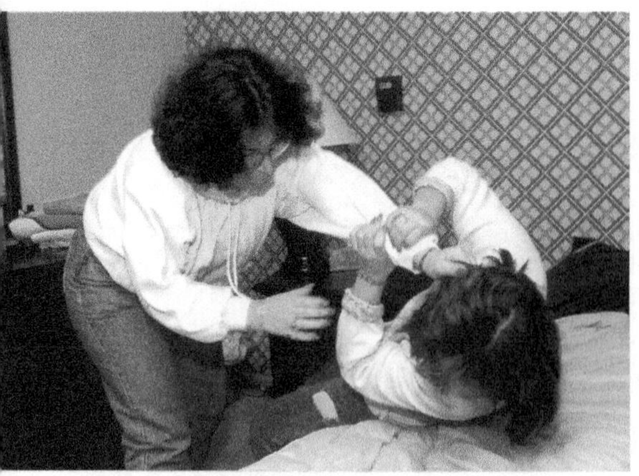

Many tired, exasperated parents punish their children's misbehavior by shouting at them or hitting or grabbing them. But this kind of punishment usually backfires, making the child angry and resentful without stopping the misbehavior. On the contrary, it teaches children what to do when they are tired and exasperated—hit someone.

one hand, you might think that punishing any behavior would reduce its frequency. On the other hand, if the punishment takes the form of an aggressive act, parents who are administering the penalty are actually modeling aggressive behavior—thereby inducing their child to imitate their action.

Does Punishing Aggression Reduce Aggression?

Let's consider the complexities of punishment. As we discussed in Chapter 6, several experiments with preschoolers demonstrated that the threat of relatively severe punishment for committing a transgression does not make the transgression less appealing to the child. But the threat of *mild* punishment, of a degree just powerful enough to get the child to stop the undesired activity temporarily, leads the child to try to justify his or her restraint and, as a result, can make the behavior less appealing (Aronson & Carlsmith, 1963; Freedman, 1965).

However, the use of *harsh* punishments to reduce aggression in children or adults usually backfires for several reasons. People may shout things they don't mean or, out of frustration, use severe methods to try to control the behavior of their children. The target of all this noise and abuse is then likely to respond with anxiety or anger, rather than with a reaction of "Thanks, I'd better correct that aggressive habit you don't like." In some cases, angry attention may be just what the offender is hoping to get. If a mother yells at her daughter who is throwing a tantrum, the very act of yelling may give her what she wants: namely, a reaction from her. Most seriously, extreme punishment—physical abuse—is a risk factor in children for the development of depression, low self-esteem, violent behavior, and many other problems (Gershoff, 2002; Widom, DuMont, & Czaja, 2007). And, finally, punishment often fails because it tells the target what not to do, but it does not communicate what the person should do. Spanking a little boy for hitting his sister will not teach him to play cooperatively with her.

Because of these drawbacks, most psychologists believe that harsh punishment is a poor way to eliminate aggressive or other unwanted behavior. In certain cases, for example when a bully is hitting a classmate, temporary physical restraint is usually called for. But is that the best strategy to keep a bully from behaving aggressively when the adult leaves the room?

All punishment is mischief; all punishment itself is evil.

—Jeremy Bentham, *Principles of Morals and Legislation*, 1789

And what if the problem is a virtual bully? Bullying, in which a stronger person intentionally humiliates or physically abuses a weaker one, has long been a fact of school life, and cyberbullying simply translates that impulse into a newer technology (Rivers, Chesney, & Coyne, 2011; Wade & Beran, 2011). Cyberbullying ranges from the less severe (prank calls and mild insults on instant messaging) to extremely severe acts (posting unpleasant or sexual photos on Web sites; sending a target photos or videos of threatening, violent scenes; and widely distributing insults, nasty text messages, rumors, and ugly accusations). It may be a one-time impulsive act or a planned campaign of harassment. According to a review prepared for the government on "Child Safety and Online Technologies," the greatest source of danger that teenagers face on the Internet does not come from pornography (which many teens themselves, usually older boys, seek out) or even from predatory adults, let alone from sexting. "Bullying and harassment, most often by peers, are the most frequent threats that minors face, both online and offline," the report found (Berkman Center for Internet & Society, 2008).

CONNECTIONS

Curbing Bullying: A Case Study in Reducing Aggression at School

Some years ago, the Norwegian government became concerned over the suicides of three young victims of bullying and the attempted suicide of several others. One sixth grader, after having been insulted, mocked, and harassed on a daily basis, was taken to the bathroom by his tormentors, who made him lie face down in the urinal. He went home and tried to kill himself. His parents found him unconscious.

Alarmed, the Norwegian government commissioned psychologist Dan Olweus (1991, 1997) to assess the problem of bullying across the entire nation and develop an intervention that might help reduce it. After surveying all of Norway's 90,000 schoolchildren, Olweus concluded that bullying was serious and widespread, that teachers and parents were only dimly aware of bullying incidents, and that even when adults were aware of these incidents, they rarely intervened. (This is also true in the United States.) The government sponsored a three-pronged campaign in every school to change the social dynamic that breeds bullies and victims.

First, community-wide meetings were held to explain the problem. Parents were given brochures detailing symptoms of victimization. Teachers received training on handling bullying. Students watched videotapes to evoke sympathy for victims of bullying. Second, students themselves, in their classes, discussed ways to prevent bullying and befriend lonely children. Teachers organized cooperative learning groups and moved quickly to stop name-calling and other aggression that escalates into bullying. Principals ensured that lunchrooms, bathrooms, and playgrounds were adequately supervised. Third, if bullying occurred despite these preventive steps, trained counselors intervened, using a combination of mild punishment and intensive therapy with the bully and counseling with the bully's parents.

Twenty months after the campaign began, acts of bullying had decreased by half, with improvements at every grade level. Olweus concluded, "It is no longer possible to avoid taking action about bullying problems at school using lack of awareness as an excuse—it all boils down to a matter of will and involvement on the part of adults" (1991, p. 415). Can you think of ways of using Olweus's techniques to reduce cyberbullying?

Using Punishment on Violent Adults The criminal justice system of most cultures administers harsh punishments both as retribution and as a means of deterring violent crimes like murder, manslaughter, and rape. Does the threat of harsh punishments make such crimes less likely? Do people who are about to commit violent crimes say to themselves, "I'd better not do this, because if I get caught I'm going to jail for a long time; I might even be executed"?

Laboratory experiments indicate that punishment can indeed act as a deterrent, but only if two conditions are met. Punishment must be both prompt and certain (Bower & Hilgard, 1981). It must follow quickly after the violence occurred, and it must be unavoidable. In the real world, these ideal conditions are almost never met, especially in a complex society with a high crime rate and a slow criminal justice system like our own. In most American cities, the probability that a person who commits a violent crime will be apprehended, charged, tried, and convicted is not high. Moreover, given the volume of cases in our courts, punishment is delayed by months or even years. Consequently, in the complex world of criminal justice, severe punishment is unlikely to have the kind of deterrent effect that it does in the controlled conditions of the laboratory.

Given these realities, severe punishment is not likely to deter violent crime. Countries that invoke the death penalty for murder do not have fewer murders per capita than those without it. American states that have abolished the death penalty have not had an increase in capital crimes, as some experts predicted (Archer & Gartner, 1984; Nathanson, 1987). A natural experiment occurred in the United States during a period that began with a national hiatus on the death penalty, resulting from a Supreme Court ruling that it constituted cruel and unusual punishment, and ended with the Court's reversal of that ruling in 1976. There was no indication that the return to capital punishment produced a decrease in homicides (Peterson & Bailey, 1988). Indeed, a study by the National Academy of Sciences demonstrated once again that consistency and certainty of punishment were far more effective deterrents of violent behavior than was severe punishment, including the death penalty (Berkowitz, 1993).

Catharsis
The notion that "blowing off steam"—by performing a verbally or physically aggressive act, watching others engage in aggressive behaviors, or engaging in a fantasy of aggression—relieves built-up aggressive energies and hence reduces the likelihood of further aggressive behavior.

Catharsis and Aggression

Conventional wisdom suggests that one way to reduce feelings of aggression is to do something aggressive. "Get it out of your system" has been common advice for decades: If you are feeling angry, yell, scream, curse, throw a dish at the wall; express the anger, and it won't build up into something uncontrollable. This belief stems from Sigmund Freud's psychoanalytic notion of **catharsis** (Dollard et al., 1939; Freud, 1933). Freud held a "hydraulic" idea of aggressive impulses: Unless people were allowed to express ("sublimate") their aggression in harmless or constructive ways, he believed, their aggressive energy would be dammed up, pressure would build, and the energy would seek an outlet, either exploding into acts of extreme violence or manifesting itself as symptoms of mental illness.

Unfortunately, Freud's theory of catharsis has been greatly oversimplified into the notion that people should vent their anger or they will suffer physically and emotionally; moreover, by venting that anger, they will become less likely to commit aggressive acts in the future. When we are feeling frustrated or angry, many of us do temporarily feel less tense after blowing off steam by yelling, cursing, or perhaps kicking the sofa. But do any of those actions reduce the chance that we will commit further aggression? Does the notion of catharsis square with the data?

The Effects of Aggressive Acts on Subsequent Aggression Following Freud, many psychoanalysts believed that playing competitive games served as a harmless outlet for aggressive energies (Menninger, 1948). But they were wrong. In fact, the reverse is true: Competitive games often make participants and observers more aggressive.

In one demonstration of this fact, the hostility levels of high school football players were measured one week before the football season began and one week after it ended. If the intense competitiveness and aggressive behavior that are part of playing football serve to reduce the tension caused by pent-up aggression, the players would be expected to show a decline in hostility over the course of the season. Instead, the results showed that feelings of hostility *increased* significantly (Patterson, 1974).

What about watching aggressive games? Will that reduce aggressive behavior? A Canadian sports psychologist tested this proposition by measuring the hostility of spectators at an especially violent hockey game (Russell, 1983). As the game progressed, the spectators became increasingly belligerent; toward the end of the final period, their level of hostility was extremely high and did not return to the pregame level until several hours after the game was over. Similar results have been found among spectators at football games and wrestling matches (Arms, Russell, & Sandilands, 1979; Branscombe & Wann, 1992; Goldstein & Arms, 1971). As with participating in an aggressive sport, watching one also increases aggressive behavior.

Fans watching aggressive sports do not become less aggressive; in fact, they may become more aggressive than if they hadn't watched at all.

Finally, does direct aggression against the source of your anger reduce further aggression? Again, the answer is no (Geen, 1998; Geen & Quanty, 1977). When people commit acts of aggression, such acts increase the tendency toward future aggression. In an early experiment, college students were paired with another student who was actually a confederate of the experimenters (Geen, Stonner, & Shope, 1975). First, the student was angered by the confederate; during this phase, which involved the exchanging of opinions on various issues, the student was instructed to give an electric shock to the confederate each time the confederate disagreed. (The shocks, of course, were phony.) Next, during a bogus study of "the effects of punishment on learning," the student acted as a teacher while the confederate served as learner. On the first learning task, some of the students were required to deliver electric shocks to the confederate each time he made a mistake; others merely recorded his errors. On the next task, all the students were given the opportunity to deliver shocks. If a cathartic effect were operating, we would expect the students who had previously given shocks to the confederate to administer fewer and weaker shocks the second time. This didn't happen; in fact, those students who had previously delivered shocks to the confederate expressed even greater aggression when given the subsequent opportunity to attack him.

Outside the lab, in the real world, we see the same phenomenon: Verbal acts of aggression are followed by more of the same. Many people feel worse, both physically and mentally, after an angry confrontation. When people brood and ruminate about their anger, talk to others incessantly about how angry they are, or ventilate their feelings in hostile acts, their blood pressure shoots up, they often feel angrier, and they behave even *more* aggressively later than if they had just let their feelings of anger subside (Bushman et al., 2005). Conversely, when people learn to control their tempers and express anger constructively, they usually feel better, not worse; they feel calmer, not angrier. All in all, the weight of the evidence does not support the catharsis hypothesis (Tavris, 1989).

Blaming the Victim of Our Aggression Imagine yourself in the experiments just described. After you've administered what you think are shocks to another person or have expressed hostility against someone you dislike, it becomes easier to do so a second time. Aggressing the first time can reduce your inhibitions against committing other such actions; in a sense, the aggression is legitimized, making it easier to carry out such assaults. Further, and more important, the main thrust of the research on this issue indicates that committing an overt act of aggression against a person *changes your feelings* about that person, increasing your negative feelings and making future aggression against that person more likely.

Does this material sound familiar? It should. As we saw in Chapter 6, harming someone sets in motion cognitive processes that are aimed at justifying the act of cruelty. When you hurt another person, you experience cognitive dissonance: The cognition "I hurt Charlie" is dissonant with the cognition "I am a decent, kind person." A good way for you to reduce dissonance is to convince yourself that hurting Charlie was not a bad thing to do. You can accomplish this by ignoring Charlie's virtues and emphasizing his faults, convincing yourself that Charlie is a bad person who deserved to be hurt. And you would be especially likely to reduce dissonance this way if Charlie was an innocent victim of your aggression. In the experiments described in Chapter 6, participants inflicted either psychological or physical harm on an innocent person who had not hurt them (Davis & Jones, 1960; Glass, 1964). Participants then persuaded themselves that their victims were not nice people and therefore deserved what they got. This certainly reduces dissonance, but it also sets the stage for further aggression, because once a person has succeeded in finding reasons to dislike someone, it is easier to harm that victim again.

What happens, though, if the victim isn't totally innocent? What if the victim has done something that did hurt or disturb you and therefore, in your opinion, deserves your retaliation? Here the situation becomes more complex and more interesting. Consider the results of one of the first experiments designed to test the catharsis hypothesis (Kahn, 1966). A young man, posing as a medical technician, took physiological measurements from college students. As he did, he made derogatory remarks about the students, which naturally annoyed them. In one experimental condition, the participants were allowed to vent their hostility by expressing their feelings about the technician to his employer—an action that looked as though it would get the technician into serious trouble, perhaps even cost him his job. In another condition, participants did not have the opportunity to express any aggression against the person who had aroused their anger. Those who were allowed to express their aggression subsequently felt greater dislike and hostility for the technician than did those who were blocked from expressing their aggression. In other words, expressing aggression did not "get it out of their systems"; rather, it tended to *increase* aggressive hostility—even when the target was not simply an innocent victim.

These results suggest that when people are angered they frequently respond with overkill. In this case, costing the technician his job was much more devastating than the minor offense the man committed with his insult. The overreaction, in turn, produces dissonance in much the same way that hurting an innocent person does: If there is a major discrepancy between what the person did to you and the force of your retaliation, you must justify that discrepancy by deciding that the object of your wrath really did something awful to warrant it.

"It's truly remarkable, Louis, thirty-seven years next Tuesday and never a cross word between us."

Charles Barsotti/The New Yorker Collection/ www.cartoonbank.com

What Are We Supposed to Do with Our Anger?

If violence leads to self-justification, which in turn breeds more violence, what are we to do with our angry feelings toward someone? Stifling anger, sulking around the house, and hoping the other person will read our mind doesn't seem to be a good solution, and neither are brooding and ruminating by ourselves, which just prolong and intensify the anger (Bushman et al., 2005; Rusting & Nolen-Hoeksema, 1998). But if keeping our feelings bottled up and expressing them are both harmful, what are we supposed to do?

First, it is possible to control anger by actively enabling it to dissipate. *Actively enabling* means using such simple devices as counting to 10 (or 100!) before shooting your mouth off. Taking deep breaths or getting involved in a pleasant, distracting activity (working a crossword puzzle, listening to soothing music, taking a bike ride, or even doing a good deed) are active ways of enabling the anger to fade away. If this advice sounds suspiciously like something your grandmother could have told you, well, that's because it is! Your grandmother often knows what she is talking about. But there is more to anger than merely controlling it, as you will see.

Venting Versus Self-Awareness Dissipating anger is not always best for you or for a relationship. If your close friend or partner does something that makes you angry, you may want to express that anger in a way that helps you gain insight into yourself and the dynamics of the relationship. You may also wish to express yourself in a way that solves the problem without escalating it by arousing anger in the other person. But for that to happen, you must express your feelings in a way that is neither hostile nor demeaning.

You can do this (after counting to 10) by making a clear, calm statement indicating that you are feeling angry and describing, nonjudgmentally, what you believe the other person did to bring about those feelings. Such a statement in itself will probably make you feel better to have "cleared the air," and because you haven't harmed the target of your anger with verbal or physical abuse, your response will not set in motion the cognitive processes that would lead you to justify your behavior by ridiculing your friend or escalating the argument. It is important that you speak in a way that does not cause your listener to become defensive or counterattack ("You're mad at me? Well, let me tell you where you're wrong, buster!"), but rather that invites problem solving ("Look, we seem to have different notions about housework standards. Can we figure out how to resolve this so that I don't get angry about your 'compulsive neatness' and you don't get angry with my being a 'slob'?"). Moreover, when such feelings are expressed between friends in a clear, open, nonpunitive manner, greater mutual understanding and a strengthening of the friendship can result.

> *I was angry with my friend; I told my wrath, my wrath did end.*
>
> —William Blake

Although it is probably best to reveal your anger to the friend who provoked it—at least if you are hoping to resolve the problem between you—sometimes the target of your anger is unavailable. Perhaps the person did something to you many years ago, or he or she has died or moved away. Then, research finds, it can be helpful to write down your feelings in a journal. In experiments with people undergoing a wide range of traumatic events, those who were instructed simply to write their "deepest thoughts and feelings" about the event felt healthier and even had fewer physical illnesses 6 months to a year later than did people who suffered in silence, who wrote about trivial topics, or who wrote about the details of the traumatic events without revealing their own underlying feelings. The benefits of "opening up" are due not to the venting of feeling, but primarily to the insights and self-awareness that usually accompany such self-disclosure (Pennebaker, 1990). For example, one young woman realized that she had been carrying a lot of anger since her childhood, over something another child had done to her. When she saw what she had written about the incident, she realized, "My god, we were both just kids." (See the Try It! on the next page.)

TRY IT!

Are you feeling angry about a personal matter in your life? Try to write your "deepest thoughts and feelings" about the event that has distressed you. Don't censor your feelings or thoughts. Do this for 20 minutes a day for a few days, and then reread what you have written. Can you see the situation differently? Do solutions offer themselves that you hadn't thought of?

Defusing Anger through Apology What if you are not the person who is feeling angry, but the one who caused it in someone else? Suppose you are taking a friend to a concert that starts at 8:00 P.M. She's been looking forward to it, and you've arranged to be at her house at 7:30. You leave your house with barely enough time to get there and discover that you have a flat tire. By the time you change the tire and get to her house, you are already 20 minutes late for the concert. Imagine her response if you (a) casually walk in, smile, and say, "Hey, it probably wouldn't have been such a good concert anyway. Lighten up; it's not a big deal!" or (b) run in clearly upset, show her your dirty hands, explain what happened, tell her you left your house in time to make it but got a flat, apologize sincerely, and vow to make it up to her. We predict that your friend would be prone toward aggression in the first case but not in the second, and many experiments support our prediction (Baron, 1988, 1990; Ohbuchi & Sato, 1994; Weiner et al., 1987). Typically, any apology sincerely given and in which the perpetrator took full responsibility was effective at reducing aggression.

Folklore has it that women apologize more than men do. Some observers believe the reason is that many men have trouble admitting they are wrong because of their "delicate egos" (Engel, 2001); others believe the reason is that women are more concerned than men with being courteous and maintaining smooth relations (Tannen, 2001); still others speculate that many men think it is not "manly" to apologize, a view reflected in Jim Belushi's book title *Real Men Don't Apologize* (cited in Schumann & Ross, 2010).

These explanations could conceivably play a role in the likelihood of a person apologizing, but the first question is whether the person believes an apology is even necessary. And here we see a clear gender difference. In a study in which young women and men kept daily diaries noting whether they committed an offense or experienced one, the researchers found that men simply have a higher threshold for what constitutes an offensive action warranting an apology. Moreover, when everyone was asked to evaluate actual offenses they had experienced in the past or come up with imaginary ones, again the men rated them all as being less severe than women did. You can imagine the unfortunate consequences of this discrepancy for romantic couples: A woman might feel angry or slighted that her partner doesn't even notice an offense that she thinks is serious enough to warrant an apology, and the man might feel angry that she is being oversensitive and thin-skinned (Schumann & Ross, 2010).

Given the importance of apologies in defusing anger, imagine the advantages that might be gained by equipping automobiles with apology signals! Suppose that every car came with not only a horn (an instrument of aggression worldwide), but also an apology signal; perhaps at the push of a button a little flag could pop up, saying, "Oops! Sorry!" One of our Eastern European readers wrote to tell us that in Poland and Hungary people apologize for their driving mistakes by using their emergency flashing lights; in the United States some motorists tap their chest as if to say "my fault" or make the V-sign meaning "peace." If these techniques were to become widely used, incidents of road rage might plummet.

Modeling Nonaggressive Behavior We've seen that children will be more aggressive (toward dolls as well as other children) if they have seen people behaving aggressively in similar situations. What if we reverse things and expose children to nonaggressive models—to people who, when provoked, express themselves in a restrained, rational, pleasant manner? This question has been tested in several experiments (Baron, 1972; Donnerstein & Donnerstein, 1976; Vidyasagar & Mishra, 1993). Children first watched youngsters behaving peacefully even when provoked. Later, when the children were put in a situation in which they themselves were provoked, they were much less likely to respond aggressively than were children who had not seen the nonaggressive models.

Warren Miller/The New Yorker Collection/
www.cartoonbank.com

Training in Communication and Problem-Solving Skills It is impossible to go through life without occasionally feeling frustrated, annoyed, angry, or conflicted. Feeling angry is part of being human. The problem is not anger itself, but the expression of anger in violent or cruel ways. Yet we are not born knowing how to express anger or annoyance constructively and nonviolently; we have to learn the right skills. In most societies, it is precisely the people who lack those social skills who are most prone to violent solutions to problems in relationships (Toch, 1980). One way to reduce violence, then, is to teach people such techniques as how to communicate anger or criticism in constructive ways, how to negotiate and compromise when conflicts arise, and how to be more sensitive to the needs and desires of others.

There is evidence that such formal training can be an effective means of reducing aggression (Studer, 1996). In a classic experiment, children were allowed to play in groups of four (Davitz, 1952). Some of these groups were taught constructive ways to relate to one another and were rewarded for such behavior; others were rewarded for aggressive or competitive behavior. Next, the children were deliberately frustrated: They were told that they would see some entertaining movies and would be allowed to have fun. The experimenter began to show a movie and hand out candy bars, but then he abruptly stopped the movie at the point of highest interest and took the candy bars away. Now the children were allowed to play freely as the researchers watched. The results? Children who had been taught constructive ways of behaving when they were frustrated or angry were far less aggressive than children in the other group. Many elementary and secondary schools now train students to use nonaggressive strategies for resolving conflict (Eargle, Guerra, & Tolan, 1994; Educators for Social Responsibility, 2001). Some schools have successfully reduced violence by teaching children problem-solving skills, emotional control, and conflict resolution (Reading, 2008; Wilson & Lipsey, 2007).

> *Man must evolve for all human conflict a method which rejects revenge, aggression, and retaliation.*
>
> —Martin Luther King, Jr., Nobel Prize acceptance speech, 1964

Countering Dehumanization by Building Empathy Picture the following scene: A long line of cars is stopped at a traffic light at a busy intersection; the light turns green and the lead car hesitates for 10 seconds. What happens? Almost inevitably, there will be an eruption of horn honking. In one experiment, when the lead car failed to move after the light turned green, almost 90% of the drivers of the second car honked their horns angrily (Baron, 1976). But if, while the light was still red, a pedestrian was hobbling across the street on crutches, only 57% of the drivers honked their horns. Seeing a person on crutches evoked feelings of empathy, which infused the consciousness of the potential horn honkers and decreased their urge to be aggressive.

Children who are taught to put themselves in others' shoes often have higher self-esteem, are more generous, and are less aggressive than children who lack skills of empathy.

As we saw, most people find it difficult to inflict pain on a stranger unless they can find a way to justify it, and the most common way of justifying it is to dehumanize the victim (Caselman, 2007; S. Feshbach, 1971). Understanding the process of dehumanization is the first step toward reversing it. By building empathy among people, aggressive acts should be more difficult to commit. The research data lend strong support to this contention. In one study, students who had been trained to empathize—that is, to take the perspective of the other person—behaved far less aggressively toward that person than did students who had not received the training (Richardson et al., 1994). In a similar study, Japanese students were told to shock another student as part of an alleged learning experiment (Ohbuchi, Ohno, & Mukai, 1993). In one condition, the "victims" first revealed something personal about themselves; in the other condition, they were not given this opportunity. Participants gave weaker shocks to the victim who had revealed personal information. It's harder to harm a stranger if you have made a personal connection with that person, and this is true whether the stranger is your neighbor, a homeless person, a sales clerk, or a civilian enemy.

CONNECTIONS

Teaching Empathy in School

"What would the world look like to you if you were as small as a cat?" "What birthday present would make each member of your family happiest?" These questions formed the basis of some of the exercises for elementary school children in Los Angeles who participated in a 30-hour program designed by Norma Feshbach (1989, 1997), who has pioneered the teaching of empathy in elementary schools. Thinking hard about the answers to such questions expands children's ability to put themselves in another's situation. The children also listened to stories and then retold them from the point of view of each of the different characters in each story. The children played the role of each of the characters and their performances were videotaped. The children then viewed the tapes and talked about how people look and sound when they express different feelings.

At the end of the program, the children not only had learned to be more empathic, but also had higher self-esteem, were more generous, and were less aggressive than were students who had not participated in the program.

At first glance, such a program may seem unrelated to academics. Yet role-playing and close analysis of stories is just what students do when putting on a play or analyzing a piece of literature. In reminiscing about his childhood, the Nobel Prize–winning physicist Richard Feynman reported that his father challenged his intellect by asking him to pretend he was a tiny creature living in their living room carpet. To do that, Feynman needed to crawl into the skin of that tiny creature and get a feel for what his life would be like in those circumstances. Such questions also encourage the kind of cognitive flexibility taught in corporate creativity programs. Accordingly, it should not surprise us to learn that students who develop greater empathic ability also tend to have higher academic achievement (Feshbach & Feshbach, 2009).

Could the Columbine Massacre Have Been Prevented?

At the beginning of this chapter we described the massacre at Columbine High School and discussed some of the speculations about what might have caused that horrifying event and the many other school shootings like it. Could these tragedies have been prevented?

One possibility is that the shooters were mentally ill. Seung-Hui Cho, the young man who murdered 32 of his fellow students at Virginia Tech in 2007, had had a lifelong history of mental problems and aberrant behavior, which had been worsening in the previous year. But it would be a mistake to dismiss the Columbine massacre and most other school shootings as being a result of individual pathology, like Cho's, and let it go at that. Such an explanation leads nowhere, because Harris and Klebold had been functioning effectively. They were getting good grades, attended class regularly, and did not present serious behavior problems to their parents or to the school authorities. True, they were loners, but so were many other students at Columbine High School; true, they dressed in Goth style, but so did other students. Their murderous spree was not readily predictable from their day-to-day interactions with parents, teachers, or friends. It was not even detected by Eric Harris's psychiatrist, who was treating the young man for depression. The adults were not negligent; Harris and Klebold's observable behavior was not far from the norm.

But more important, to dismiss this horrifying deed as "merely" the result of mental illness would lead us to miss something of vital importance, something that might help us prevent similar tragedies: the power of the social situation. Elliot Aronson (2000) argued that the school shootings were the tip of a large iceberg. Harris and Klebold were reacting in an extreme manner to a school atmosphere that creates an environment of exclusion, mockery, and taunting, making life difficult for a sizable number of students. Most high schools are cliquish places where students are shunned if they belong to the "wrong" ethnic group, come from the poor side of the tracks, wear the "wrong" clothes, or are too short, too fat, too tall, or too thin. After the shootings, Columbine students recalled that Harris and Klebold suffered greatly by being taunted and bullied by the in-group. Indeed, one in-group member justified this behavior by saying, "Most kids didn't want them there. They were into witchcraft. They were into voodoo. Sure we teased them. But what do you expect with kids who come to school with weird hairdos and horns on their hats? If you want to get rid of someone, usually you tease 'em. So the whole school would call them homos ..." (Gibbs & Roche, 1999, p. 154).

How do you suppose Harris and Klebold reacted to this relentless treatment? In the video they left behind, they spoke angrily about the insults and bullying they endured at Columbine. According to psychiatrist James Gilligan (1996), the motivation behind the vast majority of rampage killings is an attempt to transform feelings of shame and humiliation into feelings of pride. "Perhaps now we will get the respect we deserve," said Klebold on the videotape, brandishing a sawed-off shotgun.

Social rejection is, in fact, the most significant risk factor for teenage suicide, despair, and violence (Crescioni & Baumeister, 2009; Leary, Twenge, & Quinlivan, 2006; Stillman et al., 2009). When a team of researchers investigated 15 school shootings that occurred between 1995 and 2001, they found that in 13 of them the killers had been angered by bullying and social rejection (Leary et al., 2003).

In the immediate aftermath of the Columbine massacre, countless young people posted messages online, describing their anguish over being rejected and taunted by their popular classmates. None of these teenagers condoned the shootings, yet their Internet postings revealed a high degree of understanding and empathy for the suffering that they assumed Harris and Klebold must have endured. A 16-year-old girl wrote: "I know how they feel. Parents need to realize that a kid is not overreacting all the time they say that no one accepts them. Also, all of the popular conformists need to learn to accept everyone else. Why do they shun everyone who is different?"

If Aronson's analysis of Columbine is correct, it should be possible to make our schools safer, as well as more pleasant and humane, by bringing about a change in the negative, exclusionary social atmosphere. Two lines of research discussed in this chapter suggest how we might achieve this goal: the success of Dan Olweus's program to reduce bullying in the schools of Norway and Norma Feshbach's successful attempt to build empathy among schoolchildren in the United States. Similarly successful programs designed to promote empathy and cooperation will be discussed in greater detail in the following chapter.

USE IT!

Imagine that you have a younger brother who is a sophomore in high school. In a phone conversation with your parents, you learn that he seems to be having a problem with anger management. He has been getting into fistfights with some of his classmates and has even beaten up on smaller boys. Your father has recommended that he try out for the high school football team as a way of "burning off" s of his excess aggressive energy. Your mother is not that this is a good idea. They say to you, "You have t courses in psychology. What would you recomme Based on what you have learned in this chapter, what w you recommend?

Summary

What is aggression? Is it innate, learned, or optional?

- **What Is Aggression?** Aggression is intentional behavior aimed at doing harm or causing physical or psychological pain to another person. **Hostile aggression** is defined as having as one's goal the harming of another; **instrumental aggression** inflicts harm as a means to some other end. Over the centuries, philosophers and psychologists have argued about whether or not humans are aggressive by nature. Some have argued that it is in human nature to be aggressive, others that humans are malleable.
  - **The Evolutionary Argument** All over the world, males are more physically aggressive than women, starting in childhood. Evolutionary psychologists argue that aggression is genetically programmed into men because it enables them to defend their group and perpetuate their genes; males also aggress out of sexual jealousy, to protect their paternity. The hormone that fuels male aggression is testosterone. However, there is substantial variation in the degree of aggressiveness among human males and also among our two closest animal relatives, chimpanzees and bonobos. Even if aggressive behavior has survival value, nearly all animals have also evolved strong inhibitory mechanisms that enable them to suppress aggression when they need to.
  - **The Cultural Argument** Aggression is influenced by situational and cultural factors and is therefore modifiable. There is a great variation in the levels of aggression across cultures; cooperative, collectivist cultures have low levels of aggression. The degree of aggressiveness can also change within a culture over time because of changes in the situation faced by the group. In *cultures of honor*, men are raised to respond aggressively to perceptions of threat and disrespect, a response that originated in economic conditions. Multiple factors shape whether or not a culture tends to nurture aggressive behavior, including the extent to which male aggression fulfills a central part of the male role and identity.
  - **Gender and Aggression** Men and boys are much more likely than women to be physically aggressively in provocative situations, to pick a fight with strangers, and to commit crimes of violence. Men are also more likely to interpret a given situation as provocative; however, gender differences in physical aggression are reduced when women are as provoked as men or when cultural norms foster female aggression. Girls and women are more likely to commit *relational aggression*, acts that harm another person through manipulation of the relationship (backbiting, spreading rumors, shunning). Within heterosexual couples, husbands are far more likely to murder their wives than vice versa; the rate of the physical abuse of women is high around the world, especially in cultures that regard such abuse as a male prerogative.
  - **Some Physiological Influences on Aggression** Alcohol can increase aggressive behavior because it serves as a disinhibitor, reducing a person's inhibitions. Alcohol also disrupts the way people usually process information so that they may respond to the most obvious aspects of a social situation and fail to pick up its subtle elements. When people experience pain, discomfort, and heat, they are more likely to act aggressively.

What are some situational influences on aggression?

- **Social Situations and Aggression**
  - **Frustration and Aggression** The **frustration-aggression theory** states that frustration can increase the probability of an aggressive response. Frustration is more likely to produce aggression if one is thwarted on the way to a goal in a manner that is either illegitimate or unexpected. Also, *relative deprivation*—the feeling that you have less than what you deserve or less than people similar to you have—is more likely to cause frustration and aggressive behavior than absolute deprivation, as illustrated by protests and revolutions from the civil rights movement to Eastern Europe to the Middle East.
  - **Provocation and Reciprocation** Individuals frequently aggress to reciprocate the aggressive behavior of others. This response is reduced if there are mitigating circumstances or the recipient believes the other person's behavior was unintentional.
  - **Aggressive Objects as Cues** The mere presence of a gun, an aggressive stimulus, in an otherwise neutral situation increases the degree of aggressive behavior. In a classic study, participants angered in the presence of a gun administered stronger electric shocks to their "victim" than those angered in the same setting in which a tennis racket was substituted for the gun.

What evidence is there that aggression is learned by observing and imitating others?

- **Learning to Behave Aggressively** Social learning theory holds that people often learn social behavior, including aggression, by observing and imitating others.
  - **Violence in the Media** Most children are exposed to a great deal of violence in TV and movies and playing violent video games. To try to determine what effect all this violence might have on children and adults, researchers have conducted laboratory experiments and longitudinal studies. Most of the experimental evidence demonstrates that watching violence is associated with an increase in aggressive behavior, especially in children, who aren't always good at separating fantasy from reality, but not all studies find a relationship. Also, children who are already predisposed to aggression are more likely to seek out aggressive shows and games to watch and play. Exposure to violent pornography, in contrast to nonviolent erotica, increases acceptance of sexual violence toward women. As with other kinds of violent images in the media, the effects are strongest on men who are already predisposed to aggression toward women.

    In the laboratory, playing violent video games does increase hostile feelings and aggressive behavior and also has a "numbing" effect, increasing people's indifference to the needs of others. Longitudinal studies show that the more TV violence observed by children, the greater the amount of violence they exhibit as teenagers and young adults. Viewing violence also exaggerates people's perceptions of danger in the outside world and impairs their memory, making people less likely to remember a product advertised on a violent TV program.

The relationship between media violence and actual aggression is a two-way street: The former has the greatest effect on children already predisposed to violence because of a genetic predisposition, living in a violent family, or a personality trait. And many other factors have a far more powerful influence on aggression, including growing up with violent or otherwise abusive parents, living in a violent community, and being rejected socially.

- **Sexual Violence Against Women** Most crimes of rape are committed by assailants known to the victim. Acquaintance or date rape includes direct assault: drugging the victim into a blackout, sex with a victim who is drunk or otherwise incapacitated, and sex under physical coercion and threat. Sexually aggressive males who commit these acts are often narcissistic, are unable to empathize with women, may feel hostility and contempt toward women, and feel entitled to have sexual relations with whatever woman they choose. Date rape may also occur because of misunderstandings and ambiguities in the sexual **scripts** that men and women follow regarding sexual norms.

How can aggression be reduced?

How to Reduce Aggression

- **Does Punishing Aggression Reduce Aggression?** If the punishment is itself aggressive, it actually models such behavior to children and may engender greater aggressiveness. Further, severe punishment may actually enhance the attractiveness of the transgression to the child, get the attention that the child is hoping for, or backfire by making the child anxious and angry. Punishment often fails to reduce aggression because it does not communicate what the target should do, only what he or she should not do. A growing form of aggression that inflicts considerable pain on children and teenagers is cyberbullying; some interventions have been successful in reducing bullying in schools and on the Internet. For punishment to serve as a deterrent to misbehavior or criminal acts it must be both prompt and certain.
- **Catharsis and Aggression** The theory of **catharsis** predicts that venting one's anger or watching others behave aggressively would serve to make one less likely to engage in subsequent acts of aggression. Research shows the contrary: Acting aggressively or observing aggressive events or sports increases the likelihood of aggressive behavior. Ventilating anger directly toward someone who has insulted or otherwise angered you also increases blood pressure, feelings of anger, and acts of aggression. In turn, because of self-justification and the need to reduce dissonance, each act of "righteous aggression" a person commits increases the likelihood that it will be repeated.
- **What Are We Supposed to Do with Our Anger?** Venting anger usually causes more harm than good, but stifling serious feelings is often not useful either. It is more effective to become aware of the anger and then to deal with it in ways that are more constructive than yelling or hitting: cooling off; getting involved in a distracting activity; becoming more self-aware (perhaps through writing down your feelings privately); learning to communicate your feelings in a clear but nonjudgmental or insulting way; taking responsibility for acts that anger others, through understanding and apology; and strengthening empathic skills.

Could the Columbine Massacre Have Been Prevented? Social rejection is the most significant risk factor for teenage suicide, despair, and violence. Although teenagers who have committed horrifying murders in their schools had various emotional problems, what sent most of them over the edge was the anger they felt at having been bullied and rejected by their peers. Changing the atmosphere of schools is an effective way to reduce the frequency of such occurrences and improve the lives of children and teenagers.

Chapter 12 Test

Study and Review on MyPsychLab

1. ______ aggression stems from feelings of anger and is aimed at inflicting pain, whereas ______ aggression serves as a means to some goal other than pain.
   a. hostile, instrumental
   b. direct, passive
   c. instrumental, hostile
   d. passive, direct

2. Which of the following stated gender differences in aggression is *false*?
   a. Young boys tend to be more physically aggressive than young girls.
   b. Girls tend to express their aggressive feelings more covertly, such as by gossiping.
   c. Gender differences in physical aggression shrink when men and women are subjected to frustration or insults.
   d. Because violence is so rare in women, female suicide bombers are much crazier than males who carry out these attacks.

3. From a social-psychological perspective, which of the following is *not* a limitation of evolutionary theories of aggression?
   a. They fail to account for female aggression.

b. They fail to account for different rates of aggression across cultures.
c. They fail to account for men's sexual jealousy.
d. They fail to account for differences between bonobos and chimpanzees.

4. Which of the following men is most likely to act aggressively toward someone who insults him?
 a. Ray, who grew up in Minnesota.
 b. Randy, who grew up in Louisiana.
 c. Richard, who grew up in Massachusetts.
 d. Ricky, who grew up in Maine.

5. Under which of the following conditions is John *least* likely to be aggressive?
 a. His boss tells him he isn't going to get a raise he was promised.
 b. He likes to look at nonviolent pornography.
 c. He is driving to work in traffic, and another driver deliberately cuts in front of him.
 d. He has consumed enough alcohol to make him legally drunk, and a stranger bumps into him in a crowded restaurant.

6. Which of the following statements does *not* reflect the research on media violence and young children's behavior?
 a. Television advertising works better when it is shown during violent shows than nonviolent shows.
 b. Watching violent shows increases aggressive thoughts and actions.
 c. Playing violent video games may have a greater impact on children than watching TV violence does.
 d. Viewing television violence can numb people's response to violence in real life.

7. Jim has been convicted of assault and offers many reasons for his behavior. Which of the following of Jim's arguments would a social psychologist find the *least* convincing (based upon research on aggression)?
 a. "There was a gun in the room when it happened."
 b. "I used to watch my older brother beat up neighborhood kids."
 c. "I had just been fired from a job I really wanted."
 d. "I grew up in a very cold climate, in Minnesota."
 e. "I was justified—the other guy started it."

8. Tiffany is angry at Whitney for forgetting her birthday. To defuse her anger, Tiffany should
 a. think about other times Whit annoyed her and then confront Whit with all the evidence of what a bad friend she is.
 b. write about her feelings privately for 20 minutes a day for a few days, to get some perspective.
 c. write about her feelings about Whit on her Facebook page.
 d. get back at Whit by complaining about her to all their mutual friends.

9. Tiffany finally decides she is ready to confront Whitney directly. How should she express her anger (assuming she wants to keep the friendship)?
 a. She should "let it all out" so that she will feel better and Whit will know exactly how she feels.
 b. She should invite Whitney to play a game of tennis and then really try to clobber her.
 c. She should explain why she feels upset and hurt, as calmly as she can, without blame and accusation.
 d. She should explain why she feels upset and hurt, but let Whit know that she blames her for her thoughtless behavior.

10. Suppose you want to reduce the chances that your children will act in aggressive ways toward other people. Which of the following is *least* likely to work?
 a. Be a good role model; do not yell, hit, or act in other aggressive ways.
 b. Limit the time you let your children play violent video games.
 c. Teach them how to feel empathy toward other people.
 d. Encourage them to play sports where they can vent their frustrations on the playing field.

Answer Key

1-a, 2-d, 3-c, 4-b, 5-b,
6-a, 7-d, 8-b, 9-c, 10-d

SOCIAL PSYCHOLOGY IN ACTION

2 Social Psychology and Health

JOANNE HILL SUFFERED AN UNIMAGINABLE AMOUNT OF LOSS OVER A 4-YEAR PERIOD. It began when her husband, Ken, died of heart failure at the age of 55, followed shortly by the deaths of her brother, stepfather, mother, aunt, two uncles, two cousins, her cousin's partner, her stepmother, and, finally, her son, who died suddenly of a heart attack at the age of 38. Joanne helped care for several of these loved ones before they died, including her mother, who suffered from Alzheimer's and breast cancer, her brother, who died of lung cancer, and her aunt, who died of liver cancer. "Everyone I loved seemed to need help," she said (Hill, 2002, p. 21).

How could anyone endure so much loss? Surely any one of these tragedies would stop us in our tracks, and suffering so many in such a short time would surely push most of us to the breaking point, taking a severe toll on our physical and emotional well-being. But rather than crawl under a rock, Joanne made it through what she calls her "locust years" with remarkable strength, grace, and resilience. She was the executor of several of her relatives' estates and dealt successfully with complicated legal issues. She provided help and support to numerous friends and family members. She also went back to college, traveled to Europe, and wrote a book about her experiences. Life is "filled with both bright sunny places and dark stormy times," she says. "Within each I looked for the golden nuggets of wisdom and truth that helped me grow stronger, happier and healthier" (Hill, n.d.).

Maybe Joanne is one of those rare people born with a huge reservoir of inner strength, allowing her to weather any storm. But she didn't always find it easy to deal with life's slings and arrows. She had struggled with depression in childhood and beyond, was addicted to prescription medication early in her marriage, and suffered from debilitating physical ailments—so many that she had difficulty buying life insurance. "Today," she reports in her book, "in spite of one trauma after another for several years, I am healthy in body and whole in mind. Not because of Lady Luck, but because I decided to make different choices" (p. 133). Hill attributes her survival to a series of "rainbow remedies" that she learned, through hard experience, to apply to her life.

This chapter is concerned with the application of psychology to physical and mental health, which is a flourishing area of research. We will focus primarily on topics that connect social psychology and health: how people cope with stress in their lives, the relationship between their coping styles and their physical and mental health, and how we can get people to behave in healthier ways. Along the way we will return to Joanne Hill's story, discuss her "rainbow remedies," and see that at least some of them are backed up by research in social psychology and health.

FOCUS QUESTIONS

- What effects does stress have on our health?
- What can people do to cope and recover after a stressful experience?
- How can we apply social psychology to help people live healthier lives?

People are surprisingly resilient in the face of stressful events. Studies of reactions to the 9/11 terrorist attacks, for example, have found that relatively few people showed long-term signs of depression or other mental health problems.

Stress and Human Health

There is more to our physical health than germs and disease—we also need to consider the amount of stress in our lives and how we deal with that stress (Chida & Hamer, 2008; Ganzel, Morris, & Wethington, 2010; Inglehart, 1991; Park, 2010; Segerstrom, 2010; Taylor, 2010). Early research in this area documented some extreme cases in which people's health was influenced by stress. Consider these examples, reported by psychologist W. B. Cannon (1942):

- A New Zealand woman eats a piece of fruit and then learns that it came from a forbidden supply reserved for the chief. Horrified, her health deteriorates, and the next day she dies—even though it was a perfectly fine piece of fruit.
- A man in Africa has breakfast with a friend, eats heartily, and goes on his way. A year later, he learns that his friend had made the breakfast from a wild hen, a food strictly forbidden in his culture. The man immediately begins to tremble and is dead within 24 hours.
- An Australian man's health deteriorates after a witch doctor casts a spell on him. He recovers only when the witch doctor removes the spell.

These examples probably sound bizarre, like something you would read in *Ripley's Believe It or Not*. But let's shift to the present in the United States, where many similar cases of sudden death occur following a psychological trauma. When people undergo a major upheaval in their lives, such as losing a spouse, declaring bankruptcy, or being forced to resettle in a new culture, their chance of dying increases (Morse, Martin, & Moshonov, 1991). Soon after a major earthquake in the Los Angeles area on January 17, 1994, there was an increase in the number of people who died suddenly of heart attacks (Leor, Poole, & Kloner, 1996). And many people experienced psychological and physical problems after the terrorist attacks on September 11, 2001 (Neria, DiGrande, & Adams, 2011; Silver et al., 2002). One study measured the heart rates of a sample of adults in New Haven, Connecticut, the week after the attacks. Compared to a control group of people studied before the attacks, the post–September 11 sample showed lower heart rate variability, which is a risk factor for sudden death (Gerin et al., 2005; Lampert et al., 2002). On the other hand, as we will see in a moment, studies of the long-term effects of the 9/11 attacks have found relatively little evidence of prolonged negative reactions. What exactly are the effects of stress on our psychological and physical health, and how can we learn to cope most effectively?

Resilience

The first thing to note is that humans are remarkably resilient. To be sure, we all must contend with the blows life deals us, including day-to-day hassles and major, life-altering events. And although it is true that such events can have negative effects on psychological and physical health, many people, such as Joanne Hill, cope with them extremely well. Researchers have examined people's reactions over time to major life events, including the death of loved ones and the 9/11 terrorist attacks. The most common response to such traumas is **resilience**, which can be defined as mild, transient reactions to stressful events, followed by a quick return to normal, healthy functioning (Bonanno, 2004, 2005; Bonanno, Westphal, & Mancini, 2011).

Resilience

Mild, transient reactions to stressful events, followed by a quick return to normal, healthy functioning

Take life's most difficult challenge—dealing with the loss of a loved one. For years, mental health professionals assumed that the "right" way to grieve was to go through an intense period of sadness and distress, in which people confronted and worked through their feelings, eventually leading to acceptance of the loss. People who did not show symptoms of extreme distress were said to be in a state of denial that would lead to greater problems down the road. When researchers looked systematically at how people respond to the death of loved ones, however, an interesting fact emerged: Many people never experienced significant distress and recovered quickly (Wortman & Silver, 1989). Studies of bereaved spouses, for example, typically find that fewer than half show signs of significant, long-term distress (Bonanno, Boerner, &

Wortman, 2008; Bonanno et al., 2005). The remainder, like Joanne Hill, show no signs of depression and are able to experience positive emotions.

Although one might think that such people are in a state of denial, or that they were never very attached to their spouses, there is little evidence to support these possibilities. Rather, there is increasing evidence that although life's traumas can be quite painful, many people have the resources to recover from them quickly. The same pattern has been found in people's responses to other highly stressful events, such as emergency workers' reactions to the bombing of the federal building in Oklahoma City in 1995 and New Yorkers' reactions to the 9/11 terrorist attacks. Surprisingly few people show prolonged, negative reactions to these tragedies (McNally, & Breslau, 2008; Seery et al., 2008; Updegraff, Silver, & Holman, 2008). Nonetheless, some people do have severe negative reactions to stressful events. What determines whether people bounce back quickly or buckle under stress?

Effects of Negative Life Events

Among the pioneers in research on stress is Hans Selye (1956, 1976), who defined *stress* as the body's physiological response to threatening events. Selye focused on how the human body adapts to threats from the environment, regardless of the source—be it a psychological or physiological trauma. Later researchers have examined what it is about a life event that makes it threatening. Holmes and Rahe (1967), for example, suggested that stress is the degree to which people have to change and readjust their lives in response to an external event. The more change that is required, the greater the stress we experience. For example, if a spouse or partner dies, just about every aspect of a person's life is disrupted, leading to a great deal of stress. Holmes and Rahe's definition of stress applies to happy events as well if the event causes big changes in one's daily routine. Graduating from college is a happy occasion, but it can be stressful because it is often accompanied by a separation from friends and adapting to a new situation, such as looking for a job, working full time, or going to graduate school.

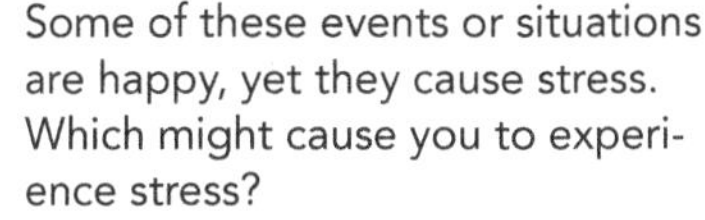

Some of these events or situations are happy, yet they cause stress. Which might cause you to experience stress?

To measure the amount of stress in your life, complete the Try It! exercise on the next page. How did you do? When the authors who developed the scale gave it to a sample of undergraduates, they found that the average score was 1,247 (Renner & Mackin, 1998). And studies have shown that the higher people score on stress inventories such as this one, the worse their mental and physical health (Almeida, 2005; Dohrenwend, 2006; Seta, Seta, & Wang, 1990).

Limits of Stress Inventories It seems pretty obvious that the more stress people are experiencing, the more likely they are to feel anxious and get sick. But the findings aren't all that straightforward. One problem, as you may have recognized, is that most studies in this area use correlational designs, not experimental designs. Just because life changes are correlated with health problems does not mean that the life changes caused the health problems (see Chapter 2 on correlation and causality). Some researchers have argued persuasively for the role of "third variables," whereby certain kinds of people are more likely to be experiencing difficult life changes and to report that they are ill (Schroeder & Costa, 1984; Watson & Pennebaker, 1989). According to these researchers, it is not life changes that cause health problems. Instead, people with certain personality traits, such as the tendency to experience negative moods, are more likely to experience life difficulties and to have health problems.

Another problem with measures such as the College Life Stress Inventory is that they focus on stressors experienced by the middle class and underrepresent stressors experienced by the poor and members of minority groups. Variables such as poverty and racism are potent causes of stress (Gibbons, Gerrard, & Cleveland, 2004; Giscombé & Lobel, 2005; Jackson et al., 1996; Myers, 2009). Moreover, the way in which these variables influence health is not always obvious. It might not surprise you to learn that the more racism minority groups experience, the worse their health. It might come as more of a surprise to learn that majority groups who express the most racist attitudes also experience diminished health (Jackson & Inglehart, 1995). Racism is often associated with hostility and aggression, and there is evidence that hostility is related to health problems such as coronary heart disease. Clearly, to understand the relationship between stress and health, we need to understand better such community and cultural variables as poverty and racism.

Perceived Stress and Health

There is another problem with measures such as the College Life Stress Inventory: They violate a basic principle of social psychology—namely, that subjective situations have more of an impact on people than objective situations (Dohrenwend, 2006; Griffin & Ross, 1991). Of course, some situational variables are hazardous to our health regardless of how we interpret them (Jackson & Inglehart, 1995; Taylor, Repetti, & Seeman, 1997). Children growing up in smog-infested areas such as Los Angeles, for example, have been found to have 10% to 15% less efficiency in their lungs than children who grow up in less-polluted areas (Peters et al., 1999). Nonetheless, some environmental events are open to interpretation and seem to have negative effects only on people who construe these events in certain ways. To some students, writing a term paper is a major hassle; for others, it's a minor inconvenience (or even an enjoyable challenge). For some people, a major life change such as getting divorced is a liberating escape from an abusive relationship; for others, it is a devastating personal failure. As recognized by Richard Lazarus (1966, 2000) in his pioneering work on stress, it is subjective, not objective, stress that causes problems. An event is stressful for people only if they interpret it as stressful; thus, we can define **stress** as the negative feelings and beliefs that occur whenever people feel unable to cope with demands from their environment (Lazarus & Folkman, 1984).

Stress

The negative feelings and beliefs that arise whenever people feel unable to cope with demands from their environment

Consider the number of losses Joanne Hill experienced in a 4-year period. According to research on life events, she should have been experiencing a great deal of stress—enough to put her at great risk for severe physical problems. The fact that she made

TRY IT! The College Life Stress Inventory

Instructions: Copy the "stress rating" number into the right column for any event that has happened to you in the past year; then add these scores.

Event	Stress Rating	Your Score
Being raped	100	______
Finding out that you are HIV-positive	100	______
Being accused of rape	98	______
Death of a close friend	97	______
Death of a close family member	96	______
Contracting a sexually transmitted disease (other than AIDS)	94	______
Concerns about being pregnant	91	______
Finals week	90	______
Concerns about your partner being pregnant	90	______
Oversleeping for an exam	89	______
Flunking a class	89	______
Having a boyfriend or girlfriend cheat on you	85	______
Ending a steady dating relationship	85	______
Serious illness in a close friend or family member	85	______
Financial difficulties	84	______
Writing a major term paper	83	______
Being caught cheating on a test	83	______
Drunk driving	82	______
Sense of overload in school or work	82	______
Two exams in one day	80	______
Cheating on your boyfriend or girlfriend	77	______
Getting married	76	______
Negative consequences of drinking or drug use	75	______
Depression or crisis in your best friend	73	______
Difficulties with parents	73	______
Talking in front of a class	72	______
Lack of sleep	69	______
Change in housing situation (hassles, moves)	69	______
Competing or performing in public	69	______
Getting in a physical fight	66	______
Difficulties with a roommate	66	______
Job changes (applying, new job, work hassles)	65	______
Declaring a major or concerns about future plans	65	______
A class you hate	62	______
Drinking or use of drugs	61	______
Confrontations with professors	60	______
Starting a new semester	58	______
Going on a first date	57	______
Registration	55	______
Maintaining a steady dating relationship	55	______
Commuting to campus or work, or both	54	______
Peer pressures	53	______
Being away from home for the first time	53	______
Getting sick	52	______
Concerns about your appearance	52	______
Getting straight A's	51	______
A difficult class that you love	48	______
Making new friends; getting along with friends	47	______
Fraternity or sorority rush	47	______
Falling asleep in class	40	______
Attending an athletic event (e.g., football game)	20	______
Sum of Your Score		______

> *Adopting the right attitude can convert a negative stress into a positive one.*
>
> —Hans Selye (1978)

it through with grace and strength suggests that there are limits to trying to predict people's reactions from a count of the number of stressful events in their lives. We need to take into account how different people *interpret* disruptions and challenges in their lives.

Studies using the subjective definition of stress confirm the idea that negative life experiences are bad for our health. In fact, stress caused by negative interpretations of events can directly affect our immune systems, making us more susceptible to disease. Consider the common cold. When people are exposed to the virus that causes a cold, only 20% to 60% of them become sick. Is it possible that stress is one determinant of who will be in this category? To find out, researchers asked volunteers to spend a week at a research institute in southern England (Cohen, Tyrrell, & Smith, 1991, 1993). As a measure of stress, the participants listed recent events that had had a negative impact on their lives. (Consistent with our definition of stress, the participants listed only events they *perceived* as negative.)

The researchers then gave participants nasal drops that contained either the virus that causes the common cold or saline (salt water). The participants were subsequently quarantined for several days so that they had no contact with other people. The results? The more stress people were experiencing, the more likely they were to catch a cold from the virus (see Figure SPA-2.1).

Among people who reported the least amount of stress, about 27% came down with a cold. This rate increased steadily the more stress people reported, topping out at a rate of nearly 50% in the group that was experiencing the most stress. This effect of stress was found even when several other factors that influence catching a cold were taken into account, such as the time of year people participated and the participants' age, weight, and gender. This study, along with others like it, shows that the more stress people experience, the lower their immunity to disease (Cohen et al., 2008; O'Leary, 1990; Stone et al., 1993).

You may have noticed that the Cohen and colleagues study used a correlational design; this must make us cautious about its interpretation. The amount of stress people were experiencing was measured and correlated with the likelihood that people caught a cold. It is possible that stress itself did not lower people's immunity but rather that some variable correlated with stress did. It would have been ethically impermissible, of course, to conduct an experimental study in which people were randomly assigned to a condition in which they experienced a great deal of prolonged stress. There are studies, however, in which people's immune responses are measured before and after undergoing mildly stressful tasks in the laboratory, such as solving mental arithmetic problems continuously for 6 minutes or giving speeches on short notice. Even relatively mild stressors such as these can lead to a suppression of the immune system (Cacioppo, 1998; Cacioppo et al., 1998).

The finding that stress negatively affects health raises an important question: What exactly is it that makes people perceive a situation as stressful? One important determinant is the amount of control they believe they have over the event.

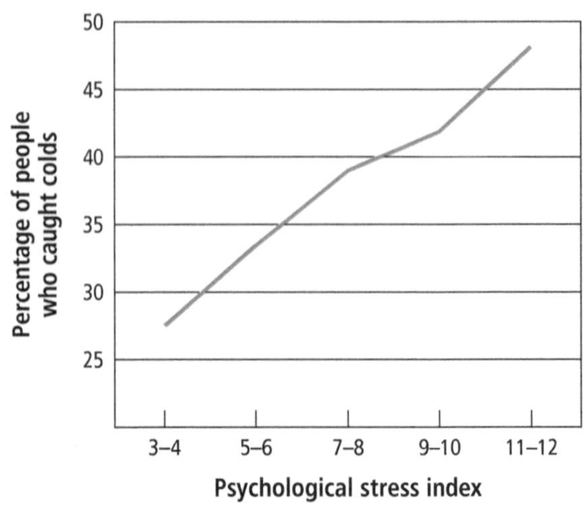

Figure SPA-2.1

Stress and the Likelihood of Catching a Cold

People were first exposed to the virus that causes the common cold and then isolated. The greater the amount of stress they were experiencing, the greater the likelihood that they caught a cold from the virus.

(Adapted from Cohen, Tyrrell, & Smith, 1991)

Feeling in Charge: The Importance of Perceived Control

"There are times in life when we feel so out of control that helplessness and hopelessness become constant companions," writes Joanne Hill. "But choice, like breath, is something that is part of us. *We always have a choice*" (Hill, 2002, p. 128). Research shows, however, that some people feel this way more than others. For example, suppose you read a series of statements and had to choose the one in each pair that you thought was more true, such as "people's misfortunes result from mistakes they make" versus "many of the unhappy things in people's lives are partly due to bad luck." Which of these two do you think is more true? These statements are part of a test of **internal-external locus of control** (Rotter, 1966), which is the tendency to believe that things happen because we control them versus believing that good and bad outcomes are out of our control. The first statement above reflects an internal locus of control, which is the belief that people can control their fates. The second statement reflects an external locus of control, which is the belief that our fates are more a matter of happenstance.

Internal-External Locus of Control

The tendency to believe that things happen because we control them versus believing that good and bad outcomes are out of our control

Perceived Control

The belief that we can influence our environment in ways that determine whether we experience positive or negative outcomes

Research by Jean Twenge and her colleagues (Twenge, Zhang, & Im, 2004) has found that between the years 1960 and 2002, college students in the United States have scored more and more on the external end of the locus-of-control scale. That is, as seen in Figure SPA-2.2, college students are becoming more convinced that good and bad things in life are outside of their control.

The reasons for this trend are not entirely clear; it may be part of an increased sense of alienation and distrust among younger generations in the United States (Fukuyama, 1999; Putnam, 2000). Whatever the reasons, research in social psychology suggests that the tendency to feel less control over one's fate is not good for our psychological and physical health. Shelley Taylor and her colleagues (Taylor, Lichtman, & Wood, 1984), for example, interviewed women with breast cancer and found that many of them believed they could control whether their cancer returned. Here is how one man described his wife: "She got books, she got pamphlets, she studied, she talked to cancer patients. She found out everything that was happening to her and she fought it. She went to war with it. She calls it 'taking in her covered wagons and surrounding it'" (quoted in Taylor, 1989, p. 178).

The researchers found that women who believed their cancer was controllable were better adjusted psychologically (Folkman & Moskowitz, 2000). Subsequent studies have found that a high sense of **perceived control**—defined as the belief that we can influence our environment in ways that determine whether we experience positive or negative outcomes—is associated with good physical and mental health (Frazier et al., 2011; Kraus, Piff, & Keltner, 2009; Leotti, Iyengar, & Ochsner, 2010; Roepke & Grant, 2011; Thompson, 1999). For example, among people who had undergone a coronary angioplasty because of diseased arteries, those who had a high sense of control over their futures were less likely to experience subsequent heart problems than people with

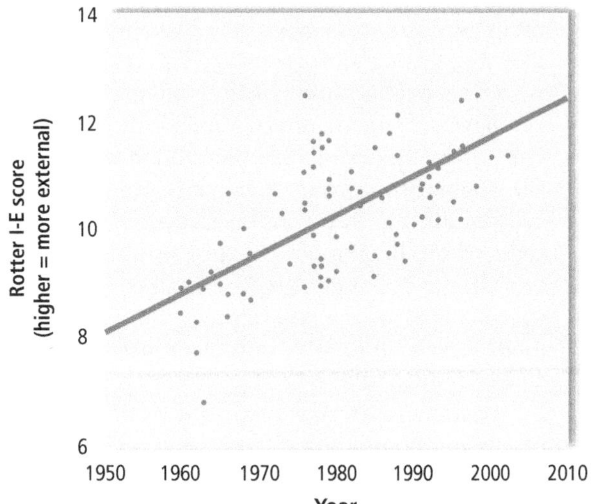

Figure SPA-2.2

Beliefs in Internal-External Locus of Control in College Students Over Time

As seen in the graph, in the past 50 years there is a trend whereby college students in the United States endorse more external beliefs about locus of control. This means that they increasingly believe that good and bad things in life are outside of their control.

(Adopted from Twenge, Zhang, & Im, 2004)

a low sense of control (Helgeson, 2003; Helgeson & Fritz, 1999). Joanne Hill recognized this lesson; one of her rainbow remedies is that the "Power of Choice is an empowering remedy that truly makes the difference whether we survive and thrive, or wither and die" (Hill, n.d.).

Increasing Perceived Control in Nursing Homes Some of the most dramatic effects of perceived control have been found in studies of older people in nursing homes. Many people who end up in nursing homes and hospitals feel they have lost control of their lives (Raps et al., 1982; Sherwin & Winsby, 2011). People are often placed in long-term care facilities against their wishes and, when there, have little say in what they do, whom they see, or what they eat. Two psychologists believed that boosting their feelings of control would help such people (Langer & Rodin, 1976). They asked the director of a nursing home in Connecticut to convey to the residents that, contrary to what they might think, they had a lot of responsibility for their own lives. Here is an excerpt of his speech:

> Take a minute to think of the decisions you can and should be making. For example, you have the responsibility of caring for yourselves, of deciding whether or not you want to make this a home you can be proud of and happy in. You should be deciding how you want your rooms to be arranged—whether you want it to be as it is or whether you want the staff to help you rearrange the furniture. You should be deciding how you want to spend your time. . . . If you are unsatisfied with anything here, you have the influence to change it. . . . These are just a few of the things you could and should be deciding and thinking about now and from time to time every day. (Langer & Rodin, 1976, pp. 194–195)

Nursing home residents who have a sense of control over their lives have been found to do better, both physically and psychologically.

The director went on to say that a movie would be shown on two nights the next week and that the residents should decide which night they wanted to attend. Finally, he offered each resident a gift of a house plant, emphasizing that it was up to the resident to decide whether to take one (they all did) and to take care of it. The director also gave a speech to residents assigned to a comparison group. This speech was different in one crucial way: All references to making decisions and being responsible for oneself were deleted. He emphasized that he wanted the residents to be happy, but he did not say anything about the control they had over their lives. He said that a movie would be shown on two nights the next week but that the residents would be assigned to see it on one night or the other. He gave plants to these residents as well but said that the nurses would take care of the plants.

The director's speech might not seem like a major change in the lives of the residents. The people in the induced-control group heard one speech about the responsibility they had for their lives and were given one plant to water. That doesn't seem like very strong stuff, does it? But to an institutionalized person who feels helpless and constrained, even a small boost in control can have a dramatic effect. Indeed, the residents in the induced-control group became happier and more active than residents in the comparison group (Langer & Rodin, 1976). Most dramatically of all, the intervention improved the residents' health and reduced the likelihood that they would die in the next year and a half (Rodin & Langer, 1977). Eighteen months after the director's speech, 15% of the residents in the induced-control group had died, compared to 30% in the comparison condition (see the left side of Figure SPA-2.3).

Another researcher increased feelings of control in residents of nursing homes in a different way (Schulz, 1976). Undergraduates visited the residents of a North Carolina nursing home once a week for 2 months. In the induced-control condition, the residents

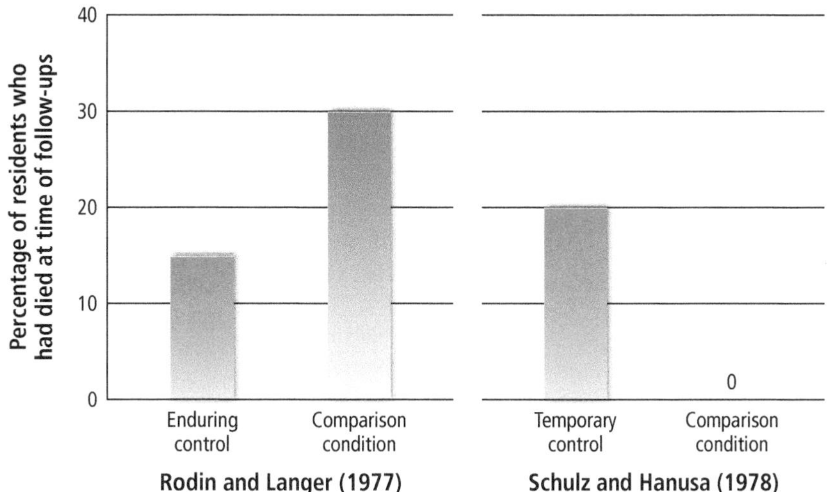

Figure SPA-2.3

Perceived Control and Mortality

In two studies, elderly residents in nursing homes were made to feel more in control of their lives. In one (Rodin & Langer, 1977), the intervention endured over time, so that people continued to feel in control. As seen on the left side of the figure, this intervention had positive effects on mortality rates. Those who received it were more likely to be alive 18 months later than those who did not. In the other study (Schulz & Hanusa, 1978), the intervention was temporary. Being given control and then having it taken away had negative effects on mortality rates, as seen on the right side of the figure.

(Adapted from Rodin & Langer, 1977; Schulz & Hanusa, 1978)

decided when the visits would occur and how long they would last. In a randomly assigned comparison condition, it was the students, not the residents, who decided when the visits would occur and how long they would last. Thus, the residents received visits in both conditions, but in only one could they control the visits' frequency and duration. This may seem like a minor difference, but again, giving the residents some semblance of control over their lives had dramatic effects. After 2 months, those in the induced-control condition were happier, healthier, more active, and taking fewer medications than those in the comparison group.

Schulz returned to the nursing home several months later to assess the long-term effects of his intervention, including its effect on mortality rates. Based on the results of the Langer and Rodin (1976) study, we might expect that the residents who could control the students' visits would be healthier and more likely still to be alive than the residents who could not. But there is a crucial difference between the two studies: The residents in the Langer and Rodin study were given an enduring sense of control, whereas the residents in the Schulz study experienced control and then lost it. Langer and Rodin's participants could continue to choose which days to participate in different activities, continue to take care of their plant, and continue to feel that they could make a difference in what happened to them, even after the study ended. By contrast, when Schulz's study was over, the student visits ended. The residents who could control the visits suddenly had that control removed.

Unfortunately, Schulz's intervention had an unintended effect: After the program ended, the people in the induced-control group did worse (Schulz & Hanusa, 1978). Compared to people in the comparison group, they were more likely to have experienced deteriorating health and zest for life, and they were more likely to have died (see the right side of Figure SPA-2.3). This study has sobering implications for the many college-based volunteer programs in which students visit residents of nursing homes, prisons, and mental hospitals. These programs might be beneficial in the short run but do more harm than good after they end.

Disease, Control, and Well-Being We end this discussion with some words of caution. First, the relationship between perceived control and distress is more important to members of Western cultures than to members of Asian cultures. One study found that Asians reported that perceived control was less important to them than Westerners did and that there was less of a relationship between perceived control and psychological distress in Asians than in Westerners (Sastry & Ross, 1998). The researchers argue that in Western cultures, where individualism and personal achievement are prized, people are more likely to be distressed if they feel that they cannot personally control their destinies. A lowered sense of control is less of an issue in Asian cultures, they argue, because Asians place greater value on collectivism and putting the social group ahead of individual goals.

Second, even in Western societies, there is a danger in exaggerating the relationship between perceived control and health. Social critic Susan Sontag (1978, 1988) perceptively observed that when a society is plagued by a deadly but poorly understood disease, such as tuberculosis in the nineteenth century and AIDS today, the illness is often blamed on some kind of human frailty, such as a lack of faith, a moral weakness, or a broken heart. As a result, people may blame themselves for their illnesses, even to the point where they do not seek effective treatment. Even though it helps people to feel that they are in control of their illnesses, the downside of this strategy is that if they do not get better, they may blame themselves for failing to recover. Tragically, diseases such as cancer can be fatal no matter how much control a person feels. It only adds to the tragedy if people with-serious diseases feel a sense of moral failure, blaming themselves for a disease that is unpredictable and incurable.

For people living with serious illnesses, keeping some form of control has benefits, even when their health is failing. Researchers have found that even when people who are seriously ill with cancer or AIDS felt no control over the disease, many of them believed they could control the consequences of the disease, such as their emotional reactions and some of the physical symptoms of the disease, such as how tired they felt. And the more people felt they could control the consequences of their disease, the better adjusted they were, even if they knew they could not control the eventual course of their illness. In short, it is important to feel in control of something, even if it is not the disease itself. Maintaining such a sense of control is likely to improve one's psychological well-being, even if one's health fails (Heckhausen & Schulz, 1995; Morling & Evered, 2006; Thompson, 2002).

Coping with Stress

No one always feels in control, of course, and sometimes it is difficult to avoid being pessimistic after something bad happens. The death of a loved one, an acrimonious divorce, and the loss of a job are extremely stressful events. Considerable research indicates that people exhibit various reactions, or **coping styles**, in the face of threatening events (Aspinwall & Taylor, 1997; Lazarus & Folkman, 1984; Lehman et al., 1993; Moos & Holahan, 2003; Salovey et al., 2000; Taylor, 2010). We examine a few coping styles here, beginning with research on gender differences in the ways people respond to stress.

Watch on **MyPsychLab**
To learn more, watch the MyPsychLab video ***Coping with Stress***.

Gender Differences in Coping with Stress

If you have ever been to a dog park, you know that dogs respond in one of two ways when they are attacked: Sometimes they respond in kind, and a dogfight occurs, with owners scrambling to remove their dogs from the melee. Other times, the dog who is attacked will take off as fast as it can, tail between its legs. Walter Cannon (1932) termed this the **fight-or-flight response**, defined as responding to stress by either attacking the source of the stress or fleeing from it. For years, the fight-or-flight response has been viewed as the way in which all mammals respond to stress. When under threat, mammals are energized by the release of hormones such as norepinephrine and epinephrine, and, like the dogs in the park, they either go on the attack or retreat as quickly as they can.

That, at least, has been the accepted story for many years. Shelley Taylor and her colleagues (Taylor et al., 2000; Taylor & Master, 2011) pointed out a little-known fact about research on the fight-or-flight syndrome: Most of it has been done on males (particularly male rats). Taylor and her colleagues argue that the fight-or-flight response does not work well for females because they typically play a greater role in caring for children. Fighting is not always a good option for a pregnant female or one tending offspring. Similarly, fleeing is difficult when an adult is responsible for the care of young children or in the later months of pregnancy.

Coping Styles
The ways in which people react to threatening events

Fight-or-Flight Response
Responding to stress by either attacking the source of the stress or fleeing from it

Females are somewhat more likely than males to develop intimate friendships, cooperate with others, and focus their attention on social relationships, particularly when under stress. This is called a *tend-and-befriend* coping strategy.

Consequently, Taylor and her colleagues argue, a different way of responding to stress has evolved in females: the **tend-and-befriend response**. Instead of fighting or fleeing, women respond to stress with nurturant activities designed to protect oneself and one's offspring (tending) and creating social networks that provide protection from threats (befriending). Tending has a number of benefits for both the mother and the child (e.g., a quiet child is less likely to be noticed by predators, and nurturing behavior leads to lower stress and improved immune functioning in mammals). Befriending involves the creation of close ties with other members of the species, which also confers a number of advantages. A close-knit group can exchange resources, watch out for predators, and share child care. As we saw in Chapter 5, human females are more likely than males to develop intimate friendships, cooperate with others, and focus their attention on social relationships. This is especially so when people are under stress; under these circumstances, women are more likely to seek out others, particularly other women (Kivlighan, Granger, & Booth, 2005; Tamres, Janicki, & Helgeson, 2002; Zwolinski, 2008).

We should be careful not to oversimplify gender differences such as these. Although gender differences in coping do exist, the magnitude of these differences is not very large (Tamres et al., 2002). Further, seeking social support can benefit both women and men—as seen in the next section.

Watch on **MyPsychLab**
To learn more about gender differences in coping, watch the MyPsychLab interview on ***Women, Health, and Stress***.

Social Support: Getting Help from Others

Joanne Hill could not have gotten through her "locust years" without the support of a good many family members and friends. When she got the devastating news that her son had died, she was at a gathering of the National Speakers Association (NSA). Joanne turned immediately to her friend Mitchell, a man who had survived both a motorcycle accident and a plane crash. Although badly scarred and wheelchair bound, Mitchell had overcome his adversity and become a successful public speaker. On that terrible day, he held Joanne's hand, shared her grief, and rode with her to the airport. Others helped too: The president of the NSA and her husband took charge of the travel arrangements, and Barbara, a woman Joanne had met just a couple of days earlier at the convention, insisted on accompanying her home. As Joanne writes,

> In my darkest hour, I was surrounded by people . . . As word spread of the devastating news, some of the speakers came to my room to hug me and give me an encouraging word. In the days and months to come, many messages of support, hope, and love came from NSA members all over the continent . . . Strangers became friends, adding their support to those most dear to me at home, my family and long-time friends. (Hill, 2002, p. 7)

Social support, perceiving that others are responsive and receptive to one's needs, is very helpful for dealing with stress (Chaudoir & Fisher, 2010; Lakey & Orehek, 2011; Taylor, 2010; Uchino, 2009). But researchers have wondered: Does social support help people physically as well as emotionally? There is some evidence that it does. Studies have shown that interventions designed to increase social support and decrease stress in cancer patients improve the functioning of their immune systems (Antoni & Lutgendorf, 2007; Andersen et al., 2004; McGregor et al., 2004; Weihs, Enright, & Simmens, 2008). And social support seems to prolong the lives of healthy people as well. In a study of a large sample of American men and women in the years 1967

Tend-and-Befriend Response
Responding to stress with nurturant activities designed to protect oneself and one's offspring (tending) and creating social networks that provide protection from threats (befriending)

Social Support
The perception that others are responsive and receptive to one's needs

to 1969, men with a low level of social support were two to three times more likely to die over the next dozen years than men with a high level of social support (House, Robbins, & Metzner, 1982). Women with a low level of social support were one and a half to two times more likely to die than women with a high level of social support (Berkman & Syme, 1979; Schwarzer & Leppin, 1991; Stroebe & Stroebe, 1996). To get an idea of the amount of social support you feel is available in your life, complete the Try It! exercise that follows.

Friendship is a sheltering tree.
—SAMUEL TAYLOR COLERIDGE (1772–1834)

It may seem obvious that social support is beneficial, but it turns out that there are some interesting qualifications in when and how it helps. First, when things are tough, the kind of social support we get matters. To illustrate, imagine that you are struggling in one of your classes and attend a study session for the final exam. Sarah, a friend of yours in the group, greets you by saying, "I know you aren't doing very well in this class, so how about if we all focus on the material you don't understand and give you an extra hand?" On the one hand, you appreciate the support and extra help. But who likes being singled out as the person who "isn't doing very well"? As we saw in Chapter 11, people don't like receiving help when it comes with the message "you are too incompetent to do it yourself." Now suppose that Sarah was a little more subtle in her support. She knows that you are having trouble with the material in the last chapter of the textbook, but rather than singling you out, she says, "A lot of us are struggling with the material in Chapter 16—I know I am. How about if we focus on that?" She steers help your way without singling you out or communicating that you are incompetent.

Research has demonstrated that the latter kind of help, which they call *invisible support*, is much more effective. This kind of support provides people with assistance without sending the message that they are incapable of doing it themselves. The former

TRY IT! Social Support

This list contains statements that may or may not be true about you. For each statement that is probably true about you, circle T; for each that is probably not true about you, circle F.

You may find that many of the statements are neither clearly true nor clearly false. In these cases, try to decide quickly whether probably true (T) or probably false (F) is more descriptive of you. Although some questions will be difficult to answer, it is important that you pick one alternative or the other. Circle only one of the alternatives for each statement.

Read each item quickly but carefully before responding. This is not a test, and there are no right or wrong answers.

1.	There is at least one person I know whose advice I really trust.	T	F
2.	There is really no one I can trust to give me good financial advice.	T	F
3.	There is really no one who can give me objective feedback about how I'm handling my problems.	T	F
4.	When I need suggestions for how to deal with a personal problem, I know there is someone I can turn to.	T	F
5.	There is someone I feel comfortable going to for advice about sexual problems.	T	F
6.	There is someone I can turn to for advice about handling hassles over household responsibilities.	T	F
7.	I feel that there is no one with whom I can share my most private worries and fears.	T	F
8.	If a family crisis arose, few of my friends would be able to give me good advice about how to handle it.	T	F
9.	There are very few people I trust to help solve my problems.	T	F
10.	There is someone I could turn to for advice about changing my job or finding a new one.	T	F

Scoring instructions appear on page 431.

(Adapted from Cohen, Mermelstein, Kamarack, & Hoberman, 1985)

type of help, which they call *visible support*, is a two-edged sword, because it singles out beneficiaries as needy and as people who can't help themselves. The moral? If you have a friend who is under a great deal of stress, find a way to help him or her unobtrusively without making a big deal of it (Bolger & Amarel, 2007; Bolger, Zuckerman, & Kessler, 2000; Howland & Simpson, 2010; Maisel & Gable, 2009).

Second, social support operates differently in different cultures. Who do you think is more likely to seek support from other people when things get tough: members of Western cultures that stress individualism and independence, or members of East Asian cultures that stress collectivism and interdependence? It might seem as though cultures that stress collectivism would be more likely to seek help from each other, but research by Shelley Taylor, Heejung Kim, and David Sherman has found just the opposite: When under stress, members of East Asian cultures are *less* likely to seek social support than are members of Western cultures (Kim, Sherman, & Taylor, 2008; Taylor et al., 2004; Taylor et al., 2007). The reason? Members of collectivistic cultures are concerned that seeking support from others will disrupt the harmony of the group and open them up to criticism from others.

Does this mean that members of collectivistic cultures receive less support from others and benefit less from it when they do receive it? Not at all. The main difference is in *how* people in different cultures seek and obtain social support. Because members of collectivistic cultures are concerned with upsetting group harmony and criticism from others, they are less likely to ask directly for help in a way that shows they are having problems. For example, they are less likely to say to a friend, "Hey, I'm having a hard time here. Can you give me a hand?" They do benefit from interacting with supportive others, as long as they do not have to disclose that they are having problems (Kim et al., 2008).

Reframing: Finding Meaning in Traumatic Events

When something traumatic happens to you, is it best to try to bury it as deep as you can and never talk about it, or to spend time thinking about the event and discuss it with others? Although folk wisdom has long held that it is best to open up, only recently has this assumption been put to the test. James Pennebaker and his colleagues (Pennebaker, 1990, 1997, 2004; Sloan et al., 2008; Smyth & Pennebaker, 2008) have conducted a number of interesting experiments on the value of writing about traumatic events. Pennebaker and Beale (1986), for example, asked college students to write, for 15 minutes on each of 4 consecutive nights, about a traumatic event that had happened to them. Students in a control condition wrote for the same amount of time about a trivial event. The traumas that people chose to write about included tragedies such as rape and the death of a sibling.

Writing about these events was certainly upsetting in the short run: Students who wrote about traumas reported more-negative moods and showed greater increases in blood pressure. But there were also dramatic long-term benefits: The same students were less likely to visit the student health center during the next 6 months, and they reported having fewer illnesses. Similarly, first-year college students who wrote about the problems of entering college, survivors of the Holocaust who wrote about their World War II experiences, and patients who had had a heart attack and wrote about it improved their health over the several months after putting their experiences in writing (Pennebaker, Barger, & Tiebout, 1989; Pennebaker, Colder, & Sharp, 1990; Willmott et al., 2011).

> *If he wrote it he could get rid of it. He had gotten rid of many things by writing them.*
>
> —Ernest Hemingway, *Fathers and Sons* (1933)

What is it about opening up that leads to better health? People who write about negative events construct a more meaningful narrative or story that reframes the event. Pennebaker (1997) has analyzed the hundreds of pages of writing his participants provided and found that the people who improved the most were those who began with rather incoherent, disorganized descriptions of their problem and ended with coherent, organized stories that explained the event and gave it meaning. Subsequent research has shown that reframing is especially likely to occur when people

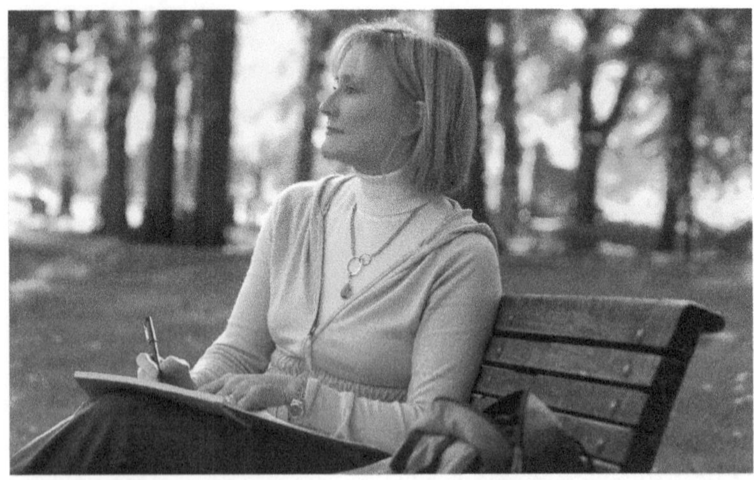

Research by James Pennebaker (1990) shows that there are long-term health benefits to writing or talking about one's personal traumas, particularly if enough time has passed to allow people to gain a new perspective on the traumatic events.

take a step back and write about a negative life event like an observer would, rather than immersing themselves in the event and trying to relive it (Kross & Ayduk, 2011). The result? Once people have reframed a traumatic event in this way, they think about it less and are less likely to try to suppress thoughts about it when it does come to mind. Trying to suppress negative thoughts can lead to a preoccupation with those very thoughts, because the act of trying not to think about them can actually make us think about them more, leading to intrusive memories (Wegner, 1994).

You may recall that in Chapter SPA-1 we discussed an intervention called Critical Incident Stress Debriefing (CISD), in which people who have witnessed a horrific event are asked to relive the event as soon as possible in a 3- to 4-hour session, describing their experiences in detail and discussing their emotional reactions to the event. As we saw, CISD has been shown, in well-controlled studies, *not* to be beneficial. But why does writing about an event help people recover when reliving it in a CISD session does not? One reason appears to be the timing. The writing exercise works best if enough time has passed to allow people to gain a new perspective on the incident. In contrast, right after the event occurs is not a good time to try to relive it, reframe it, or understand it in a different way. In fact, one problem with CISD is that it can solidify memories of the bad things that occurred, rather than helping people to reframe them. Thus, if you would like to try the writing exercise, allow some time to pass to make it easier to gain some perspective on what happened to you. You can find instructions about how to do the exercise on the Writing and Health section of James Pennebaker's Web site: homepage.psy.utexas.edu/homepage/Faculty/Pennebaker/Home2000/WritingandHealth.html

In sum, research shows that humans are often remarkably resilient in the face of adversity, particularly if they can maintain a sense of control. Seeking social support can help. If people continue to be troubled by the memories of stressful events, it may help to use Pennebaker's writing technique to help make sense of what happened and what it means.

Prevention: Promoting Healthier Behavior

Many serious health problems would be prevented if people adopted different habits and avoided risky behaviors. According to one estimate, the causes of half the deaths in the United States each year are preventable (Mokdad et al., 2004). More than 33 million people worldwide are currently infected with the HIV virus, and in 2008, 2 million people died of AIDS ("Global statistics," 2011). Most cases are in Sub-Saharan Africa, although no continent is free of the disease. Most of these cases could have been avoided if people had used condoms during sexual intercourse. Fortunately, the use of condoms is increasing in the United States; one survey found that among teenagers, 80% of males used a condom the first time they had sex. But that means that 20% did not (Martinez, Copen, & Abma, 2011). And although condom use is increasing in some African countries, in others it remains very low (UNAIDS Factsheet, n.d.).

Many serious health problems are preventable, including those resulting from unsafe sex, smoking, and overeating. Social psychologists have designed many successful interventions to improve health habits, such as programs that encourage people to use condoms.

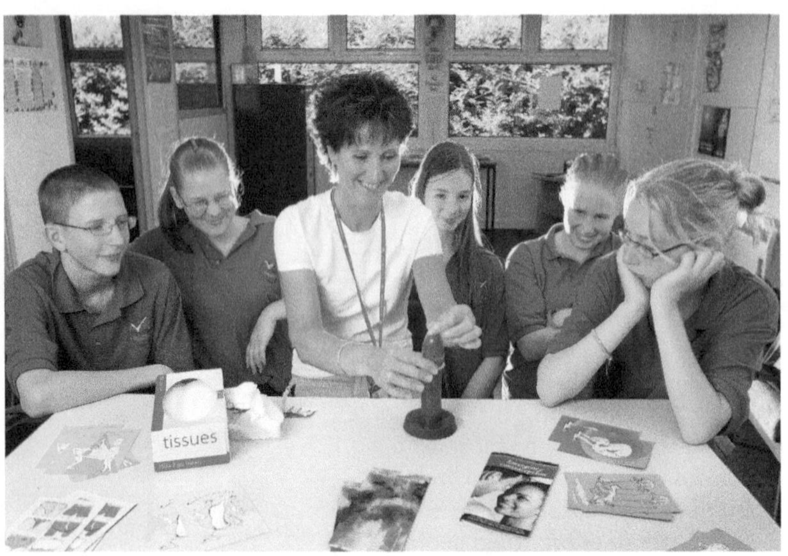

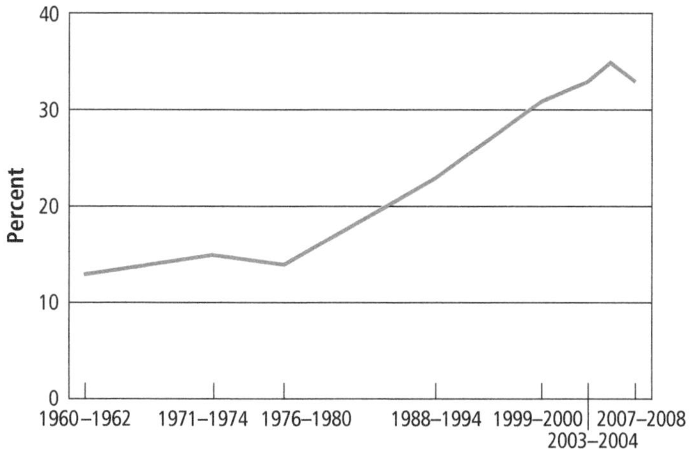

Figure SPA-2.4

Obesity Rates in the United States Over Time

The percentage of American adults who are obese (defined here as having a body mass index of 30 or above) has risen dramatically since 1960.

(Obesity and Overweight, 2011)

People could improve their health behaviors in many other areas as well, such as alcohol consumption, smoking, and overeating. Binge drinking, defined as five or more drinks in a short period of time for men and four or more for women (Wechsler & Austin, 1998), is a problem on many college campuses. Binge drinkers are at heightened risk for a number of health problems, including high blood pressure, heart disease, liver disease, meningitis, and sexually transmitted diseases. They are also more likely to be in car accidents, die by drowning, have unwanted pregnancies, experience domestic violence, and have difficulty performing sexually (Naimi et al., 2003; "Quick stats," 2008).

Americans are doing a good job of improving one unhealthy habit—namely, smoking cigarettes. Smoking rates have been declining steadily in the United States. For example, in 1995 35% of high school students reported that they smoked, but in 2009 only 20% reported that they smoked ("Trends in prevalence of tobacco use," 2009). Nonetheless, tobacco use remains the number one cause of preventable deaths in the United States. What is number two? It might surprise you to learn that it is obesity, an area in which Americans are not doing such a good job (Figure SPA-2.4). More than 1 in 3 Americans are obese, which is associated with such health problems as high blood pressure, diabetes, heart disease, and cancer of the breast, prostate, and colon ("Adult obesity," 2011).

Watch on **MyPsychLab**
To learn more about health behaviors, watch the MyPsychLab video ***You Are What You Eat.***

We realize that we have just maligned what many people consider to be the chief pleasures of life: sex, eating, drinking, and smoking. Health problems resulting from these behaviors are prevalent precisely because they are so pleasurable—in some cases (e.g., smoking), addictive. It is thus a challenge to find ways to change people's attitudes and behaviors in ways that lead to better health habits. How might we do so?

By now you know that this is a classic social psychological issue. It should be possible to put theories into action theories of attitude change and social influence to help people to act in healthier ways. Indeed, there is a great deal of research on this very question, and social psychologists have had considerable success in designing programs to get people to use condoms, quit smoking, drink less, and engage in a variety of preventive behaviors, such as using sunscreens (Noar, Benac, & Harris, 2007; Salovey & Rothman, 2003; Taylor, 2010). Many of these programs use social psychological principles covered elsewhere in this text—for example, the attitude-change techniques discussed in Chapter 7. Perhaps you can think of ways to adopt some of these approaches in your own life.

"Maybe we shouldn't have kicked all our bad habits."

Summary

What effects does stress have on our health?

- **Stress and Human Health** The relationship between stress and human health has received a great deal of attention from social psychologists.
  - **Resilience** People have been found to be surprisingly resilient when they experience negative events, often showing only mild, transient reactions, followed by a quick return to normal, healthy functioning.
  - **Effects of Negative Life Events** Nonetheless, stressful events can have debilitating effects on people's psychological and physical health. Some studies calculate the number of stressful events people are experiencing and use that to predict their health.
  - **Perceived Stress and Health** Stress is best defined as the negative feelings and beliefs that arise when people feel unable to cope with demands from their environment. The more stress people experience, the more likely they are to get sick (e.g., catch a cold).
  - **Feeling in Charge: The Importance of Perceived Control** People perceive negative events as stressful if they feel they cannot control them. In the last 40 years, college students have increasingly adopted an external locus of control, which is the tendency to believe that good and bad outcomes are out of their control. The less control people believe they have, the more likely it is that the event will cause them physical and psychological problems. For example, the loss of control experienced by many older people in nursing homes can have negative effects on their health.

What can people do to cope and recover after a stressful experience?

- **Coping with Stress** Coping styles refer to the ways in which people react to stressful events.
  - **Gender Differences in Coping with Stress** Men are more likely to react to stress with a **fight-or-flight reaction**, responding to stress by either attacking the source of the stress or fleeing from it. Women are more likely to react to stress with a **tend-and-befriend reaction**, responding to stress with nurturant activities designed to protect themselves and their offspring (tending) and creating social networks that provide protection from threats (befriending).
  - **Social Support: Getting Help from Others** Social support—the perception that other people are responsive to one's needs—is beneficial for men and women. The form of social support, however, is important. People react better to invisible than visible support. People from individualistic cultures react well when they directly ask for support, whereas people from collectivistic cultures react well when they get support without disclosing that they are having problems.
  - **Reframing: Finding Meaning in Traumatic Events** Other researchers focus on ways of coping with stress that everyone can adopt. Several studies show that reframing traumatic events, by writing or talking about one's problems, has long-term health benefits.

How can we apply social psychology to help people live healthier lives?

- **Prevention: Promoting Healthier Behavior** It also important to find ways to help people change their health habits more directly.

Chapter SPA-2 Test

Study and Review on MyPsychLab

1. After her husband died, Rachel did not experience significant distress. Within a few weeks she had returned to her usual activities and regained a cheerful outlook on life. Which is most true, according to research discussed in this chapter?
   a. Rachel's lack of distress indicates the likelihood of poor psychological adjustment.
   b. Because Rachel did not experience extreme grief, she was probably in a troubled marriage and did not love her husband very much.
   c. Although life's traumas can be quite painful, many people have the resources to recover from them quickly.
   d. Rachel is showing "delayed grief syndrome" and will probably experience grief later.

2. Bob's grandmother died recently, and he just found out that his girlfriend cheated on him. He is also in the middle of final exams. According to research on stress and health, which is most true?
   a. Because Bob is experiencing so many negative life events, he will almost certainly get sick.
   b. These life events will be stressful for Bob only if he interprets them as stressful—in other words, if he feels unable to cope with the events.
   c. When under stress, a person's immune system is stimulated. Therefore, Bob is less likely to get sick now than he normally would.
   d. If Bob feels more in control of these events than he really is, he is especially likely to get sick.

3. Lindsay does an internship at a nursing home. According to research discussed in this chapter, which of the following would be most likely to benefit the residents?
   a. Lindsay encourages the residents to talk to her about any stressful issues in their lives.
   b. Lindsay allows the residents to choose what time she will come to visit them, and when her internship ends, she decides to keep visiting the residents when they ask her to.
   c. Lindsay allows the residents to choose what time she will come to visit them, but when her internship ends, she doesn't visit the nursing home anymore.
   d. Lindsay gives the residents a plant and makes sure to water it for them.

4. Which of the following is *most true* about research on social support?
   a. Social support of all kinds has been found to be beneficial to people in all cultures.
   b. If you are thinking of helping someone, it is better to give them invisible rather than visible social support.
   c. If you are thinking of helping someone, it is better to given them visible rather than invisible social support.
   d. Members of East Asian cultures are more likely to seek help from others than are members of Western cultures.

5. Which of the following is *most true* of research on coping styles?
   a. Women are most likely to show the fight-or-flight response.
   b. Men are most likely to show the tend-and-befriend response.
   c. Women are mostly likely to show the tend-and-befriend response.
   d. Men and women tend to cope with stress in the same ways.

6. Michael's roommate has come down with a cold. In which of the following circumstances is Michael most likely to catch his roommate's cold?
   a. Michael's girlfriend just broke up with him, but he knew it was coming and doesn't view it as all that bad a thing.
   b. Michael's goldfish just died, which he views as a very negative event.
   c. Michael hasn't been exercising very much lately.
   d. It doesn't matter what is going on in Michael's life; all that matters is whether he is exposed to the virus that causes the cold.

7. Kate has had a hard time getting over her parents' divorce. According to social psychological research, which of the following would probably help Kate the most?
   a. She should spend 15 minutes a night on 4 consecutive nights writing about her feelings about the divorce.
   b. She should try to attribute the divorce to internal, global, stable things about herself.
   c. She should avoid talking about the divorce with her closest friends because it would probably just depress them.
   d. She should focus on the fact that she has low self-efficacy to improve her relationship with her parents.

8. Which of the following is *least true*?
   a. Although obesity is increasing in the United States, it is not a major health problem.
   b. Many serious health problems are preventable, and social psychological interventions have been developed to get people to act in healthier ways.
   c. Binge drinkers are more likely than others to have serious health problems.
   d. Although the percentage of people who smoke cigarettes is going down, tobacco use is still a major cause of preventable deaths.

Answer Key

1-c, 2-b, 3-b, 4-d, 5-c, 6-b, 7-a, 8-a

Scoring the TRY IT! exercises

■ **Page 426**

1. You get 1 point each time you answered true (T) to questions 1, 4, 5, 6, and 10 and 1 point for each time you answered false (F) to questions 2, 3, 7, 8, and 9.
2. This scale was developed to measure what the researchers call *appraisal social support*, or "the perceived availability of someone to talk to about one's problems" (Cohen et al., 1985, pp. 75–76). One of the findings was that when people were not under stress, those low in social support had no more physical symptoms than people high in social support did. When people were under stress, however, those low in social support had more physical symptoms than did people high in social support. Another finding was that women scored reliably higher on the social support scale than men did. If you scored lower than you would like, you might want to consider reaching out to others more when you are under stress.

In the News

The Political Effects of the Terrorist Attacks on the United States

An American Airlines flight from Boston to Los Angeles had been driven by Islamic hijackers in the north tower of the World Trade Center; here, a few minutes later, a United Airlines plane on the same flight path exploded in a fireball as it crashed into the south tower.

Three hijacked airliners struck the World Trade Center towers and the Pentagon early on the morning of September 11, 2001. By noon, about 3,000 people had been killed: the hijackers, the plane passengers, occupants of the buildings, and rescue workers among them. The actual collisions with the Twin Towers were videotaped and soon were on television throughout the world. Normal programming ceased so that the tragedy could be covered. Almost everyone watched or listened. Even those not directly connected to the tragedy cycled through intense emotions of fear, horror, and anger. Normal life ground to a halt.

Over the next few days, more information came out about the hijackers, and the U. S. government began to formulate plans to punish those who had been responsible for the attacks, to prevent further terrorist damage, and to root out terrorist activities throughout the world. Democrats joined with Republicans in bipartisan support of the administration's efforts. Public opinion surged to support the president and his plans for a long-term "war on terrorism." American flags were being displayed everywhere. Soon the Saudi millionaire Osama bin Laden was identified as a prime organizer of the extremist groups responsible for the attacks.

As time wore on, there was speculation about the long-term effects of the attack on U.S. society. The stock market plunged, the airlines and the tourist industry suffered drastic reductions in ridership and revenue, and an already weakened economy staggered. How long would the bipartisan spirit in Washington last? How would the terrorist attacks affect the outcome of the next elections, with a government balanced almost exactly evenly between Democrats and Republicans? Reports of hate crimes and discrimination against Arab Americans began to circulate. Security was being tightened in many ways, immigrants from the Mideast were being detained and prevented from flying, and surveillance of persons suspected of ties to terrorist groups were increased. How far would the new restrictions on basic civil liberties go? Some divisions of opinion began to show up in the support of costly military actions, with men more supportive than women. And there was much speculation about the long-term effects on children, who had been exposed to such vivid images of violence and death.

SOCIAL PSYCHOLOGY AND POLITICS

Focus of This Chapter

- **Public Opinion and Voting**
- **Political Socialization**
- **Group Conflict**
- **The Mass Media and Political Persuasion**
- **A New Look at the Media**
- **International Conflict**
- **Cultural Highlight: Becoming Political in America**

These questions are the stuff of political psychology. It is concerned with, among other things, voting behavior and how it is affected by partisanship and the strength of the economy; the political socialization of preadults and the role of vivid political events in it; the main group conflicts in politics and how they affect support for the civil liberties embodied in the Bill of Rights; the kinds of effects the media have and under what conditions; whether an attack on the nation usually stirs up a frenzy of patriotism and support for the president; and whether it makes people need to identify an enemy, such as Osama bin Laden. A complex series of events like these raises many questions for all of us; political psychology addresses the human side of many of them.

Public Opinion and Voting

One major focus in political psychology has been on public opinion and voting behavior. The main method of studying these topics has been public opinion surveys. The sometimes conflicting polls conducted during election campaigns can give rise to worries about their accuracy, but in reality, much of that inconsistency and volatility is due to the fact that some voters do not arrive at firm decisions until relatively late in the campaign (Abramson et al., 1998). In fact, polls taken close to Election Day generally prove to be quite accurate. As shown in Table 15–1, they came very close in 2000, though slightly underestimating the Gore vote.

How do we understand voting behavior? The most influential early study, done during the 1940 presidential campaign, found that relatively few voters changed their preferences (Lazarsfeld, Berelson, & Gaudet, 1948). About 80 percent were stably committed to one candidate or another in May, before the campaign even began. Furthermore, people ultimately voted quite consistently with their own social background. Working-class, urban, and Catholic voters supported the Democrats, and

Table 15.1

2001 Presidential Election: Final Pre-election Poll Results

	Date	Percentage for Gore	Percentage for Bush	Percentage for Other
Polls				
Gallup-USA Today-CNN	Nov. 6	46	48	6
Reuters/MSNBC	Nov. 6	48	46	6
CBS	Nov. 6	48	47	5
Voter.com	Nov. 6	45	50	4
Average		47	48	5
Actual outcome	Nov. 7	49	48	3

Note: Respondents who did not express a preference are not shown.
Source: Data from the *New York Times*, December 30, 2000; <www.pollingreport.com> November 7, 2000.

middle-class, rural, and Protestant voters supported the Republicans. Even most initially undecided voters subsequently chose a candidate consistent with such predispositions.

That study was done many years ago. Today the many polls done throughout a presidential campaign sometimes give the impression of much more volatility than that early study would suggest. Nevertheless, its basic finding holds up well today: Most voters have quite predictable preferences by the beginning of presidential campaigns, even though some say they have not decided for certain. Indeed, in recent years, statistical models have been developed that can forecast the outcome of most presidential elections within a percentage point or two on the basis of information known before the campaign even begins, such as the strength of the economy and public approval of the president (Bartels, 1993; Lewis-Beck & Stegmair, 2000). This is not to say that campaigns have no impact at all. Sometimes the ultimate winner runs behind in early polls because the campaign itself will be required to convey this information to the voters about the economy and approval of the president. And both sides' campaigns are usually run so professionally that they often simply offset each other and, in that sense, are crucial elements in achieving the predicted outcome. If one side did not campaign at all, they would most likely lose.

Party Identification

The theory of voting behavior that remains dominant today was published a few years after that early study, in *The American Voter* (Campbell, Converse, Miller, & Stokes, 1960). This theory includes two important ideas. First, it argues that voters decide primarily by deriving a candidate preference from a long-standing **party identification,** a "standing decision" to favor one party over the other. The usual approach to measuring this identification is shown in Figure 15–1. Every respondent is asked two questions, which then place the person on a 7-point scale ranging from "Strong Democrat" to "Strong Republican."

Then, by a simple process of **cognitive consistency** (as described in Chapter 5), party identification shapes the voters' attitudes toward the candidates and issues of the current election campaign. For example, lifelong Republicans tended to evaluate George W. Bush favorably and Al Gore unfavorably in 2000, approving of Bush's support for large tax cuts and increased defense spending, among other issues. These attitudes toward the candidates and issues, in turn, influence the individual's vote choice and enable us to predict it quite accurately well in advance of the election.

Even today, despite a common impression to the contrary, voters continue to be quite loyal to their traditional party moorings. The number of people who identify strongly with the two parties has not changed much in recent years. Furthermore, as shown in Table 15–2, their party loyalty in terms of presidential voting remains high. In 2000, 96 percent of the strong Democrats voted for Gore, and 99 percent of the strong Republicans voted for Bush (Abramson et al., 2000). Indeed the impact of partisan loyalties on voting behavior has steadily increased, since the mid-1970s, in both presidential and congressional elections (Bartels, 2000). Voters are increasingly likely to vote for the same party at both levels, rather than splitting their ticket. And their subjective feelings about the parties have become even more straightforwardly partisan, liking their party and disliking the opposition (Hetherington, 2001).

If party identification is such a strong factor in voting decisions, how has it happened that much of the time the presidency and the Congressional majority are held by opposite parties? Have many voters decided they actually prefer divided government, to protect against placing excessive power in the hands of either party? Do they vote against their party identification to ensure this split? There are a few people who do this. Sigelman and his colleagues (1997) found that a little fewer than 10 percent both said they preferred divided control and actually voted for it. And these deliberate ticket splitters are somewhat more politically sophisticated than the average voter (Abramowitz, 2001).

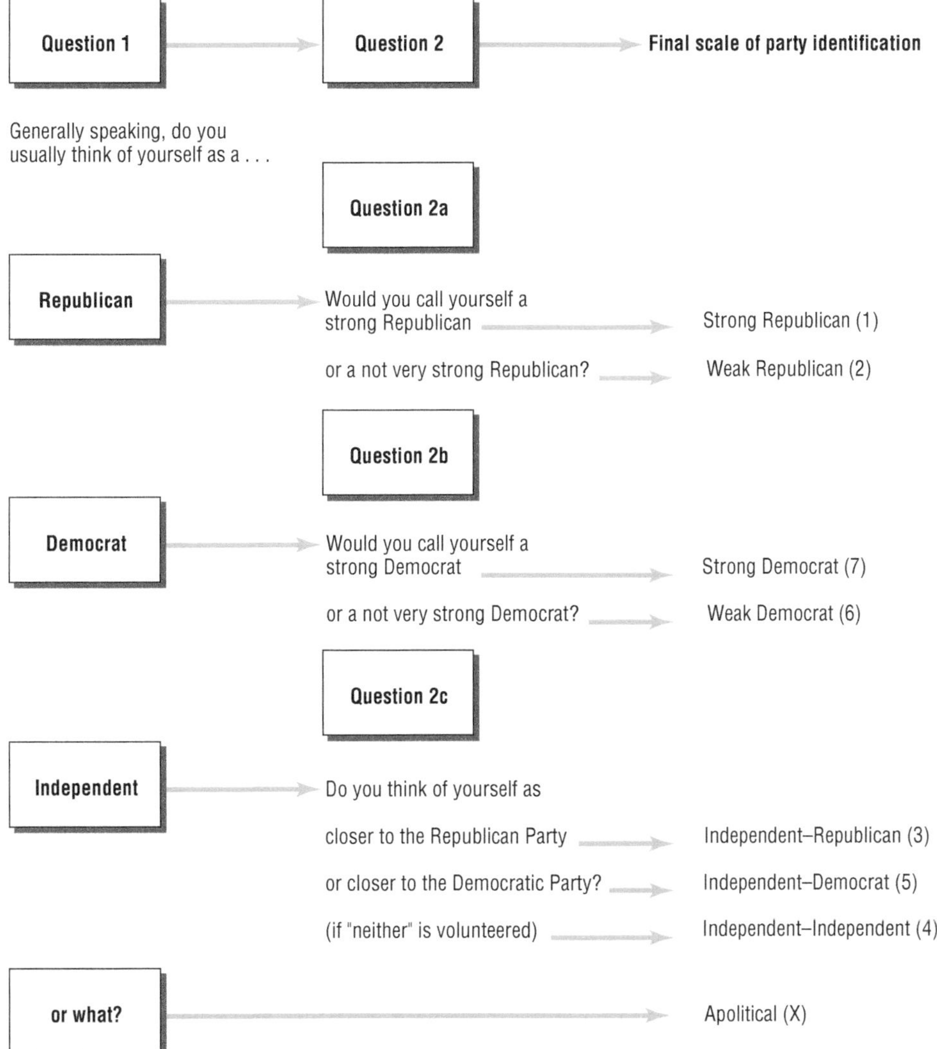

Figure 15–1 **Measuring Party Identification.**

Table 15.2

Votes for Democratic Presidential Candidate as a Function of Party Identification, in Percentages

Party Identification	1952	1976	2000
Strong Democrat	82	88	96
Weak Democrat	61	72	81
Independent, leans Democrat	60	73	72
Independent, no partisan leanings	18	41	44
Independent, leans Republican	7	15	15
Weak Republican	4	22	16
Strong Republican	2	3	1

Source: Data from Abramson et al. (2002), p. 177.

In the years since it was published, *The American Voter*'s view of party identification has been challenged in a number of ways. The revisionists' major contention is that voting choices are influenced by current political and economic realities, not simply by long-standing psychological dispositions such as party identification. They argue that voters make reasonable judgments about the performance of the current officeholder and support effective incumbents or oppose ineffective ones, even if those judgments contrast with their party identification (Fiorina, 1981). Moreover, an individual's party identification can itself shift in response to ongoing political issues and events, such as wars, crime rates, economic recessions, or unpopular candidates (Franklin, 1984; Luskin, McIver, & Carmines, 1989).

Nevertheless, over time, relatively few adult voters change their party identification much, and their voting decisions are usually quite consistent with it (Miller, 1992). So major long term changes in party balance are not common. However, there is consensus on at least one such change in recent decades: the shift of southern white voters to the Republican Party beginning in the 1950s. In 1952, almost 80 percent of white southerners were Democrats, whereas in 1994, slightly over 40 percent were (Miller & Shanks, 1996). The reasons for the shift remain a matter of debate, with some attributing it to the increasing conservatism of the Republican Party on issues of race, thereby appealing to white southerners' historic racial prejudices (Valentino & Sears, 2000), and others, to Republicans' conservatism on other issues, such as abortion, gun control, and a strong military (Petrocik, 1987).

Economic Voting

Considerable research has also focused on how people adjust their preferences based on changes in the economy. Kramer (1971) observed that the outcomes of congressional elections are strongly correlated with the health of the general economy. The president's party tends to lose ground when the economy is weak and does well when the economy is strong. These findings have been repeated many times in the United States and Europe (Lewis-Beck & Stegmair, 2000). They have led to the forecasting models mentioned earlier. Such models do a reasonably good job in predicting the outcome of presidential or congressional elections, though the prediction is considerably better when presidential job approval and issues' preferences are also considered.

Such findings might suggest widespread **pocketbook voting.** Perhaps when people are doing well personally, they support the party in power, and when they are doing poorly, they "throw the rascals out." However, voting on the basis of the strength of the economy might be explained without assuming that they are voting so self-interestedly. Even those who are doing well personally may vote against the president's party when the national economy is doing poorly, basing their vote on how good a job the president is doing for the nation as a whole, or **sociotropic voting.**

In general, sociotropic voting is much more common than pocketbook voting (Kinder & Kiewiet, 1979). Indeed, the level of pocketbook voting is usually not even statistically detectable in U.S. presidential and congressional elections, or in European parliamentary elections (Lewis Beck & Stegmeir, 2000). **Self-interest** also appears to play a minor role in determining a wide variety of other political attitudes, such as toward issues of unemployment, health care, crime, energy shortages, and even war (Sears & Funk, 1991). There are exceptions: Smokers and gun owners have been shown to be especially opposed to restrictions on cigarette smoking and gun ownership, and those who pay the most taxes are the most supportive of tax-cutting proposals (e.g., Green & Gerken, 1989; Sears & Citrin, 1985; Wolpert & Gimpel, 1998). But exceptions are relatively rare. Note that this weak role of self-interest parallels the findings discussed in Chapter 6 that material self interest also tends to play a minor role in racial and ethnic prejudices.

Why is self-interested voting rare? One answer is that the personal effects of government policies are usually not large enough, direct enough, or clear enough to the voters to influence their votes very strongly (Green, 1988; Sears & Funk, 1991). When those stakes are large and clear, self-interest does become a more powerful motive. One good example was Proposition 13 in California in 1978. This proposition promised major and specific cuts in property taxes. As shown in Table 15–3, support for it was highest among people who had expected the heaviest increases in property taxes at a time when inflation was driving tax assessments higher. However other factors played an equally important role, such as party identification, ideology, and racial attitudes (Sears & Citrin, 1985). The vote was not a matter of pure economic self-interest; it generated much standard political controversy as well.

Table 15.3

Support for Proposition 13 as a Function of a Previously Expected Rise in Property Taxes

	Percentage of Sample	Support
Expected no increase in property taxes		
Renters	36	46
Owners	4	52
Expected increase in property taxes		
Don't know amount	14	63
Up to $200	11	67
$200–$399	15	77
$400–$599	5	80
$600–$799	3	86
$800–$999	2	96
$1,000+	8	84
Total	98	

Note: Total falls short of 100 percent because of rounding error.
Source: California Poll (Sears & Citrin, 1985, p. 119).

A second answer is that voters are more likely to attribute changes in their personal financial well being to their own personal situation, abilities, and efforts than to the government or the president. If we lose our job, we blame the boss, an inept firm that is losing business, or perhaps our own lack of skill or lazy work habits. We usually do not blame the president or our congressional representative, so there is no reason to vote against either one. In contrast, people are likely to attribute responsibility for the health of the *nation's* economy to political leaders, especially to the president, an attribution providing a good reason for sociotropic voting (Feldman, 1982).

The Cognitively Limited Voter

The other main argument made in *The American Voter* was that relatively few people base their votes on informed, consistent, and sophisticated political thinking. For one thing, most citizens are not very informed about the ongoing political process. Typical examples from recent surveys are that only 3 percent could identify William Rehnquist, the Chief Justice of the U.S. Supreme Court; about 25 percent knew that U.S. senators serve 6-year terms; about 33 percent could identify Yasir Arafat, the leader of the Palestinian Liberation Organization; and about 50 percent knew which party had the majority in the House of Representatives (Gilens, 2001; Kinder, 1998).

Even if most Americans do not follow the details of politics very closely, perhaps they have clear preferences about what the government should be doing. Unhappily, that often proves not to be the case either. Converse (1970) coined the term **non-attitudes** to describe the fact that many people seem to respond more-or-less randomly when asked detailed questions about what policies the government should pursue. When asked on one occasion, they would give one answer, then many would switch when asked later, and when asked a third time, as many of the previous switchers would switch back as would stay put.

Political elites, such as legislators or convention delegates, usually do organize their attitudes in terms of a political **ideology** such as liberalism or conservatism (Jennings, 1992). But relatively few voters think about politics in such broad, abstract terms. Moreover, many do not have attitudes on the issues that follow a very consistent liberal or conservative pattern (Converse, 1964; Kinder, 1998). For example, ardent environmentalists do not necessarily favor government aid for childcare, even though both are liberal positions. Many people want tax reductions but oppose cutting government spending on the public schools or the police (Sears & Citrin, 1985). Almost everyone believes in the general principle of free speech for all, but many would not extend it to groups they dislike, such as communists, atheists, or racists (Sullivan, Piereson, & Marcus, 1982). Such inconsistencies suggest a low level of ideological thinking in the mass public.

This view of most voters as having unstable, inconsistent, and nonideological attitudes has been challenged in various ways. One set of scholars does not disagree very much with the findings of inconsistency just described but suggests that citizens may be making meaningful political choices nonetheless. Voters may be "rationally ignorant," saving time and energy by not following politics closely, and using cognitive shortcuts or heuristics (see Chapter 3) to arrive at political decisions. "On-line processing" is one such cognitive shortcut. When we hear something new about a candidate, we may use it to adjust our standing evaluation of her without committing it to memory. If a candidate for governor comes out for expanding the freeway system, we may raise our evaluation of her because of our concern about traffic congestion, but later we may not even remember that she took that position. All we need to know is that we like her; we don't need to know why. Information may be incorporated appropriately into voters' preferences without their retaining its content (Lodge & Steenbergen, 1995).

Similarly, most voters most of the time may in fact "vote correctly," in the sense of voting consistently with their own values and beliefs taken as a whole, even though they usually do not take the time to review all their thoughts very thoroughly (Lau & Redlawsk, 1997). Still, it can be shown that people with relatively little general political information do not support the issue positions that they would if they were better informed (Delli Carpini & Keeter, 2000). The same is true of information about an issue area, such as not knowing that the crime rate has been dropping for a number of years. Poorly informed people do not hold the same attitudes toward the issue that they would if they had "the facts" (Gilens, 2001). So they may be "rationally ignorant," but are they as wise as we might hope?

Another interpretation of these findings is that unstable and inconsistent attitudes may reflect a pattern of genuine **ambivalence.** After all, issues become divisive and hotly debated only when there are good arguments on both sides. People often agree with some of the arguments on both sides. In one study, this was shown by asking people for all their thoughts about whether the government should guarantee everyone a decent job or whether everyone should just get along on her or his own without government help (Zaller & Feldman, 1992). Almost half expressed both a thought emphasizing a humanitarian need to help the disadvantaged *and* a thought emphasizing the need to limit the government in some way. Similarly, almost one third of the voters typically express both positive and negative thoughts about any given presidential candidate (Lavine, 2001).

Ambivalence has a couple of important consequences. It may explain much of the apparent instability of people's attitudes over time. When asked for his opinion at one time, a person may respond in terms of whatever arguments come to his mind at the moment. When asked at a later time, different arguments might come to mind, some perhaps on the other side of the issue, so his second opinion may be somewhat different. His opinion might therefore seem inconsistent over time even though he may have held the same ambivalent set of thoughts on both occasions.

Also, ambivalence may lead to an underestimation of how grounded an attitude is in underlying values. For example, at one time a woman might think about the issue of legalized abortion in terms of women's rights to choose and might support it. The next time, she might think of her conservative religious values and might oppose it. In each case, her expressed opinion will seem inconsistent with some of her underlying values just because she is ambivalent. An observer would not understand that because he or she would not have access to the full range of the woman's thoughts about the issue; the woman was only asked whether she favored or opposed legalized abortion (Alvarez & Brehm, 1995).

Domains of Consistency

Still other scholars suggest that those examples of non-attitudes and ambivalence may have highlighted the areas in which voters look the worst. Perhaps they would look more consistent if we looked elsewhere. For one thing, on any given issue, at least a few people do have informed and meaningful attitudes. Members of the PTA are often well informed about the schools, and members of the American Civil Liberties Union (ACLU) about issues of free speech. Such people have been described as the **issue public** for that issue domain (Krosnick, 1990). Since they are well informed about that issue and have clear preferences, they are the crucial audience for any new government proposals.

Moreover, not all issues draw nonattitudes. Some attitudes are stable and consistent in many people, especially when the attitudes are grounded in fundamental values (Sears, 1983b). For example, opponents of legalized abortion tend to have quite stable and consistent attitudes toward it, based in religiosity and moral traditionalism (Sears & Huddy, 1990; Zucker, 1999). People tend to have stable and consistent attitudes about racial policies like affirmative action, grounded both in racial prejudices and in ideology (Sears et al., 1997). Attitudes about aid to the disadvantaged, such as government-supported health care or aid to the homeless, tend to be quite consistent with more general values about equality (Kinder & Sanders, 1996).

Finally, ideological self-identification—whether or not people fully understand it—has become increasingly important in recent years in partisan politics. Democrats are now sharply more liberal than Republicans on such issues as abortion, minority rights, and cuts in defense spending. And self-identification as a "liberal" or as a "conservative" has become an increasingly useful guide to party identification since the 1970's with liberals lining up as Democrats and conservatives as Republicans (Abramowitz & Saunders, 1998). Younger voters in particular seem increasingly to be choosing their political party based on ideological affinity and are more ideologically polarized than earlier generations (Miller, 1992). Basic values and ideological self-identification, then, are meaningful ways in which many voters develop their attitudes toward specific issues, the parties, and the candidates.

Political Socialization

Like many other things, our political lives begin in childhood. Fundamental political attitudes, such as party identification, basic social and moral values, racial attitudes, and other crucial predispositions, seem to be acquired before adulthood (Hyman, 1959). Therefore, we should take a close look at preadult **political socialization.**

Early Acquisition

Attitudes are assumed to be learned in the same way as any other disposition, through the basic processes of association, reinforcement, and imitation described in Chapter 5. *The American Voter* concluded that party identification, the most important determinant of voting behavior, typically develops before adulthood and is significantly influenced by one's family, and that most adults have not changed their party identifications for many years. Although there has been much research on these questions in recent years, these basic conclusions still hold up quite well.

Party identification is therefore an important starting point for examining the political socialization process. One major national survey of high school seniors showed that they strongly tended to favor the political party of their parents; only about 10 percent favored the opposite party (Jennings & Niemi, 1974). The same survey revealed that in the previous election, 83 percent of the high school students had favored the same presidential candidate as their parents. However, parent-offspring agreement was much lower in many other areas. For example, the students were as likely to disagree with their parents as to agree about how much "the people in government" can be trusted.

Why do parents sometimes have a major impact on their children's attitudes, and sometimes not? The main reason is that parents' influence is greatest on issues about which they communicate clearly and repeatedly. For example, 92 percent of the students surveyed were able, in the heat of an election campaign, to report accurately which candidate their parents favored (Niemi, 1974). Parents with the most political influence over their children tend themselves to be most politicized—those who read the political news most often and who participate in politics in the widest variety of ways (Beck & Jennings, 1991). For example, the strongest student activists in the 1960s reflected their parents' party preferences almost perfectly; also, most had been exposed to unusually strong political socialization that emphasized their standing up for their own beliefs (Braungart & Braungart, 1990). But parents do not have a major influence on all of their children's attitudes. They have more influence on simple and concrete choices that come up often, such as candidate preference or religious denomination, and less on choices that come up only once in a long while, such as attitudes toward Argentina or the metric system (Niemi, 1974).

How and when do children acquire their party identification? Is it simply a matter of dinner table ritual, such as the parent saying, "I'm a Republican, you're a Republican, now shut up!"? If so, it might seem to be a process that has little to do with rational judgments about what is going on in the political world and which side actually deserves

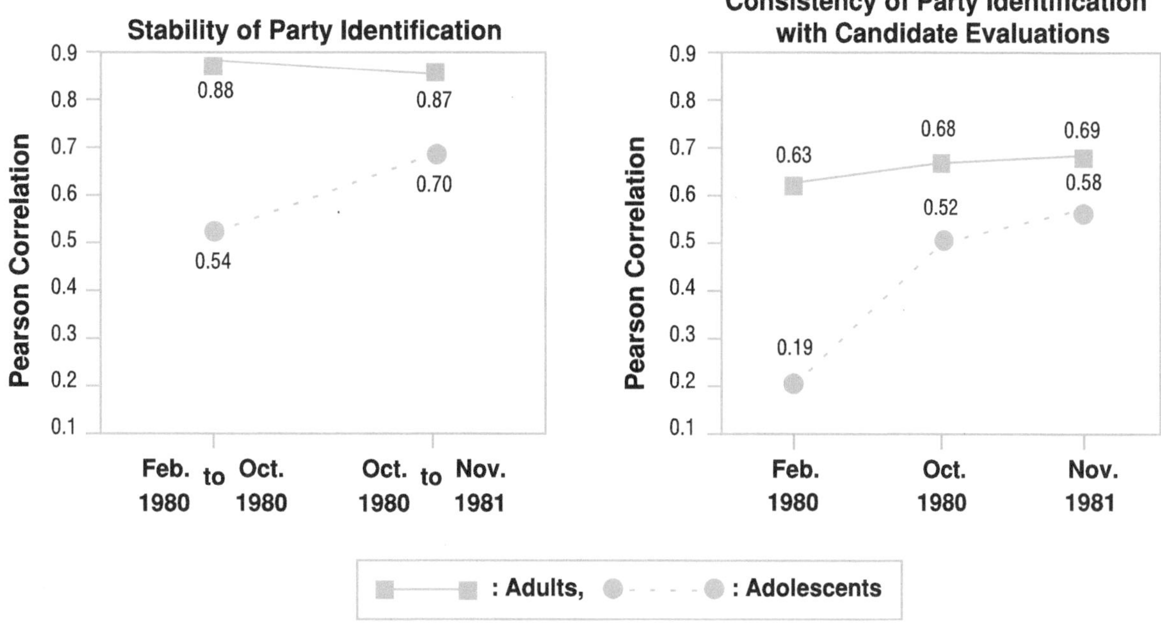

Figure 15–2 **Effects of Presidential Campaigns on Strength of Party Identification.**

Source: Sears and Valentino (1997), p. 54.

to be supported on the basis of its policies and performance. But recent research suggests that the socialization process is more closely tied to political events in the real world than that parental command would suggest. This was shown in a three-wave panel survey of adolescents and their parents, in which the first interview occurred in February 1980 before the first presidential primary, the second in October just before the election, and the third a year after the election (Sears & Valentino, 1997). The hypothesis was that the adolescents' party identifications should have strengthened more than their parents', and have done so during the presidential campaign itself, when the flow of political information was most intense.

The campaign did indeed strengthen the adolescents' party identifications substantially, as reflected both in greater consistency between their party identification and their candidate preferences and in increased stability in their party identification over time. By both tests, the adolescents' party identifications were stronger at the end of the campaign than they had been before it, as shown in Figure 15–2. No such gains occurred for the adolescents in the year following the campaign. Nor did their parents show any such gains, since most of them had a pretty well-established party identification already. The implication is that the campaign and all the information associated with it provided a powerful opportunity for the socialization of party identification. In fact, this strengthening of partisanship was greatest among adolescents who had talked most about the campaign to family and friends (Valentino & Sears, 1998). So political events such as campaigns are critical elements in the socialization process, because they stimulate talk about politics, and that discussion strengthens young people's attitudes. Most socialization does not happen in a political vacuum.

Long-Term Persistence

Do such early acquired predispositions indeed usually last throughout life, as *The American Voter* suggested? Three general hypotheses might be contrasted: (1) **persistence**—preadult attitudes remain more or less the same through our lifetime (or perhaps even strengthen with time); (2) **impressionable years**—our attitudes are still susceptible to change in late adolescence and early adulthood, when we leave the parental home and begin to establish our own identities, but thereafter they do not change much; and (3) **lifelong openness**—basic attitudes are always open to change (Sears, 1989).

Longitudinal studies that have followed individuals' political attitudes over many years provide the best tests of these hypotheses. They have found that basic political attitudes, such as party identification, racial prejudice, and political ideology, usually do not change much after early adulthood. For example, one study of a large sample of Californians found that most people had stuck with their original preferences from 1940 (when they were about 30 years old, on average) to 1977, though with a slight drift toward the Republican Party (Sears & Funk, 1999). Similar levels of stability have emerged from studies of nationally representative samples followed over shorter periods (Converse & Markus, 1979; Green & Palmquist, 1994; Jennings & Markus, 1984).

Likewise student activists from the 1960s typically maintained quite a strong commitment to their original political ideals many years later. When the high school seniors first interviewed in 1965 were reinterviewed in 1982, nearly two decades later, those who had engaged in some political protest in the late 1960s or early 1970s were still distinctly more liberal than the former nonprotestors, as shown in Table 15–4 (Jennings, 1987). Another study showed that white civil rights workers who had gone to the South in the 1960s to help African Americans register to vote still maintained liberal or radical positions on virtually all political issues 20 years later (Marwell et al., 1987).

But what happens when young people go to college? Young adults who have spent their lives in their parents' homes and surrounded by childhood friends may then be introduced to new ideas and new kinds of people. Under some circumstances, there is a profound effect. A classic demonstration was provided by Theodore Newcomb's (1943) study of Bennington College students. This small, exclusive women's college in Vermont first opened with a very liberal faculty in the early 1930s. Most of the students came from affluent, conservative Republican families and most students arrived at college with commensurate views. Yet the dominant liberal norms of the college led many students to become substantially more liberal as they progressed through school. At graduation time, many previously conservative students had switched to the Democratic Party, while there was little movement toward the Republicans among the few who had come from liberal families.

After they left school did the students' new found liberalism persist, or did they go back to their parents' conservatism? In fact, later follow ups found that their political preferences were "unbelievably stable" over time (Alwin, Cohen, & Newcomb, 1991, p. 154). The most important factor determining stability or change was their social environment after college. Their own political preferences were almost perfectly stable for nearly 50 years after graduation—if they had husbands and friends who agreed with them. The newly liberal Bennington alumnae had generally married liberal husbands

Table 15.4

Political Attitudes in 1982 among Those Who Had or Had Not Engaged in Protest between 1965 and 1973 (in Percentages)

	Protesters	Nonprotesters	Difference
Democratic party identification	74	43	+31
Liberal ideology	63	28	+35
Republican presidential vote	19	62	+43

Source: Data from Jennings (1987).

and had liberal close friends, while the few who had reverted to their parents' conservatism tended to have married husbands in occupations such as banking or corporate law and lived in a more conservative social world.

The Bennington story is more dramatic than what normally happens to college students. Still, significant changes in basic attitudes such as party identification and racial attitudes are most common during early adulthood, when these attitudes are not yet fully crystallized. For example, some high school students who had first been interviewed in 1965 were later found to have modified their party identifications in response to major political events such as the Vietnam War or racial conflict, when reinterviewed at age 25 (Markus, 1979). Similarly, their partisanship in 1982, though still predicted most strongly by their preadult party identification, had been significantly influenced by their attitudes toward the candidates and issues of the 1970s (Rapoport, 1997). This finding suggests that there is much to the "impressionable years" hypothesis.

An interesting application of this "impressionable years" idea has been to **collective memory.** These are memories that are broadly shared about events of the past. Karl Mannheim (1928/1952) hypothesized that such collective memories are especially powerful about events experienced during late adolescence and early adulthood. For example, adults of every age, when asked about their favorite music, cite something that they say first made an impression on them when they were about 16 years old (Schuman, Belli, & Bischoping, 1997). Baby boomers still love the Beatles, and U2 will not soon be forgotten.

The same is true of political events. One survey asked people to name one or two events in the past half century that they thought had been particularly important. World War II was mentioned by over 40 percent of those who had been in their early 20s at the time of the Pearl Harbor attack, but by fewer than 20 percent of those born in the late 1950s. The assassination of President John F. Kennedy was cited by nearly 20 percent of those who were then teenagers, but by only 1 percent of those who had been 50 or older. The Vietnam War was named by about 35 percent of those who had been of college age in the late 1960s, but by fewer than 5 percent of those who were then over 50 (Schuman & Scott, 1989). Political events, then, can leave powerful collective memories among people who were in the "impressionable years" when they occured.

Group Conflict

The role of groups in politics is especially important because so much political conflict revolves around group interests: "Who gets what?" is often the central political question. Social class is a key group division in most democracies, middle- and upper-class voters usually supporting conservative parties and working-class voters supporting parties that favor the redistribution of wealth downward. In the twentieth century in the United States, class-based political divisions were sharpest during the Great Depression, with the presidency of Franklin Delano Roosevelt, and during the 1980s, with the presidency of Ronald Reagan (Baum & Kernell, 2001). Now things are not so simple. The middle class is not so uniformly supportive of Republicans. Rather, many professionals have shifted to the Democrats, while the self-employed are strongly Republican. Similarly, white working-class voters are less pro-Democrat than they once were (Hout et al., 1995).

The most important group cleavages in U.S. politics today revolve around race, gender, and religion. Blacks and whites differ greatly in their party allegiances; indeed, blacks are the strongest Democratic loyalists of all. Among whites, racial attitudes clearly play an important role in people's policy preferences on explicitly racial issues such as busing and affirmative action, on evaluations of African-American political candidates, and even on seemingly nonracial issues such as welfare, taxes, and government spending reductions (Kinder & Sanders, 1996). However, as discussed in Chapter 6, there is disagreement about whether these racial attitudes date mainly from preadult socialization or are a response to realistic intergroup competition over power, status, and money. And an increasingly important political group is composed of Latino immigrants, as discussed in the "Cultural Highlight" box.

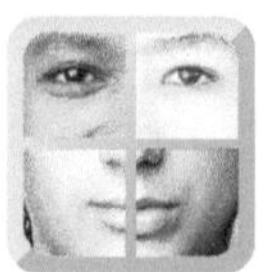

Cultural Highlight — Becoming Political in America

The rate of immigration to the United States has increased dramatically since liberalizing legislation was passed in the 1960s. What long-term political effects will this increase have? Some foresee that the new immigrants will generally follow the trajectory of the massive European immigration of a century ago (see Alba, 1990): that they will gradually, over the generations, assimilate into U.S. society, gradually replacing their original national identity with a U.S. ethnic identity, which in turn may gradually drop away. After acquiring citizenship, they will acquire a party identification, which will help guide their integration into the political system. However, some foresee a more "segmented assimilation," in which some immigrant groups follow that trajectory, while others, perhaps especially those who remain poor and with low levels of education, remain as an alienated nationality group on U.S. soil, detached from the political system (Portes & Rumbaut, 2001).

The largest immigrant group is Latino, composed primarily of immigrants from Mexico. In two recent surveys in Los Angeles County, after being asked to specify their own ethnic identity, adults were asked, "How do you primarily think of yourself: just as an American, both as an American and (ethnicity), or only as an (ethnicity)?" Table 15–A shows three distinct stages of the assimilation process. Noncitizens tended to identify themselves primarily as ethnics. Foreign-born naturalized citizens overwhelmingly said "both." The native-born were very unlikely to think of themselves primarily as ethnic and indeed resembled African Americans, almost all of whom were also native-born. With time in the United States, then, Latinos tend to assimilate to a U.S. identity, or to see themselves as hyphenated Americans (e.g., "Hispanics" or "Mexican Americans"). This pattern is not unique to Latinos: Very similar differences between immigrants and the native-born emerged in a large study of both Asian and Latino undergraduates at UCLA (Sears et al., 2001).

The European immigrants of a century ago soon became regular voters, often adopting a party identification linked to their ethnic identity in their early years of citizenship, and spurred to the polls by ethnic political organizations. What can we expect from the new waves of immigrants? Native-born Americans of all kinds usually adopt a party identification in early life, as we have seen, and it tends to get stronger as they age, as they are exposed to more information about the parties and vote more often (Converse, 1976). But immigrants often arrive at a variety of different ages. Do they follow the same pattern? Wong (2000), analyzing two large-scale surveys of Latinos and Asian Americans, found that the longer immigrants had lived in the United States, the more likely they were to have developed a party identification; how old they were did not matter much.

As these groups move through the different stages of immigration, they feel less strongly ethnic, increasingly identify with the United States, and gradually develop a party identification that will allow them to vote much as do other Americans. So far this pattern has some resemblance to the trajectory of the European immigrants of a century ago. But this area of research is just opening up, and much more needs to be learned about it.

Table 15.A

"How Do You Think of Yourself? As Just an American, as Both an American and (Ethnicity), or Just as (Ethnicity)?"

		Latinos		Blacks
	Noncitizens	Naturalized Citizens	Native-Born	All
Just an American (%)	3	15	31	33
Both (%)	42	73	69	56
Member of ethnic group (%)	55	12	0	12
	100%	100%	100%	101%
n	678	494	155	200

Source: Pooled 1999 and 2000 Los Angeles County Social Surveys.

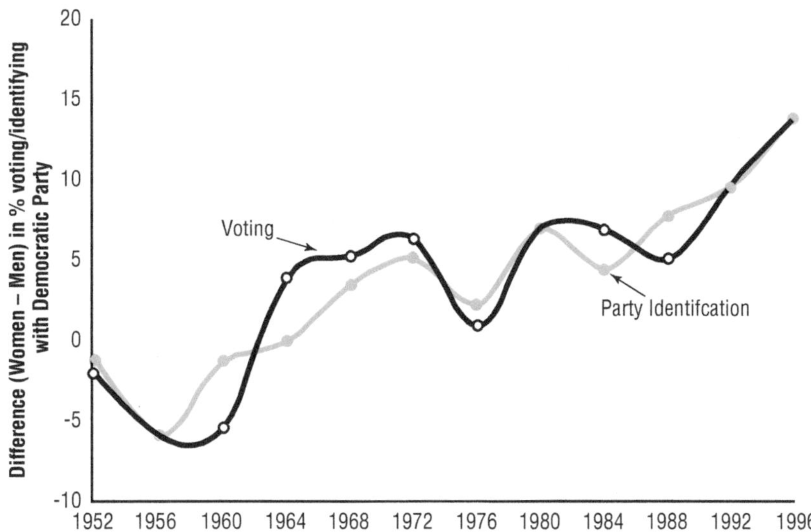

Figure 15–3 Gender Gap in Voting and Party Identification: 1952–1996.

Source: Kaufmann & Petrocik, 1999, p. 868.

The Gender Gap

Gender differences in political attitudes have become increasingly prominent and politically important. In the 1950s, men voted more for Democratic presidential and congressional candidates than did women. But now women are now consistently more likely to vote Democratic than are men, as shown in Figure 15–3. In the extraordinarily close 2000 presidential election, Al Gore led by 11 percent among women, while George W. Bush led by 11 percent among men, according to exit polls reported by CNN. These differences are usually described as the **gender gap.** It extends beyond the United States; for example, similar changes have been documented in western Europe (Vollebergh et al., 1999).

Two main theories have been proposed to explain the gender gap. One suggests that women are generally more caring about others' well-being and therefore more supportive of government efforts to help people. Such gender differences in concern for others may be a product of evolutionary endowment, or of different gender-role socialization, or both.

Women are indeed likely to be more liberal than men on so-called compassion issues, such as aid to education, public health, and social welfare (Kaufmann & Petrocik, 1999; Shapiro & Mahajan, 1986). In addition, women show greater aversion to the use of force, whether in war, building a strong military, capital punishment, or other harsh responses to crime (Mansbridge, 1985). For example, in a survey right after the Gulf War, 85 percent of the women felt a strong sense of disgust at the killing, whereas only 55 percent of the men did (Conover & Sapiro, 1993). Even the day of the World Trade Center terrorist attack, women expressed more reservations about a military response than did men: Only 57 percent of the women interviewed in one survey supported military action if innocent people might be killed, while 75 percent of the men did (CBS News, 2001).

A second hypothesis suggests that the many changes in women's roles in society since the 1950s and the women's movement have increased their group consciousness. Women today tend to be more educated and more often employed than in the past. They are also less likely to be in long-term marriages and, on average, do less full time care of small children because of both a lower birthrate and more paid day care. This change of focus from the family to the workplace may have increased sensitivity to gender inequality and thus support for a more feminist and liberal political agenda (Gurin, 1985; Klein, 1984). Consistent with this hypothesis, young, single, well educated working women contribute more to the political gender gap than do women in more traditional social roles, such as homemakers, and older, married, and less educated women. The first group is more likely to vote Democratic, to support programs that help children, the elderly, and other disadvantaged people, and to oppose the use of political and military force (Conover & Sapiro, 1993; Sears & Huddy, 1990). Second, the social changes in women's roles should also be reflected in a stronger feminist consciousness. Surprisingly enough, there is little or no gender gap in support for feminism or the women's movement more generally (Huddy et al., 2000). But feminist consciousness is a potent psychological disposition for women who have it. Women who view themselves as "feminists" are more politically liberal than either men or nonfeminist women (Conover, 1988). Women with stronger feminist consciousness were more likely to oppose the bombing of civilians in the Gulf War and more likely to feel emotionally distressed by it (Conover & Sapiro, 1993). They also have been much more favorable to presidential candidates who favored feminist issues (Cook, 1993). Issues such as abortion, sexual harassment, childcare, and parental leave are especially important when women vote for female candidates (Dolan, 1998; Paolino, 1995).

Despite these changes, and the ratification of women's suffrage in 1920, women's voices are still not heard as loudly in politics as men's are. To be sure, they now turn out to vote at almost exactly the same rate as men do (Schlozman et al., 1995). But they are substantially less likely to vote consistently with their issue preferences (Delli Carpini & Keeter, 2000). And they do not participate as actively in politics in other ways, such as in campaigns or in contacting public officials (Verba et al., 1997). This lack of participation necessarily reduces their political influence. It is not because women are too busy with family responsibilities or work; it is true regardless of whether women have children or not.

Rather, women are usually just not as interested in politics as men are. In one large national survey, women were considerably less likely to report that they enjoyed political discussions or paid a great deal of attention to national politics in the newspapers (Verba et al., 1997). One result is that women are not as politically informed as men; on average, they are about 10 percent less likely to know the right answer to any question about government and politics, a "knowledge gap" that has been strikingly constant over the past half century (Delli Carpini & Keeter, 2000). These differences are politically consequential. Among women who are as interested in politics as men, political participation is just as great. And women who are as informed as men vote just as consistently with their issue preferences as do men.

Religion

Religion is another increasingly important source of political cleavage. The early voting studies (e.g., Lazarsfeld, Berelson, & Gaudet, 1948) emphasized differences between Protestants, who tended to vote Republican, and Catholics and Jews, who were strongly Democratic. Jews still are strongly Democratic. In one recent survey in Los Angeles, 82 percent said they were Democrats, while only 48 percent of other whites said they were (Sonenshein & Valentino, 2000). However, overall differences between Protestants and Catholics are now less striking than are cleavages within each faith between people who have more orthodox beliefs and those who have more liberal religious beliefs (Wuthnow, 1988). For example, exit polls in 1988 and 1992 showed that fundamentalist religious belief was one of the strongest, if not the strongest, predictors of Republican presidential voting (Jackson & Carsey, 1999).

In particular, evangelical, fundamentalist Protestants, who often say they have been "born again" and tend to believe in the literal truth of the Bible, have shifted sharply to the Republicans, especially since the late 1980s (Kohut et al., 2000). Indeed, the political cleavages among Protestants have sharply increased. The political activation of evangelical Protestants and their shift to the Republicans party have been catalyzed by moral issues such as abortion; by traditional family values such as parental rights, traditional gender roles, and opposition to gay and lesbian rights; and by religious issues, such as prayer in the schools and the importance of religious training in the upbringing of children (e.g., Kohut et al., 2000). Traditional Republican positions on economic issues and limited government tend not to be as important to fundamentalists. Conversely, opposition to the political goals of evangelical Protestantism has come particularly from secularists and religious liberals (Bolce & DeMaio, 1999).

Political Tolerance

Conflict between groups is inevitable in political life. In fact, conflict is mostly what politics is about. But how much conflict will people tolerate? The Bill of Rights guarantees basic civil liberties to all, even to those whose ideas most people find disagreeable. Surveys have always found widespread support for abstract, general principles of free speech. Almost everyone agrees with "free speech for all, whatever their views" (McClosky & Brill, 1983). However, we saw in Chapter 5 that people also tend to reject and derogate messages that are highly discrepant from their own views, so there might also be a natural tendency to want to suppress the expression of views that we do not like. In the McCarthyite period after World War II (named after Senator Joseph McCarthy), communists, socialists, and atheists were regularly fired from teaching positions because their ideas were thought to be subversive. Today conservatives accuse the political left of insisting on "political correctness" on university campuses and on not allowing conservative ideas to be heard. Do people support the right to free expression only for people with whom they basically agree?

The main problem comes with applying these basic principles of civil liberties to unpopular groups in concrete cases. At the height of the postwar anti-communist hysteria, for example, national surveys found that two-thirds thought communists should not be allowed to speak publicly, and three fourths thought that communists' citizenship should be revoked (Stouffer, 1955). Similar though lower levels of intolerance were expressed toward socialists and atheists. In the late 1970s, John Sullivan and his colleagues (1982) still found people reluctant to grant full civil liberties to groups they loathed. These authors' respondents were first asked what group they most disliked and then whether that group should have full freedom of speech. Fewer than half were willing to grant free speech to the group they liked least, whether it was the communists, the Nazis, or the Ku Klux Klan. And the more they disliked that group, the less tolerant they were. So restricting civil liberties does indeed flow from disliking the people or groups in question.

Republican Senator Joseph McCarthy, from Wisconsin, was a leader of the anti-communist witch-hunts of the early 1950s that had a chilling effect on free political debate.

Tolerance for freedom of speech for communists, atheists, and gays has increased in recent years (Wilson, 1994). Why? It is greater among the supporters of abstract democratic principles (Sullivan et al., 1982). Moreover, younger and better-educated people are generally the most tolerant. Comparisons over time indicate that the increase is partly due to "cohort succession," the replacement of older, intolerant Americans by younger and more tolerant ones.

That replacement, in turn, has helped increase tolerance, in part because of the higher educational level of today's young people. People learn general democratic principles and, more important, the reasons for them as they become better educated. That would seem to result in a genuine increase in the willingness to hear opposing ideas and an ability to control the automatic aversion to disagreeable people and groups we discussed in Chapter 6.

But when hostilities run high, mere support for abstract democratic principles may not always be sufficient. For example, support for free speech for communists was at its lowest at the height of the Cold War, in the 1950s, when communism was widely perceived as very threatening. As detente with the Soviet Union increased and anti-Soviet propaganda became less vehement, tolerance rose, finally hitting a high point in the Mikhail Gorbachev era of openness during the late 1980s (Mueller, 1988). Similarly, tolerance of the rights of racists to speak freely, or to teach, or to have a book in the public library—a group most disliked by the best-educated, as we saw in Chapter 6—has actually decreased over time (Wilson, 1994). Increased education is not an infallible protector of the Bill of Rights. As Thomas Jefferson said, "The price of liberty is eternal vigilance."

The Mass Media and Political Persuasion

Another major area of research on political psychology focuses on the role of the mass media in politics. Everyone is familiar with seeing the president on television, watching the news at night, reading newspapers and news magazines, and the barrage of campaign ads before an election. In particular, we are said to live in a television era, in which people supposedly spend more time with television than they do with one another. Are people's attitudes as influenced by political television as it is often assumed they are?

Limited Effects

Scholarship on the political effects of the mass media has gone through three phases. The first began in the 1920s and 1930s. Radio became widely available throughout the Western world, and talking movies, with accompanying newsreels, became a source of mass entertainment. For the first time, charismatic political leaders such as Adolf Hitler, Benito Mussolini, Winston Churchill, and Franklin Roosevelt could reach huge masses of people not only through the printed word but also through radio and through movie newsreels. These leaders seemed to have an almost magical power to sway the general public. Though social scientists conducted little empirical analysis, they assumed that the political messages delivered by these public figures were extremely persuasive. Why? Because, they assumed, the audience was captive, attentive, and gullible (Institute for Propaganda Analysis, 1939).

These speculations highlighted the need for more systematic tests of media impact. A second phase of research, therefore, consisted of empirical studies on the impact of the mass media, using the new method of public opinion polling. We have already mentioned the important early study of voting in the 1940 election and its finding of relatively little change through the course of the campaign (Lazarsfeld et al., 1948). The few changes that did occur were not closely linked to mass media exposure. Rather, each candidate's campaign communications reached mainly those who already supported

Adolf Hitler delivers a speech at a Nazi rally in 1938 amid the symbols of the Nazi party.

him, a phenomenon called **selective exposure.** The major conclusion was that the media reinforced prior predispositions rather than converting people from one side to the other. A good deal of other research in the 1940s and 1950s yielded similar findings (Klapper, 1960). These were often described as fitting a **minimal effects model.**

The current era is one of renewed respect for the power of the media in politics. Many believe that television in particular has powerful persuasive effects, rendering the old minimal-effects model outdated (e.g., Ansolabehere, Behr, & Iyengar, 1993). Several social and political changes are usually cited as the reasons. There is the seeming devotion of the American public to television; supposedly the average adult spends as much time watching television as working. Campaign consultants have become increasingly expert in producing clever political commercials. Political "spin doctors" are hired by candidates to help put a positive "spin" on campaign events. Party identification is said to have declined in importance, and primary elections in which voters choose only among candidates from one party have become more important. Selective exposure should no longer be an obstacle because brief political commercials run during prime time, television news covers all sides of a campaign, televised debates present all candidates to large audiences, and television personalities like Larry King and Oprah Winfrey include candidates in their entertainment programs.

But even today, it is difficult to document cases in which the media have been successful in producing massive attitude changes. Many apparent cases of mass persuasion have, on close study, produced remarkably little real change. For example, the media events that usually draw the largest audiences in contemporary politics are the televised debates between the major presidential candidates. The debate between Jimmy Carter and Ronald Reagan in 1980, held a week before Election Day, has often been regarded as a major factor in the outcome of the election. The overwhelming journalistic consensus was that Reagan had "won" the debate and that this win was crucial in his surge to victory a few days later. But it brought only 7 percent of Carter's previous supporters to Reagan's side, according to a CBS News poll done immediately after the debate. Why was the increase so modest? Democrats and Republicans differed enormously in their evaluations of the opponents. Only 10 percent of the previously pro-Carter viewers thought Reagan had won. Only 5 percent of the previously pro-Reagan viewers thought Carter had won. In a close race, such changes are crucial, but they cannot be said to be massive. New

Table 15.5

Effects of the 1980 Presidential Campaign

June Vote Intention	Actual November Vote (%) Consistent with June Dispositions	Inconsistent with June Dispositions
Consistent with dispositions	37 (Reinforcement of predisposition)	3 (Change away from predisposition)
Inconsistent with dispositions	2 (Return to predisposition)	3 (Steadily against predisposition)
Undecided	44 (Decides to vote with predisposition)	11 (Decides to vote against predisposition)
Total (100%)	83	17

Source: Adapted from Finkel (1993), p. 15. The effects of the campaign are shown in parentheses.

information often seems to be incorporated into existing attitudes without changing them very much.

That 1980 campaign as a whole proved to resemble the 1940 campaign in the classic study by Lazarsfeld et al. (1948) described earlier. In the National Election Studies surveys, the voters' attitudes relevant to their presidential choice—party identification, presidential approval, and perceived integrity and competence of the candidates—were all measured in June, well before the nominees were even selected. But as Table 15–5 shows, the final vote was highly consistent with those precampaign attitudes. Only a handful of those with a candidate preference in June (5 percent) were converted by the campaign to a different position. Of those who had said they were undecided in June, the great majority (81 percent) ultimately voted consistently with those precampaign attitudes (Finkel, 1993). In other words, we could have predicted the voters' ultimate choices pretty well from knowing their attitudes before they were exposed to the campaign.

Another case of surprisingly modest persuasive effect is **attack advertising.** Many political consultants have made their names and fortunes in recent years by developing what were thought to be devastatingly effective negative television commercials. The conventional wisdom has been that attack ads are truly effective in changing voters' preferences, even if negative ads are widely disliked and build cynicism and reduce voter turnout. Many studies have been done to assess their effects. A careful review of over 50 such studies (Lau et al., 1999) shows that this conventional wisdom is surprisingly off the mark. "Attack ads" are indeed disliked more than positive "advocacy ads," but in the great majority of cases, advocacy ads have proved just as effective as or more effective than attack ads. And turnout is increased as often as it is decreased. However, extremely negative advertising may reduce the turnout of independents (Lau & Pomper, 2001).

Obstacles to Persuasion

Such cases suggest that the mass media continue to face major obstacles in trying to change attitudes. The first obstacle to persuasion, as people in the business of affecting public attitudes know, is reaching the people they want to influence. True, selective exposure no longer seems to be the major obstacle. It has long been known that people are not terribly motivated to seek out supportive information and avoid the opposition (Sears & Freedman, 1967). And the media today make selective exposure more difficult. People experience news magazines and television news as exposing them to a much greater variety of points of view than their friends and family members do (Mutz & Martin, 2001).

Moreover, candidates now advertise primarily with 30-second spot ads sneaked into the middle of regular programming. Even such brief ads can be effective, at least for the moment. In several experiments, inserting such ads into regular news programming increased candidate support among viewers 5 to 10 percent, compared to adults who had seen the news but not the ad (Ansolabehere & Iyengar, 1995). However, consistent with the minimal effects model, these advertising spots were more successful in solidifying support within the candidate's own party than in converting partisans from the opposite party.

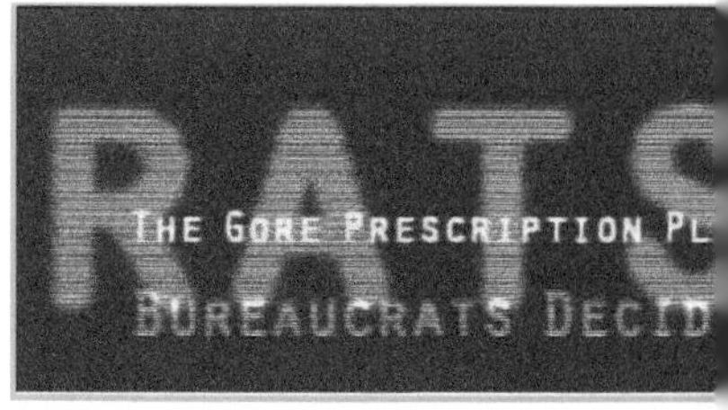

This ad, run by the G. W. Bush campaign for the 2000 elections, attacked Al Gore's Medicare plan. The ad contained an unusual brief background message, "RATS," behind the printed claims that remained on the screen long enough to be read in the usual way.

But most people just are not exposed to much political news of any kind. For example, a little more than 20 percent of U.S. households subscribe to a newspaper (Stanley & Niemi, 1999). Television news is often thought to be influential because so many people watch it. But do they? One recent study found that on an average week night, only 14 percent of the adult population watched one of the nightly national network news programs (Stanley & Niemi, 1999). Many fewer watched either CNN or PBS. Another study showed that even these relatively few watchers seemed not to have been watching very carefully. People who had watched an evening network news show could recall, later on in the evening, an average of only 6 percent of the stories it covered (Neuman, 1976).

Major political events, such as presidential debates, seem to draw large audiences. For example, in 1976, 80 million people tuned in to the first debate, and in 1992, the first debate was said to draw 62 million viewers. But the audience is not always so large. Only 47 million were said to watch the first Bush-Gore debate in 2000. And public attention to such debates may not be as deep as it is broad, according to numerous studies of the 1976 series of four debates (see Sears & Chaffee, 1979). Only a minority watched more than one debate, and only about a quarter of the public watched even one debate all the way through. Most viewers consider a situation comedy, a football game, or a good movie more interesting than a political speech or debate.

The second obstacle to persuasion is that even a communicator who has been successful in getting the message through to the target is a long way from changing the target's opinion. Often the message confronts strong attitudes that are resistant to change. Why is that so, if many apparent attitudes are really just "nonattitudes"? The reason is that the few communications that draw a large audience usually tend also to be those that will encounter strong, highly committed attitudes in many viewers. The biggest advertising budgets are for presidential campaigns. To start with, each side is often neutralized by the other, because both sides are quite expert and well funded. In addition, all those clever ads tend to confront strong partisan attitudes. When the wall of inattention is broken through, people are likely to use a variety of modes of resolution other than attitude change to restore cognitive consistency, as discussed in Chapter 5. They reject outright arguments that are discrepant from their own previously held attitudes, derogate the ads that attack their candidate, and distort the positions on issues taken by the candidates to make them more consistent with their own preferences.

Not all attitudes are emotionally laden and deeply held, of course, as discussed earlier. The media may have a major persuasive impact on attitudes toward relatively new and unfamiliar attitude objects, such as a relatively obscure military officer who decides to go into politics or the leaders of a coup in a large African country. The media may also be a more influential factor in primary and nonpartisan elections when not combating the obstacle of party identification. Few people have ever heard of the candidates in the Democratic primary contest for lieutenant governor, and so almost all the voters are probably open to influence. But if neither candidate has enough money to advertise much, Election Day is likely to come and go before we will ever see a single ad from either one. And most will never have heard of that African country.

Thus, in politics and public affairs, the percentage of the potential audience reached by any message is often quite small. Also, given the relatively poor attention and recall of those who are reached by it, massive attitude change seems unlikely. And even if

One of the most poignant moments in the funeral procession following the assassination of John F. Kennedy came as his casket passed his saluting son, John F. Kennedy, Jr., his daughter Caroline, his widow Jacqueline, and his brothers Edward (Ted) and Robert Kennedy.

many watch and pay close attention, they may well resist persuasion by using modes of resolution other than attitude change.

Massive Exposure

There are always exceptions. Not all political events suffer from public inattention. Truly massive public exposure to political events does occur and can produce major attitude changes. A classic example is the assassination of President John F. Kennedy. The three major television networks covered the events immediately following the shooting virtually nonstop for 4 days, from the confusion at the hospital where the dying president was taken; the swearing in of his successor, Lyndon B. Johnson; the murder of Lee Harvey Oswald, the alleged assassin; the funeral services; the cortege to Arlington Cemetery; the burial there; several processions through the streets of Washington; and countless retrospectives and interviews with prominent people. The networks devoted, on the average, almost 70 hours to these events, and the average American adult watched 34 hours of this coverage (Rubin, 1967; Sheatsley & Feldman, 1965).

The attitude changes were no less impressive. Before the assassination, Kennedy had not been thought of as a particularly exceptional president. He had won the election by a narrow margin and was rated by the public as doing no better a job than most presidents. Yet, in a national survey conducted just after the assassination, half the sample rated Kennedy as one of the best two or three presidents in history, and only 2 percent rated him "somewhat below average." It is impossible to separate the effects of the assassination itself from those of its television coverage in producing this change. However, it is widely agreed that the television coverage was instrumental in making the event among the most memorable in U.S. history.

Similarly massive media exposure occurred in the aftermath of the terrorist attacks on September 11, 2001. In a poll taken that evening, 99 percent of the respondents said they had watched or listened to news reports (ABC News, 2001). Less than a week later, 37 percent recalled that they had watched news coverage all that first day, and 63 percent said they "couldn't stop watching" the coverage of the attacks (*Los Angeles Times,* 2001; Pew Research Center, 2001). The predominant initial emotional reaction was shock and horror, but many soon reported feeling very angry at the perpetrators (CBS News, 2001). As a result, support for a major military response soon emerged. Only 2 days later, 85 percent said they supported strategic air attacks against military targets, 81 percent supported assassination of those responsible, and 55 percent supported (38 percent opposed) a ground invasion even if it would cost U.S. lives (Time.com, 2001).

Sudden international conflicts generally do attract massive media attention. Surprisingly enough, the public's approval of the president often improves even if the crisis involves a setback for the nation. For example, in 1961, President Kennedy's approval ratings increased after the humiliating defeat of a CIA-led invasion of Cuba in the Bay of Pigs. The approval of George W. Bush's job performance as president rose from 51 percent just before the terrorist attacks to 80 percent a few days later, although little that was concrete had yet been done (Pew Research Center, 2001).

Scholars have described this increased public approval as the **rally-round-the-flag effect,** attributing it to patriotism: When the United States has been challenged, the U.S. public rushes to the president's support (Mueller, 1973). But this increased public approval is partly contingent on the media. The rally effect following negative events seems to occur only if there is little prominent political opposition to the president's actions. For example, when the Iran-Contra scandal broke in 1986, the opposition Democrats were highly critical of President Reagan and his administration. There was a substantial drop in his support, one third of his previous supporters disapproving of his overall job performance (Brody, 1991). However, the more usual case is that leaders of both parties support the president in major international conflicts, as in the case of the terrorist attacks. If so, the public should rally, at least in the short run, regardless of the consequences of the president's actions.

Long-Term Exposure

Most studies of media impact deal with relatively brief or short term mass communications: a debate on TV, an attack ad, or coverage of a particular political event over a period of a few days. However, many important changes of attitude may result from exposure to the media over long periods of time. One careful study (Page & Shapiro, 1992) investigated 80 different instances in which public opinion polls repeated exactly the same question over a period of several months or more. Half the cases showed some systematic (although usually relatively modest) attitude change over time that was a function of the amount and direction of news coverage of the issue. Similarly, in a long war, public disapproval tends to mount as the casualty rate increases, presumably as the media focus attention on casualties (Mueller, 1973).

However, voters' responses to long-term media exposure depend on two factors, which Zaller (1992, 1997) has nicely modeled. One is whether political elites are largely agreed on a common position or are putting forward competing messages. The second is the voter's **habitual news reception,** as indexed by the amount of political information the individual has. If elites are largely in agreement, heavy exposure to the news should drive people toward that common position. We might call that a "mainstream effect." If the two sides disagree, however, their messages will tend to align people's attitudes with their predispositions, polarizing voters into partisan camps rather than changing their attitudes toward one side or the other. Those most exposed to the news should polarize the most. We might call that a "polarization effect."

Both principles are illustrated by the public's response to the Vietnam War. In the early phases of the war, in 1964, both parties supported intervention in Vietnam. The more an individual tuned in to the media's coverage of the war, the greater his or her support for the "mainstream" position, that is, support for the war. This support is shown to the left in Figure 15–4. In the late 1960s, however, increasing antiwar protest led to great divisions between prowar and antiwar elites. As a result, greater exposure to the media led people to polarize around their basic predispositions. That is, greater exposure led "hawks" (those with a general tendency to support foreign wars) to become more supportive of the war and "doves" (those preferring to work out disagreements with other nations through negotiation and bargaining) to become more opposed to the war, as shown to the right in Figure 15–4.

But even massive and seemingly one-sided media coverage, sustained over a long period of time, does not guarantee that the public will be much persuaded. The intensely negative media scrutiny of Bill Clinton's affair with Monica Lewinsky throughout 1998 is a striking example. This scandal became public in January 1998 and went on for more than a year. It featured almost nonstop media condemnation of Clinton's conduct, fueled by the investigation led by Kenneth Starr, the special prosecutor; grand jury testimony; charges about other kinds of sexual misconduct; the votes to impeach Clinton by the House of Representatives' Judiciary Committee and the full House; and the Senate vote not to remove him from office, with several major television appearances by Clinton himself along the way.

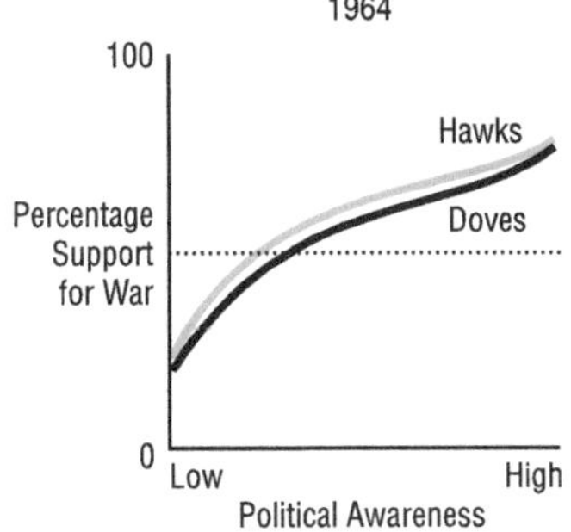

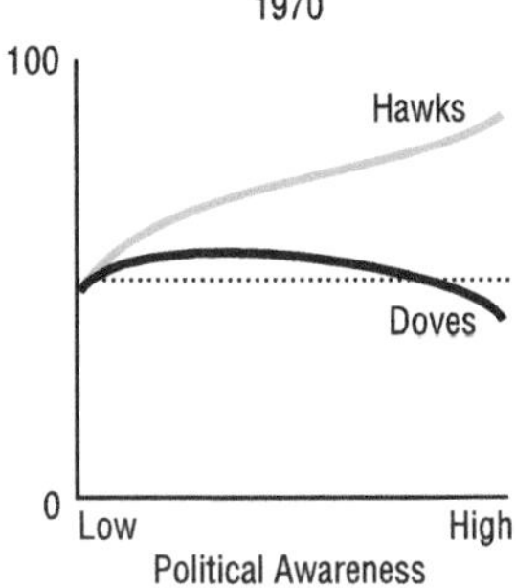

Figure 15–4 **Partisan Polarization on the Vietnam War.**

Source: Zaller (1992), p. 210.

The public clearly frowned on extramarital sexual activity; in one survey at the time, 76 percent said they thought it was "always wrong." And indeed, over the course of the year, there was a substantial long-term erosion in the public's perceptions of Clinton's honesty and trustworthiness (Newport, 1999). But this avalanche of bad publicity, along with only the second presidential impeachment in American history, had astonishingly little effect on Clinton's political support. A little over 60 percent continued to approve his performance at almost every sounding throughout the year (Newport, 1999; Pew Research Center, 1998a). To be sure, immediately after the scandal first broke, and then again after the Starr report became public, his job approval dropped by around 5 percent, but then it rebounded after a few days. In contrast, both his State of the Union address shortly after the scandal broke and the Republican vote in the House for his impeachment generated larger and longer-lasting increases (Pew Research Center, 1998a, 1998b; Zaller, 2000). Overall, though, his public support changed little over the course of the year.

Why was the massive media coverage of this scandal not more effective in discrediting Clinton, despite his violation of consensual moral values? There are two reasons. First of all, by the end of the year, the public as a whole, by a 2-to-1 margin, had concluded that the affair was a private, not a public, matter and had rejected the Starr investigation and the Republican impeachment vote as simply partisan. Indeed, in the 1998 congressional elections, Clinton's own party, the Democrats, actually picked up strength in both the House and the Senate. Attitudes about the scandal hurt Republican candidates most among voters who had been most exposed to it (Abramowitz, 2001). Simply put, in this case, the voters listened to their own judgment and not to the media talking-heads.

Second, the intense media coverage, with attacks on Clinton by Republicans and support for him by Democrats, simply served to polarize the public around their party identifications (Zaller, 2000). All the votes in Congress were extraordinarily narrowly divided and broke almost exactly down party lines. Democrats overwhelmingly believed that the affair was a private matter, and that the Starr investigation and the impeachment vote were motivated by partisanship. Most Republicans believed just the opposite. On all these questions the polarization of the two sets of partisans was greatest among those who were regularly most intensively exposed to the mass media, as shown in Figure 15–5 (Zaller, 2000).

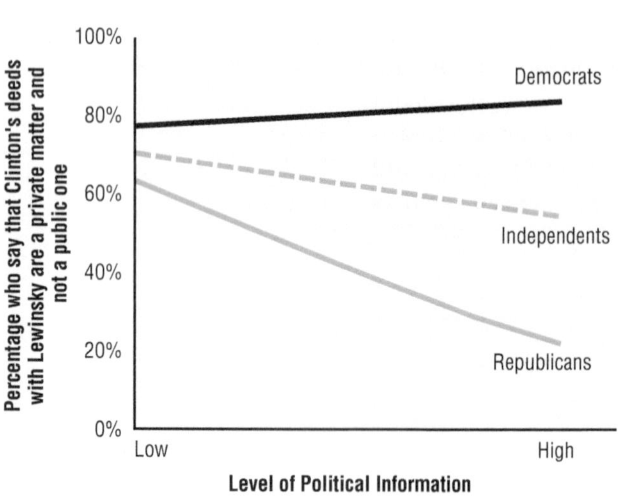

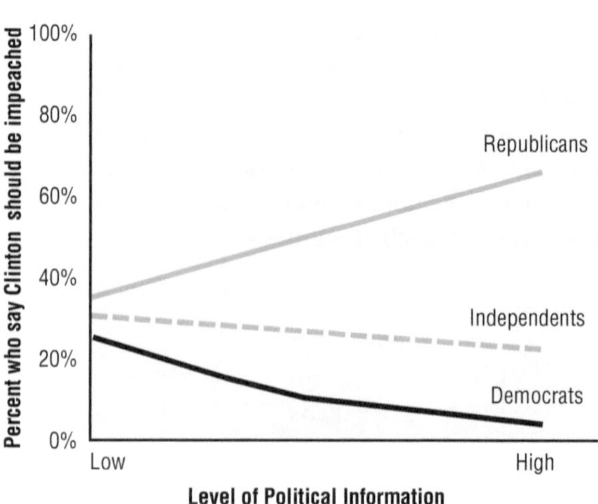

Figure 15–5 The Effect of Political Information and Partisanship on Attitudes Toward the Lewinsky Matter.

Source: 1998 National Election Study (Zaller, 2000.).

Even massive short-term exposure or long-term exposure to conflicting messages, then, often leads to polarization around previous predispositions rather than systematic attitude change. The tendency of intense media coverage to polarize voters around their prior attitudes, rather than to persuade them that one side is right and the other side is wrong, is a major reason why the media often have only a modest persuasive impact.

A New Look at the Media

Because of the many demonstrations of the limited persuasive impact of television, researchers have increasingly considered other ways in which it might influence voters.

Conveying Information

Most people say that television news is their primary source of political information. And the media do indeed have considerable success in providing information. Children learn a great deal from television programs, ranging from *Sesame Street* to weather forecasts (Comstock et al., 1978). They are more likely to learn about presidential campaigns if they watch television news or read a newspaper (Chaffee & Kanihan, 1997). Regular attention to television news also contributes significantly to adults' knowledge of candidates' positions (Zhao & Chaffee, 1995). Watching presidential debates increases adults' familiarity with the candidates' positions on campaign issues (Sears & Chaffee, 1979).

Yet the informing function of television news should not be exaggerated. For one thing, the audience for "hard news," as reflected in the networks' nightly news and in newspapers, is shrinking. Just in the last decade, the number of regular viewers of network news has dropped from almost 80 percent to below 60 percent. And with the expansion of cable TV, the competition for the public's attention has heated up. As a result, the content of "hard news" has gotten "softer": News stories increasingly have little public policy component and focus instead on human interest, crime and disaster, and sensationalism in general. Even election coverage by television news tends to focus to a surprising degree not on policy proposals, but on "the horse race"—who is winning, how big campaign audiences are, what the advertising strategies are, and who made the latest mistake (Patterson, 1993). For example, one third of all the television news stories on the 1988 primaries referred to the candidates' poll standings (Ansolabehere, Behr, & Iyengar, 1991). In contrast, the candidates' 30-second spot television commercials are often quite informative about their positions, especially in very high profile, and expensive, campaigns (Zhao & Chaffee, 1995).

Agenda Setting

In recent years, much attention has also been paid to the media's role in political **agenda setting.** When issues are given a great deal of media coverage, the public comes to see them as more important. In this sense, the media are said to set the agenda for political discussion: They influence not *what* the public thinks, but what the public thinks *about.*

The public's attitudes toward crime are a good example of this media-driven agenda-setting effect. In 1991, only 1 percent felt that crime was the most important problem in the United States, but by August 1994, 52 percent did (Hagen, 1995). Why? Was a real surge in crime itself the reason? That seems unlikely because the rate of serious crime actually dropped in that period (Ellsworth & Gross, 1994). Rather, scholars pointed to the media coverage of violent crime, particularly in local television news programs. For example, one study found that over half the local news broadcasts in Los Angeles used crime as the lead story; 78 percent of all crime stories focused on violent crime, although only 30 percent of all the crimes in Los Angeles were violent (Gilliam et al., 1996).

Do such findings merely reflect a decision by the media to cover the problems already worrying the public, rather than the influence of media coverage on the public's priorities? Undoubtedly, media coverage sometimes mainly reflects public concerns, such as when a war breaks out. And even though the crime rate was evening out in the early 1990s, it still must have seemed like a serious threat to many people. However, a number of careful experiments have indicated that greater television news coverage can increase concern about an issue regardless of the viewers' previous priorities. In these studies, adults viewed television newscasts in which the amount of coverage given particular issues was varied experimentally. Such manipulations significantly influenced the perceived importance of these issues, even on questionnaires given 24 hours later (Iyengar & Kinder, 1987).

Such experiments show that the media *can* set the public agenda. But they cannot tell us whether the media normally *do* set it. The media may simply reflect what politicians are talking about, or they may follow the stories the public is most interested in. In general, politicians, media, and public all seem normally to go together fairly harmoniously: Politicians are trying to please the voters by addressing the issues the voters care about, and the media generally cover both what the politicians are talking about and what they think will interest the public (Dalton et al., 1998).

Priming

Media coverage of a particular issue affects which attitude comes to the voter's mind, and therefore which attitude is weighed most heavily when people arrive at their political choices. This is an example of **priming.** In the studies just described that experimentally varied which issue was covered in a television news broadcast, the viewers not only rated the issues presented as more important but tended to base their approval of the president's *overall* performance on his handling of the *particular* issue made salient in the broadcast. For example, when the news covered energy shortages, viewers tended to evaluate the president's overall performance in terms of how well they felt he was handling energy problems (Iyengar & Kinder, 1987).

A real world example comes from the first President Bush's handling of the Persian Gulf War in 1991. This event received a tremendous amount of media attention. A national sample was interviewed both before the United States took any military action and then again several months after the war was over. Over that time, evaluations of President Bush became more closely linked to appraisals of his specific performance in the Gulf crisis. However, they did not become more closely linked to his performance on the economy, which had received much less media attention (Krosnick & Gannon, 1993). During that period, his popularity was quite dependent on his management of the Gulf crisis.

As mentioned earlier, television seems to have added to public concern about crime in the early 1990s. Since black men commit more than their share of violent crimes, television news coverage of those crimes might well prime whites' racial attitudes. Some have suggested that the first George Bush used black crime in his 1988 campaign as a vehicle for attracting more support from prejudiced whites without seeming to make an explicit appeal to racism. He attacked his Democratic opponent, Michael Dukakis, for having an "ultraliberal, ultralenient approach to crime." He often told a story about Willie Horton, a convicted first degree murderer, who, while on weekend furlough from prison, raped a Maryland woman and assaulted her husband. Mendelberg (1997) hypothesized that this story primed racial prejudice because it was consistent with conventional stereotypes about black violence. She showed students either a network news broadcast about Bush's use of the Willie Horton case or a Bush campaign ad criticizing Dukakis for harbor pollution in his state, an ad unlikely to prime racial attitudes.

Viewing the Willie Horton news broadcast indeed primed racial attitudes, strengthening their association with attitudes toward racial policies such as affirmative action. Viewing the ad on pollution had no such effect. Mendelberg (2001) then analyzed survey data on the 1988 campaign to see whether this priming effect had occurred then. Evaluations of the two candidates had indeed been strongly associated with racial attitudes during the campaign, especially in its middle phase, when Bush featured a "revolving-door" campaign ad showing swarthy criminals quickly revolving in and out of jail. If the Bush campaign had intended the Horton case and this ad to prime racial prejudice, it seems to have been successful.

Finally, how do candidates decide which issues to put on the agenda and therefore which attitudes to prime? The parties differ in what policy goals their core supporters want accomplished. The Democrats usually promote the "compassion" issues described earlier, such as assistance to the poor or elderly, or health care, or education, while Republicans focus more on lower taxes, a strong military, and crime control. So if we want stronger social security, we vote for the Democrats, and if we want tax cuts, we vote for the Republicans. This has been called **issue ownership** (Petrocik, 1996). Each party tries to have the issues it "owns" dominate the public agenda, priming attitudes that will bring the most support to the party.

Willie Horton, a convicted murderer and rapist, was the celebrated criminal used by George H. W. Bush to discredit his opponent, Michael Dukakis, during the 1988 presidential campaign.

Framing

The implication of the agenda setting and priming effects is that the salience of an issue is crucial to its political impact. It also implies that the **framing** of any given issue is also important. Framing makes some aspects of the issue especially salient in order to promote a particular interpretation of it. Framing does so by invoking particular metaphors, catchphrases, and condensing symbols.

National leaders often need to mobilize public opinion in support of war. How the war is framed may be crucial. A classic example concerns the public's attitudes toward U.S. military intervention in Korea in the early 1950s (Mueller, 1973). The public strongly supported intervention when they were asked, "Do you think the United States was right or wrong in sending American troops to stop the communist invasion of South Korea?" However, when "the communist invasion" was not included in the question, the public was mostly opposed to intervention. Apparently the communist-invasion frame stimulated the strong anticommunist sentiment of the day and so produced much more public support for military action.

Another example comes from the Gulf War. In the debates before the war, some compared Saddam Hussein to Hitler in the 1930s, as two dictators taking over small nations on the way to domination of a whole region. Others compared the situation to the Vietnam War, in which a small, early commitment led to a quagmire of inconclusive conflict. Consistent with the "collective memory" effect we discussed earlier, older people initially preferred the Hitler analogy, and younger people the Vietnam analogy. Preferring the Hitler analogy was associated with much more support for military action. Once the war began, however, President Bush focused entirely on the Hitler analogy, and it became the dominant one for people of all ages. Support for the war rose accordingly (Schuman & Rieger, 1992).

Different kinds of framing of domestic issues can also produce large swings in public support. An important debate between the political parties is between the small, limited central government usually favored by Republicans and the more expansive (and expensive) federal government usually favored by Democrats. The difference can be framed in the abstract (between a smaller government with less spending, and a larger government with more services) or more concretely in terms of specific programs, such as Social Security, Medicare, and public transportation. Support for more limited government is far greater when it is framed in the abstract than when it is framed in terms of specific programs that most people want (Jacoby, 2000; Sears & Citrin, 1985). Not surprisingly, Republicans prefer to argue for smaller government in the abstract, an issue they "own," and Democrats prefer to argue for specific services issues they "own."

International Conflict

Another major focus of attention in political psychology has been on international conflict. During the 1950s and 1960s, the Cold War inspired much psychological research on international conflict, just as today much work is focused on international tensions in and around the Middle East and the Balkans. Specific crises have also been a focus of attention, such as the Cuban Missile Crisis or the negotiations at Munich in 1938 that led to Hitler's takeover of parts of Czechoslovakia.

Images of the Enemy

A convenient starting point is the images that contending adversaries hold of themselves and each other. These images can focus on nations, political leaders, or populaces. For one thing, people seem to delight in having a foreign enemy; consequently, they develop passionately held **enemy images.** In general, enemies are perceived as having bad intentions, a lack of morals, and negative traits (Finlay, Holsti, & Fagen, 1967). A strongly held enemy image, in turn, produces such biased images as "the diabolical enemy," "the moral self," and "the virile self" (White, 1970).

For example, after the September 2001 terrorist attacks, U.S. decision makers perceived Osama bin Laden as the primary enemy, a man described as filled with hatred and as ruthless, heartless, and deceitful. That image may well have been accurate, but social psychologists are especially interested in patterns of misperception. Cognitive consistency theories (see Chapter 5) predict that perceptions will be biased toward consistency with basic attitudes. When people have a strong commitment to viewing another nation as the enemy, many of their other perceptions fall into line. For example, when Slobodan Milosevic started the war in Bosnia, he portrayed Muslims as diabolical enemies who would threaten Serbs' lives. To be sure, there was some reason for Serbs to be suspicious and fearful, but Milosevic greatly exaggerated it, depicting the Muslims as implacably hostile, even though at the time, they were among the most secular and tolerant Muslims in the world (White, 1996).

Perhaps the enemy images that have received the most attention are those held during the Cold War by Soviet and U.S. decision makers (Larson, 1985). Some scholars believe that the Americans misperceived the Soviets as fundamentally hostile to the United

After the terrorist attacks of September 11, 2001, the American government assigned primary responsibility to the Arab militant Osama bin Laden, and described him as the nation's greatest enemy.

States, perhaps motivated by an ideological desire that communism should dominate the world. But much of the Soviets' foreign policy might have been basically defensive, since Russia had been decimated by the Germans in two world wars. Still others believe that Soviet leaders were in fact isolated and ignorant about the United States, exaggerating the threat that Americans might invade the USSR and, as a result, being more ready to go to war than they would have been with more realistic perceptions.

Group serving biases cause some of these problems. Images of the enemy lead to favorable attributions of the actions taken by one's own nation and to negative attributions of those taken by the enemy. This can be seen in explanations for either aggressive or humanitarian actions. First of all, we tend to view our own nation's military actions as defensive and the enemy's military actions as aggressive desires for power. In one study, 57 percent of a sample of California adults provided negative attributions for the Soviet invasion of Afghanistan, whereas only 27 percent gave negative attributions for the U.S. invasion of Grenada (Burn & Oskamp, 1989).

Second, if our nation does a positive act, we explain it positively, but not if the enemy does a positive act. In another study (Sande, Goethals, Ferrari, & Worth, 1989), Americans were given a newspaper story describing the heroic action of an icebreaker in cracking an escape route through the Arctic ice that allowed 1,000 trapped whales to escape. When the vessel was described as a U.S. boat, the participants explained the action in altruistic terms (e.g., "to save the whales"). When the vessel was described as a Soviet boat, the action was explained as self-serving (e.g., "to generate favorable publicity"). In general, the United States was evaluated as acting on a more moral basis than was the USSR. This contributes to the **mirror image** (Bronfenbrenner, 1961). We believe that our enemy is aggressive and immoral, and the other side believes the same thing about us. Each side believes it has peaceful intentions, and each is afraid of the other because it is perceived as aggressive and threatening. One's own militarism is justified as self defense.

Still another enemy image is called the **blacktop illusion,** the tendency to see the enemy's government as evil, but the people of that country as basically good (White, 1970). To test for this illusion, Burn and Oskamp (1989) asked a sample of Californians to rate the Soviet and U.S. people and government with a series of adjectives, such as "friendly" or "peace loving" or "bad." They found that in general, the participants rated the United States more favorably than the USSR, but they rated the people of the USSR more favorably than the USSR government.

Enemy images serve a variety of functions for leaders and followers alike, sometimes justifying actions that might otherwise be improper or illegal, and at other times diverting attention from other pressing and more difficult problems. As Finlay and colleagues (1967) indicated, "It seems that we have always needed enemies and scapegoats; if they have not been readily available, we have created them" (p. 7). Taking a broader perspective is some protection against these potentially dangerous biases. In one experiment, respondents summarized speeches about the U.S.–Iraqi conflict by President Clinton and Saddam Hussein. They distorted those speeches less when reviewing them from the perspective of a historian than from the perspective of a U.S. military officer (Kemmelmeir & Winter, 2000).

Belief Systems

A central tenet of social cognition theories in psychology (see Chapter 3) is that information processing tends to be theory-driven rather than data-driven. One particularly interesting set of theories held by decision makers involves the **lessons of history** they have learned (Jervis, 1976). In line with the collective-memory effect described earlier, these lessons are often learned from particularly vivid events that occurred when the decision maker was young. For example, Franklin Roosevelt, who was secretary of the navy at the end of World War I, was much impressed by President Woodrow Wilson's failure to bring the United States into an international peacekeeping organization, and so at the end of World War II, he was willing to make important concessions to the Soviet Union to ensure that all nations would join the United Nations. On the other hand, John F. Kennedy, whose father was ambassador to Great Britain when the British government was appeasing Hitler at Munich, later in life was resolutely opposed to making concessions to the Soviet Union. Each had learned from history during his formative years, but quite different lessons.

There is some value in learning from history, as reflected in the familiar quote from George Santayana: "Those who cannot remember the past are condemned to repeat it." On the other hand, knowing history has its dangers. Too often, its lessons are learned early in life in a particular historical context and are applied much later in circumstances that make that original context irrelevant or misleading. The complaint that military leaders are always "fighting the last war" reflects this sometimes dated quality of the lessons of history. Another danger, as with cognitive biases in general, is that the lessons of history give too much weight to firsthand or vivid experiences, or to efforts that were only accidentally successful (Jervis, 1976).

An overarching question motivating much of the research on the psychology of international conflict is whether foreign-policy decision makers are making rational or irrational decisions. A formal definition of rationality, involving a conclusion logically consistent with the decision maker's values and based on full information, would surely not fit most of the cases we have discussed. Many errors and biases intrude. A more flexible definition of rationality is needed. Simon (1985) offered the notion of **bounded rationality,** which suggests that practical decision makers tend to be rational within their limits: They do not have all the information, they do not have all the time necessary to evaluate the information available, they take various cognitive shortcuts, they choose alternatives that are "good enough" rather than "perfect," and they are subject to a wide variety of irrational pressures. But they are often as rational as can be expected under the circumstances. This view has been much influenced by the research on social cognition described in Chapter 3.

Crisis Management

How do political leaders deal with international (or even domestic) crises? In 1962, the Kennedy administration discovered that the Soviet Union had placed nuclear missiles in Cuba. This discovery led to a confrontation between the United States and the USSR that took the world to the brink of nuclear war. When John F. Kennedy and his advisers attempted to deal with the crisis, what determined whether they would be successful or not? Clearly they could have triggered war, but they did not. On the other hand, they might have defused the crisis without risking war, and they did not. What makes leaders more or less successful in dealing with such crises?

One factor inherent in international crises is psychological stress. Such stress can have a number of negative effects, such as reducing the complexity of information processing, and it can lead to defensive avoidance and wishful thinking. Janis and Mann (1977) developed a theory of decision making for occasions when the issues are strongly emotion-laden. They described the various patterns of coping behavior common in such conflicts and their consequences for decisional rationality. They offered various techniques for coping constructively with stress, primarily relying on vigilance. Decision makers need to inform themselves adequately beforehand not only about the decision, but also about the emotions likely to accompany the decision and its aftermath, and to come to grips with these emotions.

Most foreign policy decisions are also made with extensive small group deliberation. One of the most influential findings by a political psychologist (Janis, 1982) is the identification of groupthink. As discussed in Chapter 10, this occurs when a group of people working together form a highly cohesive group with high morale. Subtly they begin to reject people who don't agree with the group, they reject differing ideas, and they perceive the group as invulnerable. They then begin to exhibit many symptoms

During the Cuban Missile Crisis, many meetings were held in the White House of deeply worried members of the Kennedy administration. Some, like this one, involved the full Cabinet. President Kennedy is seated in front of the middle window.

of poor decision making, such as incompletely surveying alternative possibilities, failing to examine the risks of the preferred choice, and adopting selective biases when evaluating information.

On the other hand, things can be done to prevent or minimize groupthink. The group leader can encourage each member to air objections and be critical of the group's consensus. Outside experts can be called in to challenge the group's decision. Devil's advocates or subcommittees can be formed within the group to come up with plausible alternatives. Indeed, Janis suggested that the Kennedy administration's handling of the Cuban Missile Crisis exhibited some of these desirable features. The president even arranged to be absent from some key meetings so that the others would not feel compelled to please him by agreeing with whatever he said.

The psychological approach to politics is distinctive in two respects. First, it tends to be a comprehensive approach: The political psychologist tries to take into account any and all forces that affect human behavior. Second, the political psychologist emphasizes distinctively psychological factors, such as stress, cognitive consistency, cognitive biases, and group influence. These factors tend to emphasize irrational influences on the individual's behavior. A rival point of view, in many respects, is the **rational choice theory** derived from neoclassical economics, which views people as more narrowly motivated by the rational pursuit of material interests.

As with many other topics discussed in this book, this contrast of perspectives provides a creative tension that helps to enlighten us about the many complex aspects of the human species. One point often overlooked is that two approaches may have somewhat different strengths and weaknesses. We have seen that ordinary people often have relatively little political information, often have inconsistent attitudes, do not seem preoccupied with their own material self-interest, and do not seem to respond especially rationally to new information. But it can be argued that in the long run, public opinion in the aggregate emerges as rather responsive to social, economic, and political change. Democratic citizens may do pretty well as a group, emerging with reasonably coherent decisions from a "sea of noise," even if up close, as individuals, their political views seem uninformed and chaotic (Kinder, 1998; also see Page & Shapiro, 1992). Whether that greater coherence means that their collective decisions meet the standard of sufficient rationality remains open to debate (Converse, 2000).

Summary

1. The dominant theory of voting behavior views a long-standing party identification, acquired early in life, as the major influence on the vote. Voters are thought to be generally ill-informed and nonideological, and to have rather inconsistent attitudes on issues.
2. This theory has been challenged in recent years by the view that voters do respond in a moderately informed manner to the realities of life, in terms of economic conditions, issue differences between candidates, and presidential performance. People are often ambivalent rather than simply inconsistent. Ideology also plays a more central role now than it once did.
3. Basic political attitudes are often acquired before adulthood. They are vulnerable to change in early adulthood but are quite persistent thereafter. Party identification is influenced to some extent by one's parents, although not as exclusively as was once thought.
4. Intergroup conflict is currently receiving much attention in the field of political psychology, especially racial, gender, and religious conflict. The "gender gap" is becoming an important political reality, as are divisions between fundamentalist Christians and more secular voters.
5. In the 1930s, the mass media were thought to be an awesomely powerful new weapon, and in the 1940s and 1950s, to have minimal effects. Today there is renewed respect for their role. Nevertheless, far ranging attitude changes are rarely produced by the media.
6. Major obstacles to attitude change through the media include lack of exposure to discrepant information and the fact that highly committed attitudes are resistant to change.
7. The media can produce major changes in political attitudes on those rare occasions when there is massive exposure to the political arena, or through repeated exposure over long time periods, or by changing low commitment attitudes.
8. The media can also be effective by providing information, setting agendas, priming strong attitudes, and framing issues.
9. International conflict generates a number of common misperceptions, including the need to identify an enemy, the mirror images that contending powers have of each other, and the tendency to overuse the lessons of history.
10. Elite decision making in international relations is also subject to bias owing to imperfect information processing, the stress and emotionality inevitably associated with that activity, and the group dynamics of decision making elites.

Critical Thinking

1. Think about your own opinions about affirmative action and/or legalized abortion. How do they fit the contending descriptions given in this chapter, in terms of stability over time, internal consistency or ambivalence, and a base in more general liberal or conservative ideology?
2. Parents are important, but not the sole, influences in the political socialization process. Think about your own party preference, racial attitudes, and moral and religious values. How would you explain the pattern of influences that has brought you to your current views?
3. Reflect on the Monica Lewinsky scandal. Why do you think there were such large differences between Democrats and Republicans? Do you think those differences would have occurred, in that form, if a Republican president was involved? How does the account here compare to what you perceived your own responses to the scandal to be, and your friends, and your parents?
4. Think of someone your age who came from an immigrant family. It could be yourself or a friend. How does that person think about the balance between an ethnic identity and identity as an American? You might ask some people from immigrant families if you know some.
5. Some believe there may be a psychological need to have enemies, resulting in the various "enemy images" described in this chapter. What theories presented in earlier chapters would be relevant to such a tendency?

Key Terms

agenda setting
ambivalence
attack advertising
blacktop illusion
bounded rationality
cognitive consistency
collective memory
enemy images
framing
gender gap
group-serving biases
habitual news reception
ideology
impressionable years
issue ownership
issue public
lessons of history
lifelong openness
minimal effects model
mirror image
nonattitudes
party identification
persistence
pocketbook voting
political socialization
priming
rally-round-the-flag effect
rational choice theory
selective exposure
self-interest
sociotropic voting